Covert colonialism

Manchester University Press

STUDIES IN IMPERIALISM

General editors: Andrew S. Thompson and Alan Lester

Founding editor: John M. MacKenzie

When the 'Studies in Imperialism' series was founded by Professor John M. MacKenzie more than thirty years ago, emphasis was laid upon the conviction that 'imperialism as a cultural phenomenon had as significant an effect on the dominant as on the subordinate societies'. With well over a hundred titles now published, this remains the prime concern of the series. Cross-disciplinary work has indeed appeared covering the full spectrum of cultural phenomena, as well as examining aspects of gender and sex, frontiers and law, science and the environment, language and literature, migration and patriotic societies, and much else. Moreover, the series has always wished to present comparative work on European and American imperialism, and particularly welcomes the submission of books in these areas. The fascination with imperialism, in all its aspects, shows no sign of abating, and this series will continue to lead the way in encouraging the widest possible range of studies in the field. 'Studies in Imperialism' is fully organic in its development, always seeking to be at the cutting edge, responding to the latest interests of scholars and the needs of this ever-expanding area of scholarship.

To buy or to find out more about the books currently available in this series, please go to: https://manchesteruniversitypress.co.uk/series/studies-in-imperialism/

Covert colonialism

Governance, surveillance and political culture in British Hong Kong, c. 1966–97

Florence Mok

MANCHESTER UNIVERSITY PRESS

Copyright © Florence Mok 2023

The right of Florence Mok to be identified as the author of this work has been asserted in accordance with the Copyright, Designs and Patents Act 1988.

Published by Manchester University Press
Oxford Road, Manchester M13 9PL

www.manchesteruniversitypress.co.uk

British Library Cataloguing-in-Publication Data
A catalogue record for this book is available from the British Library

ISBN 978 1 5261 5819 2 hardback
ISBN 978 1 5261 8233 3 paperback

First published 2023

The publisher has no responsibility for the persistence or accuracy of URLs for any external or third-party internet websites referred to in this book, and does not guarantee that any content on such websites is, or will remain, accurate or appropriate.

Typeset by Newgen Publishing UK

*To my late grandparents, who lived through the history that
I am writing.*

Contents

List of figures and tables	*page* viii
Preface and acknowledgements	ix
List of abbreviations	xi
Introduction	1
1 Constructing 'public opinion' through Town Talk and MOOD	24
2 The Chinese as the official language movement	53
3 The anti-corruption movement	85
4 The campaign against telephone rate increases	125
5 The campaign to reopen the Precious Blood Golden Jubilee Secondary School	155
6 The changing immigration discourse and policy	176
7 The British Nationality Act controversy	208
8 Overt public opinion surveys and shifting popular attitudes towards proposed and implemented constitutional reforms	232
Conclusion	254
Select bibliography	262
Index	272

Figures and tables

Figures

1.1 Structure of the Public Relations Office in 1957. HKRS 160-1-23, 'The Organisation of the Public Relations Office', by J. D. Duncanson, December 1957 — page 27
1.2 Chain of command in MOOD's operation in 1977. HKRS 925-1-1, 'Information Paper for Recipients of MOOD: How MOOD is Produced', MOOD, 5 May 1977, pp. 2–4 — 42

Tables

1.1 Quota of each occupation group in ten city districts in December 1970 — page 38
1.2 Classifications of social stratifications adopted in Town Talk in early 1975 — 40
3.1 Complaints made to the ICAC — 109
3.2 Percentage of identifiable complaints made to the ICAC — 111
3.3 Percentage of corruption reports made in person — 111
3.4 Number of reports received by the ICAC — 112
3.5 Modes of reports for ICAC consideration — 112
4.1 Applications received and lines installed by the Hong Kong Telephone Company — 127
4.2 Telephone take-up rate in Hong Kong (direct lines) — 129
6.1 Legal immigration from China to Hong Kong in 1978 — 180
6.2 Number of illegal immigrants arrested in 1978 — 180
6.3 Statistics of illegal immigrants repatriated in 1980 — 198

Preface and acknowledgements

My pursuit of history can be traced back to the time when I was nine. The idea of how history encompassed humanity, understanding, diversity, perspective-taking and empathy but also destruction, violence and exploitation intrigued me. The contentment, sorrow and pain which I found when immersing myself in history is unexplainable: 'it is as if a hand had come out and taken yours'. Since then, I have aspired to become a historian. Along the way, I have been extremely fortunate to meet numerous history mentors at different stages of my life, including Hilda Yam, Rosaline Kwong, Jonathan Miller and Richard Bunce who have inspired and enlightened me, and encouraged me to follow the path I have taken. These mentors played an important role not only in my academic journey, but also my life. Sometimes history does not necessarily have the answers we are looking for. And even though we fight and try, we may not be able to achieve what we firmly believe in. Perhaps this is the powerlessness of history: things changed but things still stayed the way they were.

Going to York is probably one of the best decisions I have made in my life. Special thanks must go to David Clayton, who has been a perfect mentor over the past seven years. David is definitely the best supervisor one could possibly ask for: always patient, supportive and enthusiastic. He taught me the art of being a historian, and reminded me of the importance of history in this time of turbulence. When I was in doubt, he was always there to back me up, offering insightful advice and support. I will never forget the words he told me after my graduation: 'Our relationship has changed: we are now equal. And you can always come back to me if you need advice at work and in life.' Without his encouragement, none of my achievements would have been possible. It has been a great pleasure and honour being your student and collaborator, David. Thank you for having so much trust in me. I will always be deeply indebted to you for your tremendous support, academic and pastoral.

I would like to express my gratitude to Jon Howlett, Oleg Besnech and Stevi Jackson for their invaluable guidance at York. Special thanks too to scholars in Hong Kong studies who offered important academic and career advice selflessly during and after my PhD, in particular Robert Bickers, John Carroll, Edmund Cheng, Mark Hampton, Carol Jones, Agnes Ku, Lam Wai-man, Lee Ching Kwan, Loretta Lou, Lui Tai-lok, Ma Ngok, Chi-kwan Mark, Michael Ng, Alan Smart, John Wong, Ray Yep and members of the Society for Hong Kong studies. Big thanks also go to the Hong Kong studies study group, in particular Grace Cao, Doris Chan, Kelvin Chan, Charles Fung, Ken Fung, Vivian Kong, Adonis Li and Allan Pang. The solidarity that all of you have shown is what makes research meaningful and worthwhile despite the difficult times that we are in. And I must acknowledge the support I received from colleagues in the History Department and the Hong Kong Research Hub in Nanyang Technological University, in particular Scott Anthony, Kiu-wai Chu, Jack Greatrex, Kaman Ho, Jonathan Hui, Sam Lai, Tapsi Mathur, Hallam Stevens, Chun Chun Ting, Els von Dongen, Ivy Yeh, Michael Yeo, Zhang Yun and Taomo Zhou. And without your encouragement and emotional support, I do not think I could have made it this far: Alvin Au, Jessica Chan, Meng Hui Chew, Matthew Chin, Catherine Chong, Yousun Chung, Yiyun Ding, Weiying Eng, Maria Fernanda, Fiona Fok, Sally Ho, Charlie Hung, Llewellyn James, April Kwan, Surina Lai, Kenneth Lam, Ivy Leong, Edwin Leung, Leo Shum, Florence Tsui, Yien Chyn Tan and Victor Zhuang.

Over the past twenty years, my parents have never questioned the path I have taken and have always offered unconditional support. (And how can I not mention my three cats, who spent countless nights with me revising my work?) Thank you for everything.

And lastly, I must thank my hometown, Hong Kong. In 2019, I saw the best and worst of humanity. It reminded me why my job is important and why we must get the history right. I will never forget the obligation of being a historian and will always try to make a tiny difference to the world through history.

Abbreviations

BC	British Citizens
BDTC	British Dependent Territories Citizens
BN(O)	British National Overseas
BOC	British Overseas Citizens
CBDT	Citizens of the British Dependent Territories
CCOL	The Federation for the Promotion of Chinese as an Official Language in Hong Kong operated by the Campaign for Chinese as an Official Language
CDC	City District Commissioner
CDO	City District Officer
CUKC	Citizens of the United Kingdom and Colonies
DO	District Officer
GIS	Government Information Services
HAD	Home Affairs Department
HKDN	*Hong Kong Daily News*
HKFS	Hong Kong Federation of Students
HKS	*Hong Kong Standard*
HKT	*Hong Kong Times*
ICAC	Independent Commission Against Corruption
IRA	International Research Associates
KSDN	*Kung Sheung Daily News*
KSEN	*Kung Sheung Evening News*
LO	Liaison Officer
MAC	Mutual Aid Committee
MOOD	Movement of Opinion Direction
NCNA	New China News Agency
OSU	Opinion Survey Unit
PRC	People's Republic of China
SAR	Special Administration Region
SCA	Secretariat for Chinese Affairs

SCMP	*South China Morning Post*
SRH	Survey Research Hong Kong
STMP	*Sing Tao Man Pao*
STYP	*Sing Tao Yat Pao*
TTYP	*Tin Tin Yat Po*
UMELCO	Unofficial Members of the Executive and Legislative Councils
UN	United Nations
WKMP	*Wah Kiu Man Po*
WKYP	*Wah Kiu Yat Po*
WPCOL	All Hong Kong Working Party to Promote Chinese as Official Language

Introduction

In post-handover Hong Kong, there has been a growing sense of nostalgia for the late colonial period, particularly among the young generation and anti-China activists.[1] They view Beijing's interference in politics, education and media as an encroachment on Hong Kong's autonomy, which was guaranteed for fifty years after the end of British rule in 1997. Yau Wai-ching, the former Legislative Councillor who faced disqualification due to her political agenda, described the colonial regime as 'relatively enlightened' and argued that China was undermining a 'well-developed political and constitutional framework' 'step by step'.[2] Andy Chan Ho-tin, the convenor of the Hong Kong National Party, described the last two decades since the handover as 'a period of regression rather than progress': 'The situation is so dire that we dare say Hong Kong never experienced such horrid colonialism until 1997.'[3] In 2019, when the Extradition Bill was proposed, Hong Kong's last Governor, Chris Patten, argued that the law would 'remove the firewall between Hong Kong's rule of law and the idea of law which prevails in communist China' – which 'are sometimes pretty obscure, are rolled all together'.[4] These statements directly and indirectly acknowledged British colonial legacies in Hong Kong. The blue flag of colonial Hong Kong, inscribing the Union Flag with the coat of arms of the colony, was also repeatedly waved by some of the protesters and political groups in anti-China demonstrations, including the recent anti-extradition bill and anti-national security law protests in 2019 and 2020, either requesting British intervention or advocating the Special Administrative Region (SAR)'s secession from mainland China.[5] Some protesters argued that the colonial flag represented 'certain values embodied by the colonial government', in particular 'personal freedoms, rule of law and clean governance'.[6] How these young activists constructed colonialism has raised an important question: To what extent does the Hong Kong public have an accurate historical understanding of state–society relations in British Hong Kong?

These statements about British colonialism are an expression of serious discontent towards China's intervention in Hong Kong. However, it is important to note that these selective historical memories do not reflect history accurately. They are used by activists and politicians to support their political stances, sustain legitimacy and solicit support for their campaigns. It is essential therefore to have a thorough understanding of the relationship between the colonial state and the Chinese communities in Hong Kong under British rule. This book responds to this agenda by undertaking the first comprehensive archive-based study to explore colonial governance and Hong Kong political culture from 1966 to 1997. The overarching research question is: How did state–society relations evolve in the period before the handover of Hong Kong from Britain to China in 1997? The book tackles this question by asking two interrelated questions: What strategies were employed by popular social movements, and do they reveal a shift in mass political culture?[7] How did the perceptions of 'public opinion' held by bureaucrats appointed to run Hong Kong influence the colonial government's ruling strategies? In this book, political culture is defined as political attitudes and political orientations. It mainly examines the attitudes of Hong Kong Chinese towards the colonial government, their ideas about rights and entitlement, and their sense of how to advocate for reforms. In addition, the book explores how these attitudes and orientations influenced political actions.[8] In particular, it investigates what forms of political action were considered acceptable by contemporaries.

By focusing on these questions, this book hopes to contribute to a new understanding of the changing mechanisms used by the colonial government to monitor shifting popular sentiment, and the role played by social movements and public opinion in policy changes and shifting political culture in Hong Kong. Using under-exploited archival records and unofficial published sources in Hong Kong and London, it offers a new perspective on state–society relations in British Hong Kong, revising the existing work, which has mainly been written by political scientists and sociologists. Following new work in social science and historical literature, this book rejects an older concept of Hong Kong as a 'laissez-faire' state. It brings together the hitherto disjointed revisionist research on the colonial state and Chinese communities in Hong Kong. The book contributes to the history of Hong Kong, the late British Empire and modern China, and to emergent scholarship on the comparative study of late colonialism.

Hong Kong: an anomaly in the British Empire?

After the end of the Second World War, a range of factors led to decolonisation in Asia and Africa. Strategically important bases were lost during the war and in the early post-war period, which weakened Britain's ability to deploy coercive power globally and symbolised Britain as an imperial power in decline. The independence of India in 1947 was 'a major turning point'.[9] Without the Indian troops which could be mobilised to the East and the West when needed, Britain lost its 'keystone of the arch' of its Commonwealth defence. Its ability to exert influence on Asia had therefore been reduced substantially.[10] The withdrawal from Egypt in 1951 implied that the Canal Zone could 'no longer be considered a base for defence of the Middle East'.[11] The Suez Crisis in 1956 further exposed Britain's limited military power and fragile sterling economy, in contrast to the rise of the United States (US) as a 'superpower', which Britain now could not act independently without.[12] The shift in the international climate which divided the world into contesting ideological blocs also suggested Soviet aggression had to be checked, which was an expensive task. The continued occupation of Germany alone cost £100 million a year in 1946.[13] By the end of the war, Britain had lost its geopolitical advantages and incurred a lot of overseas debts and borrowing.[14] At a time when the incumbent Labour government was committed to reconstructing the domestic economy and implementing social reforms, Britain needed to cut its overseas defence costs.

In addition, after the early period of post-war reconstruction, the economic value of the empire to Britain was on the wane. The failure of development projects in the colonies and the decreased value of colonial earnings made British economic interests in the colonies less significant.[15] The 'double taxation' system, which required British businesses that invested in the colonies to pay tax in both the United Kingdom and the dependent territories, also placed them at a disadvantage compared to foreign competitors, further deterring investment in colonial ventures.[16] By the late 1950s, trade within the Sterling Area was shrinking and Britain's links with its Sterling Area members were weakening.[17] Simultaneously, Britain's trading interest had shifted towards the more advanced economies in Europe, as indicated by its agreement to join the European Free Trade Area, which was formed in 1960. Retaining a formal colonial empire had become increasingly uneconomical and unattractive.[18] Supporting 'decolonisation', by withdrawing from a commitment to rule colonial dependencies and replacing this formal empire with informal ties between Britain and its ex-colonies was, by the late 1950s, a timely and rational strategy for Britain to pursue.[19]

Decolonisation was also, however, a product of changes in the international arena due to increased criticism of colonialism in the post-war period. Under the United Nations (UN) Charter, formal colonialism became internationally illegitimate. The fact that the French and Belgians had already retreated from their empires left Britain's position even more awkward, subjecting it to increased abuse and criticism in the UN under the influence of Cold War politics.[20] Britain had become 'public enemy number one' for many former colonies, intensifying the global momentum towards decolonisation.[21]

Transformations in colonial societies, such as new kinds of consumption, increased literacy and new communication techniques, also strengthened anti-colonial nationalism in particular colonies in Asia and Africa.[22] Due to the rise of resistance to colonial rule, a previous method of collaborating with native social elites to legitimise foreign administration became far less effective.[23] Educated elites started forming larger coalitions, exploiting pervasive social discontent over administrative autocracies.[24] Ordinary people also mobilised to revolt against colonial rule.[25] For example, the Malayan Spring marked the beginning of a new era, whereby 'new moods, vocabularies and techniques were introduced into political life' and people started to 'test the limits of the new freedom'.[26] The British proposal of the Malayan Union provided further impetus for Malay nationalism to flourish, pressing Britain to instead form a federal government to maintain their ethnic majority in governance.[27] Communal tensions and the British eviction of Chinese squatters from forest reserves led to the Malayan Emergency in 1948.[28] Anti-colonial movements also flourished in Singapore, such as the language campaign organised by the educated Chinese. Communist infiltration was particularly successful in Chinese middle schools. In May 1954, when students did not register for national service despite the passage of the National Service Ordinance, a riot broke out.[29] During the transitional period, different means were employed by the British to contain opposition and win the 'hearts and minds' of natives. Strategies ranged from conducting psychological tests and surveys targeting radicals and introducing representative electoral systems, to the use of propaganda and repression, such as the creation of interrogation camps during the Mau Mau Uprisings and the deportation of Chinese suspects during the Malayan Emergency.[30] However, counter-insurgency operations did not enable Britain to retain its colonies, and the eruption of anti-colonial nationalism in a large number of British colonies speeded up decolonisation.

Hong Kong did not conform to this general pattern of decolonisation. As John Darwin has pointed out, the case of Hong Kong constituted an anomaly in the British Empire which proved to be 'an embarrassing puzzle' for historians of decolonisation:

> Hong Kong's political history makes nonsense of the decolonising process as it is usually imagined. Until after its political future was settled, it underwent no significant constitutional change. It will never travel the colonial *cursus honorum* from crown colony rule to representative and then responsible government. It has never experienced the growth of an indigenous Hong Kong nationalism nor the demand for self-rule by as well as for its inhabitants.

Unlike practically every other territory in the former British Empire, the end of British rule will bring not sovereign independence but reabsorption into the state out of which the colony was originally carved.[31]

The peculiar development of Hong Kong raises further questions about state–society relations in the colony: To what extent and how was repression used to control the population? What propaganda were deployed to win the locals' 'hearts and minds'? How does the 'decolonisation' of Hong Kong compare with the decolonisation of Malaya and Singapore, where there were also large Chinese communities which had migrated from China? What formal channels were used by the Hong Kong colonial government to communicate with Chinese communities before the mid-1980s when electoral reforms were first introduced? How did the government solicit public opinion without encouraging a process of uncontrollable decolonisation? How do we explain why anti-colonial nationalism was so mooted in Hong Kong compared to Malaya and Singapore? Were, as was argued by the first generation of social scientists studying life in the colony, Hong Kong Chinese people politically apathetic, unwilling to engage in politics? In addition, why did Britain hold on to Hong Kong until 1997 rather than withdrawing from the colony in the late 1950s and early 1960s when decolonisation was accelerating in Asia and Africa?

Hong Kong represents a unique case study that is 'too important to be simply ignored'.[32] The changing state–society relations in Hong Kong can be used to identify similarities and differences in experiences of decolonisation in the British Empire, setting up a transnational comparative framework for further studies.

The significance of Hong Kong

Since its establishment, the People's Republic of China (PRC), which believed that the treaties that governed Hong Kong's status were unequal and invalid, had always asserted that Hong Kong was part of its territory and perceived British administration in the colony to be temporary.[33] However, in 1949, Mao Zedong and Zhou Enlai had decided not to take back Hong Kong immediately. The Chinese Communists perceived it as advantageous if Hong Kong remained in British hands temporarily. Using the colony as a window, China could trade with the West and generate foreign exchange, especially when a trade embargo was imposed on China by the US.[34] This decision to accept the continuation of British rule was also influenced by Cold War politics. According to Wang Gungwu, the colony retained a 'unique position for Chinese both inside and outside China' as it allowed both Chinese Communists and Nationalists to 'disseminate information and disinformation to seek to reach out to as many Chinese as possible'.[35]

Through Hong Kong, China could disseminate propaganda to overseas Chinese communities in Southeast Asia.[36] In addition, China could provoke unrest and exploit issues in Hong Kong to split the Anglo-American alliance. Therefore, instead of liberating Hong Kong, China's Hong Kong policy focused on 'long-term planning and full utilisation'.[37] Despite China's toleration of British presence in Hong Kong, Britain was always concerned that China would attack Hong Kong if a Sino-American war broke out due to conflicts over Korea or Taiwan, given that Hong Kong was militarily indefensible.[38] Although Hong Kong's garrison was strengthened shortly after the PRC was founded, it was soon scaled down in 1950 because of the outbreak of the Korean War and high maintenance costs.[39] As Britain's strategic interest in retaining the colony had diminished greatly after the Second World War, in 1952, the British government had abandoned its plans to defend Hong Kong in the event of a full-scale communist invasion.[40] Hong Kong's vulnerability was further aggravated by the reluctance of the US to defend it.[41] Given Hong Kong's vulnerability, the colonial regime 'avoid[ed] provoking [China] unnecessarily'.[42] To prevent giving China the impression that it was challenging its sovereignty and 'open[ing] the door to a confrontation between left-wing and right-wing supporters',[43] a representative electoral system was not introduced in Hong Kong.[44] The colony's political system remained largely unreformed after the Second World War. Direct channels for political participation were limited. The Legislative Council was entirely comprised of official and unofficial members appointed by the Governor. The members of the Executive Council, an organ to advise the Governor in policymaking, were also appointed either by the Queen or the Governor. Although the Urban Council was partially democratically elected, it had little financial autonomy and executive power.[45] Institutional and constitutional reforms were only implemented after the mid-1980s.

Why did Britain remain in the colony until 1997? As a 'fault line' in the Cold War, Hong Kong was important for Britain strategically: it provided a base for the capitalist bloc to monitor activities in mainland China and acted as a bulwark against the spread of communism to Southeast Asia.[46] Unlike other British colonies which required high cost of maintenance, Hong Kong was also relatively self-sufficient, and even eventually made a contribution towards the cost of the British garrison in the colony.[47] Moreover, Hong Kong was a major financial contributor to the Sterling Area until 1972, holding its large public reserves of sterling in London. Apart from the construction of two local universities, it rarely required financial help from the metropole.[48] As Chi-kwan Mark has suggested, it was 'too valuable to be willingly abandoned'.[49]

Although Britain ruled Hong Kong until 1997, as scholars have argued, 'informal devolution of power' and 'decolonisation' still took place in Hong

Kong. Leo Goodstadt, for example, pointed out that there had been an informal devolution of power from the metropole to Hong Kong since the 1950s, 'a partial substitute for Hong Kong's control of its own administration'.[50] John Darwin argued that Hong Kong had been effectively 'decolonised' by 1952, in effect controlled by China rather than Britain.[51] Chi-kwan Mark referred to a different timeframe, suggesting that 'decolonisation' was completed by 1968, when the bureaucratic mentality revealed that Britain had lost both the 'means' and 'will' to control Hong Kong.[52]

A period of transformation

The period from 1966 to 1997 was a pivotal period of Hong Kong history. Politically, the colonial government's ruling strategies changed drastically. Since 1965, Sino-British relations had been moving 'in a downward spiral'.[53] The escalation of the Vietnam War and Britain's open support for the US had led to rising Anglo-Chinese tensions.[54] The official propaganda in Beijing had intensified its attack on Britain.[55] However, the waning economic power of the British Empire and the 'East of Suez' policy shift in 1967 meant Britain's ability to defend Hong Kong had been reduced significantly. The vulnerability of Hong Kong to social unrest and political revolution was revealed by the Star Ferry riots of 1966 and the leftist riots of 1967.[56] The 1966 riots show 'the existence of considerable social discontent' and a communication gap between the government and the society.[57] The 1967 riots, a spillover of Cultural Revolution, revealed that Hong Kong's internal and external security were inseparable, leading Britain to realise that the colony was 'indefensible against Chinese military attack'.[58] It also demonstrated clearly how domestic developments in Hong Kong could adversely affect Sino-British relations.[59] By 1969, Britain understood that 'Hong Kong's future must eventually lie in China' and its withdrawal was inevitable.[60] To avoid similar incidents from happening, it was crucial for the colonial government to develop a sense of 'civic pride' among the Hong Kong Chinese as a substitute for 'national loyalty', which would be an important bargaining chip in future negotiations with China.[61] The colonial administration therefore took the initiative to respond to these internal and externally inspired events through political and social reforms, which mark the starting point of the analysis in this book. The issue was how could the governance of Hong Kong be reformed without risking further unrest or discrediting British rule.

Before the 1970s, the Urban Council was the only political institution with democratically elected members. The cadet system, which recruited expatriate elites directly from universities in Britain and trained them as interpreters to be used in courts and administration, was used in Hong

Kong until 1960. In other words, almost 'all' high-ranked civil servants were 'British subjects of pure European descent' who came from a 'solid, though not rich, upper middle-class' background.[62] The language requirement further prevented Chinese people who had low English proficiency from serving in the colonial bureaucracy. An effective communication channel was absent. A 'gap' between the colonial government and the Chinese population was the central problem to be resolved. With the size of the state expanding, senior civil servants acknowledged that the existing law and order was 'unsustainable' and sought 'new forms of legitimation'.[63] As the introduction of a democratic electoral system was unfeasible, a City District Officer (CDO) Scheme was implemented in 1968, with the aim of restoring confidence, enhancing the legitimacy of the colonial bureaucracy and improving communications between the government and the people. The City District Office had multiple functions. It was 'a communication agent, a community organiser and a trouble-shooter for the people'. On the one hand, it facilitated communications between the government and the Hong Kong Chinese and explained policies to the public; on the other hand, it addressed people's grievances and fed 'public opinion' to the policymakers in the bureaucracy.[64]

State–society relations underwent further changes during the rule of Murray MacLehose from 1971 to 1982, a pivotal period which laid the foundations for political, social and economic changes in Hong Kong. The long 1970s is always described by historians as 'a paradoxical decade' and 'a crucial period of change and adjustment' that reshaped the contours of global history.[65] This was no exception for Hong Kong; it was during the 1970s, the focus of this book, that the colonial government altered its governance strategies and became increasingly responsive to popular demands. A series of legislative and institutional changes were introduced to improve political communications, enhance the colonial regime's legitimacy and eradicate petty bureaucratic corruption practised by civil servants, including the formalisation of Chinese as the official legal language of Hong Kong, the enactment and the abolition of the 'Touch Base' policy, and the formation of the Independent Commission Against Corruption (ICAC), all of which will be discussed using newly available archival evidence.[66] Some of these reforms were initiated or endorsed by London. In the 1970s, Labour politicians and left-wing activists, who believed in the necessity of creating 'a rapid and comprehensive' 'social security system', paid increased attention to the colony's condition, especially people's living standards and workers' conditions, which to some extent resembled industrial maladies in Dickensian England.[67] However, in some cases, it was the colonial government that took the lead and implemented the reforms. Regardless, these reforms and developments continued to affect Hong Kong's governance, discourse and political culture after the 1970s, even in the post-handover era when political tensions heightened.[68]

The 1980s and 1990s witnessed further political changes in the colony. To safeguard Hong Kong's 'high degree of autonomy' post-1997, attempts were made by the colonial government to democratise the political system. In 1982, the District Boards were formed and their first direct election was subsequently held. In 1983, the Urban Council's electoral franchise expanded and its membership increased.[69] In July 1984, a Green Paper on electoral reform was issued by the government, aiming to 'develop progressively a system of government the authority for which is firmly rooted in Hong Kong'.[70] In 1985, indirect election was introduced in the Legislative Council. Nevertheless, extensive political reforms were inviable due to opposition from China. Xu Jiatun, China's representative in the colony, argued that democratising Hong Kong's political system during this transitional period would have been a breach of the Sino-British agreement. No significant reforms should be introduced until the Basic Law was promulgated in 1990.[71] Nonetheless, the electoral reforms proposed by Chris Patten in the early 1990s, which suggested broadening the electorate base in Legislative Council elections, still met with strong resistance from China.[72]

Despite the lack of progress with making the Hong Kong government more accountable to the people, the colonial administration advanced a number of long-term social reforms. The Ten-Year Housing Programme provided accommodation for approximately 1.8 million people. Free primary education was introduced. Social welfare services, public assistance, transport, labour legislation as well as the medical and health system were expanded.[73] The period also saw a surge in political mobilisation. Since the late 1960s, there had been a shift in political culture, particularly among the post-war baby boomers, who started developing a sense of belonging to Hong Kong.[74] The emergence of these young activists and the increased responsiveness of the colonial state encouraged discussions of current affairs in the public domain.[75] The Sino-British negotiations further politicised Chinese elites, leading to the formation of various political groups in the 1980s, such as the Meeting Point in 1983, the Hong Kong Affairs Society in 1984 and the Association for Democracy and People's Livelihood in 1986.[76] Besides, both legal and illegal immigration from China continued to be an important issue, placing pressure on the colony's housing and welfare system, and creating tensions between locals and mainland Chinese. It is possible that a Hong Kong identity was constructed in opposition to a mainland Chinese identity.

Economically, Hong Kong continued to experience rapid growth through the 1970s and beyond. Hong Kong's Gross Domestic Product had increased by 117 per cent during the period from 1968 to 1973.[77] Significantly, the index of real wages increased from 100 in 1964 to 184 in 1982.[78] This further widened the gap between living standards in Hong Kong and China, but the slow convergence of living standards between Hong Kong and South China began soon afterwards. In 1978, the Open Door Policy was implemented by Deng Xiaoping. A number of special economic zones were set up, including Shenzhen, encouraging foreign investment. China's inexpensive labour and land led many Hong Kong industrialists to relocate their factories to the mainland. These economic changes gradually transformed Hong Kong from a 'manufacturing base' in the 1970s to a 'leading financial and service centre' in the 1990s.[79]

The period was also significant for the constitutional settlement of Hong Kong. Sino-British negotiations started when MacLehose visited Beijing in 1979. In 1981, the British Nationality Act was passed, stripping two and a half million Hong Kong Chinese of their right of abode in Britain. This provoked 'a sense of betrayal'. Optimism further waned after the British Prime Minister, Margaret Thatcher, visited China in 1982: 'By the time Thatcher left Beijing, it was clear that China would try to recover Hong Kong in 1997.'[80] Although the Sino-British Joint Declaration signed in 1984 suggested that under 'One Country, Two Systems', Hong Kong would enjoy a high degree of autonomy, public confidence in Hong Kong's future dropped, especially after the Tiananmen Square incident in 1989, resulting in a panic in financial markets and waves of emigration.

This period was the precursor to political and social changes in postcolonial Hong Kong. An exploration of the relationship between policy-making and political culture in this period is necessary to understand reforms and responses initiated by the colonial state and changing Sino-British relations, leading to the handover of Hong Kong in 1997. Although scholars have recently refuted the notion of a 'minimally-integrated social-political system' and have pointed out that considerable social conflicts had broken out in the post-war period, there remains a paucity of detailed archive-based studies on how social movements were organised and how the public and the state responded to political activism.[81]

The historiography of Hong Kong's 'minimally-integrated social-political system'

In 1964, George Endacott first described the colonial state in Hong Kong as 'a minimum of government' in the style of 'Benthamite laissez-faire', with Chinese communities having a limited impact on policy formation and the state having a weak relationship with social groups.[82] The notion that Chinese society had limited contact with the colonial state was endorsed by political scientists and sociologists, such as Norman Miners, J. S. Hoadley and Ambrose King, who observed in the 1970s that the colony was politically stable. Sustained civic advocacy for constitutional reforms was absent. The level of political participation of Hong Kong Chinese in formal politics was also low.[83] According to these scholars, this phenomenon was attributable to a general lack of interest in political participation, influenced by a 'refugee mentality' and Confucian values, which created 'a deep-rooted anti-political attitude among the people'.[84] The government's practice of administrative co-option, such the recruitment of elites into the administrative system and the incorporation of grassroots opinions through implementing the CDO Scheme, also provided channels for ordinary Hong Kong Chinese to express their opinions in policy formation, minimising the possibility of public resistance.[85]

In the 1980s, sociologist Lau Siu-kai reinforced the notion of a laissez-faire state and a politically apathetic Chinese society, describing Hong Kong as a 'minimally-integrated social-political system'. According to Lau, there were limited links between the 'autonomous bureaucratic polity' and the 'atomistic Chinese society'. The colonial state dominated the political sector and was largely free from interference by social and economic forces. It lacked 'organisational penetration' into Chinese society. The only linkages between it and Chinese society were via some Chinese elites, intermediate organisations and state-sponsored schemes, but the mechanisms of integration were weak.[86] The underlying social ethos was 'utilitarianistic familism'. Even in a hyper urban-industrial setting, familial interests remained the primary consideration among most Hong Kong Chinese, placed above communal interests. This resulted in 'political aloofness', and subsequently a low level of political participation.[87] Within these familial groups, economic interdependence and mutual assistance were emphasised. In other words, the Chinese households did not demand the state to intervene to redistribute resources.[88]

However, this portrayal was erroneous. First, 'political stability' does not necessarily equate to the complete absence of political activism. Throughout the post-war period, the colony witnessed a number of political and social mobilisations, which indicate a considerable degree of political participation among the Chinese population. Adhering to the narrow definition of political participation, sociologists neglected informal political activities. For example, the Star Ferry riots in 1966 signified the emergence of anti-colonial sentiment among some Hong Kong Chinese. The 1956 and 1967 riots were inspired by the ongoing confrontation between Kuomintang, the Chinese Communist Party and the colonial government.[89] Second, these studies were ahistorical due to the over-reliance of these sociologists on social science theories and interview data from a limited sample size. For example, Lau acknowledged that his adoption of a 'basically theoretical approach' inevitably had led to the omission of 'many historical and empirical details'.⁹⁰ Demographic variables, in particular education, income and occupation, were crucial factors that determined political attitudes and orientations. By dismissing the importance of these factors, Lau's approach overlooked 'class differences within the Chinese community', misinterpreting the Hong Kong Chinese as a homogenous and amorphous social entity.⁹¹ The poor methodological construction and the failure to take the historical context into consideration resulted in partial and inaccurate knowledge of Hong Kong's political culture.

Revisionism

Since the 1990s, revisionists have contested the notion of a 'minimally-integrated social-political system' and have convincingly argued that it misrepresented the state–society relations in Hong Kong. There are two strands in this literature: one analysing colonial statecraft and the other examining political culture in Chinese society. Scholars working on the colonial state argued that the existing literature had grossly simplified the complex nature of British colonialism in Hong Kong.⁹² In reality, the colonial state was far from 'a politically neutral state', which 'disengaged itself from societal affairs'. Its reach into Chinese society was 'far more penetrating'.⁹³ The synoptic view that emerged was that state–society relations in Hong Kong were 'complex and contingent upon particular situations'.⁹⁴ Sometimes the ruling elites acted benevolently and rewarded their followers. Sometimes, through the deliberate creation of 'social cleavages' and collaborations with various social groups, the colonial state 'exercise[d] leverage and manoeuvre[d] events into the desired directions'.⁹⁵

Rather than practising non-interventionism, the state intervened in Chinese society. Like other British colonies, there were 'severe controls on freedom of expression' in Hong Kong.⁹⁶ The newspapers in the colony were 'continuously and systematically monitored and pervasively censored through the collaborative efforts of executive actions, legislative provisions and judicial decisions'.⁹⁷ Similar rules were applied to films due to the worries that they could become 'an ideological weapon' in the context of the Cold War.⁹⁸ As Ma Ngok has argued, 'the mutual non-intervention between polity and society was overstated'.⁹⁹

The strongest revisionist challenge came from efforts by historians and social scientists to reconstruct social movements, with particular emphasis given to the disturbances of 1966 and 1967. These were viewed as 'a watershed in Hong Kong's political history'.¹⁰⁰ Before the mid-1960s, Hong Kong's political discourse was largely influenced by communist

China and Kuomintang Taiwan. There was little concern over local politics. Nevertheless, the sojourner mentality ended when Hong Kong Chinese gradually turned into a settled population due to the tightening of border controls between Hong Kong and China in the 1950s, and gradually this facilitated the formation of a new political culture.[101] After the outbreak of the Star Ferry riots in 1966, the political culture shifted among the locally born young generation. The disturbance led them to 'reflect on their life and their role in the local society, and voice their views in a significant way for the first time'.[102] This 'new political and social climate' encouraged political affairs discussions in public discourse.[103]

Scholars have also investigated the state-led reforms of the 1970s, which enhanced the government's credibility and fostered a sense of belonging among the locals.[104] In addition, rapid economic development enabled people in Hong Kong to travel abroad and compare their homeland with other cities. Increased economic affluence led to the rise of a local popular culture industry. In local television programmes, movies and music, 'the cultural differences between Hong Kongers and mainland Chinese' were emphasised.[105] As a result, the notion that 'Hong Kong was politically and culturally separated from China' was reinforced.[106] As John Carroll has observed, from the 1970s, the emergence of this local consciousness led many activists in Hong Kong to start making more demands to the colonial government.[107]

In 2004, Lam Wai-man expanded the formerly narrow definition of political participation to include informal and unlawful activities, such as protests, signature campaigns, petitions and discursive discussions, showing that political mobilisation had never been absent in Hong Kong. Lau's claim that Chinese society lacked the 'will and ability' to challenge the colonial state therefore was unjustified.[108] These forms of political mobilisation conveyed different ideologies, ranging from nationalism and anti-colonialism to the concept of universal human rights and gender equality. Although a 'culture of de-politicisation' existed, which bounded the ability of social movements to radically reorder social relations and transform the state, it did not stop political activism. Instead, it gave rise to 'gradualism and reformism within a framework of stability and prosperity', which in turn benefited the colonial government.[109] Like much of the revisionism to date, Lam relied on published sources to present case evidence. She did not use the standard historical source, state records, which can potentially show how the colonial government perceived these social movements and whether this public opinion had been channelled into the policymaking process. Using state records and a wide range of published records, this book addresses deficiencies in the existing literature by examining the strategies and rhetoric employed by activists, the public reception of these campaigns and how they influenced policymaking.

Approach and methodology

The significance of this research lies in the richness of the unexplored primary sources. Most existing research has been carried out by political scientists, sociologists, linguists and anthropologists. This book is timely and important. It is the first to use comprehensive archival sources to explore political culture and public policymaking in a crucial period for Hong Kong. Departing from existing methodologies and focus, it provides a longer perspective using historical discipline, aiming at bridging the gap between the past and present. This book asks a series of questions to explore the changing relationship between the government and the residents of Hong Kong. How did unorthodox mass political activities interact with bureaucracy and alter the existing political establishment and order? How did political attitudes of Hong Kong Chinese of different social classes and age groups shift over time?

An inductive method was employed in the research for this book. Evidence was obtained from archives in both Hong Kong and London. The state records in the Hong Kong Public Records Office and the National Archives in Kew were confidential and have only been released into the public domain recently. These under-exploited files provide a novel understanding of how social movements were organised and how the state responded to political activism. They capture social change and can be used to examine the development of associational life, a manifestation of 'political activism'. The way officials and activists described social movements in private correspondence and petitions illustrates participants' political orientations and how activists and organisations were mobilised. Official surveys and observations record how ordinary Hong Kong Chinese viewed political activism, which can be used to analyse the political culture of different groups in the colony. Correspondence between policymakers evaluates the contemporary mood and explains the reasons behind administrative, legislative and institutional changes. Unofficial records, such as newspapers, pamphlets and student newsletters, have also been collected and consulted. Both Chinese and English newspapers have been used as sources. The mass media played a significant role in constructing the collective sense of Hong Kong community. Some of the campaigns, such as the *China Mail* anti-corruption campaign, were centred on the media.

The partiality and limitations of these sources must be acknowledged. Some of these records are fragmentary. Some documents that discuss individuals who are still alive have not been released into the public domain. Files containing sensitive content which may influence the present relationship between Britain and China are retained. Some incriminating archival records may also have been destroyed on the eve of decolonisation or are

Introduction 15

still stored in the Migrated Archives at Hanslope. The disclosure of these documents might embarrass the British government and compromise intelligence information. Therefore, they are not in the public domain.

Structure and argument

This book consists of eight chapters. Chapter 1 explains how the colonial state solicited public opinion indirectly and directly, and how they influenced ruling strategies. The other seven chapters are case studies on major events of political participation which stimulated heated public discussion from 1966 to 1997. They have either been inadequately covered by the existing literature or under-studied using the newly released archival records. These cases do not only include positive responses from the government, but also negative responses. Examination of these cases can therefore identify under what circumstances social movement and public opinion could exert pressure on the colonial government and successfully influence its policies.

Chapter 2 details the Chinese as the official language movement from the late 1960s to 1970, which has not been fully covered by existing literature using archival sources. The campaign was substantial and significant. The formalisation of Chinese as the official legal language of Hong Kong removed the communication barrier between the colonial regime and Chinese society. The stake of Hong Kong Chinese in politics was also drastically enhanced as more of them could now serve in the colonial government.

Chapter 3 explores the relationship between a number of anti-corruption campaigns and the formation of the Independent Commission Against Corruption (ICAC), the most important institutional change in British Hong Kong in the 1970s. The ICAC was largely successful in restoring public confidence in the colonial government. It also played an important role in changing Hong Kong's political culture. People started to identify themselves when reporting cases of corruption. Their fear of officialdom had been greatly reduced.

Chapter 4 examines how telephone rates were regulated in Hong Kong and how this influenced consumer movements, and vice versa. The movement was significant since there was an anti-colonial agenda behind the protests against rising prices. Poor regulation was condemned and state intervention was demanded. It also indicated a changing political culture. Hong Kong Chinese, including those at the grassroots level, demonstrated considerable skills at mobilising support when their interests were at stake.

Chapter 5 documents the Golden Jubilee incident in 1978, which reveals young activists' remarkable capacity for organisation and effective communication with post-secondary students and MPs in London. The colonial state countered the political activism of teachers and students by setting up a Committee of Inquiry. The shifting opinions monitored by the colonial government however suggested that political culture in Hong Kong was divided: the grassroots groups and middle-aged and elderly households largely disapproved of confrontational political activism initiated by the educated young generation.

Chapter 6 explores the changing immigration policy in Hong Kong. The scale of illegal immigration from China strained the colony's limited housing stock and under-developed welfare and education systems since the 1960s. The exclusionist immigration policy of the colonial state facilitated increased discrimination towards and stereotypes of mainland Chinese, which influenced how Hong Kong Chinese identified with the colony and led many of them to engage in intensive discursive debates, demanding reforms and prioritisation of their access to economic resources and social services. The changing popular sentiment led to the formation and abolition of the 'Touch Base' policy in 1974 and 1980.

Chapter 7 examines how people of different social classes and age groups in Hong Kong responded to the enactment of the British Nationality Act. The British Nationality Act passed in 1981 stripped the rights of abode of Hong Kong Chinese in Britain, provoking 'a sense of betrayal'. This chapter analyses the public discourse and investigates to what extent that affected policymaking and political allegiance to the colonial and British governments.

Chapter 8 explores constitutional reforms in Hong Kong in the 1980s and 1990s, in particular the setting up of District Boards and their election in 1982, the Green and White Papers on the development of Hong Kong's representative government in 1984 and 1985 and the subsequent Legislative Council elections, and the electoral reforms proposed by Chris Patten in 1992. It investigates how the public reacted to these changes and proposed reforms and whether demands for democratisation escalated in the late 1980s and 1990s, especially after the Sino-British Joint Declaration was agreed in 1984 and the Tiananmen Square Incident took place in 1989. Although Hong Kong Chinese people did not play an active part in drafting the Joint Declaration in 1984 and the Basic Law in 1990, colonial bureaucrats implementing major electoral reforms before the handover had to take into account how Hong Kong people viewed this controversial settlement to ensure a smooth transition into 1997, sustaining Britain's political and economic interests. The chapter also investigates why the colonial government increasingly shifted from 'covert colonialism' to using scientifically organised overt public opinion polls undertaken by commercial firms and post-secondary academic institutions in the 1980s and questions whether democratisation and quantitative polling in the 1980s and 1990s completely replaced the covert mechanisms used in Hong Kong since 1968.

The book argues that activists employed collaborative strategies to mobilise the public from 1966 onwards. Activists often resorted to informal means, such as petitions, signature campaigns and setting up ad hoc organisations, to pull resources, rally support from external parties and pressurise the colonial government to introduce changes. Activists deployed ideological and instrumental reasoning, which were sometimes inseparable. Increased political activism suggests that the general political culture in Hong Kong had shifted since the 1970s. Moderate informal political channels were gradually accepted. However, in the aftermath of the 1967 riots, political activism which directly confronted the colonial regime was still not widely acknowledged. Political conservatism persisted in the 1980s and 1990s despite the opening up of the colonial polity and the emergence of political parties, especially among the grassroots groups and business and industrial sectors, which did not support rapid democratisation in Hong Kong and believed it would jeopardise the colony's political stability.

This book also argues that shifting popular sentiment played an important role in administrative, legislative and institutional changes in Hong Kong despite the absence of a democratic electoral system. The reformist colonial state had developed an increasingly scientific and sophisticated covert polling exercise, Town Talk in 1968 and MOOD in 1975, to monitor and assess changing public opinion in Chinese society. This polling device provided the colonial government with the organisational capacity to conduct surveillance, monitoring Chinese society closely, a manifestation of 'covert colonialism'.[110] It also functioned as a substitute for representative democracy, enabling the undemocratic colonial government to widen the channels of political participation for ordinary people in a state-controlled manner without provoking China's resistance nor politicising the Hong Kong Chinese. With Town Talk and MOOD's existence being concealed from the public, the colonial government had the leeway to decide when to follow public opinion. This technique, which both enhanced and limited the ability of the public to influence the policymaking process, was vital to sustaining the legitimacy of the undemocratic government, which was challenged by surging anti-colonial sentiment and increased aspirations among the public to engage in political activities amid widespread decolonisation in Asia and Africa. It also provides historians with a new way of revealing how the mentalities of bureaucrats were changing as Hong Kong 'decolonised'. The covert polling exercise survived until the 1990s but became less significant when scientifically organised overt public opinion surveys were increasingly used from the 1980s, a time when increased democratic electoral reforms were introduced to Hong Kong's political system.

As the chapters reveal, social movements pressurised the colonial government to respond to shifting popular sentiment. The procedure normally started with the supply of intelligence on social movements and covert public opinion by local organisations to senior officials. Preliminary advice was given by these civil servants who observed the community secretly. If the event attracted considerable attention from the public, a Special Committee or a Commission of Inquiry was set up to investigate the issue, after which the public was invited to take part in consultation. This was usually followed by the publication of reports explaining the Committee's findings to the society. Lastly, the colonial state determined whether a new administrative approach was to be adopted based on the findings in these extraordinary reports. During this policymaking process, nonetheless, a number of factors, such as Britain's interests and its diplomatic relations with China, could have had a greater influence on policymaking than shifting popular sentiment as imperfectly revealed to bureaucrats by secret and public polling.

The intelligence gathered by colonial bureaucrats provides new insights into how political cultures differed in accordance with social classes and age groups. The upper class was in general reluctant to engage in political activism. They despised informal means of political participation as they believed that these activities were undignified and undermined political stability. The middle class on the whole was pro-establishment and indifferent to informal political engagement. The working class and the grassroots level were mainly driven by instrumentalism. Despite their capacity to mobilise, they were unaware of the implications of an increasingly responsive reformist colonial state. Influenced by traditional Chinese values, the middle-aged and elderly groups mostly believed that political activism should be checked as it might get out of hand, threatening the order and stability of the colony. The young generation was largely divided. Some students were reluctant to take part in social movements. Yet, those in higher education tended to consider informal political participation to be an appropriate way to express themselves and adopt relatively radical strategies to pursue their ends. In general, the young generation held a less favourable view of the colonial state than their seniors.

The recent anti-extradition bill protests and the enactment of the National Security Law, which have divided generations and social classes, have regenerated discussions regarding Britain's colonial legacies, as well as debates on Hong Kong's changing governance and political culture. By revealing the colonial government's effort to manage public opinion and how it interacted in complex ways with a diverse variety of Chinese communities engaging with new political movements and generating pro-democratic discourse, this book provides an innovative long-term perspective of the constitutional crisis in today's Hong Kong and contributes to the public debates on Hong Kong's past as a British colony and its future in the hands of Beijing.

Notes

1 Gary Cheung, 'Beijing Finds Hong Kongers' Nostalgia for Colonial Era Hard to Fathom', *South China Morning Post* (*SCMP* hereafter), 1 October 2012; 'In Pictures: Better Times? Hong Kong's British Nostalgia Trip', *Hong Kong Free Press* (*HKFP* hereafter), 28 May 2017; Jason Wordie, 'In Former Colonies Hong Kong and Taiwan, "National" Identity Often Emerges from Fanciful Nostalgia', *SCMP*, 29 March 2019.
2 Yau Wai-ching, 'Democracy's Demise in Hong Kong', *New York Times*, 16 September 2018.
3 Jeff Lam and Alvin Lum, 'Hong Kong Separatist Party Leader Andy Chan Ho-tin Calls China "A Threat to All Free Peoples in the World" in Fiery Foreign Correspondents' Club Speech', *SCMP*, 14 August 2018.
4 Helen Davidson, 'The Last Fight for Hong Kong: Activists Gear Up over Extradition Law', *The Guardian*, 7 June 2019.
5 Richard Lloyd Parry and Raphael Blet, 'Colonial Nostalgia Rules in Hong Kong as Young Refuse to Accept China's Authority', *The Sunday Times*, 14 June 2019.
6 Holmes Chan, 'Explainer: The Conflicting Messages Behind Protesters' Use of the Colonial Hong Kong Flag', *HKFP*, 13 July 2019. This view and the 'myths of our colonial past', however, are increasingly contested in public discourse. See Yehua, 'Hong Kong's Former Coloniser Cannot be Our Saviour: We Must Critically Confront the Injustices of Britain's Past and Present', *Lausan*, 3 March 2020.
7 According to Gabriel Almond and Sidney Verba, levels of political participation and attitudes towards politics vary in different political cultures. There are three types of political cultures, which can be categorised as 1) parochial, 2) subject and 3) participant. 1) The parochial political culture refers to societies where there are no or minimal or specialised political roles and expectations of changes initiated by the political system. People often do not have knowledge and/or interest in politics. They may be aware of the presence of a central political regime but their feelings towards the political structure are often uncertain or negative. 2) The subject political culture refers to societies in which people are aware of politics and political phenomenon. Yet, their orientations to engage in politics ('input objects') 'approach zero'. Due to their heavy subjection to decisions made by the central government, they are, hence, 'subjects'. 3) The participant political culture is one in which members of the society 'tend to be explicitly oriented' to both the political and administrative structure and process. In other words, they engage in politics actively and are able to exert their influence on the government. See *The Civic Culture*, pp. 17–18.
8 Almond and Verba's concept of political culture has been contested and criticised by other scholars since the 1960s. One of the main criticisms is that the theory does not offer 'an ontology and epistemology of its own' and merely suggests a 'dimension of comparative analysis without having fundamentally specified what it is and how it works'. It does not offer explanations for attitude

operationalisation. Therefore, this book will not only investigate the political attitudes and orientation of Hong Kong Chinese, but also question how they affected people's level and forms of political participation, and interaction with the colonial state. This will help to integrate culture and state studies in a more unified framework. See Welch, *The Political Culture Theory* and Voinea and Neumann, 'Political Culture', p. 335.

9 Hyam, 'The Primacy of Geopolitics', p. 44.
10 Alanbrooke, *Triumph*, p. 533.
11 Darwin, *The Empire Project*, pp. 563–4.
12 Ibid., pp. 590, 607–8.
13 Ibid., p. 532.
14 Peden, *The Treasury*, p. 407.
15 Darwin, *The Empire Project*, p. 528.
16 Daunton, *Just Taxes*, pp. 237–9.
17 Cain and Hopkins, *British Imperialism*, p. 672.
18 Ibid., Chapter 26; Hopkins, 'Macmillan's Audit', pp. 234–60; Schenk, 'Decolonisation', pp. 444–63.
19 Louis and Robinson, 'The Imperialism of Decolonisation', pp. 462–511; Gallagher and Robinson, 'The Imperialism of Free Trade', pp. 1–15.
20 Hyam, 'The Primacy of Geopolitics', p. 43.
21 Louis, 'Public Enemy Number One', pp. 186–213.
22 Darwin, 'Empire and Ethnicity', p. 386.
23 Robinson, 'Non-European Foundations', pp. 117–42.
24 Wallerstein, *Africa: The Politics*; Hodgkin, *Nationalism in Colonial Africa*.
25 Low, 'The Asian Mirror', pp. 1–29; Grimal, *Decolonisation*.
26 Harper, *The End of Empire*, p. 75.
27 Turnbull, 'British Planning', pp. 239–54.
28 Harper, *The End of Empire*, p. 95.
29 Yeo, *Political Development in Singapore*, pp. 173–5.
30 Linstrum, *Ruling Minds*, pp. 155–6 and 175–82; Anderson, 'British Abuse', pp. 700–19 and Low, 'The Repatriation of the Chinese', pp. 363–92.
31 Darwin, 'Hong Kong in British Decolonisation', p. 16.
32 Ibid.
33 Tsang, *Hong Kong: An Appointment*, p. 69.
34 Ibid.
35 Wang, 'Hong Kong's Twentieth Century', pp. 6–7.
36 Lu, 'The American Cold War', p. 130; Mok, 'Disseminating and Containing Communist Propaganda', pp. 1–21.
37 Jin, *50 Years of Memories*, pp. 30 and 35; Wong, *China Resumption of Sovereignty*, pp. 34 and 96.
38 Mark, 'Defence or Decolonisation?', pp. 53–5.
39 Tsang, *Hong Kong: An Appointment*, pp. 76–7.
40 Miners, *The Government and Politics*, pp. 19, 25 and 223.
41 Tsang, *Hong Kong: An Appointment*, p. 76; Tsang, *A Modern History*, p. 157.
42 HKRS 742-15-22, 'Aims and Policies of the Hong Kong Government: Text of an Address by the Defence Secretary at a Seminar, September 1970', M. D.

A. Clinton to heads of departments and Secretariat branch heads, 7 October 1970, p. 2.
43 HKRS 742-15-22, 'The Government in Hong Kong: Basic Policies and Methods', 14 May 1969, enclosed in 'Countering Subversion: Government Policies', Hugh Norman Walker to D. C. C. Luddington, 16 May 1969, pp. 2 and 5.
44 In the 1950s, British officials were uncertain whether China would object to Hong Kong's democratisation. However, in the mid-1960s, the idea that China would not accept any attempts to democratise Hong Kong became widely accepted by senior officials in Britain and Hong Kong. This notion was derived from China's opposition to any changes in Hong Kong's constitutional status and how Britain associated the introduction of democracy with self-government and independence based on their experiences in other colonies. By 1967, colonial bureaucrats were convinced that China would object to any democratic development in Hong Kong. See Tsang, *A Modern History*, pp. 206–7; FCO 40/42, Hong Kong to the Foreign and Commonwealth Office (FCO hereafter), 18 March 1967; Hong Kong to FCO, 20 March 1967.
45 Endacott, *Government and People*, pp. 230–1; Scott, 'Bridging the Gap', p. 138.
46 Wang, 'Hong Kong's Twentieth Century', p. 5.
47 Mark, 'Lack of Means', p. 57.
48 Ibid., p. 47.
49 Ibid., p. 70.
50 Goodstadt, *Uneasy Partners*, p. 55.
51 Darwin, 'Hong Kong in British Decolonisation', pp. 20 and 30.
52 Mark, 'Lack of Means', p. 47; also discussed in Hampton, 'The Uses of Monarchy', pp. 226–7.
53 Mark, *The Everyday Cold War*, p. 108.
54 Ibid., pp. 80–3.
55 Ibid., p. 83.
56 In 1965, the colonial government announced that the Star Ferry Company had applied for a fare increase of between 50 and 100 per cent. The Transport Advisory Committee approved the increase in March 1966. A protest initiated by So Sau-chung and Lo Kei took place in April 1966 but was suppressed by the colonial government. Subsequently, the peaceful demonstrations turned into a violent riot. In 1967, demonstrations broke out in May due to labour disputes in shipping, taxi, textile, cement and artificial flower companies. Pro-Beijing trade unions were involved. The demonstrations soon developed into violent riots between pro-Beijing leftists and the Hong Kong government, which did not subside until October. See Bickers and Yep (eds), *May Days in Hong Kong*.
57 Tsang, *A Modern History*, p. 189.
58 Mark, 'Lack of Means', pp. 64–5.
59 For how the 1967 riots affected Sino-British relations, see Fellows, 'Colonial Autonomy', pp. 570, 574–6 and 579; Mark, *The Everyday Cold War*, pp. 118–127; FCO 40/113, Hong Kong Police Special Branch, 'Action against the Communist Press – Reappraisal at 24th October, 1967', 24 October 1967.

60 Mark, 'Development without Decolonisation', p. 323; Cheung, *Hong Kong's Watershed*, p. 140.
61 FCO 40/329, M. MacLehose to Leslie Monson, Wilford, Morgan and Laird, 16 October 1971; also quoted in Yep and Lui, 'Revisiting the Golden Era', p. 253.
62 Lethbridge, 'Hong Kong Cadets', pp. 36–43.
63 Scott, 'Bridging the Gap', pp. 132–3, 138 and 144.
64 King, 'Administrative Absorption of Politics', in King and Lee (eds), *Social Life and Development*, p. 138; Mok, 'Public Opinion Polls', pp. 67–8.
65 Roberts, 'Introduction', p. 1; Borstelmann, *The 1970s*, p. 3.
66 In 1974, the colonial government announced that all Chinese immigrants who failed to 'touch base', that is, reach Hong Kong's urban area, would face repatriation. See Mok, 'Chinese Illicit Immigration', pp. 339–67.
67 England, *Hong Kong*. For dynamics between the British and Hong Kong government, see Yep and Lui, 'Revisiting the Golden Era', pp. 249–72.
68 Hampton and Mok, 'Remembering British Rule'.
69 Lo, *The Politics of Democratisation*, p. 83.
70 Hong Kong Government Printer, *Green Paper: The Further Development of Representative Government*, p. 4; also quoted in Tsang, *A Modern History*, p. 231.
71 Tsang, 'Realignment of Power', p. 35.
72 Ma, *Political Development*, p. 139.
73 Carroll, *A Concise History*, p. 161; Mark, 'Crisis or Opportunity', p. 264.
74 Tsang, *A Modern History*, pp. 180–8; Tsang, *Government and Politics*, p. 248; Carroll, *A Concise History*, pp. 167–76; Lui and Chiu, 'Social Movements', p. 105.
75 Lui and Chiu, 'Social Movements', p. 106.
76 Ma, *Political Development*, p. 137.
77 Carroll, *A Concise History*, p. 168.
78 Miners, *The Government and Politics*, p. 34.
79 Carroll, *A Concise History*, p. 169.
80 Ibid., pp. 178–80.
81 The concept of 'minimally-integrated social-political system' was coined by Lau Siu-kai in *Society and Politics*. Revisionists, such as Tak-wing Ngo, Ma Ngok and Lam Wai-man, refuted this erroneous view of state–society relations in the 2000s.
82 Endacott, *A History of Hong Kong*, p. 121.
83 Miners, *The Government and Politics*, p. 32; King, 'Administrative Absorption of Politics', p. 424; Hoadley, 'Political Participation of Hong Kong Chinese', pp. 605, 610 and 612.
84 Miners, *The Government and Politics*, p. 32; King, 'Administrative Absorption of Politics', p. 427; Hoadley, 'Hong Kong is the Lifeboat', pp. 210–11; Hoadley, 'Political Participation of Hong Kong Chinese', pp. 612–13; Lau and Kuan, *The Ethos of the Hong Kong Chinese*, p. 70.
85 King, 'Administrative Absorption of Politics', pp. 431–4; Endacott, *Government and People*, p. 229.

86 Lau, *Society and Politics*, pp. 2, 14–20, 122 and 157.
87 Lau, *Society and Politics*, pp. 68–85 and 102; Lau, 'Chinese Familism', pp. 978–86.
88 Lau, 'Chinese Familism', p. 988.
89 On 10 October 1956, the National Day of the Republic of China, riots broke out at the Lei Cheng Uk Resettlement Estate when Resettlement Department staff removed Nationalist flags and decorations. Violence soon ensued, resulting in over 6,000 arrests and 443 injuries. See Lam, *Understanding the Political Culture*, pp. 88–91; Mark, 'The "Problem of People"', p. 1164.
90 Lau, *Society and Politics*, p. 21.
91 Leung, *Perspectives on Hong Kong Society*, p. 26.
92 Ngo, 'Colonialism in Hong Kong', p. 2.
93 Ibid., p. 3.
94 Clayton, 'From Laissez-faire to "Positive Non-interventionism"', p. 2.
95 Ngo, 'Colonialism in Hong Kong', p. 5.
96 Goodstadt, *Uneasy Partners*, p. 79.
97 Ng, 'When Silence Speaks', p. 425.
98 Ng, 'Inhibition vs. Exhibition', p. 24.
99 Ma, *Political Development*, p. 25.
100 Scott, *Political Change*, p. 81.
101 Tsang, *A Modern History*, pp. 180–2.
102 Tsang, *Government and Politics*, p. 248.
103 Lui and Chiu, 'Social Movements', pp. 105–6.
104 Carroll, *A Concise History*, pp. 172–6.
105 Ma, 'Reinventing Hong Kong', pp. 329 and 332.
106 Ma, *Culture, Politics and Television*, p. 17.
107 Carroll, *A Concise History*, pp. 169–70.
108 Lam, *Understanding the Political Culture*, pp. 47–52 and 181.
109 Ibid., pp. 184–5, 211–30.
110 The term 'covert colonialism' was used by Martin B. Van Der Weyden to explain how developed countries continued to practise colonialism covertly in the healthcare and medical sectors and exploit health professionals from the developing world in the post-colonial era. See 'Covert Colonialism', p. 185. However, 'covert colonialism' in this book carries different meanings. It refers to the covert control and surveillance that the colonial government exercised over Hong Kong's Chinese society through opinion polls that were concealed from the public.

1
Constructing 'public opinion' through Town Talk and MOOD

According to Lau's concept of 'minimally-integrated social-political system', the links between the 'autonomous bureaucratic polity' and the 'atomistic Chinese society' were extremely limited. The colonial state had no 'organisational penetration' into the Chinese communities and Chinese households were politically apathetic, reliant on familial networks and self-regulating. As a result, 'boundary maintenance' was sustained. Politics only took place at the boundary between the colonial government and the Chinese communities. These political interactions were 'not highly institutionalised in formal or legal sense'. In other words, political institutions which allowed non-bureaucratic outsiders to exercise political power were absent.[1]

As the introduction has demonstrated, Lau's work was ahistorical, based primarily on an unrepresentative set of interview data. It failed to examine the actual relationship between the colonial state and Chinese communities in Hong Kong 'in a particular structural-historical context'.[2] Although revisionists refuted this erroneous view of state–society relations, the history of interactions between the people of Hong Kong and bureaucrats ruling over them is under-explored.

The colonial administration solicited public opinion, creating a Public Relations Office that monitored press coverage and a Secretariat for Chinese Affairs (SCA) that advised on Chinese customs and assessed shifting trends in public opinion through local Chinese leaders.[3] Historians have, however, a poor understanding of how these agencies of the colonial state functioned. In 1968, the CDO Scheme was introduced to bridge the communication gap between the colonial state and Chinese society. However, it has not been subject to close historical examination. For example, the work of Steve Tsang, John Carroll and Ian Scott only provided a short institutional history of the scheme, focusing on the background in which it was established and its key functions.[4] Scott's recent work further pointed out that the scheme, an administrative solution, was introduced to widen channels of political participation without introducing democratisation or delegating further executive power to the Urban Council because there was a general 'antipathy' among senior colonial bureaucrats towards elections and devolution of government functions.[5] Ambrose King's work contained the most detailed account of the scheme. Nonetheless, his article was published in 1975, and was based on a few published sources, supplemented by some oral interviews.[6] Our understanding of this reform remains impressionistic. This existing literature neglects to discuss how the colonial state constructed and monitored 'public opinion' using Town Talk and Movement of Opinion Direction (MOOD), two state-funded opinion polling exercises which were not officially included in the scheme but were, as shall be argued, the most innovative aspect of this reform.[7] These devices did not only absorb the ordinary Chinese at the grassroots level into the administrative system but also incorporated them into the policymaking process. The Town Talk and MOOD files have only recently been released into the public domain, enabling historians to investigate the mechanism used by the colonial state to monitor changing public opinion at the local level.

Using archival evidence, this chapter addresses how the colonial administration in Hong Kong solicited changing popular sentiment using indirect mechanisms before 1968, namely through the Public Relations Office and the SCA. It then investigates how a reformist state monitored and gauged public opinion through covert polling exercises. It examines Town Talk and MOOD, two bureaucratic instruments introduced by the colonial state after the Star Ferry riots and the leftist-inspired riots to monitor the shifting mood in Chinese society under the coordination of the Home Affairs Department (HAD) and the City District Offices. Town Talk reports were first produced in 1968. In 1975, advanced methodologies were adopted to collect public opinion at the district level. Town Talk was then given a new name: MOOD. MOOD was used at least until 1980 and was then replaced by Talking Points in the late 1980s.[8] This chapter details the changing methodologies bureaucrats employed to enhance the credibility of this data. It also explains how this constructed 'public opinion' was channelled back into the policymaking process.

This chapter argues that the implications of this mechanism are twofold. On the one hand, Town Talk and MOOD reveal that the colonial government possessed the 'means and will' to monitor changing popular sentiment in Chinese society closely. This state surveillance was a manifestation of 'covert colonialism'. On the other hand, the fact that these constructed opinions influenced the state's administrative strategies shows that the 'public' was involved in the policy formulation process. The exercises were adopted as a substitute for democracy. Significantly, the presence of these polling exercises was concealed from the public and therefore people may have been taking part in policy formulation unconsciously. Channels of political participation were widened covertly in a state-controlled manner.

High-ranked officials, however, were fully aware of Town Talk and MOOD, which were embedded in the CDO programme. The covert nature of these devices provided the government with the leeway to decide when to follow public opinion; their function as an intelligence device was prioritised over the aim to increase popular political participation. Town Talk and MOOD therefore supplied colonial bureaucrats with information on the strategies and rhetoric employed by activists to mobilise the mass population in social movements, aiding state surveillance and policymaking.

The covert nature of the exercises can also be explained by the colonial government's concern that China would react strongly if democratisation was to take place in Hong Kong. Overt democratic reforms also risked promoting politicisation among the Chinese population, which might lead to a rise of anti-colonialism and increased demands for extensive constitutional reforms. Although the public's engagement was strictly controlled by the state, which had the complete discretion to decide what opinions they should adopt, these exercises still indicate some degree of 'decolonisation' in the bureaucratic mentality. Unlike Lau's beliefs, Town Talk and MOOD demonstrate that political interactions between the state and Chinese society were formally institutionalised within the CDO Scheme. Containing substantial amounts of valuable qualitative insights into the lives of ordinary Hong Kong Chinese, they provide a new opportunity to examine social hierarchies in Hong Kong, and thus how divisions along class lines and generational differences influenced prevailing political cultures. These reports, alongside confidential state correspondences and newspapers, will be used in the first six case studies in this book as primary sources to deconstruct the political culture in accordance with social classes and age groups. Since MOOD reports beyond 1980 are unavailable in the archives and scientifically organised overt public opinion polls were increasingly used, the latter will be used to analyse the shifting discourse on proposed and implemented constitutional reforms in the last case study. Other state records, such as correspondence between the Governor and the Foreign and Commonwealth Office, will also be examined. The first six case studies investigate how this constructed 'public opinion' was channelled into the policymaking process and influenced administrative, legislative and institutional changes in Hong Kong. This chapter provides a foundation for this later analysis.

Indirect rule: Public Relations Office and the SCA

Before 1968, the colonial government continued to practise indirect rule in Hong Kong as democratisation was infeasible. Although there had been an informal devolution of power from London to Hong Kong since the 1950s

Constructing 'public opinion' 27

in the economic and social domains, 'a partial substitute for Hong Kong's control of its own administration', political changes remained insubstantial.[9] The colony was still jointly administered by expatriates and Chinese 'community' leaders. Bureaucrats often consulted Chinese elites and advisory boards before policies were implemented but they did not consult the public directly. If the colonial administration gained a sense of 'public opinion', it came via the operations of the Public Relations Office and the SCA, a de facto home office, which had a diffuse set of responsibilities as discussed later. The official conceptualisation of 'public opinion' generated by these bureaucratic offices, however, typically channelled the views of Chinese social elites and community leaders about ordinary people. The voices of ordinary Hong Kong Chinese remained unheard.

Public Relations Offices were set up in a range of British colonies during the Second World War to augment wartime propaganda, that is, keeping subjects informed of the progress of an unprecedented total and global war, and making known 'the ways in which they could best support the war effort'.[10] Hong Kong, which was occupied by Japan from 1941, did not have a Public Relations Office until 1946. When it was established, it had two main functions. First, to present the case of the colonial and British governments to the citizens in the colony through local mass media 'as clearly, forcefully, comprehensively and promptly as possible'. Second, to show the situations of Hong Kong people to the colonial regime and places outside Hong Kong, either through British mass media or the Information Department of the Colonial Office.[11] The Office monitored different channels of communication closely, including newspapers and films. It had four divisions (see Figure 1.1). The Press Division issued information through 'Daily Information Bulletin' to the press. It also reported Chinese-language newspapers' reactions to government policies by compiling 'Daily Press Summaries' (later known as the 'Chinese Press Review'): 260 copies of an eight-page summary were produced and disseminated to different departments on a daily basis. Foreign comments about the colonial administration

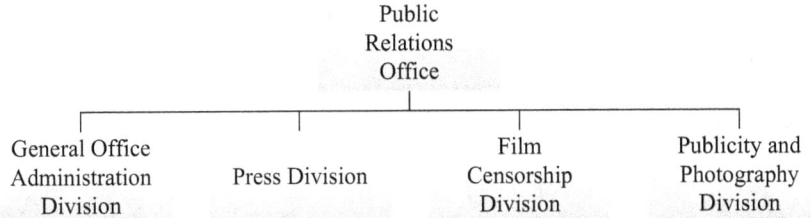

Figure 1.1 Structure of the Public Relations Office in 1957. HKRS 160-1-23, 'The Organisation of the Public Relations Office', by J. D. Duncanson, December 1957.

were also analysed, albeit irregularly in a separate report, 'Hong Kong As Others See It'.[12] In 1959, the Office was renamed as the Government Information Services (GIS). By 1964, its Press Division was analysing twenty-five Chinese-language newspapers, which it was estimated had a total circulation of 700,000 copies.[13]

The Public Relations Office failed to obtain a representative view of changing public opinion by monitoring the Chinese press. Due to constraints in resources and manpower, not all Chinese newspapers were analysed. Fourteen other Chinese-language newspapers, which accounted for a daily circulation figure of 248,000, were not consulted.[14] The rapid population growth and the lack of direct channels of communication also constituted difficulties in 'keeping in sufficient touch with public feeling and thinking at the level of man-in-the-street'.[15] Two years before the outbreak of the Star Ferry riots, the weaknesses of the existing indirect mechanism had been recognised: 'In any event, the impression is that we lack sufficient means of keeping our fingers on the pulse of public thinking at common level.'[16] These inadequacies and the changing political and social context suggest that even before the shocks of the riots of 1966 and 1967, there was a need for an alternative mechanism to improve communications between the colonial state and society.

The SCA was the colonial government's 'main channel of direct communication with the Chinese people' before 1968.[17] The department liaised with social elites. It sought the opinion of the Chinese members of the Legislative and Executive Councils.[18] It developed a close relationship with kaifong associations, indigenous mutual aid organisations which had been set up to fulfil the local community's needs for basic welfare services, including education and medical care;[19] retained a link with the Tung Wah Hospital, the 'main informal governing body for the Chinese community' which provided various social services, ranging from the organisation of relief for victims of disasters to the burial of unclaimed dead bodies;[20] and liaised with leaders of village communities that were not located in the New Territories, Hong Kong's large rural hinterland which had a different governance structure.[21] The Secretariat's main responsibility was to assist the administration to assess shifting trends in public opinion, advise on Chinese customs and present official policy to the Chinese public. The Secretary for Chinese Affairs advised 'on any aspect of relationships between government departments and Chinese residents', and he paid close attention to social issues such as Chinese marriages, housing, squatters, narcotics and anti-corruption, with heads of departments required to consult and cooperate with him in 'matters affecting or concerning the Chinese population in general or any considerable section of it'. The areas overseen by the Secretariat included urban areas and rural areas outside the New Territories.[22]

By the late 1950s, in a situation of rising anti-colonialism in Asia and Africa, colonial bureaucrats sought to cultivate a sense of loyalty among the Hong Kong Chinese. The Assistant Secretary for Chinese Affairs recognised the need to reform existing ruling strategies:

> In short, we cannot expect the people of Hong Kong to commit themselves to active support (a very different thing from mere acceptance) of our policy unless we are prepared to commit ourselves to saying what it is.[23]

In addition to practical responsibilities, the Secretariat was obliged to build up 'a feeling of local citizenship' based on two 'essential ingredients': 'profitable self-interest' and 'selected and sectional traditional loyalties'.[24] The 'non-political' nature of 'local pride and local citizenship', however, was emphasised.[25] Officials believed that this psychological policy could strengthen colonial rule by stabilising the society and turning the colony into 'a counter to Communist China, for the ultimate preservation of our society'.[26] To carry out these duties, the Secretary for Chinese Affairs possessed executive power. He held membership of both the Executive and Legislative Councils.[27]

Nevertheless, the Secretariat, arguably, was unable to adjust to the pace and form of social change in post-war Hong Kong. In 1957, E. B. David, the Colonial Secretary, observed that 'civic spirit' was already growing rapidly due to 'changing political and social environments':

> The large proportion of the Chinese communities, including local born and refugees, will no longer treat Hong Kong as a transit camp, temporary shelter or adventurer's paradise, but as their permanent and real home where they can settle down peacefully to bring up their young generation with determination and confidence. Moreover, the average men nowadays are not only interested in making their own living or improving their skill and profession, but are proud to have a share in contributing to the wealth and prosperity of the community, in which, he may be promised a fair place in the complicated social and political organisation of today.[28]

Reforms were necessary to improve how the state communicated with Hong Kong residents, that is, how bureaucrats understood the needs of people and how they informed the people of government policies. One option to resolve this universal problem, introducing direct democracy, was however not perceived to be viable in the context of the ongoing Cold War and China's refusal to recognise the legitimacy of British rule. Due to inadequate resources and manpower, systematic direct consultation was also not feasible. David's interim solution was to 'cultivate good leadership' among 'voluntary organisations', such as kaifong associations. He commented that it would be as 'dangerous for government to ignore or overlook as to discourage or whip up their immature enthusiasm'.[29] The government was seeking to accommodate but not to actively stimulate civic activism. At this stage, these traditional Chinese organisations remained a safe source of opinion for the Secretariat in the 1950s but the information gathered on the people via this mechanism was partial: in 1957, kaifong associations had over 300,000 members, equivalent to one-tenth of Hong Kong's population.[30]

By the late 1950s, the Secretariat's inefficacy was commonly acknowledged by colonial bureaucrats. J. C. McDouall, the Secretary for Chinese Affairs, even suggested that both officials and the public failed to understand the department's functions: 'Even the Chinese members of Councils, the Chinese press and many members of the Chinese public generally, only had in the main a feeling that the SCA had provided and should continue to provide some vital but undefined links between government and the Chinese population.'[31] Similar observations were made by an Assistant Secretary for Chinese Affairs. While serving as a member in the Cadet Selection Board, he realised that most candidates 'just don't know what it's [the government] doing nor why'.[32] There was a communication gap between the colonial state and Chinese society.

The Secretariat became less important within the colonial administration due to a range of factors. First, the growth of other departments which sometimes dealt directly with the public. Second, there was a higher standard of education which increased people's English proficiency, so that they could increasingly comprehend policies and directives, as reported by newspapers and as communicated directly to the people. Third, Ronald Ruskin Todd, the former Chinese Affairs General, had been reluctant to expand the department's responsibilities and activities during the period from 1949 to 1955.[33] Despite the rapid growth of the population concentrated in the urban areas of Hong Kong Island and Kowloon, the Secretariat's manpower decreased. In internal correspondence with the Secretary for Chinese Affairs in 1958, the Assistant Secretary complained about the department's inadequacies and argued that a direct means of political communication was urgently needed:

> The S.C.A., if it did not exactly stand still, moved a lot more slowly than anything else … Consequently, I fear, many people, thinking they can do nothing, accept with resignation for vituperation – something that could in fact be changed if they knew the right way to go about it … It is not enough for the S.C.A. to be a channel of communication with organised Chinese bodies. It is very necessary that it should be able to help unorganised non-English speaking Chinese individuals.[34]

McDouall also recognised the weakness of the Secretariat; in particular, the S.C.A.'s 'inadequate direct and indirect contacts with the bulk of usually inarticulate population' could be 'increasingly dangerous'.[35]

As a result, the Secretariat was reorganised in 1958. It had a clearer division of labour. The Secretary for Chinese Affairs was responsible for contacting Chinese members of the Executive and Legislative Councils, the Urban Council, the Housing Authority, statutory Chinese committees and non-Chinese boards. The Assistant Secretaries for Chinese Affairs and Cadet Officers liaised with all other government departments, Chinese religious organisations and the Chinese press. They also dealt with miscellaneous issues, including narcotics and deportation cases. The Tenancy Inquiry Bureaux handled landlords and tenants. The District Watch Force contacted village and rural communities. Liaison Officers (LO) and Assistants managed kaifong associations, district commercial associations, clansman societies and significant Chinese individuals. The number of staff in the Secretariat increased from 102 in 1956 to 113 in 1960.[36] The positions of Senior Community Development Officers were added to cope with the 'rapid increase of work', operating under the Assistant Secretaries.[37] These reforms and the expansion of the SCA suggest that the colonial regime in Hong Kong was determined to improve the monitoring of popular sentiment among Hong Kong Chinese, even in a situation where the bureaucracy was struggling to keep pace with the dramatic increase in the population.

Post-hoc official conceptualisation of public opinion through Town Talk

By the mid-1960s, the reach of the colonial government into the society was still limited. As noted in the introduction, and as discussed by political scientists in the 1970s, the Urban Council was the only institution which possessed both executive power and democratically elected members. Nonetheless, only two of ten were elected councillors and its franchise remained extremely limited. There were few channels for the public to raise their grievances. The colonial state was reluctant to introduce a relatively democratic political system, in part because senior civil servants believed that, in a relatively small city-state, a centralised administration was more efficient. They were also concerned that an increasingly democratic local government would lead the Chinese government to believe that Hong Kong was moving towards independence, provoking strong reactions and a potential military attack.[38] As E. B. Teesdale, the Colonial Secretary, had observed, 'these measures, this machinery [the Public Relations Office and the SCA] still leave a good deal of ground untouched'.[39] The colonial administration strove, consequently, to make greater use of other departments which were 'in daily touch with people', 'keeping ear of government to the ground' and channelling useful information to 'those who ought to know it'.[40] These departments included the Education Department, the Hong Kong Police Force, Medical and Health Services and the Resettlement Department.[41] Junior civil servants in these departments were advised to make more contributions as they often 'hear[d] much useful opinion expressed'.[42] Nigel J. V. Watt, the Director of GIS, suggested that these junior ranks could be brought together by occasional discussions on topical matters of public concern, under the supervision of the Secretariat's Training Unit.[43] Plans were also made to expand the scope of 'Daily Press Summaries' beyond the existing twenty-five Chinese-language newspapers.[44] However, the colonial administration was still reluctant to gather public opinion systematically: 'It would seem essential to avoid any stereotyped or standardised system of reporting; or any procedures which would give the impression that government servants are spies or agents of "Big Brother".'[45]

There is some evidence that the absence of formal political channels to express public opinion contributed to a sense of 'alienation' that was felt strongly by many people during the 1960s and beyond.[46] By the mid-1960s, kaifong associations were in decline, unable to recruit young leaders.[47] The riots in 1966 and 1967 gave colonial bureaucrats justification to advance reforms advocated since 1958. No opinion polls were conducted on a regular basis at this point. Public opinion was only gauged on an ad hoc basis in response to the riots, when a Commission of Inquiry, the Secretary for Chinese Affairs and the police force investigated these serious disturbances.[48]

Despite the need to reform, the British and colonial governments both acknowledged that democratisation was infeasible in Hong Kong:

> Many people will tell us – and often do – that none of this is as effective in promoting the rights of the citizen as democratic self-government but it is commonly held that the Chinese government will accept the status of Hong Kong only for as long as there are no constitutional developments which might be interpreted as pointing towards self-government ... You will therefore not find in government policy any intention to promote sophisticated western democratic institutions. We have to get our public participation in other ways.[49]

In a break from the past, and to improve political communications in new ways, the CDO Scheme was introduced as a solution in 1968. The scheme aligned with the informal devolution of power in social and economic domains in the 1950s, sharing the same governance objectives of ensuring that 'the people of Hong Kong [would] realise that the policies of Hong Kong government' were 'in their best interests' and a 'sound method of local government' could be developed so that the colonial government could 'govern' and 'determine, in partnership' with the local population 'what is right for Hong Kong' without abdicating to 'external pressure'.[50] It widened the channels of political participation without granting democratisation or delegating executive power to the Urban Council.[51] The government used the idea of the People's Association and Citizens' Consultative Committees in Singapore as a point of reference.[52] The scheme was 'a multifunctional political structure'. Ten City District Offices were set up to provide policymakers with intelligence about public opinion, to explain the state's policies, to answer public enquiries and to manage district affairs. These Officers were 'intended to be political officers'.[53] Although they had 'little executive authority initially', their influence on government policies was 'considerable'.[54] They were expected to 'foresee local problems and conflicts' and 'initiate proposals for changes' when needs were 'apparent'.[55]

CDOs were required to report to the City District Commissioners (CDCs) regarding political situations in their districts on a weekly basis. Their findings were comprised into a political report and presented verbally by the Secretary for Chinese Affairs at the Government House every Friday morning. In addition, each month, CDOs had to produce a political report in 'greater depth', which was given 'a wider circulation within government'.[56] This reform sought to incorporate the lower strata of the society into the administrative authority without democratisation. CDOs observed people in their everyday lives and surveyed them collectively via District Monthly Meetings and Study Groups, new devices 'geared primarily to reach local leaders'; Town Talk, a new confidential official publication, was oriented towards ordinary people.[57]

Since the introduction of the scheme in 1968, CDOs were required to organise the opinions they heard and gathered into weekly written reports, the circulation of which was restricted only to department heads and high-ranked government officials. These confidential reports were known as Town Talk. As implied by its name, Town Talk's objective was to capture talk and the qualitative aspect of opinions of the Hong Kong Chinese in 'town', Kowloon and Hong Kong Island, the colony's urban areas.[58] Town Talk was a covert opinion monitoring exercise that served as a substitute for representative democracy as 'western democratic institutions' could not be promoted in Hong Kong and 'other ways' for political participation had to be sought.[59] Being 'one of the most important channels for soliciting public opinions', the exercise aimed to 'detect any strong current of public feeling' and record views of the 'man in the street' from 'different walks of life' in urban areas.[60] It excluded the opinions of the bureaucrats. Instead, the City District Officers recorded what they heard in public places and on social occasions, both private and public. Public opinion was gathered primarily by observing and having casual conversations with ordinary people. Town Talk was a key innovation among 'a variety of methods' which were developed in response to the criticisms of 'the lack of constitutional development in Hong Kong'.[61] The public opinion collected and phenomena observed were summarised into reports, which were used by high-ranked colonial bureaucrats in policymaking:

> When policies and programmes are being formulated much attention is focused upon the relevance of informed and independent opinion; indeed this process is probably taken further in Hong Kong than in most territories ... In particular, the CDO Scheme opens up new opportunities in this direction, and every advantage should be taken of the scope it offers for consulting public opinion on particular district projects.[62]

The direct mechanism allowed the undemocratic colonial government's performance to be compared 'reasonably well with that achieved by more formal democratic process that exist[s] in the west', especially in 'entertaining complaints and consulting the public'.[63] With Town Talk, the colonial state was able to incorporate Chinese society into the policymaking process covertly.

To acquire an accurate understanding of shifting public opinion, the colonial state invested a substantial amount of time and manpower in the preparation of Town Talk, expanding its organisational capacity to observe and survey Hong Kong Chinese covertly. Town Talk was prepared mainly by Liaison Assistants, LOs and CDOs. In 1969, there were as many as 100 reporting officers spread over the urban areas in Hong Kong. These officers were responsible for collecting opinion independently from these ten city districts. CDOs also attended routine staff meetings with field staff in different departments, such as the Tenancy Inquiry Bureaux and the Resettlement Department, to gather the comments they picked up, which were also included in the report.[64] Apart from LOs and CDOs, Town Talk was prepared by 'all officers in the department'. In other words, senior officers and clerical staff in the Secretariat for Home Affairs also made contributions.[65] A considerable amount of time and money was spent on Town Talk. Each publication took approximately 110 hours, with input from at least ninety-three staff, and cost $1,310, which was a sum that was higher than the minimum monthly salary of a Class II Executive Officer and four times that of a clerk's wage in the late 1960s.[66] At this early stage, according to the Secretary for Home Affairs, Town Talk was a 'by product', which arose from listening into casual conversations and attending meetings with individuals whose views were incorporated into the reports.[67] The comments CDOs solicited were not necessarily sensitive. Sometimes they were 'almost random', especially in the weeks 'when nothing much seems to catch the public interest and imagination'.[68] Staff normally did not ask for views on any particular topic but only reported what they overheard. However, the Secretariat did on occasions request CDOs to assess the reaction of the people to specific matters.[69]

Who, then, did Town Talk observe and who did CDOs interview? To enhance the diversity and representativeness of the opinions collected, the importance of not relying on the same people was repeatedly emphasised in Town Talk: 'strangers are a good source and you should acquire the trick of striking up acquaintance around the district'. The opinion poll primarily targeted the Chinese population. The 'wealthier non-government, non-Chinese people' were considered contacts that were 'not good'. To avoid, as far as was possible, a skew towards certain types of people, CDOs tried not to interview too many people of the same social status, and they were given clear definitions of some social groups; for example, being 'middle class' meant living in a household with a monthly expenditure of approximately $500.[70]

To understand the opinions of different social classes, the HAD continued to expand its contact list. Initially, the Secretary for Home Affairs defined 'public opinion' as 'a majority opinion of adults'. In 1969, the contacts which the CDOs had were still very limited. They were mostly 'more public-spirited middle class men, older students, housewives, the white-collar class and well-to-do-men whose English proficiency was limited'. As it came to better understand the constraints it was operating under, the HAD increased contact with grassroots members, such as factory workers and hawkers. To assess the representativeness of a comment, the officials had to provide general descriptions of the respondents, including their social class, occupation and geographical area, such as educated middle class and textile worker.[71] The continual expansion of Town Talk's contact list to include a larger number of interviewees from different social classes and age profiles highlights how the colonial administration was determined to obtain a representative sample of public opinion. Nonetheless, there was no clear guidance on the number of people they should interview or talk to: this was not 'a statistically justifiable sample of expressions of public opinions'.[72] As a result, terms such as 'majority', i.e. exceeding 50 per cent, were used with caution.[73] Town Talk was not robust.

Although Town Talk was never based on a statistically representative sample of residents of urban Hong Kong, the qualitative data that it generated allowed officials to obtain a richer and more in-depth understanding of interviewees' attitudes and feelings. To ensure that the data collected was free from official bias, officers were instructed to follow certain techniques. First, it was advised that comments 'should arise without prompting', as to do so would 'colour what you hear'. When questioning the respondents, staff were asked to frame the questions 'in a neutral way'. During the course of exchanges with people, if serious misconceptions were encountered, CDOs were obliged to 'correct them on the spot if possible'. The surviving files do not allow us to understand to what extent and how misconceptions of government policies were corrected but this practice shows how Town Talk was a dynamic, interactive process of informing as well as recording the views of the people. CDOs also had to anticipate how the information would be used within the government. They were encouraged to consider follow-up actions, such as explaining the proposals and relaying particular words being used by the public to the relevant departments.[74] The over-riding aim was to prevent misunderstandings and miscommunication between the colonial state and Chinese society, which may have contributed to the colony-wide confrontations of 1966 and 1967.

After gathering opinions from different respondents, meetings were held to finalise the report, which then reached the policymakers. Either the CDOs held an informal meeting during which staff reported on what they heard in the past week or the LOs compiled all the comments in the offices. The CDOs then decided what to include in Town Talk and were responsible for summarising and editing the report. It was advised that, in particular, topics which people talked about 'outside personal affairs' or had some connections with the governing of Hong Kong should be included. Unexpected views and serious misunderstandings among the public had also to be recorded. A meeting specifically on Town Talk was subsequently held between the CDOs, CDCs and the Deputy Secretary of Home Affairs to compare and cross-check the findings. CDCs and the Deputy Secretary of Home Affairs then weaved these solicited comments into narratives: the aim was to create 'coherent' narratives, 'if possible', but if there was evidence of 'confusion' among those who had been monitored by the CDOs, narratives were left 'incoherent'. These comments were followed by a 'fairly long or thoughtful reflection' on the subject. After the report was finalised, it was disseminated only to high-ranked officials. The Governor would 'take time to read it' and 'often discuss it with head[s] of departments', who were also recipients of Town Talk.[75] Being classified as 'restricted', the existence of Town Talk was concealed from the public: 'We do not particularly want it to become publicly known that such a preparation is produced.'[76] It was the responsibility of the heads of departments to ensure that the report did not 'get into hands of junior officers'.[77]

There are two implications of this analysis of the government files. On the one hand, the mechanism of Town Talk constituted a surveillance instrument used by the colonial state to observe changing public opinion, a manifestation of 'covert colonialism'. On the other hand, it indicated that 'decolonisation' was changing the character of colonialism in Hong Kong, albeit subtly. The exercise's covert nature suggests that this 'public opinion' was constructed and fed into the policymaking process in ways that were controlled by bureaucrats, and without the public knowing. This provided the colonial government with the leeway to decide when to follow public opinion. The innovative mechanism therefore was not simply a 'devolution of power'; instead, this carefully constructed colonial statecraft represented the state's dual attempt to expand its organisational capacity to gather intelligence on public opinion and widen channels of political participation at the discretion of the colonial state, without having to introduce democratic electoral reforms that would provoke China's resistance and promote politicisation among the Chinese population.

The relatively unsystematic and unscientific nature of Town Talk attracted criticism from bureaucrats, who questioned the report's credibility. As early as in 1969, the Secretariat for Home Affairs recognised that the selection of contacts was 'often not methodical' although it was 'unlikely' that any subject that was widely talked about would be missed.[78] David Lai, the CDC of Kowloon, had noticed the absence of a consistent and systematic method in compiling the report: 'Different methods are employed by different districts to compile the paper.'[79] For example, in Kwun Tong, the CDO determined the importance of each item depending on the number of times it had been mentioned by the LOs. Only 'occasionally' were instructions given to LOs to solicit opinion on specific issues. In Mong Kok, however, the Assistant CDO pinned up items of special interest on a noticeboard as 'general guidance'.[80] These incoherent practices affected the report's selection of themes and representativeness. Town Talk's presentation was also disorganised, containing miscellaneous comments. It was 'too long for weekly reading'.[81]

To improve Town Talk's quality, a clearer chain of command was first introduced. CDOs were asked to personally prepare Town Talk. Assistant CDOs were responsible for coordinating the contributions from LOs. Second, to help policymakers reading the findings, the revised Town Talk was divided into two parts: the first being comments on general topics by more than one district and the second being remarks made by individual citizens on specific issues. Third, recipients were reminded of the limitations of the report, which they should read 'in the right perspective'. Lastly, Town Talk was limited to at the most four pages, with CDOs' contributions not exceeding one page and those of the CDCs being kept under three pages.[82]

In late 1970, the Secretariat for Home Affairs acknowledged that the views expressed in Town Talk were 'impressionistic rather than quantified'. Samples were 'not truly representative of the Hong Kong adult population'. In general, more views were gathered from the 'professional class', which only accounted for less than 5 per cent of the working population. The LOs, who were responsible for contacting respondents, were also not trained interviewers, and therefore they sometimes used 'leading' questions.[83] Changes were introduced. From December 1970 onwards, CDOs followed a quota sampling system. Three LOs from each district collected opinion from a previously determined quota sample. Twenty persons were allocated to each LO, forming a total sample size of 600 people. The sample was arranged 'district by district' based on the census data in 1966, to reflect the distribution of gender, age and occupation in each area 'proportionately'. (See Table 1.1 for quota of each occupation group determined in different districts.) A random sampling method was not adopted because it was considered impracticable due to 'various reasons', including 'expense, time, staff'.[84]

By 1972, there were accusations both within and outside the Secretariat for Home Affairs arguing that the way public views were solicited in Town Talk was 'mostly unsystematic' and that comments were largely 'impressionistic and without statistical support'. Some officers still defended its methodologies. For instance, Stephen Y. S. Ho, the CDO of Central argued that it was intentional that Town Talk was compiled 'in an unscientific manner quite different from a statistical research'. The usefulness of the opinion poll relied on the fact that it was 'an album of human expressions manifested through personal contact and human relations'. Nevertheless, it was also agreed that after four years since the first Town Talk was produced, the Secretariat for Home Affairs should address its limitations. Was it capturing views from different sectors of the community? Why were views from youth and students 'comparatively rare'? Why were so many insights not incorporated in the reports? Why were they so imprecise, with references to the opinions of 'several housewives' or 'a few kaifongs'?[85]

Table 1.1 Quota of each occupation group in ten city districts in December 1970

Area	District	White-collar workers	Blue-collar workers	Homemakers	Total
Hong Kong Island	Central	21	33	6	60
	Eastern	15	33	12	60
	Wan Chai	15	36	9	60
	Western	18	33	9	60
Kowloon	Kowloon City	12	39	9	60
	Kwun Tong	9	45	6	60
	Mong Kok	15	36	9	60
	Sham Shui Po	12	42	6	60
	Wong Tai Sin	3	51	6	60
	Yau Ma Tei	18	33	9	60

HKRS 286-1-9, Secretariat for Home Affairs, 'Town Talk: Result of the Public Opinion Survey Conducted on 18 December 1970', 24 December 1970, p. 3.

Constructing 'public opinion'   39

To improve the quality of Town Talk, the state refined its surveying methodology. To ensure that only important matters were included in the reports, the staff focused on 'hot topics' of the week, as decided by individual CDOs. The Assistant CDOs acted as the coordinators of Town Talk in different districts. The department also continued to expand its contact list and seek more contacts from various sources as people of different social classes had different mentalities and reactions to the same issue. Hoping to enhance the representativeness of the opinions they gathered, the Secretariat for Home Affairs considered a number of recommendations. Rather than merely reporting what they had overheard randomly, 'a more positive method' was perceived to be needed and CDO staff were asked to approach different sectors in the community for opinions. Nonetheless, this recommendation was rejected as officials did not want Town Talk to explicitly solicit the view of people. With limited resources, the present method used in compiling Town Talk remained largely unchanged. Town Talk continued to be a weekly survey to capture the 'immediate reaction of the public on controversial issues'.[86] The failure to introduce major methodological changes, however, was arguably beginning to cast doubts on the reliability of the report's findings.

To strengthen the authoritativeness of Town Talk, the HAD and the CDOs experimented with a new version in February 1975. The new Town Talk written report was divided into five sections. The first section was 'popping points', which consisted of main issues of public concern that high-ranked civil servants needed to be informed about, such as increases in telephone charges, corruption and unemployment. The second section outlined popular misconceptions on the state's policies and actions the HAD should take to correct them. The third section contained immediate reactions to 'hot issues'. The fourth section included rumours which could be formerly found in 'Small Talk'. The last section assessed how public opinion was influenced by television, radio and the press. To avoid ambiguity and offer a perspective on social stratification, Town Talk indicated the type of persons holding the views reported. Respondents were classified into the groupings in accordance with their age, social class, educational level, type of residence, gender and occupation. The type of settlement respondents lived in was particularly important as living conditions, such as overcrowding and poor hygiene in squatters, were likely to be a source of discontent. The government's responses varied depending on whether the complaints arose in public or private housing estates (See Table 1.2). Staff also ranked how prevalent certain insights were using one to four stars, ranging from a small minority to the majority. In terms of procedure, the CDOs now chaired the District Town Talk meetings and reported to the Deputy Director of Home Affairs every Tuesday afternoon. During each week's meeting, CDOs also

Table 1.2 Classifications of social stratifications adopted in Town Talk in early 1975

Types	Classifications			
A. Age	Young (A1)	Middle-Aged (A2)	Old (A3)	
B. Social Class	Lower Class (B1)	Middle Class (B2)	Upper Class (B3)	
C. Educational Level	Primary Education (C1)	Secondary Education (C2)	Post-secondary Education (C3)	
D. Type of Residence	Group A Estate (D1)	Group B Estate (D2)	Squatters (D3)	Others (D4)
E. Gender	Male (E1)	Female (E2)		
F. Occupation	Blue-Collar (F1)	White-Collar (F2)	Professionals (F3)	

HKRS 413-1-2, 'Town Talk', A. K. Chui to CDOs, 5 February 1975, p. 2.

indicated whether the comments they reported were solicited by staff or simply overheard.[87]

From 1968 to 1975, the covert Town Talk exercise was the main device the colonial state adopted to monitor and gauge shifting public sentiment in the Chinese communities directly, improving political communications and widening political participation without introducing democratic changes that might provoke China, lead to increased politicisation of the Chinese population and give rise to anti-colonialism. To obtain a representative sample of public opinion, the colonial government invested a considerable amount of manpower, money and time on Town Talk. These polling exercises were not conducted explicitly in public and the reports derived from them were highly restrictive. Only high-ranked officials who were involved in the policymaking process had access to them. This created a false impression that the public was not involved in the policy formulation process. Nonetheless, as later chapters will demonstrate, this constructed 'public opinion' had a direct impact on the colonial state's ruling strategies.

A selective qualitative survey, Town Talk enabled officials to have a better understanding of shifting popular attitudes and sentiment, which could be used to devise appropriate policies and strategies to strengthen colonial rule and minimise social discontent. High-ranked civil servants in Hong Kong and London considered this information before introducing administrative, legislative and institutional changes in the colony. The exercise was an embodiment of both 'covert colonialism' and 'decolonisation' in bureaucratic mentality. The fact that the HAD continued to introduce

Constructing 'public opinion' 41

methodological advancements to the exercise also suggests the colonial state's determination to increase its organisational capacity to monitor shifting sentiments in Chinese society and the report's value to colonial bureaucrats. The next section explains why MOOD replaced Town Talk, and how the colonial state improved MOOD in the second half of the 1970s.

From Town Talk to MOOD

To provide policymakers with accurate political intelligence, Movement of Opinion Direction (MOOD) was introduced in March 1975. It intended to be a 'more authoritative and therefore influential' public opinion poll to replace Town Talk.[88] Similar to Town Talk, MOOD was a confidential report generated by the HAD, the main purpose of which was 'to draw attention to subjects which are currently or potentially of public concern, and to assess public reactions, attitudes and feelings in appropriate instances'.[89] Nonetheless, MOOD focused on a number of aspects Town Talk did not pay attention to. MOOD placed its priority on collecting opinions that were not found in the media. It also examined voices of 'the less articulated classes' who 'cannot get their views heard and have therefore suffered in silence'. Controversial topics and anti-government activities were investigated, as well as the opinions of civil servants who disagreed with state policies. MOOD was important for colonial bureaucrats. It was stated clearly that MOOD was given 'the first priority over all other work' as it was 'read by the Governor and his policy advisers every week, and was referenced during policymaking'.[90] Due to the sensitivity of the intelligence gathered, the reports only circulated among senior officials.[91] Heads of departments were reminded to store their MOOD reports 'securely all the time'.[92] Its highly restrictive nature suggests MOOD findings were acknowledged and handled carefully.

Opinion polling was evidently valuable to bureaucrats. The colonial state continued to provide funding to improve this source of intelligence. As the existing polling exercise was 'not comparable with that of a professional public opinion survey', which reduced its accuracy, the administration sought to further improve the methodologies of MOOD. Compared to Town Talk, archival evidence suggests that MOOD was a sizeable unit with a clear chain of accountability. The total number of staff involved increased from 100 in Town Talk to about 280 to 380 in MOOD (see Figure 1.2). Records also reveal that the HAD was systematic in observing and soliciting public opinion. Unlike Town Talk, MOOD was no longer a by-product derived from random conversations. A sophisticated and systematic polling scheme was developed to collect public opinion. CDOs no longer had the

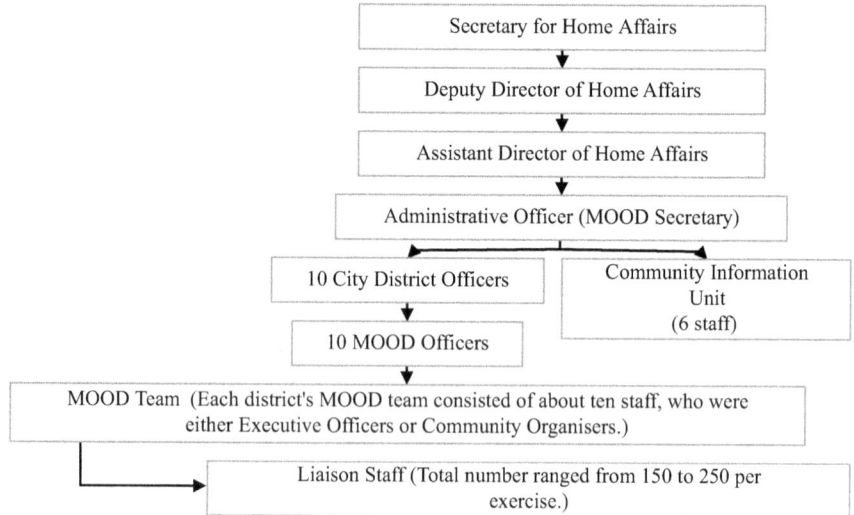

Figure 1.2 Chain of command in MOOD's operation in 1977. HKRS 925-1-1, 'Information Paper for Recipients of MOOD: How MOOD is Produced', MOOD, 5 May 1977, pp. 2–4.

discretion to choose the subject of investigation. Instead, the topic of each exercise was selected by the Deputy Director of the HAD. During the period from March 1975 to June 1976, the government used MOOD to examine public attitudes towards a number of ad hoc issues, including public reactions to the Labour Relations Bill and the proposed increase in public transport charges, school fees and electricity prices. The colonial government also displayed a clear interest in general political attitudes and identities.

Each MOOD exercise began with the debriefing given by the Deputy Director at the HAD Headquarters after the subject was selected. Policy papers were provided to ensure MOOD Officers, who were nominated by CDOs, had 'an intelligent and accurate understanding of the subject [topic]'. Similar documents were disseminated to the Community Information Unit in the HAD, which consisted of six experienced liaison civil servants. During each meeting, the CDOs were given a topic and the number of respondents required. On the next day, every CDO, assisted by his or her MOOD Officer, held a meeting to explain and discuss the subject with the district MOOD team. To reach the grassroots level, the MOOD staff then created samples using data supplied by Mutual Aid Committees (MACs) and kaifong associations, under the liaison of community leaders. Each monitor had a fifty-person contact list, of which every week, one-third of the people were removed from the list and replaced by new contacts. On special occasions, the CDOs could add the contacts back to the list and use them

Constructing 'public opinion' 43

more than once.[93] On the other hand, the Community Information Unit monitored comments made by the mass media which attempted to determine the sentiments of groups and areas that were potentially sensitive, such as coolies and hawkers in some circumstances. It also conducted random sampling through telephone calls, using the data provided by the Census and Statistics Department.[94] Each MOOD drew data from approximately 2,500 people, which was four times Town Talk's sample size.[95] MOOD also advised its staff to be indirect and pay close attention to their interviewing technique. This avoided giving the impression of surveillance and could 'take the respondents off their guards'.[96] When the reports were returned, the CDOs convened a meeting in which findings were checked, discussed, analysed and compiled in note form. A final MOOD meeting, attended by all MOOD Officers, the Deputy Director and the Assistant Director, was then held at the HAD Headquarters. During the meeting, feedback obtained from all districts was examined as a whole and compared with data obtained by the Community Information Unit.[97] An editor analysed the findings to produce one MOOD report for circulation. In 1975, MOOD was printed every Thursday for circulation on Friday.[98] In 1977, to allow sufficient time for thorough investigation, MOOD became a bi-weekly report.[99]

By 1977, there were between 150 and 250 monitors, who were either full-time Executive Officers or part-time Community Organisers working outside office hours. The HAD built up a regularly updated contact list of about 10,000 people.[100] This cohort was selected by the HAD staff as they were known to be 'responsive and well-informed about life and problems in their respective social sectors' and 'ready to offer information, views and suggestions on public issues'. This was not a random representative sample derived from population census data. The list was regularly revised to ensure constant turnover. Old contacts, perceived to be less useful, were removed and new contacts were added, increasing the total number of respondents progressively. It was claimed to 'cover a wide cross-section of occupation groups, stratified in respect of age (15–24, 25–44, 45 and above) and educational background (primary and below, secondary, post-secondary and above)'.[101] About 300 to 400 people were selected from the list for each MOOD issue. Apart from interviewing people on the contact list, the HAD staff spoke to people in the community. The number of these incidental samples varied in different districts. They ranged from 2,000 to 3,000 in total. In normal circumstances, no respondent was interviewed more than once in less than four months. As the Chief Secretary and the Secretary for Administration imposed the duties of assessing and predicting public reactions towards proposed and existing policies, on request, the HAD was now obliged to report opinion trends on specific topics to the relevant department directly.[102] Apart from the normal contacts, a random sample of 20,000 households was selected by the Census and Statistics Department and passed to the City District Office staff. This was to ensure that regular and reliable new contacts spreading across the full spectrum of social strata in different urban areas were added.[103]

MOOD was a research project concerned with obtaining qualitative information and public sentiment. It adopted an informal interviewing system and modelled input on the Osaka Feedback Scheme and the Japanese Monitor System for National Policy.[104] Unlike Town Talk, each report had tailor-made topics and targeted groups. Tests and pilot surveys were carried out in advance, such as checking the sample coverage and anticipating non-response rate. This was done to determine the method used in soliciting views, for example, whether through observations, sending out questionnaires or interviews.[105] If it was in the format of interviews, 'informal' techniques were employed. Questions were not standardised. Staff could tailor the wording and alter the order of the questions which they believed were appropriate for the contacts. Such an unstructured approach, it was judged, succeeded 'better than set questions in getting to the heart of the respondent's opinion'.[106]

Nevertheless, by 1977, bureaucrats were still questioning the credibility of MOOD. The Commissioner of Census and Statistics, for example, pointed out that 'MOOD method has areas where it can be improved', such as the choice of samples and statisticians' conduct.[107] As better-informed respondents were still contacted frequently, reports did not 'truly reflect the attitudes and thinking of an average citizen or a man in the street'.[108] In no way was MOOD a representative sample. Another criticism of MOOD was that it could be biased. Officials used MOOD as 'an axe of their own to grind'.[109] CDOs' and monitors' personal opinions distorted public attitudes. People also may have acted reservedly, knowing the approaching person was a civil servant.

To further improve the methodology of MOOD, it was recommended that a departmental representative should attend discussions if that report was requested by a particular department. As the current MOOD only covered Kowloon and Hong Kong Island, the presence of the staff of the New Territories administration, such as the District Officer (DO) of Tsuen Wan, was useful. Not only could they learn the contacting techniques, but information from the New Territories could also be gathered and used for comparisons. On important topics, such as Green Papers on constitutional development, the department used 'more scientific methods' to check public views regularly.[110] To enhance the report's credibility, three-quarters of the contacts in each issue of MOOD became incidental casual respondents. The established contact lists in different districts were now renewed and the categorical breakdowns, such as age and occupation of respondents, were sent to the Census and Statistics Department.[111] These new arrangements were made possibly because CDOs and monitors still approached better-informed, responsive respondents repeatedly, affecting the representativeness of MOOD. These changes also lowered the risks that officials carried out fewer interviews than MOOD required them to.

By 1979, the HAD was still reluctant to change the sampling method extensively, as it would have involved 'extra work', and was thus impractical given 'limited resources'.[112] MOOD was instead issued on a monthly basis, allowing more time for fieldwork.[113] It was not until April 1980 that the HAD switched to a quota sampling method. The selection of contacts in terms of their gender, age and occupation was now in proportion to the number and distribution of the overall population in the area. The most updated general population breakdown in terms of gender, age and occupation was supplied by the Census and Statistics Department every three months. This new method was probably adopted because of the changing geographical distributions of Hong Kong's population. According to the government census in 1971, 25 per cent of the total population lived in Hong Kong Island, 18 per cent in Kowloon, 37 per cent in New Kowloon and 17 per cent in the New Territories. By 1981, the distribution had changed, with a large increase in the New Territories: 24 per cent of the total population lived in Hong Kong Island, 16 per cent in Kowloon, 33 per cent in New Kowloon and 26 per cent in the New Territories.[114] The new methodology reduced the sample size from 2,500 to 993, with the latter now including people living in the districts of Tsuen Wan and Kwai Chung.[115]

Apart from the quota sampling method, the random sampling method was also adopted in household interviews in 1980. In every MOOD exercise, household members of selected living quarters in one district were randomly interviewed. The selection of the 300 living quarters was based on a sample frame provided by the Census and Statistics Department, using systematic random techniques. All household members aged fifteen and above in the chosen quarters were interviewed. A questionnaire approach was adopted. Questions were set out, including alternative answers. The exact same questions were asked and were in the same order. The answers provided by the respondents were subsequently coded. Coding sheets were then processed using a manual data processing method and table formats were compiled. This enabled the analysis of responses and reactions on a 'strictly scientific basis'.[116]

In the second half of the 1970s, the government invested a substantial amount of resources to improve the methodology and hence the reliability of the polling exercise, indicating the value of MOOD to the bureaucracy. The HAD introduced MOOD to replace Town Talk in 1975. Compared to Town Talk, MOOD was far more organised and scientific. In terms of content, MOOD examined more aspects than its predecessor. This included comments made by the press, and how they influenced popular sentiment and the opinions of the lower strata of the society. The theme of each report also became more focused. Rather than recording everything officials overheard, only topics that were significant for both the public and the bureaucrats were selected and investigated. Statistically, respondents were sourced from an increased number of different channels, including the Census and Statistics Department. To enhance the report's representativeness, incidental contacts were increased and the sample size was largely expanded. By 1980, quota sampling and random sampling methods were introduced to ensure that high-ranked officials had an accurate understanding of shifting opinions of different age groups and social classes in each district. While statistical techniques had been improved, MOOD preserved Town Talk's essence, drawing on the local intelligence of CDOs. MOOD continued to be used by colonial bureaucrats to understand changing popular opinion until at least late 1980. It was then replaced by Talking Points and other scientifically organised overt opinion polls in the 1980s, the mechanisms and impact of which will be discussed in further detail in the last chapter.

Conclusion

This chapter has demonstrated how the colonial bureaucracy in Hong Kong shifted from indirect mechanisms to covert direct opinion polls. In the postwar period, the colonial state devoted increased manpower and resources to understanding the attitudes and opinions of Chinese society. These were complementary activities, in theory, improving policymaking and providing a feedback loop. Shifting popular sentiment of the Chinese communities was initially gauged through the Public Relations Office, which monitored Chinese newspapers closely, and the SCA, which liaised with local Chinese leaders in kaifong associations and clansman societies. By the late 1950s, it was evident that these devices were failing to gather the views of people at the grassroots level. Since the late 1950s, colonial bureaucrats had started advocating changes in these existing mechanisms amid rising nationalism and anti-colonialism in British colonies in Asia and Africa. The SCA was reorganised and expanded. There were discussions that the public should be consulted more directly. Nonetheless, democratic electoral reforms were infeasible due to China's resistance. Direct opinion polling was also not introduced, primarily due to constraints in resources, as well as the continued significance of kaifong associations.

The 1966 and 1967 riots reconfirmed that state–society political communications had to be improved to strengthen colonial rule and minimise the possibility of future outbreak of disturbances. To close the communication gap with Chinese people, the CDO Scheme was introduced in 1968, under which the colonial government regularly collected and closely monitored shifting public opinion, which, as shall be argued subsequently, aided policy formulation and widened channels of political participation in a state-controlled manner. The state's opinion poll soon evolved from the by-product Town Talk to the systematic prototype of MOOD in a scientific manner. When Town Talk was first introduced in 1968, it primarily recorded what officials overheard and the random conversations they had with Chinese residents in different districts. The report was not, in hindsight, statistically robust. It was based on a small sample of ordinary people that was selected by bureaucrats using existing contacts, and captured the views of those who were willing to discuss their sentiments. These people were consulted repeatedly. Techniques changed dramatically over time. The contact list of the HAD was renewed regularly with the addition of new contacts of different social classes and age groups. Indirect interviewing techniques were adopted by officials in interviews to ensure that the opinions they gathered were free from bureaucratic bias. To further enhance the representativeness of the exercise, the state refined its methodologies and introduced MOOD in March 1975.

MOOD collected the views of the people on issues and events that were of interest to both Chinese communities and high-ranked bureaucrats. In particular, it focused on the opinion of the lower social classes and the impact of the press on public opinion. MOOD was more scientific than Town Talk. Its contact list was large and the inclusion of incidental contacts probably increased its representativeness. The size of the sample of each exercise certainly increased from 600 in 1970 to 2,500 in 1975. Areas covered also rose from merely ten City Districts to the New Territories. By 1980, the quota sampling method and random sampling method were adopted. Compared to devices used by the colonial state to monitor public attitudes before 1968, both Town Talk and MOOD were more organised and scientific.

Town Talk and MOOD, which were used as a substitute for representative democracy, were important direct mechanisms by which ordinary Chinese people were consulted on government policy. They contrast with older indirect methods, in which the colonial state worked through social elites and local leaders who in theory represented their communities. This constructed 'public opinion' was new, and could be used to deconstruct the political culture in accordance with social classes and age groups.

Although it remains difficult for historians to determine exactly how this information was used and surviving records are partial, piecemeal evidence in archives suggests that both Town Talk and MOOD were read by high-ranked officials and fed into the policymaking process. This sensitive 'public opinion' circulated restrictively among senior policymakers, including the Governor and his policy advisers, and senior staff in the Foreign and Commonwealth Office. They were referenced in policy formulation, as noted in subsequent chapters. Nevertheless, both polling exercises were not included in the official programme of the CDO Scheme; their existence was concealed from the public. In other words, the public influenced the colonial state's ruling strategies implicitly. This suggests that on the one hand, these polling exercises provided the colonial government with the organisational capacity to conduct surveillance, monitoring changing sentiments in Chinese society closely, a manifestation of 'covert colonialism'; on the other hand, this covert mechanism skillfully allowed ordinary people to take part in the policy formulation process in a state-controlled manner without provoking China's resistance or advocating the public to pursue more political rights and extensive constitutional reforms, indicating that the bureaucratic mentality was shifting towards 'decolonisation'.

The following six case studies, namely the Chinese as the official language movement, the anti-corruption campaign, the campaign against telephone rate increases, the Golden Jubilee incident, changing immigration discourse and policy, and the British Nationality Act controversy demonstrate how this constructed 'public opinion' influenced the colonial state's ruling strategies from 1968 to 1980. Along with newspapers and other state records, Town Talk and MOOD provide valuable information on the strategies and rhetoric employed by activists to mobilise the masses and achieve their political agenda in each specific context. In the last case study, overt opinion polls conducted by the colonial government and research institutions will be used to examine how the public reacted to proposed and implemented constitutional changes in the 1980s and 1990s.

Notes

1 Lau, *Society and Politics*, pp. 13–21, 121 and 157–9.
2 Ibid., pp. 21 and 157.
3 Ho, *The Administrative History*, pp. 20–6, 308–11.
4 Tsang, *A Modern History*, p. 190; Carroll, *A Concise History*, p. 159; Scott, *Political Change*, pp. 107–10.
5 Scott, 'Bridging the Gap', p. 131.
6 King, 'Administrative Absorption of Politics'.
7 King did not discuss Town Talk in his work extensively but claimed that it might have been 'one of the most important channels for soliciting public opinion'. Ibid., pp. 433–4.
8 The last issue of MOOD accessible at the Hong Kong Public Records Office was printed in November 1980.

9 As the British Empire declined, the expertise and resources available in London to oversee Hong Kong affairs were also reduced substantially. In addition, colonial officials started to realise that the local population would be dissatisfied if the government policies were 'blatantly designed to exploit Hong Kong for the United Kingdom's profit'. To present the colonial administration as defending the Chinese communities' interests, London granted colonial bureaucrats greater autonomy over policymaking. See Goodstadt, *Uneasy Partners*, pp. 52–4 and 62.
10 HKRS 160-1-23, 'The Work of Information Departments in the Colonies', enclosure to Circular Despatch, 15 July 1948, p. 1.
11 HKRS 160-1-23, 'Reorganisation of Public Relations Office', Synopsis of Memorandum and Priority Suggestion, memo to J. F. Nicoll, 28 November 1950.
12 HKRS 160-1-23, 'The Organisation of the Public Relations Office', by J. D. Duncanson, December 1957, pp. 3–4.
13 HKRS 160-4-4, 'Newspapers Read for Compilation of Press Summaries', 1964.
14 HKRS 160-4-4, 'Newspapers Not Read for Compilation of Press Summaries', 1964.
15 HKRS 160-4-4, Note enclosed in telegram from E. B. Teesdale to Nigel J. V. Watt, 5 November 1964.
16 Ibid.
17 HKRS 163-1-2176, 'General Orders 2190 and 2530–2532', Secretariat Temporary Circular no. 75, C. B. Burgess to heads of departments, 22 September 1958.
18 HKRS 163-1-2176, 'S.C.A.', J. C. McDouall to C. B. Burgess, 10 April 1958.
19 The term 'kaifong' (街坊) refers to people living in the same neighbourhood. Kaifong associations (街坊會) are non-governmental mutual-aid organisations that emerged in Hong Kong after the Second World War. Wong, *The Kaifong Associations*, p. 18.
20 Tsang, *A Modern History*, p. 69; Sinn, *Power and Charity*, p. 90.
21 Due to the New Territories' rural character, a separate administrative system was set up to administer the area. DOs were appointed to administer the New Territories, serving as a link between the colonial state and rural villagers. Tsang, *Government and Politics*, pp. 37–42.
22 'General Orders 2190 and 2530–2532'.
23 HKRS 163-1-2176, A.S. 2 to S.C.A., 14 April 1958.
24 'S.C.A.', McDouall to Burgess, 10 April 1958.
25 HKRS 163-1-2176, Deputy Colonial Secretary to C. B. Burgess, 20 September 1958.
26 A.S. 2 to S.C.A.
27 HKRS 163-1-2176, 'Secretary for Chinese Affairs', J. C. McDouall to Chinese members of the Executive and Legislative Councils, 17 February 1958.
28 HKRS 934-17-47, 'Increase of Staff 1958/59: Community Development Office', enclosed in memo from E. B. David to J. C. McDouall, 16 September 1957, pp. 1–2.
29 Ibid., p. 2.

30 Ibid.
31 HKRS 934-17-47, 'S.C.A.', J. C. McDouall to C. B. Burgess, 16 June 1958.
32 A.S. 2 to S.C.A.
33 Ibid.
34 Ibid.
35 'S.C.A.', McDouall to Burgess, 16 June 1958.
36 'Increase of Staff 1958/59: Community Development Office', p. 6.
37 Ibid.
38 Scott, 'Bridging the Gap', p. 138.
39 Note enclosed in telegram from Teesdale to Watt, p. 1.
40 Ibid., p. 2.
41 Ibid., p. 3.
42 HKRS 160-4-4, 'Public Opinion', Nigel J. V. Watt to E. B. Teesdale, 20 November 1964.
43 Ibid.
44 Ibid.
45 Note enclosed in telegram from Teesdale to Watt, p. 2.
46 Lui, *The Old-so Familiar 1970s*, p. 56.
47 Lau, *Society and Politics*, p. 133; Wong, 'Chinese Community Leadership', pp. 592, 597, 600–1.
48 Scott, 'Bridging the Gap', pp. 132–7.
49 'Aims and Policies of the Hong Kong Government', p. 8.
50 'The Government in Hong Kong: Basic Policies and Methods', pp. 2 and 4.
51 Ibid., p. 144; Lui, *The Old-so Familiar 1970s*, p. 21.
52 HKRS 934-17-34, US Government Circular, J. M. Patrick to J. Cater, 29 November 1967, pp. 1–5.
53 HKRS 934-17-34, 'CDO Scheme and Reorganisation of the SCA', D. C. Bray to M. Gass, 26 June 1968, p. 1.
54 HKRS 934-17-34, D. R. Holmes, 'Directive to CDO', 20 March 1968, p. 3.
55 Ibid., p. 2.
56 Ibid., p. 8.
57 King, 'Administrative Absorption of Politics', pp. 433–4; Mok, 'Town Talk', pp. 1–22.
58 Town Talk was translated as '街談巷議' in Chinese. See HKRS 413-1-2, D. R. Holmes, 'The Preparation of Town Talk: A Guidance Note', 11 October 1969 and its translation.
59 'Aims and Policies of the Hong Kong Government', p. 8.
60 HKRS 413-1-2, 'The Preparation and Significance of Town Talk', 27 November 1969, p. 3.
61 'Aims and Policies of the Hong Kong Government', pp. 6–7. Other methods included monitoring columns in Chinese-language newspapers and having regular contact with rural committees in the New Territories through the District Administration.
62 'The Government in Hong Kong: Basic Policies and Methods', p. 2.
63 'Aims and Policies of the Hong Kong Government', p. 7.

64 Ibid., p. 4.
65 The SCA was renamed as the Secretariat for Home Affairs in 1969, which was then renamed as the Home Affairs Department in 1973. Holmes, 'The Preparation of Town Talk: A Guidance Note', pp. 1–2.
66 HKRS 502-2-4, 'Appendix II: Estimate Cost of Town Talk Based on Hours Spent by All Officers Concerned in the Compilation', 'Town Talk', David Lai to Deputy Secretary for Home Affairs (hereafter DSHA), 25 July 1969; HKRS 160-1-23, 'Departmental Information and Publicity Units and the Special Publicity Unit', Nigel J. V. Watt to Establishment Officer, 29 December 1967, p. 1.
67 Holmes, 'The Preparation of Town Talk: A Guidance Note', p. 1.
68 'The Preparation and Significance of Town Talk', p. 2.
69 Ibid., p. 4.
70 Ibid., pp. 2 and 4.
71 Holmes, 'The Preparation of Town Talk: A Guidance Note', pp. 1–2.
72 Ibid., p. 2.
73 Ibid.
74 Ibid., pp. 1–3.
75 Ibid., p. 3.
76 'The Preparation and Significance of Town Talk', p. 3.
77 Holmes, 'The Preparation of Town Talk: A Guidance Note', p. 4.
78 'The Preparation and Significance of Town Talk', p. 3.
79 HKRS 502-2-4, 'Town Talk', David Lai to DSHA, 25 July 1969, p. 1.
80 'Appendix I: Description of Mechanism Used in Each C.D.O. to Compile Town Talk', attached to ibid.
81 Ibid., p. 3.
82 Ibid.
83 HKRS 286-1-9, Secretariat for Home Affairs, 'Town Talk: Result of the Public Opinion Survey Conducted on 18 December 1970', 24 December 1970, p. 1.
84 Ibid., p. 2.
85 HKRS 489-4-25, 'Town Talk', Stephen Y. S. Ho to CDC (HK), 27 January 1972, pp. 1–2.
86 HKRS 413-1-2, 'Note of Meeting Held on 5 December 74 and 11 December 74 at Wan Chai City District Office to Discuss Ways and Means of Improving the Quality of Town Talk', December 1974, pp. 1–2.
87 HKRS 413-1-2, 'Town Talk', A. K. Chui to CDOs, 5 February 1975, pp. 1–3.
88 HKRS 394-27-9, 'Town Talk', A. K. Chui to all CDOs, 24 February 1975, p. 1.
89 HKRS 925-1-1, 'MOOD: Movement of Opinion Direction', 13 March 1975, p. 1.
90 'Town Talk', Chui to all CDOs, 24 February 1975, pp. 1 and 3.
91 The circulation rate of MOOD varied throughout the 1970s, ranging from 153 to 167 copies. They were only sent to policymakers and high-ranked officials, such as the Chief Secretary, the Secretary of the Local Intelligence Committee and the Director of GIS.
92 'MOOD: Movement of Opinion Direction', p. 2.
93 'Town Talk', Chui to all CDOs, 24 February 1975, pp. 1–3.

94 HKRS 394-27-9, Extract from minutes from Governor's Committee, 21 March 1975.
95 'MOOD: Movement of Opinion Direction', p. 1; The estimated total population of Hong Kong was 4,045,300 and 4,402,990 in 1971 and 1976, respectively, according to the government censuses. 2,500 was about 0.0618 per cent and 0.0568 per cent of the estimated total population in 1971 and 1976. See Hong Kong Census and Statisticss Department, *Hong Kong Population and Housing Census*, p. 9; *Hong Kong 1981 Census Main Report*, p. 15.
96 HKRS 394-27-9, 'Needle Point, Session on MOOD', minutes of HAD meeting held on 21 July 1975, 28 July 1975, p. 2.
97 HKRS 925-1-1, 'Information Paper for Recipients of MOOD: How MOOD is Produced?', MOOD, 5 May 1977, p. 4.
98 'MOOD: Movement of Opinion Direction', p. 1.
99 'Information Paper for Recipients of MOOD', p. 4.
100 Ibid., pp. 1–3.
101 HKRS 394-27-9, Christine Chow to Lam Chow-lo, enclosed in MOOD Review Paper, 6 January 1977, p. 2.
102 'Information Paper for Recipients of MOOD', pp. 1–2.
103 Chow to Lam, pp. 2–3.
104 'Information Paper for Recipients of MOOD', p. 1.
105 Chow to Lam, p. 5.
106 Formal and informal interviewing, content extracted from Moser and Kalton, *Survey Methods in Social Investigation*, in Chow to Lam, Annex A.
107 HKRS 394-27-9, D. S. Whitelegge to A. K. Chui, 6 April 1977.
108 HKRS 394-27-9, 'Some Observations on MOOD Methodology', 7 May 1979, p. 1.
109 Whitelegge to Chui.
110 HKRS 394-27-9, 'Note of a Meeting to Discuss Possible Improvement on MOOD Methodology Held on 11.5.79 at 2.30 p.m.', 15 May 1979.
111 HKRS 394-27-9, 'Note of a Discussion on Improvement on the MOOD Methodology Held on 17.5.79 at 3.00 p.m.', 21 May 1979.
112 'Some Observations on MOOD Methodology', p. 1.
113 Ibid., p. 3.
114 *Hong Kong 1981 Census Main Report*, p. 63.
115 HKRS 471-3-2, 'MOOD Methodology, MOOD', 10 April 1980.
116 HKRS 394-27-9, Alice Lai, 'Notes on MOOD Methodology', 12 September 1980, p. 2.

2

The Chinese as the official language movement

In 1974, the Chinese language was recognised as the official language of Hong Kong under the Official Languages Bill. The Official Languages Bill was the result of a prolonged struggle led by a large number of organisations, student bodies and individual activists. The language movement was the largest social movement during the long 1970s, and is investigated in this book using newly available archival sources, complemented by published primary sources, notably newspapers and student newsletters.

Demand to make Chinese the official language of Hong Kong can be traced back to the mid-1960s, the beginning of a new era when a new political culture and Hong Kong identity started to emerge. It was a time when the Chinese population of Hong Kong gradually turned into 'a settled one' and the sojourner mentality dissipated.[1] In particular, the young generation, who were locally born and had no experience with the PRC started to reflect on their lives and their roles in Hong Kong, and express their grievances, as in the 1966 Star Ferry riots.[2] The popular mood further shifted after the 1967 riots. These post-war baby boomers reconsidered their relations with colonialism.[3] This context, along with rapid economic development, increased economic and cultural exchange between Hong Kong and China, and the colonial government's effort to build credibility and respond to public demands facilitated the rise of a 'distinctly local political culture'.[4] With the introduction of the CDO Scheme in 1968, political communications between the bureaucracy and the grassroots public improved.[5] The public was increasingly involved in current affairs and politics. Due to a wider cultural shift and bureaucratic reforms, political discourse became 'spontaneous' and 'issue-driven'.[6]

Despite the importance of the language movement and its potentially strong effects on local political culture, the campaign has not been covered in depth by existing literature. J. S. Hoadley merely used the campaign to demonstrate that the Chinese population mobilised on a temporary basis.[7] When looking at the aftermath of the 1967 riots, Ian Scott has also mentioned the development of the language movement, but did not explain its significance.⁸ Lam Wai-man examined the development of the language campaign and how it impacted on Hong Kong's political culture.⁹ For Lam, the campaign possessed 'numerous political meanings': that Hong Kong society was 'moving away from its past'; that local identity was starting to emerge; that members of the young generation were searching for political allegiance and had become active political actors. She argued that practical demands and ideological concerns were mutually reinforcing and a culture of depoliticisation persisted.¹⁰ A recent article written by Charles Fung revisited the rationale and process of the colonial state's incorporation of the Chinese language in the 1970s, pointing out that Pierre Bourdieu's theories of state formation 'paid insufficient attention to the international context'.¹¹

This existing literature, however, has not closely explored the strategies and rhetoric employed by the activists and the mechanism of policymaking. This chapter uses a wide range of sources obtained from archives in Hong Kong and London to answer the following questions: What motivated the participants to engage in the movement? Did the movement suggest a general shift in political culture? And what role did political activism and public opinion play in making Chinese the official language in 1974?

Shifting public sentiment in the 1960s

Since the early 1960s, there had been discussions about the status of the Chinese language in public discourse. Hong Kong and Kowloon Joint Kaifong Association Research Council had advocated the equality of use for both Chinese and English since 1963. As neighbourhood organisations which provided charitable works and welfare services, kaifong associations served as one of the main informal channels of communication between the colonial government and the Chinese communities. They represented the interests of the Chinese communities to the authorities, and publicised and explained governmental policies to the public.¹² Kaifong leaders mostly worked in the tertiary sector, whose 'outward appearances', 'living styles' and 'outlook' showed 'very little sign of having been "westernised"'; their English proficiency was low.¹³ With the decline of kaifong associations in the 1960s due to their inability to recruit young leaders, government officials were 'increasingly reluctant' to treat kaifong leaders as 'spokesmen of Chinese society'.¹⁴ Therefore, the request of kaifong leaders for wider use of the Chinese language in governmental affairs could be interpreted as instrumentalism, an ambition to maintain and raise their personal status.

Another advisory body, Heung Yee Kuk, a rural advisory council established to advise the government's administration in the New Territories in

1926, also demanded that Chinese be legalised as an official language. In September 1967, the Executive Committee of the Kuk unanimously supported the proposal of its former Chairman, Chan Yat-sun. According to Chan, villagers often received communications from the government in English and had to seek assistance. By making Chinese the official language, the communication barrier between the colonial state and the villagers could be lowered.[15]

Since 1964, the language issue also started capturing the attention of Urban Councillors. In a meeting of the Urban Council in October 1964, Brook Bernacchi, a lawyer and an elected Urban Councillor, proposed that the status of official language should be granted to the Chinese language.[16] He argued that arrangements should be made to enable bilingual proceedings and establish simultaneous translations in the Council to remove the communication barrier between the government and the people. As an elected member of the Council and the founder of the Reform Club, which advocated the setting up of democratically elected colonial institutions, Bernacchi also believed that more Chinese-speaking people could serve the colonial administration if Chinese became the official language. In 1965, another elected Urban Councillor, Henry Hung-lick Hu demanded equality between the English and Chinese languages. As the Vice Chairman of the Reform Club, Hu believed that by making Chinese the official language of Hong Kong, unfair government measures could be reduced: 'A sense of equality and true social justice among the inhabitants of this colony' could be promoted. To pursue language equality, Hu argued that a Chinese translation should be attached in all documents of the Urban Council and the Urban Services Department. In October 1970, Hu put forward a motion at the Urban Council: for 'the betterment of Hong Kong as a whole and for achieving the fundamental fairness of its inhabitants', the colonial government should resolve the language problem by introducing a system to ensure that all Chinese correspondence would be responded to in Chinese. The motion was carried with eighteen votes for, nil against and five abstentions.[17] In December 1966, another Urban Councillor, Elsie Elliot similarly called for the formalisation of Chinese as the official language at the Urban Council Annual Conventional Debate: 'The government of Hong Kong must regard all permanent inhabitants of Hong Kong as citizens, with citizen rights, by respecting the language of the over 90 per cent majority, which should be introduced either as the official language or as equal with English.'[18]

The status of Chinese as a bureaucratic language triggered a simultaneous discussion by student organisations. In December 1964, the Current Affairs Committee of the Hong Kong University Students' Union Council issued a press statement on behalf of its members, persuading the government to enhance the official status of the Chinese language. These students argued that it was 'imperative' for both the English and Chinese languages to be given 'an equal place'. An unfair language policy could be misinterpreted as 'the colonial government's indifference to promoting Chinese culture as a kind of suppression of native culture and language'.[19] In February 1965, the language issue captured students' increased attention when a dispute over the language of instruction emerged in a student forum held at the University of Hong Kong. Subsequently, many students requested another meeting to secure reforms. More than 500 students attended this meeting, held in April 1965. It was agreed that both Chinese and English could be used as the languages of instruction in any future meetings.[20]

In 1967, a three-year Chinese–English Dictionary project was announced by the Chinese University of Hong Kong, the first university in the colony to adopt Chinese as the medium of instruction. To promote Chinese Studies and provide a basic reference work which was similar to the *Concise Oxford Dictionary* in English, Dr. Lin Yutang, a philology expert and writer, was personally responsible for translating Chinese phrases into idiomatic English.[21] The project was timely and provided the general public with 'a more adequate and up-to-date reference work'.[22] These developments further stimulated discussions over the status of the Chinese language.

In the student newsletter of the University of Hong Kong, *Undergrad*, students argued that the leftist riots broke out mainly due to the presence of a communication barrier between the colonial state and the Chinese communities. To improve political communications and strengthen people's sense of belonging to Hong Kong, the newsletter argued that Chinese should be legalised as the official language.[23] In December 1967, *Undergrad* conducted a survey. The results suggested that a majority of the undergraduates at the University of Hong Kong favoured Chinese being legalised as an official language: 60 per cent of the interviewed students supported the notion that Chinese should be made the official language of Hong Kong; and 74 percent believed that the general status of Hong Kong Chinese would be greatly enhanced if the government granted the Chinese language official status.[24] In May 1968, *Undergrad* criticised the absence of a concrete governmental proposal granting the Chinese and English languages equal legal status. Students expressed their discontent about the colonial state's lack of plans to solve technical problems in the implementation of wider use of Chinese in administration, such as translation services and employment of interpreters. They urged the setting up of a Language Committee to investigate the impact of making Chinese an official language in the existing political and educational system. The government should, they argued, implement language reforms gradually.[25]

In late October 1967, the university students' first joint publication argued that the colonial state should legalise Chinese as an official language since the majority of the Chinese population in Hong Kong did not speak English but Chinese: 'With Chinese as an official language, we can rightly make use of those otherwise left out to enhance efficiency.'[26] In January 1968, due to the students' increased interest, seven post-secondary institutions organised a seminar on the language issue at Chung Chi College in the Chinese University of Hong Kong. The seminar concluded that the use of Chinese as an additional official language would help to improve the effectiveness of the administration by removing the communication barrier between the bureaucracy and the Chinese population.[27] The fact that demands of political elites and students were linked to a perceived failure of political communication, which was alluded to as the cause of the 1967 riots, laid the foundation for a wider movement in 1970.

Political activism and increased press coverage

To arouse attention from the British government, Urban Councillor Denny Huang Mong-hwa sent a letter to a British newspaper on 4 June 1969, demanding a 'wholly local, internal, self-governing administration' in the colony.[28] In late 1969, to make Chinese the official language and seek educational reforms, Huang set up the Society to Promote Chinese Education. The Society was 'supported by a number of leading persons in education circle, notably heads of private secondary Chinese schools having close connections with Taiwan'. According to Town Talk, after the formation of the Society, the language issue 'had been given intermittent publicity in the leading Chinese press, particularly *Wah Kiu* and *Kung Sheung*'.[29] In 1970, the movement gained momentum. Previously uncoordinated and unconnected organisations and bodies now joined together to form ad hoc coalitions, fighting for the official status of the Chinese language. Three prominent organisations started to campaign for the official status of the Chinese language actively in mid-1970: the All Hong Kong Working Party to Promote Chinese as Official Language (WPCOL), the Federation for the Promotion of Chinese as an Official Language in Hong Kong operated by the Campaign for Chinese as an Official Language (CCOL) and the Hong Kong Federation of Students (HKFS).

The WPCOL was formed in 1970. It comprised nineteen bodies, which included the Chinese Civil Servants Association, the Heung Yee Kuk, the Chinese Manufacturers' Association of Hong Kong and four student unions.[30] Its individual supporters included kaifong members and academic figures in Hong Kong and Southeast Asia. Denny Huang was elected as the

Chairman of the organisation. As the Urban Councillor during the period from 1967 to 1986, Huang was publicly known as a critic of the colonial government. During his service, he requested the colonial state to introduce elections in the Legislative and Executive Councils. The organisation's agenda mainly focused on promoting equality between the Chinese and English languages. In the early 1970s, many ordinary citizens in Hong Kong still encountered 'language discrimination': for example, the *Tiger Standard* noted that 'colonialism still pervades the atmosphere in this city to such a degree that it is almost mandatory for a Chinese to speak English in order to receive decent service from these [bureaucratic] organisations'.[31] According to James So, the CDO of Wong Tai Sin, many respondents he contacted tended to believe that correspondence to the colonial government written in English 'would be dealt with more expeditiously and favourably than one written in Chinese'.[32] The *Far Eastern Economic Review* argued that such 'language discrimination' was not atypical:

> Unable to obtain satisfaction from the complaints department of a public utility, a Chinese rang off, then called again, this time speaking in English instead of Cantonese. Immediately, the haughty attitudes of the official he addressed switched to one of deference and helpfulness ... Although 98 per cent of the population [in Hong Kong] is Chinese, English is the official language and many Chinese use it daily for reasons that vary from commercial necessity to snobbishness.[33]

By legalising Chinese as an official language used in the Legislative and Urban Councils, the WPCOL believed that discrimination against people who did not speak English could be reduced. By making available a Chinese version of all official communications and documents, information could also be transmitted from the bureaucracy to the Chinese communities without any barriers. The Chinese population could have better understanding of government policies. Activists predicted that language reform would lead to more Chinese people getting directly involved in bureaucratic politics.

Both the CCOL and the HKFS were student bodies. The CCOL consisted of eleven student bodies. The HKFS represented nine post-secondary colleges, including Baptist College, Northcote Teachers Training College, New Asia College, Technical College, Sir Robert Black Teachers Training College, Chung Chi College, United College, Lingnan College and the University of Hong Kong. These student activists believed that Chinese school graduates would have better career prospects if official status was granted to the Chinese language. Racial equality could also be achieved if English competency was no longer the only standard requirement for appointment to most administrative posts. As students of Raimondi College had pointed out in their publication, if the language policy was revised, non-English educated Chinese with great capability could enjoy equal opportunity with their counterparts, and could be elected as members of the Urban Council and serve the public.[34]

In mid-1970, activism increased. A signature campaign was initiated by the WPCOL under the supervision of Huang. During the first weekend of December 1970, more than 30,000 signatures were collected in Wong Tai Sin.[35] By March 1971, the Chinese language campaign was said to have collected 330,000 signatures.[36] As the activists adopted a door-to-door strategy and started their signature campaigns in Wong Tai Sin, where a large number of resettlement blocks were located, they were able to collect a substantial amount of signatures within a short period of time.[37] However, according to the Chairman of the Wong Tai Sin Kaifong Welfare Association, some people only gave their signatures because 'they did not want to be pestered by the campaigners'.[38] The number of signatures was therefore not a reliable indicator of the level of popular support for the movement.

Meanwhile, the CCOL gave the government a deadline of 29 August 1970 to issue a definite statement in response to the language issue. For propaganda purposes, the CCOL also produced some yellow-fisted T-shirts for sale, on which the Chinese as an official language slogan was stamped. Handbills were subsequently distributed to the public. In September 1970, the Chairman of the CCOL, Lam Hung-chow, announced that plans had been made to boycott classes if the government continued to neglect the language issue. Lam publicly 'urged students to do something more meaningful than just attending classes'.[39] Almost at the same time, 30,000 copies of language pamphlets were printed and distributed by the HKFS. They also planned to carry out a survey to ascertain public views on the language issue in ten city districts and five districts in the New Territories.

The campaign was not a unitary movement with one goal. Apart from instrumental concerns and personal interests, ideological motivations, including the pursuit of localisation and democratisation, the notion of racial equality and cultural nationalism, played an important role in determining people's positions in the campaign. Whenever activists found it possible and saw it fit, they were willing to inhabit various ideas and exploit the mass population for their own benefit. Among the middle-aged and elderly groups of Hong Kong Chinese, a tendency to avoid political participation was accounted for by the following attributes: 'acquiescence, transience, fear of China, satisfaction, conservatism, rationality and reluctance to share power'.[40] To appeal for support from the bulk of the population, activists often avoided overt political overtones in their activities and slogans. They never limited themselves to nationalistic doctrines and political ideologies. This flexibility was particularly important given the influence of communism on local political life. Many Hong Kong Chinese of the older generation fled to Hong Kong as refugees to escape from political turmoil in mainland China, such as the Great Leap Forward, the Hundred Flowers Movement and the Cultural Revolution. The 'indiscriminate bombing campaign' in the 1967 riots by the leftists added further weight to this view.[41] Knowing that many Hong Kong Chinese were sceptical towards the Chinese Communist Party, all three organisations suspended their activities on the Chinese National Day, 1 October 1971, to avoid association with the Party. Rhetoric employed in slogans was also intentionally apolitical to make the language campaign more welcoming to the public. The Hong Kong University Students' Union's poster, for instance, used the slogan, 'Justice, Hearts of Public, a People, Her Dignity'.[42] The meaning behind the term 'official language' was vague and rarely defined. Another pamphlet issued by the students also did not mention constitutional reform. Instead, it focused on racial equality and appealed to the cultural aspect of the movement: 'There is four million Chinese population in Hong Kong, and Chinese has not been used for a hundred years. Why? Culture and tradition of five thousand years has been forgone. Why cannot Chinese use Chinese?'[43] These tactics depoliticised the campaign, which was presented as a technical and cultural issue to improve political communications and preserve Chinese culture, not to change policies or institute democracy.

As the majority of the language activists were educated social elites, such as students and Urban Councillors, they were particularly aware of the approaches they used to pursue their ends and how it would affect their professional reputations. To avoid being labelled as radicals and isolating support from the masses, the activists presented themselves as orderly citizens who complied with the law. They resorted to moderate and legitimate means: inter alia, Huang's petition sent to the UN, open letters issued by the HKFS, and forums, public opinion polls and signature campaigns jointly coordinated by organisations. For example, in his letter to Anthony Royle, a British MP, James Chui, the Chairman of the HKFS Language Action Committee, pointed out the contrast between the approaches adopted by the police force and the student activists. He stressed that, on the one hand, 'only peaceful means, such as public polls, forums and signature campaigns etc., were employed' by the students; on the other hand, the Hong Kong police force and Urban Council were 'mishandling' a 'peaceful demonstration'.[44] This disparity captured the attention of the public. People tended to sympathise with the activists. In addition, demands were presented as the public will. For example, in the position paper, Chui argued that 'though the political set-up of Hong Kong is not a democracy, it has proved in the past not too unwilling to take note of public opinion'. Therefore, 'the popular desire of making Chinese an official language should be heeded'.[45]

The Chinese as the official language movement 61

Nevertheless, the student activists were not as moderate as they portrayed themselves in public. In Chui's letter to Royle, the student representative first hinted that the movement was powerful in numbers: it was not only supported by the majority in Hong Kong, but also by a number of overseas Chinese student associations and international bodies. For example, the National Union of Students of the United Kingdom alone consisted of 500,000 members. He threatened to escalate actions, which would affect public order, if the colonial government failed to respond to their demands:

> Reluctance of the Hong Kong government to take swift and decisive actions to heed public desire will convince the public, in particular students, that peaceful means through negotiations, are ineffective in the promotion of social justice. Undoubtedly such loss in confidence in the authorities is detrimental to the interest of the community at large and will only invite troubles to all parties concerned.[46]

Similar language could be found in the HKFS's letter to F. K. Li, the Deputy Secretary for Home Affairs.[47]

The radicalness of the student activists can also be seen when the student activists tried to draft their own legislation. The fourth report of the Chinese Language Committee was issued in July 1971, in which the Committee recommended that the government consider declaring both Chinese and English 'Fat Ting U Man' (official languages). However, it came to the students attention that the Committee 'has failed to recommend government how Chinese and English should be declared official languages'. Being impatient at the slow progress made by the government to implement the new language policy, the Legal Sub-committee of the Chinese Language Study Committee of the HKFS decided to draft their own legislation, presented to Anthony Royle, J. Sweetman, the Deputy Secretary for Home Affairs, and Sir Kenneth Ping-fan Fung and P. C. Woo, unofficial members of the Executive and Legislative Councils. The proposition, which was divided into four parts, provided a schedule for implementation. According to the HKFS, the new language policy should be carried out in four stages. 'The more important ordinances and subsidiary legislation affecting the general public' should be first translated into Chinese. Laws 'affecting the general public, are nevertheless of comparatively lesser importance' should be translated into Chinese at stage two. And the translation of the ordinances 'affecting special sections of the public' and 'of limited interest' should be scheduled for the third and fourth stages.[48] Despite their reiteration that the draft was 'merely an example, open to alternation after due consultation', along with the language of coercion employed, this move could be interpreted as a subtle attempt to alter the existing policy and system.[49] According to the constitution, the Legislative Council was the only institution that possessed the power of enacting and amending laws and ordinances. Throughout the campaign, on the one hand, language activists portrayed themselves as orderly moderates by adopting the tactics of depoliticisation and resorting to legitimate means to mobilise public opinion; on the other hand, they employed coercive language and attempted to perform the duties of the Legislative Council by proposing a new draft of legislation. These strategies reinforced each other, pressurising the colonial government effectively.

The activists' depoliticised strategy successfully captured the attention of the press. The Chinese Press Review compiled by the GIS made the following observation:

> Since the beginning of July 1970, there have been intermittent reports in the Chinese press in connection with making Chinese another official language in Hong Kong. Out of the sixteen major non-communist Chinese papers, eleven gave editorial comments on this issue. All of them endorsed the principle that Chinese must be made an official language alongside English.[50]

Over the next month, newspaper coverage increased. In late September 1970, the Chinese Press Review recorded that reports about the language movement 'appear[ed] in Chinese non-communist press almost daily'. The newspapers did not only cover actions taken by organisations and individuals, but they also published editorial comments on the language campaign. All sixteen major non-communist Chinese papers 'agreed that in principle Chinese should also be made an official language in Hong Kong'.[51] The rhetoric employed in newspapers indicated that the campaign was received positively. *Wah Kiu Yat Po* (*WKYP*) suggested that wider use of the Chinese language by the colonial administration was 'constructive' as it would help to 'build up trust and mutual reliance between the government and the public'.[52] The *Hong Kong Standard* (*HKS*) described the campaign as a 'language crusade'.[53] Historically, the term 'crusade' was often used to refer to 'the holy war' which was undertaken according to 'the will of God' from the eleventh to the thirteen century, liberating the suppressed Christians in the East. It therefore carried the connotation of justice, suggesting that the cause of the language movement was legitimate. The choice of the term 'crusade' also implied that the rights of Hong Kong Chinese were suppressed by the colonial regime.

Government responses and public reception

The colonial government was aware of increased interest in the language issue. During the meeting of the Legislative Council on 28 February 1968, the Governor, David Trench, said that the colonial government would start 'considering further' 'ways and means of giving our two main languages here, Chinese and English, as near equality of use and status as it is practically possible to do'.[54] Trench reassured the public that Chinese would continue to be used as a medium of communication for official purposes. However, there were practical difficulties if laws had to be written in Chinese. Moving towards a bilingual society was 'a process' that required 'taking numerous small and specific steps, not of making one sweeping gesture'. Therefore, the colonial government needed time to 'iron out the practical difficulties of using both languages, without creating confusion, in as many selected circumstances as possible'.[55]

After Trench's speech, on 30 March 1968, circulars about the official use of the Chinese language were issued to the heads of all departments by A. T. Clark, the Principal Assistant Colonial Secretary. In the circular, Clark suggested that although many departments had already adopted the practice of writing letters in Chinese or sending Chinese translations with formal replies, 'the effect that one or two offices do not reply to Chinese letters in Chinese, and still issue important printed or cyclostyled notices, warning or advice to humble people' continued to attract public criticism. Clark sent the department instructions on the subject to these high-ranked bureaucrats and ordered them to make 'suitable arrangements' within one month.[56] Besides, a report was written by C. K. K. Wong, both the Assistant Secretary and the CDO of Sham Shui Po, to assess to what extent had Chinese been used in government departments and the inadequacies so far. Wong uncovered that although a number of departments had already adopted the practice of using Chinese more widely in correspondence, they had misplaced the emphasis on 'translation':

> Between English and Chinese, the linguistic differences are immense and their modes of presentation of ideas are not easy to reconcile. I myself find that, in an alarming proportion of translated letters and notices, much of the original subtlety in putting across an idea is lost in the course of translation.[57]

The current translators did not possess enough special subject knowledge to provide accurate and precise interpretations of letters and notices. Instead of translating the English documents and letters into Chinese literally, Wong recommended that all official publications which affected the Chinese communities should be rewritten in Chinese.[58] Other CDOs responded to Wong's paper. Despite the internal investigations and communications, no official language reform was introduced in the late 1960s.

In 1970, the language issue was revived. The fact that information related to the movement could be found in almost all newspapers reflected 'the public's increasing interest in the development of this issue'.[59] The increased press coverage on the language movement influenced public opinion. Town

Talk stated that at a public forum, 'a unanimous stand' was taken by the secondary and post-secondary student bodies that 'Chinese must be made an official language in Hong Kong and be given equal status'.[60] In response to the society's increasing interest in the language issue and the pressure exerted by these organisations, the colonial government announced that a Chinese Language Committee was to be set up on 18 September 1970. The Committee was responsible for examining the use of the Chinese language in administration, legislation and education. It consisted of five members, including T. L. Yang, a District Judge, T. C. Lai, who was from the Department of Extra-Mural Studies in the Chinese University of Hong Kong, G. M. B. Salmon, who represented the Hong Kong General Chamber of Commerce, M. A. B. Steveson, the Deputy Director of the GIS and F. K. Li, the Deputy Secretary for Home Affairs. The colonial government relied on mechanisms embedded in the CDO Scheme to assess public feelings on the language policy and movement. Apart from Town Talk, the CDOs were required to produce a weekly situation report and forward that to the CDCs.[61] These 'special arrangements' were made with the CDOs' 'to see, on behalf of the [Chinese Language] Committee, members of the public who wish to make known their opinion on this matter'.[62] The CDOs then conveyed these views to the Language Committee. They were also responsible for submitting another bi-weekly report to the Committee, which was a collection of specific examples of cases where an English letter or document should be accompanied by a Chinese translation.

The formation of the Chinese Language Committee was positively received by the majority of the public. According to the CDO of Wan Chai, although some people suspected that the formation of the Committee 'was only a tactical move calculated to silence the critics without intending to do anything', most people 'welcomed government's proposal to set up a committee to study the issue'.[63] Some press welcomed the setting up of a formal Language Committee. The *Hong Kong Times* (*HKT*), for instance, believed the setting up of the Committee was 'a positive step' taken by the colonial state to respond to public opinion. *Wah Kiu Man Po* (*WKMP*) also suggested that 'this move taken by the government shows it pays heed to public opinion'.[64]

However, activists remained dissatisfied with the government's arrangement. Denny Huang condemned the government-appointed Committee as an unrepresentative bureaucratic 'farce', in which four of five members were connected with the colonial state: 'The Committee was not what people want because it did not include in its terms of reference the study of Chinese being made an official language.'[65] To express his discontent, Huang claimed that he would ignore the Committee and would not submit any representation to it. The Chairman of the Hong Kong University Students' Union,

John Ng, similarly argued that the Language Committee only represented 'to a great extent the point of view of government rather than that of a cross section of the society'.[66] To protest against the lack of representativeness of the Committee's membership, the language leaders announced that they would boycott the Committee in October 1970.

According to a report written by the Kowloon CDC, David Lai, the cause of the language movement was widely supported by the public:

> There is widespread endorsement and sympathy with this agitation among the public ... For the average person the need for better communication with government is still felt despite the actions taken by government so far in using Chinese as an alternative medium of communication. There is a widespread feeling that the use of Chinese by government departments so far has not been as widespread and certainly not as effective as Colonial Secretary has suggested in his speech in Legislative Council.[67]

The majority of the population believed that to improve political communication, 'Chinese should be made an official language'. Many held that 'unless Chinese was made an official language, users of English would still be given preferential treatment'.[68]

This shifting popular sentiment influenced the colonial state's ruling strategies. However, instead of appointing some 'representative' members to the Language Committee, the colonial state attempted to weaken the movement by communicating with the public through CDOs. The CDOs were instructed to brief their staff on the official line of thinking before they started talking to the general public. They should explain to the public that the language issue was 'more complicated than it appears to be' and point out that the government 'has been making genuine effort to meet the need of non-English speaking people'. They were also told to 'act systematically and discreetly' to 'isolate the support for the movement, particularly for Denny Huang's group'. For example, in their conversations with their contacts, they should hint that Huang's enthusiasm was associated with him seeking re-election to the Urban Council in April 1971.[69] In 1971, the Chinese Language Committee examined the intelligence supplied by CDOs closely and produced the first report in February. The Committee took public opinion into consideration and advised that simultaneous interpretation in English and Cantonese should be provided in any open meeting of the Legislative and Urban Councils. Similar facilities should also be introduced in boards and committees with members who did not speak English.[70]

Reactions to the first language report were mixed. Urban Councillors D. J. R. Blaker and Elsie Elliott both welcomed the introduction of simultaneous interpretation in the Councils, considered that to be the first stage of enabling more Chinese to participate in political affairs. Chinese-language newspapers were also supportive. *Sing Tao Man Pao* (*STMP*) suggested that if the recommendations of the Committee were to be carried out, the status of the Chinese language would be enhanced substantially. They were confident that the Governor would seriously consider the advice offered by the Committee.[71] *WKYP* believed that all the suggestions of the Committee were 'reasonable' and 'realistic'. They were 'happy to note the alacrity with which the Committee has tackled its job'.[72] Nevertheless, some press and activists held a completely opposite view. The *Hong Kong Daily News* (*HKDN*), for instance, expressed its disappointment and suggested that there was 'a feeling' that the appointment of the Committee was merely 'a delaying tactic'.[73] Huang was also 'disappointed' that the Committee made no mention of making Chinese the official language in its report. The Chairman of the HKFS, James Chui, said that he was 'not very happy with the report'. To Chui, the Committee was relying on 'a delaying tactic' and the recommendations were only a 'small success' in the whole language campaign.[74]

The Committee submitted the second report on 28 April 1971, in which it responded to the activists' demands. It recommended the colonial government give Chinese and English 'equality of use and status as far as practically possible'. A senior officer should be appointed 'to keep a constant check on government's performance' in the use of Chinese in official business. The government should 'pool existing facilities for the translation of technical terms to stimulate further translation and to provide all departments with official glossaries'.[75]

The second report was received favourably by *Tin Tin Yat Po* (*TTYP*), which 'applaud[ed] the Committee' for its 'wonderful recommendation that could lay down a fixed rule for all government officers concerned'.[76] *WKMP* also pointed out that 'people from all walks of life fully endorse the "equality of status" of Chinese in government documents to the public'.[77] Even the HKFS supported the second report 'whole-heartedly' despite their suggestion that the government should show more sincerity and speed up dealing with the language issue.[78] However, the report was criticised by Urban Councillor Henry Hu, who asserted that 'the current language campaign would not have been necessary if government had followed its declared policy on "near equality of use and status" for both Chinese and English'.[79] The *Truth Daily* also criticised the Committee's recommendation and argued that if the English version was serving as the basis, it implied that the Chinese version was less important. This would consequently be 'a heavy blow' for the status of the Chinese language.[80]

In the face of the negative responses, the Governor announced in May 1971 that recommendations made in the first report of the Committee had been accepted. The third report, which mainly dealt with the use of the Chinese language in courts, was published by the Committee in late June.

The Chinese as the official language movement

The Committee recommended that all bills and ordinances should be published in both languages in the future. Present legislation should be translated into Chinese in stages. In the lower courts, oral proceedings should be conducted in both Cantonese and English. However, the Committee also suggested that 'equal status does not necessarily imply equal use in every single instance': 'Status denotes the rank of one language in relation to another, whereas use concerns communication'. In higher courts, the existing system should be preserved and court records should continue to be kept in English.[81]

At this point, public interest in the language issue subsided. The inconsistency of the Committee statements and the third report, however, provoked a bitter response from the student activists. To express their discontent, a report was submitted by ten law students from the University of Hong Kong to the Legal Sub-Committee of the Chinese Language Committee. In July 1971, the HKFS issued a position paper and forwarded it to the Committee to reiterate their demand of making Chinese the official language of Hong Kong:

> The Chinese Language Committee has stated time and time again that it is working on the principle of giving 'as near equality in status and usage to the Chinese language as English'. We strongly dissent from this ... We strongly advocate that legislation to be enacted to the effect of declaring both Chinese and English official languages of Hong Kong, equal in status, with the usage of Chinese language defined in specific areas.[82]

The HKFS subsequently sent a letter using similar language to Anthony Royle, who was now the Parliamentary Under-Secretary of State at the Foreign and Commonwealth Office. They argued that it was 'the popular desire of all sectors of all community that [the] Chinese language [should] be recognised officially as equal in the status to the English language'. The HKFS accused the Committee of adopting 'a delaying tactic' and did not make any concrete recommendations of making Chinese the official language of Hong Kong despite a nine-month investigation.[83]

On 26 July 1971, the Committee finished and published the fourth and final report, in which they recommended the colonial government to train a class of specialist translators. The Director of Education should also examine how the standard of both languages could be improved in secondary schools. They also recommended the government to consider 'promulgating a firm policy, in a suitable manner, that Chinese and English are "Fat Ting U Man", that is to say, official languages'.[84]

Despite the Committee's recommendation, there were little signs indicating that the government was going to enact legislation to make Chinese an official language of Hong Kong immediately in 1971. To exert more pressure on the colonial government, the HKFS escalated their action. On

30 August 1971, the HKFS wrote to both the Acting Secretary for Home Affairs, F. K. Li, and Anthony Royle to reaffirm their demand. Being impatient at the slow progress, the students 'decided to draft their own legislation making Chinese an official language in Hong Kong'.[85] The law members from the HKFS had prepared a detailed legal document 'telling the government how it should declare an official language'.[86] The draft, passed to the Secretariat for Home Affairs, was discussed in the meeting held between the HAD and the student representatives in September 1971. On 10 September, 30,000 copies of language pamphlets were printed and distributed by the students to advocate a legislative declaration of Chinese as an official language. An open letter was then issued to the Unofficial Members of the Executive and Legislative Councils (UMELCO) on 14 September, which subsequently led to a meeting between the UMELCO and the HKFS on 17 September. Besides, the HKFS sought support from student bodies and figures of political importance outside Hong Kong. For example, they approached the National Union of Students in London, which later agreed 'to give full support' to the campaign.[87] James Johnson, a Labour Party MP, raised the language issue in the House of Commons in November 1971. An open letter was sent to the new Governor, MacLehose, on 1 December to 'urge him to remove government red-tape' on the language issue.[88]

In response, on 15 December 1971, the Colonial Secretary, Hugh Norman-Walker, reiterated that the Language Committee's first report, which dealt with the use of Chinese at meetings of the Legislative and Urban Councils, had been accepted by the Governor. Norman-Walker also stated that the Governor would soon approve the second report, which would then be passed to the Financial Committee of the Legislative Council. The third report, which contained many controversial recommendations, would be submitted to the Executive Council after it had been considered by the Chief Justice, the Attorney General and the departments concerned. The extent to which the recommendations in the fourth report would be adopted depended upon the decisions made on the other three reports. Although the colonial state was unable to give a definite date, the new simultaneous interpretation system should be in full operation by mid-1972.[89]

The punctual response of the government was well received by the public. The focus of the political discourse shifted away from the language movement to other topics, such as the Diaoyu Islands movement. As a result, the language movement became less prominent. Nonetheless, London was aware of the tensions over the language issue in Hong Kong:

> During the past twelve months the Chinese language issue has been the subject of representations from various quarters and in November and December it was the subject of Parliamentary Questions by Mr. James Johnson and Mr. James Sillars to which Mr Royle replied on 16 November and 7 December.[90]

Copies of the Committee's reports were sent to the Foreign and Commonwealth Office in late 1971.[91] In the course of the next three years, the colonial administration trained translators and promoted the wider use of Chinese in administration. A new division, the Development, Training and Research Division, was set up in April 1973 and improved translation standards.[92] To ensure that the government would use Chinese as widely as possible in different departments and official business, the Chinese Language Branch was also set up. The Director of Home Affairs had been appointed as the Chinese Language Authority in January 1974. In February 1974, the prolonged struggle of the language activists finally paid off. The Official Languages Bill passed its final reading in the Legislative Council.[93] The language requirement for Urban Council membership was revised in late 1974: people who only spoke Cantonese and were able to read and write Chinese were eligible to serve the Council.[94] Both Chinese and English now possessed equal status. Although some ordinances and bills were still enacted in English, Chinese terms were used and Chinese translations of the bills were published. In magistrates' courts, juvenile courts, labour tribunals, tenancy tribunals and any inquiry by a coroner, judiciary proceedings were henceforth 'conducted in either the English language or the Chinese language as the court thinks fit'.[95]

The language movement had demonstrated that mass political activism could influence policy formation. These activists organised informal political activities to mobilise the masses. They successfully captured the attention of the press and the public. Public opinion shifted, favouring formalisation of Chinese as the official legal language of Hong Kong. In response, the colonial state set up the Chinese Language Committee. To understand shifting popular sentiment, CDOs were instructed to monitor and solicit public opinion covertly on a weekly basis on behalf of the Committee. This constructed 'public opinion' was taken into consideration by the Committee in drafting the four reports. These processes reveal that the reformist colonial administration became increasingly responsive to popular demands.

Political culture in Hong Kong

Through observing the attitudes and motivations of participants who engaged in the language movement, we can reveal what encouraged people to engage in the campaign and make inferences about Hong Kong's political culture in the early 1970s. Despite having the common goal of promoting wider use of the Chinese language in official communications, the language campaign was far from monolithic, with supporters holding a range of beliefs.

The young generation was politically conscious and ideologically driven. To many students, the language campaign was a movement through which self-determination could be pursued. Since the late 1960s, political awareness had increased, particularly among higher education students. They were critical of the colonial administration and advocated increased political participation as a citizen's obligation. For instance, the editor of *Undergrad* criticised the current educational system as failing to address the needs of civic education fully, resulting in the absence of public political consciousness. He therefore urged the young generation to acquire better understandings of the existing social and political problems.[96] In another article titled 'From Apathy to Inertia' in *Undergrad*, published in May 1968, the author criticised the university students, saying that they were 'supposed to have more understanding on the nature of these voting rights than other youths in Hong Kong'. They were, however, not fulfilling their civic responsibilities. The author argued that holding a press conference was insufficient and advocated students to be more politically active. In particular, the HKFS 'should take up a leading role in pushing students to participate in social affairs'.[97] An editorial in the student newsletter of the Chinese University of Hong Kong, *CU Student*, also encouraged students to take up 'intellectual responsibility' and provide solutions to improve the condition of Hong Kong: 'We students have a dual role as learners about problems and their various solutions, and as intellectuals who identify problems and suggest new solution.'[98]

Influenced by the social climate, the young generation, in particular the university students, viewed participation in the language movement as a civic duty. They believed that only by granting the Chinese language official status would Chinese-speaking people take up appointed or elected positions in the colonial administration. According to *Undergrad*, the campaign had 'very profound implications'. The movement was interpreted by 'a sector of' participants as 'the beginning of popular political movements in Hong Kong'. It was viewed as 'the first step towards democratisation and decolonisation of this community': 'We must all understand that ultimately we are actually bargaining for the power of the people of Hong Kong to decide their own affairs.' The student press also stressed that it was crucial for students to develop this perspective: 'The campaigners of the Chinese language movement should not be afraid to pronounce their long-term ideals to reform the political system of Hong Kong.'[99] Student motivations reveal a shifting political culture: these post-war baby boomers held a less favourable view of the colonial state than traditional elites and considered political engagement an obligation.

Similar political attitudes were found among some educated elites. For example, the organiser of the campaign, Denny Huang, was well known as a critic of the colonial administration. Huang criticised the Committee's suggestion as having 'very little effect' as it did not provide grounds for non-English speaking people to become councillors. Like the student activists, Huang was politically motivated. He admitted that the ultimate goal of the movement was to see people who spoke only Cantonese become councillors, 'a real step forward' to 'make Chinese feel they had a real stake in the Councils'. The WPCOL was pragmatic but the ultimate agenda of Huang and student activists was to empower the Chinese population and increase their participation in public affairs.[100]

Some students were by contrast motivated by nationalism. Their political allegiance towards the PRC could be observed from the rhetoric they employed in the movement. In late 1970, Denny Huang and some student committee members had a 'very hot discussion' on whether the Chinese in Hong Kong should be called 'Hua Ren' (華人, ethnically Chinese) or 'Zhongguo Ren' (中國人, which had multiple meanings, and could be used to refer to people associated with China, either by reason of ancestry, nationality, citizenship, heredity, place of residence or other affiliations) in the campaign.[101] Although the term 'Hua Ren' was not adopted in the end, mainly because of activists' deliberate attempt to exclude Chinese who were British subjects by birth or naturalisation from their movement, the choice of word definitely reflected some students' political orientation towards mainland China in the 1970s. For example, in a HKFS pamphlet, the theme of nationalism was adopted: 'The era when Chinese are second-rate people is gone; we are no longer people being pushed around; Chinese people in Hong Kong have risen to roar at any unreasonable things.' Most importantly, it was stressed that Hong Kong was 'an integral part of Chinese territory'.[102] Positive attitudes towards China were attributable to the belief that China would be more liberal and open in the near future. Students' optimism could be observed in an editorial called 'Hong Kong is Ours' in *CU Student*:

> After going through the disturbances, most people feel at heart that Hong Kong lacks a sense of security. Some even note that it will only be a little over twenty years before Kowloon is returned to China and by that time people will have to live under communist rule ... Actually those people who worry too far into the future and as a result lose faith in Hong Kong are troubling themselves without a sound cause. Apart from the possibility that many changes may occur in twenty years' time in this ever-changing world, even if Hong Kong is returned back to China, we will only be moving from a colony back to our mother country – and instead of being colonial subjects, we will become masters of this piece of land ... In twenty years' time even if the ruling authority in China remains unchanged, its internal organisations will most certainly have undergone changes. According to the observation of sociologists, a forecast

into the future of capitalism and communism is that as the former is gradually moving towards the Left while the latter towards the Right, someday the two will finally meet at a mid-point and the two systems will be merged into one.[103]

Throughout the movement, unlike the middle-aged and elderly groups who tended to hold a negative attitude towards China, some student activists repeatedly identified themselves as Chinese politically. They showed no hesitation in revealing to the public that they were campaigning for a national cause. Although that does not necessarily suggest they were leftists or allegiant to the PRC, the majority of students definitely held a positive attitude towards the Chinese Communist regime. In essence, although the aim of the language movement was to introduce language reforms in administration, legislation and education in Hong Kong, it was inseparable from Chinese nationalism.

The language movement also had a cultural dimension. As the CDO in Eastern District, M. Leung had observed that, unlike any other political agitation for constitutional reforms, the language campaign was 'one with a cultural appeal'.[104] Participants did not treat the language campaign only as a political movement. Many supporters of the campaign were driven by cultural nationalism: enthusiasm to promote Chinese culture, enhance the status of the Chinese language and achieve racial equality. The theme of promoting Chinese culture was adopted by the HKFS in their position paper:

> The cultural heritage of the Chinese civilisation has a history of over 4,000 years. It is a great asset to the whole community. Preservation and development of the Chinese culture would be greatly facilitated and encouraged by giving Chinese an official status.[105]

In his report in mid-1970, Wong Tai Sin CDO James So stated that student bodies were 'motivated by a sense of national pride'.[106] According to So, most students were 'in favour of the movement' and their reaction to it was 'filled with emotion'. These students considered it 'an insult to the Chinese community in Hong Kong' to not be able to use the Chinese language in the colonial administration.[107] An editorial in *CU Student* even described the campaign as 'a call of an ethnic group': 'One can ignore the voice of an individual, one can ignore the voice of an organisation, but the voice of an ethnic group could never be unheard.'[108]

The claims made by the Chairman of the To Promote Chinese as an Official Language Committee of Hong Kong Baptist College Student Union, Dominic Shui, supported So's assessment. Shui suggested that his organisation was 'campaigning for a national cause', 'a succession' of the May Fourth movement.[109] Since 1969 was the Jubilee of the movement, throughout the year, details and impacts of the movement were widely covered by student newsletters and magazines. The *Undergrad* even published a 'May

Fourth Special Edition' on 4 May 1969. Students were influenced by the ideas of the May Fourth movement and saw a parallel between it and the current language movement. The May Fourth movement symbolised criticism against traditional ideas and the existing system. By coining the term 'May Fourth movement', the student activists tried to show that they upheld the 'sacred duty to arouse [the] Chinese community to respect the Chinese culture'.[110]

Western-educated elites in an Asian society were inclined to find the concept of nationalism appealing when they challenged the status quo. After the 1967 riots, there was an 'identity-crisis'. These intellectual youths, as a result, were 'vulnerable to political ideologies which [could] offer them new identities'. As the notion of nationalism placed cultural identity at the centre of its concern, the young generation could construct a new political identity from the concept of nationalism. On the one hand, nationalism legitimated their claims to political self-determination; on the other hand, the concept allowed them to refer to their indigenous identity. Within this new identity, the student activists and elites could 'play the leading role' in pursuing increased local autonomy while recreating local culture.[111]

In addition, the language campaigners justified their demand by appealing to universal human rights. For instance, in the position paper issued by the HKFS in 1971, a language of universalism was adopted by students to justify their claims:

> Social and political equality are basic human rights in a society. It is a gesture of respect to make the language of an ethnic group an official language. The demand to make [the] Chinese language an official language is a political right that should not be denied then.[112]

The language movement merged hopes for self-determination, cultural nationalism and calls for universalism.

The demands of the movement were paradoxical. On the one hand, activists demanded the enhancement of the status of their native language as the official language; on the other hand, many participants still viewed the Chinese language as inferior to the English language. In a letter to the editor of the *Truth Daily*, a supporter of the campaign recommended that in any cases of dispute, especially regarding legal and technical issues, 'the English version should prevail'.[113] The suggestion of using the English clauses as 'the basis' of the Chinese version indicated that the notion of English being a more appropriate language to be used in formal occasions was still deeply rooted in many people's minds. A contemptuous attitude towards the Chinese language remained common in the early 1970s. Prejudice that English-written correspondence should be given preferential treatment and the status of the Chinese language was inferior compared to that of English 'existed not only in the mind of many government officials but also the general public'.[114] The fact that a number of supporters still showed a degree of contempt towards the Chinese language sub-consciously suggested that the rhetoric employed in the slogans should not be taken at face value.

Nonetheless, some students did engage in the movement because of non-ideological concerns: their future career prospects. Both the CDC of Kowloon and the CDO of Wong Tai Sin observed that the student activists mostly came from schools and universities using Chinese as the medium of instruction. David Lai observed that 'the hard-core of the agitation lies in the Federation of Hong Kong Catholic Students and the College Students Association of Hong Kong', the membership of which largely consisted of Chinese University students and post-secondary college students who felt that 'they are being discriminated against in terms of job opportunities'. They therefore viewed 'the adoption of Chinese as an official language as a means to improve their prospects'.[115]

James So also agreed with Lai's observation and argued that these students joined the movement because they were 'not able to compete on a par with graduates from H.K.U. for jobs'. They therefore considered that 'if Chinese could be made [the] official language they would stand a much better chance in competing with H.K.U. graduates for jobs'.[116]

These findings suggest that the political culture within the young generation was far from uniform. In fact, many secondary school students were reluctant to politicise the campaign. Most of those who participated in a language seminar held at Ying Wa College on 17 November 1970 were 'scared to associate themselves too closely with any of the campaign promoters, and therefore, made no reference to any of the three organisations throughout the seminar'.[117] The political culture within the young generation was divided between those in secondary and tertiary education.

Denny Huang's declaration of his personal decision to run for the next Urban Council election further fractured the pluralist movement. Some post-secondary students expressed their disappointment by calling Huang a 'hypocrite' and asserted that he only started the movement with a 'self-seeking purpose'.[118] Some student representatives felt that Huang wanted to dominate the movement.[119] Many gradually withdrew, 'fed up' that the campaign representatives never consulted them and had never informed them how their donations were spent.[120]

As the editor of *WKYP* pointed out, many people engaged in the movement due to pragmatism: they wanted Chinese to be used in their workplace. These people were reluctant to politicise the movement.[121] This tendency was particularly prevalent among the middle-aged and elderly groups, who were more likely to be influenced by 'the tradition of paternalism in Chinese politics, and the refugee experience'.[122] For the older generation, their engagement in the language movement was often driven by instrumental and pragmatic concerns. For example, for non-English-speaking middle-aged community leaders, such as the kaifong leaders, their involvement in the language campaign was often neither politically nor culturally driven, but 'dictated by considerations of personal status that were somehow impeded by their insufficient English and the inferior position of Chinese language in official usage'.[123]

By the early 1970s, some governmental documents and letters were only available in English. As the Colonial Secretariat had pointed out in January 1971, many documents were still found either without a Chinese version or with one but were never used.[124] For example, in the Inland Revenue Department, many forms and letters, including notice for recovery of tax, salaries tax, assessment and demand for tax, were only written in English.[125] This practice had brought serious inconvenience to the Chinese people who did not read English. It also caused a large number of people coming to City District Offices requesting their staff to translate and explain the content.[126]

Given the diverse motivations, participants disagreed on tactics and timing. For some activists, the declaration of Chinese as the official language was 'tantamount to putting the cart before the horse' and had neglected 'the feasibility and practicability of employing Chinese as a lingua franca in every sector of the administration'.[127] Many also questioned the meaning of 'official' and the necessity of making Chinese an official language. The middle and upper classes, in particular, found the campaigners' tactics, such as organising class boycotts and sending petitions to the authorities, radical. They 'favoured a milder and patient approach'. For instance, C. P. So, the Chairman of a multi-storey building in Tsim Sha Tsui, supported the idea that the Chinese language should be used widely but did not side with the students and become involved in the campaign directly as he found it 'unnecessary'; he believed that the colonial government 'was already making a hard attempt to widen the use of Chinese'.[128] Industrialists and businessmen were relatively 'indifferent' to the issue. Many professionals were also reluctant to engage in the movement. The CDO of Kowloon City interviewed two anonymous company executives regarding their views towards the language campaign. Both suggested that 'they did not mind signing' for the movement but 'did not want to be too much involved' and put down their addresses.[129] Civil servants also criticised the active involvement of Tsin Sai-nin, the Chairman of the Hong Kong Chinese Civil Servants Association. They argued that his cooperation with the WPCOL would 'give the impression that all members of Chinese civil servants supported the campaign', which was 'far from truth'.[130] Diverging opinions suggested that divisions existed among participants and the political culture in Hong Kong was far from uniform. The middle and upper classes despised 'radical' informal political activities and were reluctant to engage in the movement directly. Compared to most of the students, they were politically conservative.

Most of the working class and lower-income groups were either uninterested in the language issue or simply avoided getting involved. By late 1970, most people in the grassroots groups interviewed by the CDOs confessed that 'they had not bothered to acquaint themselves with the issue'.[131] In his assessment of public reaction to the language issue in October 1970, the Kowloon CDO made the following comment: 'During the last week, although my staff made a special effort to elicit opinions on this use, our contacts did not seem to be very interested.'[132] James So similarly pointed out that 'generally speaking, this movement fails to arouse much interest among people in the district'.[133] By contrast some workers were openly hostile. For example, Huang received a letter of death threat from 'a group of workers', who clearly believed Huang's organisation did not represent all workers and did not want to be involved in the movement. They asked Huang not to 'do something which has nothing to do with the masses' and 'sacrifice the public' for himself. An accusation was also made against Huang of 'using the workers as tools' to pursue his own political ambition.[134] Town Talk also suggested that there was 'a general sense of apathy and indifference' towards the language movement 'among the working class and the lower and lower middle income groups' that officials had contacted.[135] Nonetheless, some factory workers and apprentices in Kowloon City expressed that they 'would support the campaign heartily because they did not know English'.[136] This indicates that sweeping conclusions cannot be always made about the relationship between political attitudes and social classes.

One divisive issue was 'nationalism', which aroused suspicion of inclining towards the Chinese Communist Party. In a letter to the editor of the *South China Morning Post* (*SCMP*), a reader described the language movement as a 'ballyhoo' and called the organisers of this 'trouble-making campaign' 'rats' who were receiving support from the leftists and plotting against the colonial government.[137] For some others that did not support the movement, Mandarin rather than Cantonese 'should be taught early and well': 'To say Cantonese should be official is like saying that the Yorkshire dialect should be the language of England, the Kentucky drawl the language of America or Breton the language of France.'[138]

By 1971, the CDO of Central, Ng Chak-Lam, observed that the movement had waned: 'Some heat has apparently been taken out of this issue, and I doubt if it is still worthwhile to compile a weekly report.'[139] Jack So also pointed out that 'people in the district are no longer interested in the issue' and his staff were therefore 'unable to collect any prompted comments of significance'.[140] In a meeting of the Kowloon City District Council in December 1970, most CDOs reported that there was no special activity launched by the student activists.¹⁴¹ As the government's response was well received by the public, student activities seemed to have died down. People who joined the campaign because of pragmatism gradually showed less interest in the campaign. By late March 1971, the heat of the language campaign had subsided. The Deputy Secretary of Home Affairs, F. K. Li, ordered the CDOs to discontinue the bi-weekly returns.¹⁴²

Conclusion

The language movement shows that a reformist colonial administration was responsive to shifting popular sentiment. In response to a coalition demanding legal status for the Chinese language, the colonial government set up the Chinese Language Committee to investigate the issue. In the absence of democratic reforms, to better understand changing public opinion, high-ranked policymakers and the Committee relied on Town Talk and weekly situation reports produced by the CDOs, which contained diverse views of different social classes and age groups. The colonial government understood the importance of respecting and responding to public opinion – a way to strengthen its rule and enhance its legitimacy. This 'public opinion' constructed by the covert mechanism and recommendations made by the CDOs were transferred to and accepted by the Committee, indicating widened channels of political participation and the potential for the 'decolonisation' of the mentalities of colonial bureaucrats. Simultaneous translation was provided in Urban and Legislative Council meetings. Interpreters were recruited and trained. In 1974, the Chinese language finally gained official status.

As the Legislative Councillor Hilton Cheong-leen had said during the second reading of the Official Languages Bill, 'In the years to come, the Official Languages Bill would be seen to have done much to reaffirm the cultural dignity and pride of the Chinese residents of Hong Kong.'¹⁴³ In hindsight, the later generations attributed the pursuit of the equality and promotion of Chinese culture as the main cause of the movement. Archival evidence, however, shows that the language movement was far from monolithic but as having multiple agenda: the quests for political self-determination, cultural nationalism, racial equality, career prospects, social status and even more convenience in everyday life were all important in driving the movement. Ideological and instrumental concerns intertwined.

A distinctive Hong Kong identity, which was built upon the differences between the colony and mainland China, had not taken full shape in the early 1970s. Activists consistently appealed to both cultural and political nationalism to justify their resistance to the colonial government's language policy. Although language activists and movement supporters often only identified themselves as Chinese culturally and rarely made direct associations with the Chinese Communist regime, optimism towards Hong Kong's return to China and the future development of the PRC was expressed. In essence, although the aim of the language movement was to introduce language reforms in administration, legislation and education in Hong Kong, the campaign was inseparable from Chinese nationalism.

Lastly, the language movement demonstrated that Hong Kong had many political cultures. The young generation, which was often portrayed by scholars as politically active, was far more divided. University students and elites, who were both ideologically and instrumentally motivated, vigorously engaged in social movements. They were critical of the colonial administration and politically conscious. They also perceived informal political engagement as their right and an appropriate means to express their grievances. The secondary students, however, held a more cautious attitude towards political activism. The middle-aged and elderly groups were relatively indifferent to politics. Many of them joined the movement solely due to instrumental concerns. In general, the upper and middle classes showed concern over the language issue but displayed contempt towards informal political activities, which they considered 'radical'. Many were reluctant to participate in the movement. The working-class and grassroots groups were predominantly indifferent. Some expressed concerns over political activism due to their fear of officialdom and political instability.

The passage of the Official Languages Bill removed the language barrier between the bureaucracy and the public, and increased the stake of the Chinese population of Hong Kong in politics. More Chinese-speaking people could now serve the government. These changes paved the way for increased political activism and a more open political culture in the mid- and late 1970s, which are discussed in the next chapter.

Notes

1 Tsang, *A Modern History*, pp. 180–1.
2 Tsang, *Government and Politics*, p. 248.
3 Lui and Chiu, 'Social Movements', p. 105.
4 Tsang, *A Modern History*, p. 223; Carroll, *A Concise History*, p. 167.
5 Leung, *Perspective on Hong Kong Society*, p. 163; Tsang, *Government and Politics*, pp. 216–19.
6 Lui and Chiu, 'Social Movements', p. 105.
7 Hoadley, 'Political Participation of Hong Kong Chinese', pp. 608–12.
8 Scott, *Political Change*, pp. 110–13.

9 Lam, *Understanding the Political Culture*, pp. 125–36.
10 Ibid., pp. 134–5.
11 Fung, 'Colonial Governance and State Incorporation', p. 59.
12 Lau, *Society and Politics*, pp. 131–2; Wong, 'Chinese Community Leadership', pp. 590–1.
13 Ibid., pp. 596–7.
14 Lau, *Society and Politics*, p. 133.
15 HKRS 70-3-26-3, 'Chinese as an Official Language', *SCMP*, 29 September 1967.
16 Hong Kong Government Printer, *Hong Kong Urban Council, Official Record of Proceedings*, pp. 306–13.
17 Henry Hu, 'The Language Issue from a Councillor's Point of View', *CU Student*, 2:7, 15 October 1970.
18 HKRS70-3-26-2, Extract from the speech by Elsie Elliot at the Urban Council Annual Conventional Debate, 1 December 1966.
19 HKRS 70-3-26-2, 'Do Not Suppress Chinese Language, Students Urge', *SCMP*, 3 December 1964.
20 Lam, *Understanding the Political Culture*, p. 126.
21 HKRS 70-3-26-3, 'Chinese University's Dictionary Project', *SCMP*, 31 January 1967; *University Bulletin*, 3:7, February 1967, p. 4.
22 *University Bulletin*, 9:3, December 1972, pp. 2–3.
23 '中文應與英文共列為官方語言', *Undergrad*, no. 14, 1 November 1967, p. 1.
24 HKRS 70-3-26-2, 'Students Want Chinese Made Official', *Hong Kong Standard* (*HKS* hereafter), 17 December 1967.
25 '請即成立「中文為官方語言」調查委員會', *Undergrad*, no. 9, 1 May 1968, p. 4.
26 HKRS 70-3-26-2, 'Make Chinese Official: Students', *HKS*, 31 October 1967.
27 HKRS 70-3-26-2, '崇基研討會昨發表公報：中文列為官方語言裨益市民有助施政', *Hong Kong Times* (*HKT* hereafter), 23 January 1968.
28 Moss, *No Babylon*, p. 247.
29 HKRS455-4-4, 'Special Supplement on the Use of Chinese as an Official Language', Town Talk, 27 August 1970, p. 1.
30 The Chinese Manufacturers' Association represented most of the small-scale factories and was critical of the colonial government's commercial, industrial and social policies. See Clayton, 'From "Free" to "Fair" Trade', p. 271.
31 HKRS 70-3-26-2, 'Resolution', *Tiger Standard*, 1 January 1967.
32 HKRS 455-4-4, James Y. C. So, 'Report on Chinese as an Official Language', August 1970, p. 2.
33 D. Baird, *Far Eastern Economic Review*, vol. 35, 27 August 1970.
34 HKRS 488-3-36, 'Weekly Progress Report: Chinese as an Official Language', 23 November 1970, CDO (Central) to CDC (Hong Kong), pp. 1–2.
35 HKRS 488-3-36, Extracted from minutes of CDC (Kowloon)'s meeting with the Kowloon CDOs, 16 December 1970.
36 HKRS 285-1-1, '促進中文運動 據稱遭阻難 仍有卅三萬人簽字', *Nam Wah Man Po*, 1 March, 1971.
37 HKRS 455-4-4, 'Chinese as an Official Language: Assessment of Public Reaction for the Week Ending 8 December', CDO (Kowloon City) to CDC (Kowloon), 8 December 1970, p. 1.

38 HKRS 455-4-4, 'Chinese as an Official Language, Weekly Progress Report (9.12.70-15.12.70)', CDO (Wong Tai Sin) to CDC (Kowloon), 15 December 1970.
39 HKRS 455-4-4, Notes on open forum organised by student union of HKU at the City Hall, 19 September 1970, p. 1.
40 Hoadley, 'Political Participation of Hong Kong Chinese', p. 614.
41 Tsang, *A Modern History*, p. 187.
42 HKRS 285-1-1, 'Chinese as Official Language', S.H.A. to Colonial Secretary, 7 September 1970.
43 HKRS 488-3-36. The extract is found in the lyrics of the Chinese Official Language Song. The song could be found on the poster produced by the HKFS with the title '中文必須成為法定語文' ('Chinese Must be Made the Official Language) (date unspecified).
44 FCO 40/341, James Chui, Hong Kong Federation of Students to Anthony Royle, 22 July 1971, pp. 2–3.
45 FCO 40/341, Hong Kong Federation of Students, *Position Paper of the Hong Kong Federation of Students on the Matter of Recognition of Chinese as an Official Language of Hong Kong Presented to the Government Chinese Language Committee on the 16th July, 1971*, 16 July 1971, p. 1.
46 Ibid., p. 2.
47 FCO 40/341, James Chui to F. K. Li, 30 August 1971, p. 2.
48 FCO 40/341, Hong Kong Federation of Students, *Position Paper of the Hong Kong Federation of Students on the Matter of Legislative Declaration of Chinese as an Official Language of Hong Kong*, July 1971, pp. 3–4.
49 Ibid., p. 2.
50 HKRS 285-1-1, GIS, 'Chinese Press Review: Chinese as an Official Language', 11 August 1970, p. 1.
51 HKRS 285-1-1, GIS, 'Chinese Press Review: Chinese as an Official Language Part III', 23 September 1970, p. 1.
52 HKRS 285-1-1, '本港新聞:港政府外籍官員最好能對民眾暢所欲言 通曉中國語文 藉此與民眾建立同情與信賴之良好關係 對中文成為法定語文一事亦有極大幫助', *WKYP*, 18 October 1970.
53 HKRS 285-1-1, 'Dr Huang to Report Today on his Language Crusade', *HKS*, 25 April 1971.
54 Hong Kong Government Printer, *Official Report of Proceedings*, p. 50.
55 Ibid., pp. 50–1.
56 HKRS 1443-1-13, A. T. Clark, Principal Assistant Colonial Secretary, 'Official Use of Chinese Language', 30 March 1968, p. 2.
57 HKRS 1443-1-13, C. K. K. Wong, *Report on the Use of Chinese by Government as a Medium of Communication*, 31 July 1968, pp. 3–4.
58 Ibid., p. 5.
59 HKRS 285-1-1, GIS, 'Chinese Press Review: Press Response to the Second Report of Chinese Language Committee', May 1971, p.1.
60 'Special Supplement on the Use of Chinese as an Official Language', p. 1.
61 HKRS 488-3-36, Minutes of CDC's meeting with Kowloon CDOs held at CDC (Kowloon)'s Office on 23 September 1970, p. 2.

62 HKRS 488-3-36, DSHA to CDCs and CDOs, 26 October 1970.
63 HKRS 455-4-4, 'Chinese as Official Language: Report for the Week Ending 10.10.70', CDO (Wai Chai) to CDC (Hong Kong), 19 October 1970, p. 1.
64 'Chinese Press Review: Chinese as an Official Language: Part III', p. 3.
65 HKRS 70-3-26-21, P. Mak, 'Language Leader to Boycott Committee', *HKS*, 23 October 1970.
66 HKRS 285-1-1, 'Language Committee "Leans on Govt Side"', *SCMP*, 22 October 1970.
67 HKRS 488-3-36, 'Chinese as an Official Language: Initial Report on Public Feelings by Kowloon C.D.O.s', CDC (Kowloon) to S.H.A., 26 August 1970, p. 1.
68 HKRS 455-4-4, 'Chinese as Official Language: Report for the Week Ending 10.10.70', CDO (Wai Chai) to CDC (Hong Kong), 19 October 1970, p. 1.
69 HKRS 488-3-36, Minutes of CDC's meeting with Kowloon CDOs held at CDC (Kowloon)'s Office, 23 September 1970, p. 1.
70 HKRS 285-1-1, GIS, 'First Report of the Chinese Language Committee Recommends Simultaneous Interpretation', *Daily Information Bulletin*, 28 February 1971, pp. 1–2.
71 HKRS 285-1-1, GIS, 'Chinese Press Review: Press Response to the First Report of the Chinese Language Committee', 4 March 1971, pp. 1–2.
72 Ibid.
73 Ibid., p. 1.
74 HKRS 285-1-1, 'Mixed Views on Language Report', *SCMP*, 2 March 1970.
75 Hong Kong Government Printer, *The Second Report of the Chinese Language Committee*.
76 The article of *Tin Tin Yat Po* (*TTYP* hereafter) mentioned was published on 1 May 1971, recorded in 'Chinese Press Review: Press Response to the Second Report of the Chinese Language Committee', p. 1.
77 '官方對民眾文件中文英文並重 各方力表贊', *WKMP*, 30 April 1970, also recorded in ibid., p. 6.
78 Ibid., p. 3.
79 HKRS 285-1-1, 'Language Drive Could Have Been Avoided', *SCMP*, 30 April 1970.
80 'Chinese Press Review: Press Response to the Second Report of the Chinese Language Committee', p. 2.
81 Hong Kong Government Printer, *The Third Report of the Chinese Committee*, p. 6.
82 *Position Paper of the Hong Kong Federation of Students on the Matter of Recognition of Chinese as an Official Language of Hong Kong Presented to the Government Chinese Language Committee on the 16th July, 1971*, pp. 2–3.
83 Chui to Royle, p. 2.
84 Hong Kong Government Printer, *The Fourth (and Final) Report of the Chinese Language Committee*, p. 9.
85 FCO 40/341, 'Students Step up the Pressure on Language', *HKS*, 11 September 1971.

86 FCO 40/341, 'Students in Language Bid', *HKS*, 17 September 1971.
87 FCO 40/341, Richard Molienux, Manager of the International Policy Group within the National Union of Students to James Chui, 22 September 1971.
88 FCO 40/341, 'Sir Murray in Student Language Row', *HKS*, 1 December 1971.
89 FCO 40/341, GIS, 'Simultaneous Interpretation Facilities for Council Meetings: New System Expected to be Fully Operational by Mid-1972', Daily Information Bulletin, 15 December 1971.
90 FCO 40/341, E. O. Laird to L. Monson, 1 December 1971.
91 FCO 40/341, 'Parliamentary Question by Mr. Johnson', MacLehose to FCO, 1 December 1971.
92 FCO 40/536, 'New Chinese Authority Announced', *Registry Records*, 11 January 1974, p. 3.
93 FCO 40/536, 'Language Bill Passed: Call for Further Improvement in Standard of Chinese', *Registry Records*, 13 February 1974, p. 3.
94 FCO 40/536, 'Language Requirement for URBCO Membership to be Revised', *Registry Records*, 26 July 1974, p. 7.
95 HKRS 70-6-249-2, Hong Kong Government Printer, *Legal Supplement No.3*, C3-4.
96 '中學教育應重視政治知識', *Undergrad*, no. 1, 1 January 1968, p. 6.
97 'From Apathy to Inertia', *Undergrad*, no. 10, 16 May 1968, p. 4.
98 'Editorial: Intellectual Responsibility', *CU Student*, 2:11, 15 February 1971, p. 1.
99 'Language and Politics', *Undergrad*, no. 15, 16 October 1970, p. 4; 'Language Committee "Leans on Govt Side"', *SCMP*, 22 October 1970.
100 HKRS 285-1-1, 'Chinese for Equal Status', *HKS*, 2 March 1971.
101 HKRS 455-4-4, 'Chinese as an Official Language Weekly Progress Report', CDO (Kwun Tong) to CDC (Kowloon), 3 November 1970.
102 However, the pamphlet was soon denounced by the Secretariat for Home Affairs, which argued that its content was 'un-factual'. Activists were asked to cross out this sentence along with a few others. HKRS 285-1-1, 'Students Strike out Sentences from Language Handbill', *HKS*, 10 September 1971.
103 '香港是我們的', *CU Student*, 2:6, 15 September 1970, p. 1.; translated version enclosed in HKRS 285-1-1.
104 HKRS 455-4-4, 'Chinese as an Official Language', CDO (Eastern) to DSHA, 20 October 1970, p. 2.
105 *Position Paper of the Hong Kong Federation of Students on the Matter of Recognition of Chinese as an Official Language of Hong Kong Presented to the Government Chinese Language Committee on the 16th July, 1971*, p. 1.
106 So, 'Report on Chinese as an Official Language', p. 1.
107 Ibid., p. 2.
108 '民族的呼喚', *CU Student*, 2:8, 15 November 1970, p. 1.
109 Similar to the language movement, the May Fourth movement was initiated by the youths, intellectuals and students. It was a Nationalist movement that took place in 1919 after the allied powers secretly agreed to accept Japan's position in Shandong during the Versailles Peace Conference. In response to

the unfair agreement, students organised protests in Beijing. To strengthen China's national power, Confucian values, such as the classical relationships between the emperor and his ministers, and fathers and sons, were denounced. Efforts were also made to promote the vernacular language to allow highly educated intellectuals from institutions to communicate with ordinary people. See Harrison, *China: Inventing the Nation*, pp. 172–4.
110 HKRS 488-3-36, A. Bennett (CDO of Kowloon City), 'Weekly Progress Report: Use of Chinese as an Official Language', 29 October 1970. The definition of 'Chinese culture' here was ambiguous as the representatives did not elaborate what they meant by that explicitly in detail. It was likely that the student representatives were referring to the linguistic tradition of the Chinese language.
111 Breuilly, *Nationalism*, pp. 28–9.
112 *Position Paper of the Hong Kong Federation of Students on the Matter of Recognition of Chinese as an Official Language*, p. 1.
113 Editorial in *Truth Daily*, 29 April 1971, recorded in 'Chinese Press Review: Press Response to the Second Report of Chinese Committee', p. 2.
114 HKRS 455-4-4, 'Special Issue, Chinese as an Official Language', 26 November 1970.
115 HKRS 455-4-4, Draft CDC (Kowloon) to Hon. S.H.A., 1970, pp. 1–2.
116 So, 'Report on Chinese as an Official Language', p. 1.
117 HKRS 1443-1-13, CDO (Mong Kok) to CDC (Kowloon), 19 November 1970.
118 HKRS 455-4-4, 'Chinese as an Official Language, Weekly Progress Report (30.12.70–5.1.71)', CDO (Wong Tai Sin) to CDC (Kowloon), 1 January 1971, p. 1. Huang visited Taiwan frequently and was a member of the Kiangsu-Chekiang Native Association. There is archival information suggesting that Huang 'may be connected with Taiwan' and was helping Taiwan to expand its influence in Hong Kong, although no source of financial support could be traced. See 'Special Supplement on the Use of Chinese as an Official Language', Town Talk, pp. 6–7 and 9.
119 HKRS 1443-1-13, 'Chinese as Official Language Weekly Progress Report', CDO (Kwun Tong) to CDC (Kowloon), 1 December 1970.
120 HKRS 1443-1-13, 'Weekly Progress Report (11–17 November, 1970)', CDO (Wong Tai Sin) to CDC (Kowloon), 17 November 1970, p. 1.
121 HKRS 285-1-1, '再論爭取中文法定地位運動', *WKYP*, 12 October 1970; '爭取中文合法化不是政治運動', *WKYP*, 23 October 1970.
122 See Hoadley, 'Political Participation of Hong Kong Chinese', p. 613; Hong Kong Government Printer, *Report of the Working Party of Local Administration*, p. 11; Hoadley, 'Hong Kong is the Life-boat', p. 60.
123 'Special Supplement on the Use of Chinese as an Official Language', Town Talk, p. 4.
124 HKRS 1443-1-13, Colonial Secretariat to Hon. Secretary for Home Affairs, 25 January 1971.
125 HKRS 455-4-4, 'Weekly Progress Report: Use of Chinese as an Official Language', CDO (Sham Shui Po) to CDCs (Hong Kong and Kowloon), 6 October 1970, p. 3.

126 HKRS 488-3-36, 'Official Forms Printed in English Only', Commissioner for Resettlement to Secretariat for Home Affairs, 18 December 1970.
127 HKRS 285-1-1, 'Moving towards a Bi-lingual Society', *SCMP*, 2 March 1971.
128 HKRS 488-3-36, 'A Supplement to Town Talk Ending 17.11.70: Chinese as an Official Language', CDO (Yau Ma Tei) to CDC (Kowloon), 17 November 1970, p. 2.
129 HKRS 455-4-4, 'Chinese as an Official Language: Assessment of Public Reaction for the Week Ending 16/12/1970', CDO (Kowloon City) to CDC (Kowloon), 16 December 1970.
130 HKRS 1443-1-13, 'Chinese as an Official Language, Weekly Progress Report (25.11.70–1.12-70)', CDO (Wong Tai Sin) to CDC (Kowloon), 1 December 1970.
131 'Special Supplement on the Use of Chinese as an Official Language', Town Talk, p. 5.
132 HKRS 455-4-4, CDO (Kowloon City), 'Chinese as an Official Language: Assessment of Public Reaction for the Week Ending 20 October', 20 October 1970.
133 So, 'Report on Chinese as an Official Language', p. 1.
134 HKRS 285-1-1, 'Dr Huang Receives Threat', *SCMP*, 22 October 1970.
135 'Special Supplement on the Use of Chinese as an Official Language', Town Talk, p. 5.
136 HKRS 285-1-1, '中文教育與法定語文', *WKYP*, 5 October 1970; 'Why Change', *SCMP*, 25 September 1970.
137 HKRS 285-1-1, 'Too Much Ballyhoo', *SCMP*, 29 September 1970.
138 HKRS 285-1-1, 'Childish', *SCMP*, 6 October 1970; HKRS 285-1-1, 'One out of 10, Try Again', *China Mail*, 2 March 1971.
139 'Weekly Progress Report: Chinese as Official Language', CDO (Central) to CDC (Hong Kong), 23 November 1970, p. 2.
140 HKRS 1443-1-13, 'Chinese as an Official Language, Weekly Progress Report 16.12.70–22.12.70', CDO (Kwun Tong) to CDC (Kowloon), 22 December 1970.
141 HKRS 455-4-4, Extracted from the minutes of CDC (Kowloon)'s meeting with Kowloon CDOs, 30 December 1970.
142 HKRS 1443-1-13, 'Use of Chinese in Official Business', DSHA to all CDOs, 31 March 1971.
143 Hong Kong Government Printer, *Hong Kong Legislative Council, Official Report of Proceedings*, pp. 454–5.

3

The anti-corruption movement

By the 1960s, bureaucratic corruption was systematically operating in various governmental departments in Hong Kong. For the colonial government, it arose from Chinese culture, built on social 'relationships' instead of 'laws and regulations', exacerbated by language barrier between the administration and various Chinese communities.[1] After the 1966 Star Ferry riots and the 1967 riots, the colonial state increasingly responded to popular demands to enhance legitimacy and close the 'communication gap' between itself and the Chinese communities. As Chapter 2 has demonstrated, the language policy was widely perceived as a prerequisite for improved colonial rule. Another major reform was the formation of the Independent Commission Against Corruption (ICAC) in 1974, 'one of the most important developments in Hong Kong since 1945'.[2] The ICAC 'generated invaluable political dividends for British rule', enhancing the credibility of the colonial state.[3] It symbolised the emergence of a 'local political culture', creating an impression that Hong Kong was more civilised than other Asian countries, including China, where corruption remained entrenched.[4]

The ICAC has become a subject of recent revisionism, which has placed stress on incremental shifts rather than changes brought about by the creation of the ICAC. Mark Hampton has explored British legal and political culture, including how it adapted to the context of Hong Kong.[5] Observing the transforming anti-corruption measures from the Prevention of Bribery Ordinance 1968 to the setting up of the ICAC, he argued that despite Britain's establishment of an anti-corruption culture at home, its 'good government' idea, in an imperial context, emphasised trusteeship rather than imposing this British value on its colonies; the Hong Kong colonial government therefore did not tackle the issue of corruption actively until it became a problem for the Hong Kong Chinese.[6] British legal norms, in particular, the Fugitive Offenders Act, however, served as an obstacle to eradicate corruption in Hong Kong, as will be detailed later.[7] Ray Yep has emphasised decades of cumulative efforts made by Governors ruling before

MacLehose, including Robert Brown Black and David Trench. Reforms pushed by these former Governors in the context of escalating tensions between the Hong Kong community and London in the 1960s and 1970s, such as the passage of the Prevention of Bribery Bill in 1970, paved the way for the setting up of the ICAC.[8] Lam Wai-man has provided a brief account of the student-led anti-corruption movement after the escape of Peter Godber, the Deputy District Police Commander of Kowloon, in 1973.[9] In June 1973 Godber was put on the watch list after evidence indicating that he possessed a huge amount of unexplained wealth. His disappearance in Hong Kong resulted in public criticism. Students subsequently initiated an anti-corruption movement. Lam examined how students mobilised the public. The campaign received 'extensive' publicity and the scale of participation was 'considerable'.[10] It demonstrated the 'political sophistication of the young political forces'.[11]

These scholars nevertheless have not considered fully how anti-corruption movements facilitated the formation of the ICAC and how general political culture was affected by it. Although Hampton asserted that the setting up of the ICAC 'was the culmination of anti-corruption campaigns emerging from Hong Kong's Chinese grassroots during a period of political crisis', he did not examine the anti-corruption public discourse and the network of activists closely.[12] Yep focused on how changing dynamics between the British and colonial governments led to anti-corruption reforms in 1974. He only noted the 'growing local frustrations' among the Chinese communities.[13] Lam failed to analyse non-student-led anti-corruption movements, and relied on published sources, such as student magazines and newspapers. We have a fragmentary understanding of the anti-corruption movement, which was initiated by newspapers, student activists and individual campaigners, and supported by the wider public.

Using state records and newspaper articles on corruption from London and Hong Kong, complemented by the manuscripts of Elsie Elliott (later known as Elsie Tu) held at the Baptist University Library, Hong Kong, this chapter provides a comprehensive study of anti-corruption social movements. This analysis shows that anti-corruption reforms were implemented after the emergence of various social movements, suggesting that the legislative and institutional changes were responses to shifting public sentiment, and state records show that the colonial administration was actively investigating changing popular opinion. The surviving data is fragmentary but supports two notions: first that, as argued previously, the colonial government had enhanced organisational capacity, and thus could monitor the changing sentiments of Chinese society; second, that this constructed 'public opinion' was, as to be expected, feeding into the policymaking process, primarily via the CDO Scheme.

This chapter investigates various anti-corruption campaigns, including the *China Mail*'s opinion poll campaign, the student-led anti-corruption movements and campaigns started by Elsie Elliot, James Johnson and Alan Ellis, and the connections between them. It also analyses confidential correspondence between Hong Kong and London to reveal the relationship between social movements and policy formulation, explaining how activism led to the formation of the ICAC instead of the appointment of an external inquiry in 1974. It then studies the public reactions towards the Commission throughout the 1970s and how political culture in Hong Kong shifted due to its activities.

Increased press coverage and shifting public sentiment

Serious corruption had existed in Hong Kong in different governmental departments since the post-war period. Taking the Commerce and Industry Department as an example, it was commonly known that officers welcomed gifts at Chinese seasonal festivals and businessmen viewed this as 'an accepted practice'.[14] During the Korean War, the embargo imposed by the US on China created even more opportunities for corruption. Many officials actively assisted big companies to import and export a large quantity of 'strategic goods' to the mainland.[15] By 1962, a report by the Anti-Corruption Branch of the Hong Kong police estimated that 90 per cent to 95 per cent of the Inspectorate (about 200 officers) were or had been corrupt.[16] Prior to the 1970s, measures to prosecute corruption were insufficient and ineffective. The Misdemeanours Punishments Ordinance enacted in 1898 was the first piece of corruption-related legislation. Any public servant who received a bribe or person who offered a bribe was liable to two years' imprisonment and a fine not exceeding $500. Nonetheless, a department which dealt with corruption specifically did not emerge until 1948 when the Anti-Corruption and Narcotics Branch was formed. In 1948, the Prevention of Corruption Ordinance was enacted, outlining that when an accused person who was in possession of pecuniary resources disproportionate to his/her source of income failed to explain the wealth, magistrates could accept this as the evidence of corruption.[17] However, corruption investigations were still carried out by the police force, which was most notoriously known for corrupt practices. In spite of the introduction of the Prevention of Bribery Ordinance in 1970, which outlined that officials were liable to dismissal if they were unable to provide a satisfactory account to explain why they were living beyond their salaries, bureaucratic corruption continued to exist.[18]

By 1970, scandals of corruption within the police force were widespread, from police officers collecting 'protection fees' from gamblers and triads to them receiving promotion fees within the Police Department. The public was dissatisfied with the police force. As Elsie Elliott pointed out, 'this deep mistrust of the existing machinery is colony-wide' in the early 1970s.[19] Discussions of corruption increased during the enactment of the Prevention of Bribery Bill. Town Talk made the following observation:

> This, again, is a subject which has attracted widespread attention. There seems no doubt that the consensus of opinion among a wide variety of people is that the proposed measures seem likely to be more effective than the existing legislation, though some people wondered whether they would be really effective against big racketeers.[20]

Most people, however, believed that the Anti-Corruption Branch should be detached from the police force: 'People just do not seem to think that the Anti-Corruption Branch can give the legislation the full effect that government, and the public desire.'[21]

By November 1969, 'the most widespread comment' continued to be 'the effect that the Anti-Corruption Branch should not locate within the police force but [be] independent'.[22] The Bill also increased press coverage of corruption. Many newspapers criticised the colonial administration's attitude to corruption. *HKS* regarded corruption in the colony as 'the way of life in Hong Kong' and a 'social cancer', which was 'too deep rooted to be up-rooted and too rewarding to be stamped out'; the government's 'laissez-faire devil-may-care attitude' and the current 'permissive system' were blamed.[23] *China Mail* even commented that one 'would have to be deaf, dumb and blind not to realise corruption is rampant in Hong Kong'.[24] The colonial government was increasingly criticised for its 'ostrich-like attitude' towards corruption.[25] Chinese press, such as *Kung Sheung Daily News* (*KSDN*), *Kung Sheung Evening News* (*KSEN*) and *HKT*, similarly complained that the colonial government's attempts to eradicate corruption were inefficient. Instead of catching 'tigers', only 'small fry' was caught.[26] When Tom Pendry, the Labour MP, visited Hong Kong in 1973, he found that bureaucratic corruption had caused 'a great deal of anti-British feeling' in the colony.[27]

The situation was made worse in June 1973, when Peter Godber, the former Chief Police Superintendent, was able to flee to the United Kingdom even though he was under investigation and had failed to explain his wealth of $4.3 million. Within two months, another Police Superintendent Ernest Hunt was charged due to corruption. These episodes led to escalated public discontent over police corruption. Anti-corruption campaigns were initiated by journalists, student organisations and individual activists. Newspapers, such as *STMP* and *HKS*, started calling for the separation of the Anti-Corruption Branch from the police force.²⁸ In October 1973, the *SCMP* recorded how social attitudes were changing:

> From silent, resentful tolerance of corruption and big boys who get away with it, the mood of the people has changed to an indignant and censorious outcry against both those who accept bribes and the administration who allows them to abuse the norms of society with such profligacy and contumely.²⁹

Eradicating corruption was declared 'the unanimous demand of all citizens in Hong Kong'.³⁰ This shift in public sentiment had numerous components, which will be analysed separately in the following sections.

Political activism

China Mail campaign

China Mail, a tabloid in Hong Kong, started protesting against corruption in 1970, before the escape of Peter Godber. The circulation figure of *China Mail* was approximately 21,300 copies in 1970. With an estimated readership of 76,000 in 1971, it was the 'most widely-read afternoon English language newspaper in Hong Kong'.³¹ Its audience comprised young adults (30,000 aged between twenty and thirty-four) and educated readers. The majority were bilingual (58,000).³² Its campaign called for the intervention of Scotland Yard to set up an independent public inquiry into corruption. The newspaper disclosed the seriousness of corruption within the bureaucracy. Citizens' experiences of being exploited by the police were regularly published. Practical and ideological concerns were inseparable and reinforced each other. Readers sometimes engaged for instrumental reasons: 'I work in the off-course gambling organisation. I can say that if we do not pay, there is no chance of doing business.'³³ Social injustice was also a motivator:

> Corruption in Hong Kong has become unofficially legalised. I feel that corruption is inseparable from the social structure and its judiciary system ... What's more, I wonder if you have heard of the Rent Collectors. They make more money than the Governor.³⁴

Many sympathised with the exploited 'weak and poor' who still had to give money to police.³⁵

To enhance the credibility of its claims and appeal for public support, *China Mail* published first-hand accounts of policemen:

> I have been working in the force for over fifteen years but I must say I have achieved nothing ... The outsiders' belief is right that there is corruption in the police force. But do you know that senior officers are more corrupt?

They squeeze money from their subordinates ... You can never guess how much a detective sergeant Class I had to give his superior. Now I tell you, it was about $100,000 ... Do you know that a detective superintendent got more than $100,000 a month? He was very much better off than the Governor.[36]

In March 1973, the newspaper escalated its campaign. It set up a hotline for its readers so that they could report corrupt practices without providing their names and information. Opinion polls were also carried out to collect readers' views on corruption and reforms, and replies were published, before being sent to Governor MacLehose.

The campaign captured further elite attention and galvanised the young generation. More than 800 replies were received by 26 March 1973, less than a month after the campaign began. These replies were perceived to be representative of public opinion, which should be listened to by the colonial government: they were 'from all walks of life', including doctors, lawyers, housewives and even policemen.[37] And the number reached more than 1,000 by early April 1973.[38] The poll results in March suggested that the public had 'no confidence in the police, the fire services and of the government': 97 per cent of respondents believed there was corruption in the police force, 95 per cent argued that there were corrupt practices in the fire services; 94 per cent was convinced that there was corruption in the government. 95 per cent demanded an inquiry to be ordered, with 85 per cent hoping that the inquiry would be in public. In terms of the appointment of the investigators, *China Mail* claimed that only approximately 16 per cent wanted a combination of Hong Kong and English investigators; 20 per cent believed that the inquiry should be carried out by local investigators. The majority (57 per cent) expressed their demands of having English investigators.[39]

The campaign attracted mixed responses. Some readers were pessimistic: 'I compliment you on your attempt to do something, but I fear that you will be beaten by the Establishment. Good luck and keep trying.'[40] However, most published comments supported that idea that the Anti-Corruption Branch must be divorced from the police force.[41] 'Make it Independent' even became the headline on 6 June 1973.[42] While the orientation of the press was supported by Sir Ivo Rigby, the Chief Justice of Hong Kong, some disagreed and argued that 'Hong Kong's affairs and legislation, and Hong Kong's problem should be solved by and in Hong Kong': the 'Godber incident' should not 'be the precedent of Britain interfering in Hong Kong's domestic politics'.[43] P. C. Woo, the unofficial member of the Executive and Legislative Councils, similarly asserted that corruption in Hong Kong should be dealt with at a local government level by locals.[44]

China Mail's campaign was influential and important because it provided an independent source of information for MPs in London and raised awareness about corruption in Hong Kong. The campaign gained good publicity in Britain. James Johnson, for example, agreed that 'an official enquiry' was 'the only way' to deal with corruption and praised the *Mail*'s efforts: 'This kind of thing [corruption] concerns me a great deal. The *China Mail* is doing a fine job in campaigning [for] corruption.'[45] Johnson submitted a parliamentary question to the Foreign Secretary using similar wording to that found in *China Mail*: 'If he is aware of the widespread anxiety among the public in Hong Kong regarding corruption in the police force, fire services and government departments, and if he will institute an inquiry?'[46] On 28 March 1973, Johnson and a group of retired Hong Kong civil servants started a campaign in London to pressurise Whitehall to set up an inquiry into allegations of corruption within Hong Kong's civil service. The *China Mail* campaign was also reported by *The Guardian*.[47] In April, Johnson, along with two other Labour MPs, Kenneth Marks and Daniel Jones, announced their plans to visit the colony to investigate corruption through *China Mail*.[48]

On 20 September 1973, *China Mail* published a petition to the Governor. The paper mentioned the 1967 riots and implied that political stability would be undermined if corruption was not addressed in new ways. The Godber incident made this campaign timely and gave it a strong resonance:

> Hong Kong today is living through its greatest crisis of confidence since the bloody days and nights of 1967 ... This atmosphere of cynicism and distrust, if allowed to continue, will destroy the confidence of Hong Kong to tackle the very real problem that face the colony in an increasing competitive world ... Today, because of Peter Godber, the standing and reputation of Hong Kong police – unjustly perhaps – has never been lower in public esteem. The one bad apple, it is argued, must have polluted half the barrel.[49]

The newspaper then recommended institutional reforms and the appointment of Jack Cater, the Secretary of Home Affairs, to investigate corruption.[50]

The *China Mail* campaign was, however, limited as it was restricted to its elite bilingual audience, and lasted for a relatively short period of time. The campaign continued to pay attention to corruption after the ICAC was formed in February 1974. For example, in March, the paper criticised that some people could not reach ICAC through its hotline.[51] It also reported the changing relationship between the ICAC and the police force.[52] Nonetheless, the campaign ended in August 1974 due to the closure of the newspaper itself.[53] The campaign was regardless significant. It demonstrated increased engagement in political discourse among the young generation and elites, who paid close attention to the issue of corruption. The campaign was also influential as it informed both the MPs in London and other press in Hong Kong. For example, the interview with Charles Sutcliffe, the Commissioner of Police with *China Mail*, was 'picked up' by 'a number of Chinese newspapers'.[54]

Influenced by newspaper campaigning led by *China Mail*, the public was mobilised, and it became evident that most people who engaged in the debate favoured the separation of the Anti-Corruption Branch from the police. According to Town Talk, there were 'reports from four districts on public feelings on the question of whether the Anti-Corruption Branch should be separated from the Police, all of which were in favour of such [a] move'.[55] From her public contacts, Helen Lai, the Yau Mai Tei CDO, asserted that the majority of the population believed that the creation of an independent establishment was necessary: 'The general public thinks that there should be some kind of a watch-dog over the entire government and perhaps especially over the police.'[56]

Student movements

Students also expressed discontent over the way the colonial government handled corruption. Students at the Chinese University of Hong Kong, for example, considered the Prevention of Bribery Ordinance enacted in 1970 'unacceptable', as it had 'apparently violate[d] certain rights customarily granted people under British rule'. They were sceptical about the notion that evidence from unknown sources could be used and the law's potential negative impacts on innocent people:

> If anonymous evidence could be considered valid in a court of law – a questionable item in itself, the government could use this dubious right to deprive a man of his inalienable innocence only to protect one who may be a misinformer ... Here the law is so broad that citizens are totally dependent on the intelligence and integrity of the court's individual interpretation of justice, and have little guaranteed legal protection.[57]

Most importantly, the students argued that the Anti-Corruption Branch should be separated from the police force: 'For one thing, the police, primary target of graft accusations are still the authority used to investigate corruption cases. If so, they will not be so dependably vigilant against their self-interests.'[58]

The Godber case captured the attention of university students. In the summer of 1973, the HKFS, along with about 1,200 post-secondary students, started a signature campaign to pursue Godber's extradition. Apart from uprooting the problem of corruption in Hong Kong, there were a number of ideological factors which mobilised students to engage in the movement. The pursuit of social justice was one. Many university students aimed at exposing the misdeeds of the colonial state and establishing a just social system.[59] Students presented the anti-corruption movement as endorsed by the people of Hong Kong:

> Corruption is serious in various departments in the colonial government, which threatens the lives of four million citizens in Hong Kong. We promote the anti-corruption movement based on the interest of the entire society ... Therefore, the movement is just, and is the unanimous will of all residents in Hong Kong.[60]

Students were generally anti-colonial in outlook. For example, students at the Chinese University attributed the problem of corruption to the unjust nature of colonialism:

> When we look at the Godber incident, we should not look at the surface of the problems but analyse why and how it happened, in order to bring out the 'new problem'. Understanding the nature of this event would deepen our understanding of the society: a society like this, with the system of colonialism, is a system designed for rulers.[61]

The HKFS also adopted an anti-colonial slogan: 'Anti-capitalism, Anti-colonialism and Anti-imperialism'.[62] Some participants even compared the movement to Sun Yat-sen's revolution to overthrow the Qing Dynasty.[63] Others joined the campaign as they believed the state had violated freedom of speech. On 12 July 1973, the colonial government announced the possibility of suing three local newspapers for 'disclosing identity of the persons being investigated'. The Federation condemned this move as an 'irritating measure of attempted suppression of the freedom of speech', which they had to protest against.[64] These different ideologies added weight to students' claim that institutional reforms were necessary to eradicate corruption in Hong Kong.

Despite different motives, most students believed that the escape of Godber demonstrated that senior officials were involved in corruption. To press for the extradition of Godber and the order of a public inquiry, they petitioned both the Prime Minister, Edward Heath and the opposition leader in the UK Parliament, Harold Wilson. The HKFS expressed anger in response to the British government's reluctance to extradite Godber:

> The general public in Hong Kong are indignant over the escape of Godber. It is no answer to the question 'why isn't Godber brought back to Hong Kong' to say that 'because the UK law says that he is not returnable under the UK law'. This may well be a good answer to the question 'why should Godber be protected by the UK law?' Is it because the UK endorses the conduct and behaviour of Godber? Is it because the UK considers herself to be under a moral obligation to protect Godber? Or is it because the UK government is minded to 'accord to the colony an imperial brush off'?[65]

Student representatives demanded the British government to amend the Fugitive Offenders Act enacted in 1967, which outlined that an offence was only extraditable if it was also an offence in British law. Apart from petitioning, students also organised a signature campaign. The signature campaign portrayed the student-led anti-corruption movement as a mass movement and hence legitimated their demands of extraditing Godber. The campaign was later joined by twelve other student organisations and developed into the Thirteen Anti-Corruption Group in August 1973, including the 70's Biweekly Group.[66] To strengthen the movement, student activists rallied for external support. In August 1973, the Group and local student bodies agreed to cooperate with six leftist students' and workers' unions in England, namely the International Marxist Group, Fourth International, International Socialists, Labour Party Young Socialists, Social Labour League and Solidarity, to press for the extradition of Godber.[67]

To appeal for public support, the HKFS organised public forums and put up posters across the colony. The satirical poster portrayed Godber as a man who was 'podgy' because of 'high-ranking office and excellent living environment', with the hobby of 'collecting $500 notes'. It described him as having the speciality of being 'able to move in and out freely under supervision' due to his 'extraordinary friendship with world's big financial bosses'.[68] The Federation successfully collected 50,000 signatures.[69] The ineffectiveness of the existing anti-corruption measures also led student organisations to plan setting up an anti-corruption force of its own.[70] This could be interpreted as a radical plan to perform the duties of the existing Anti-Corruption Branch. Students intended to equip the squad with 'spy-eye cameras'. However, instead of sending the evidence to the Anti-Corruption Branch, they would disclose their findings to the public through the mass media.[71] Nonetheless, the plan was not executed, possibly due to a lack of funding. Compared to the *China Mail* campaign, the student anti-corruption signature campaign was of a much bigger scale, targeting supporters of all social classes and age groups. Rather than appealing merely to bilingual elites, posters and pamphlets printed in Chinese could be easily understood by the general public. Public forums were also organised to educate and mobilise the public.

Nonetheless, compared to the *China Mail* campaign, the student movement's influence was confined to Hong Kong. According to Town Talk, it 'produced mixed reactions': 'Those in favour said that the campaign was more meaningful than [the] Senkaku issue while others commented that the students had no right to display misleading posters as if Godber was already a convicted criminal.'[72] The adult members of the society tended to be pro-status quo and held a politically conservative attitude towards propaganda used by the students. They argued that the design of the posters 'damaged the image of the police to quite a large extent'. For example, area committee members argued that the colonial state 'should control the design of handbills and posters more strictly'. A headmaster pointed out that the government was 'far too patient' in handling post-secondary school students.[73] The general public also 'did not believe the students efforts would bear fruits'.[74] Different responses towards the signature campaign were recorded in various districts. For instance, in Western District, 'the general public were generous in giving their signatures in support'.[75] Yet in Kwun Tong, 'many sensible people', which were mostly of the middle-aged and elderly groups, including some kaifong leaders, teachers and headmasters, did not 'approve the signature drive' and felt that 'the government was already trying its best'.[76] In Mong Kok, many parents showed little interest to the signature campaign and expressed their hopes that students 'would not stir up any trouble regarding the issue'.[77] Political conservatism persisted among middle-aged and elderly groups before the formation of the ICAC.

Student organisations subsequently demonstrated. The HKFS held three 'Bring Godber Back' rallies, with the last one held in Morse Park, a venue which was not approved by the government. According to the Colonial Secretary, Hugh Norman-Walker, 'there has been some backing for the proposed demonstrations among students, especially the HKFS'.[78] However, the student demonstrations failed to appeal to the general public. Norman-Walker anticipated that the demonstrations would be poorly attended: 'We are nevertheless not expecting any mass support: the preliminary police estimate is that there may be up to 500 involved in the Victoria Park meeting.'[79] Although the meeting was 'better attended', the general atmosphere was 'unexciting'.[80]

According to Town Talk, sympathisers believed the rallies were 'held for a good cause'. Young leaders were praised for the 'sensible and orderly manner' they had when organising the rally in Victoria Park. Yet, only 'a few people' found the slogan 'Is it true that an anti-corruption rally is a crime whilst corruption itself is not a crime' appealing.[81] The general response was indifferent due to the absence of adequate publicity and people's reluctance to take part in rallies.[82] Views towards the Morse Park demonstration were more 'divided'. While 'the overwhelming majority' considered students' interest in corruption 'a healthy sign', they believed that demonstrating was 'unreasonable'.[83] Many 'adult members' argued that students 'should have cooperated by holding [a] rally where it was permitted'.[84] Well-educated people within the upper and middle classes, such as teachers and white-collar workers, 'strongly criticised the students who insisted in organising the anti-Godber rally at Morse Park'.[85] The 'older people' were also 'critical of the organisers' as they worried that holding a mass gathering close to former resettlement estates might spark off riots. They expressed concerns over the possibility that 'young people had become so radical and restless' and might 'get out of hand', which could be 'a threat to the social stability and good order'.[86] A few contacts even stated that the government should consider taking action against the organisers for holding 'an illegal rally'.[87]

These Town Talk reports show that different age groups had contrasting outlooks. The middle-aged and elderly groups evidently valued political stability. The young generation, by contrast, endorsed political activism. In general, they 'approved of the rally' and considered that 'the most popular way' to 'express themselves'.[88] The older generation viewed political activism 'with dislike and concern', and worried that 'social order and discipline will inevitably be undermined'. The upper class in general considered political engagement 'undignified and unbecoming of their status'.[89] As a respondent pointed out, most people would not engage in social movements but 'render[ed] their moral support to the students in their rally against corruption'.[90] The student movement gradually waned in late 1973.

Individual campaigners

Elsie Elliott, who had been an anti-corruption pioneer in Hong Kong since the 1960s, continued her campaign in the 1970s. Elliott, an Urban Councillor, was known as 'one of the colony's longest campaigners against corruption'.[91] Believing that the police force was corrupt and the existing anti-corruption devices were ineffectual, she started pursuing the establishment of a Royal Commission of Inquiry from the 1960s. From time to time, she wrote to Governors, MPs and officials in the Foreign and Commonwealth Office to press for an institutional change. She visited London in 1966 but failed to convince the Labour government to set up a Royal Commission to report on the problem. Elliott was liable to 'publish anything she received'.[92] She had good connections with a number of newspapers, including the *China Mail*, the *HKS*, the *SCMP* and the *Star*, and requested them to investigate cases.[93] Back in the 1960s, her demands were deemed radical by politicians in London. For instance, Nigel Fisher, an MP in the House of Commons, described Elliott as 'a very irrational person of somewhat extreme views' despite his acknowledgement that 'some corruption does exist in Hong Kong'.[94]

Elliott's strategy was to portray herself as a representative of ordinary Chinese citizens whose voices were unheard. For example, in a petition to MacLehose, she argued that 'public opinion is growing against corruption as more young people are educated'.⁹⁵ In 1973, she tactically exploited the Godber incident and employed the rhetoric of 'law and order' to justify her cause:

> As to Godber, he has bought a lot of suffering to a lot of Chinese families, and should not be allowed to use his privilege[d] position as an Englishman to get away with it. The Chinese people cannot be expected to respect law and order if Godber is allowed to escape.⁹⁶

Similar rhetoric is found in her petitions and open letters: 'One can only conclude that the injustices in the recent amnesty and the continual use of tainted witnesses against those under indictment, as well as the failure of all channels of communication between the upper and lower ranks, pose a threat to public law and order.'⁹⁷ She also implied that 'revolution, rioting, strikes and disturbances' would occur if the government failed to strengthen anti-corruption measures and extradite Godber.⁹⁸ As a public figure, her letters received attention and replies from policymakers.

In contrast to the *China Mail*'s campaign, Elliott's movement was supported by ordinary people whose grievances could not be addressed through formal political channels. A citizen, for example, expressed his respect to Elliott in his letter:

> We should thank you for the good and valuable service that you have rendered to the public of Hong Kong. I personally admire your courage, justice and untiring effort to fight for right and justice for the welfare of the public and I can earnestly say you are the best Urban Councillor I have ever known.⁹⁹

With widespread distrust in the police force, Elliott was a conduit for personal appeals for redress. As she noted: 'people want to report crime, and often report it to me'.¹⁰⁰ They sent their complaints to Elliott, who then forwarded their letters to high-ranked civil servants and relevant departments in the colonial and London governments. Due to a fear of victimisation, many of these complaints were anonymous.¹⁰¹ This indicates that although fear towards officialdom continued to exist among the grassroots groups, they would report to trustworthy civil servants when their interests were at stake: they were less passive.

As noted above, Elliott's personal network enabled her to take this campaign outside Hong Kong, and she wanted to use this campaign to open a wide-ranging critique of colonial governance. As such, she maintained a good relationship with a number of MPs. When she was being accused of having given $5,000 to encourage demonstrators to take part in the 1966 riots, she was supported in the House of Lords by the Opposition Deputy Leader, Lord Shepherd and his Labour party colleague, Lord Brockway, who pleaded to clear her name. In the 1970s, she worked particularly closely with James Johnson to press for an anti-corruption institutional change and the introduction of limited democracy. She often passed information in Hong Kong to Johnson through letters.[102] Elliott and Johnson both believed that the fundamental reason behind corruption was the absence of democracy in Hong Kong:

> It is an appalling scandal that the government possess not one elected member, either in Legislative Council or at a higher level, to go on the Executive Council ... it is impossible for the people to have their grievances dealt with, or even considered adequately, unless there are some members who plea their cause and put their case in public in the Legislative Council.[103]

Johnson was a prominent figure in the campaign against corruption in Hong Kong. In 1967, he argued that the appointment of a Royal Commission of Inquiry was necessary to address corruption in the colony. He also proposed that members of the Commission should be led by 'a man of unquestioned integrity'. In other words, a person who was not 'directly connected with Hong Kong'. Members should include an MP from each of the three parties (Conservative, Labour and Liberal) and people with wide experience of working in the police, for example the Inspector General of Colonial Police.[104] From time to time, he pressed for changes during parliamentary discussions.[105] To allow MPs in London to better understand the situation in Hong Kong, he compared corruption and crimes in Hong Kong to Switzerland: 'Bodies, human beings, gold, narcotics and so on are smuggled between the colony and the mainland. It seems to be like an oriental Switzerland.'[106] Johnson also initiated meetings with the staff in the Foreign and Commonwealth Office to urge the British government to strengthen anti-corruption measures in Hong Kong.[107] To wipe out corruption, he argued that the introduction of limited democracy in the colony was necessary.

As with the press and student campaigns, Elliott's cause received more attention from the press and the public due to Godber's escape. The *Star*, for example, published Elliott's lengthy editorials and comments about corruption in 1974.[108] The *Star* showed its endorsement of Elliott by suggesting including her in the Anti-Corruption Commission as an advisory committee, which would be 'a step in the right direction' and 'one of the most welcome moves'.[109] Apart from approaching local newspapers, Elliott shared corruption stories with newspapers in the United Kingdom. In late 1973, she gave *The Guardian* information about corruption within the police force and explained how that 'amounted to a widespread system of alternate taxation'.[110]

As Hampton has noted, Elliott was in close contact with Alan Ellis, a former police officer in Hong Kong. In 1963, Ellis was dismissed on the grounds of his temperamental unsuitability. However, he believed that his discharge was related to corruption and maladministration within the police force. Since then, he had petitioned the press and the British government to urge the investigation of the termination of his probationary appointment. In November 1973, when it was rumoured that there might be a plot against Elliott, Ellis wrote to Anthony Royle and supported Elliott publicly, noting: 'She is a dear, courageous, sincere and sometimes dotty friend of mine. Dotty, I say, because in her relentless pursuit of truth and justice from the cancer of administration corruption, she does things which you and I might never at least without great self-thought do.'[111] Like Johnson and Elliott, Ellis supported the setting up of an externally appointed Commission of Inquiry and was critical of the franchise of the Legislative Council. Royle had written to Ellis to reaffirm his decision not to intervene in April 1972 as he believed that the action taken in respect of the case was proper. Despite Royle's earlier reply, Ellis continued writing to different newspapers to press for reforms. For example, he emphasised the seriousness of corruption in Hong Kong and shared his story of dismissal with *China Mail* and *The Guardian* to draw the attention of the audience in Hong Kong and Britain.[112] He also wrote to politicians in the British government, including MPs Johnson and Enoch Powell, Anthony Royle and Andrew Stewart, claiming that his inquiry of 1963 had had many defects. In his letters, Ellis often invoked the danger of undermining the principle of the rule of law: 'you will know that it is most undesirable for any civil servant, of whatever rank, to feel confident that he is above the rule of law and the system of public accountability upon which the constitution of this country relies.'[113] He similarly warned the Foreign and Commonwealth Office that if no stringent anti-corruption measures were introduced, 'civil disturbances' may break out.[114]

His campaign led the Hong Kong and Indian Ocean Department to request the Overseas Police Adviser to re-investigate his case in April 1973: 'In order to get rid of Mr Ellis, the Minister said he would ask you to look through the papers.'[115] However, the Foreign Office concluded that the action taken 'was not only proper but within the discretion of the Commissioner of Police'. The allegations of maladministration and corruption of senior officers in the police force were 'totally unsubstantiated'.[116] Ellis continued his campaign by writing to newspapers after April 1973.[117] He wrote to Royle to reassert that an externally appointed judicial inquiry was 'the best way to examine the matter [corruption] long term' even after the announcement of the formation of the ICAC.[118]

Many civic organisations and local leaders echoed individual campaigners and urged the colonial administration to implement legislative and institutional changes. Edmund Chow, the Secretary of the Civil Association, said he was 'shocked' that the report did not recommend an outright separation, which to him should be the 'first recommendation'.[119] Wu Shing-sheun, the Chairman of the Hung Hom Kaifong Association, similarly voiced his concern: he was 'very disappointed' that the report did not suggest an independent Commission.[120] As Town Talk reported confidentially, 'virtually all our contacts expressed disappointment and dismay because there was no definite proposal to set up an independent anti-corruption organisation'.[121]

Unlike the *China Mail* campaign and the student-led movement, the campaign initiated by these individual activists did not stop in 1974. In 1975, Elliott expressed her disappointment with ICAC's first-year performance: 'The Commission is costing Hong Kong too much money and puts too few people in jail for too short a term'.[122] She continued to ask for a Royal Commission. Elliott's claim was supported by Urban Councillor Tsin Sai-nin and Ellis.[123] She still wrote to newspapers, such as the *SCMP* and the *Times*, and was interviewed by their journalists, taking these opportunities to raise ongoing concerns of corruption and criticise the ICAC. She called the ICAC 'little more than a cosmetic exercise', which only had arrested 'a lot of small fry, but none of the high-ups'.[124] She also argued that people who were 'less fortunate' could not afford lawyers. Therefore, they were unlikely to be able to prove themselves innocent under the new anti-corruption legislation.[125] Elliott cooperated with Johnson after the ICAC was formed. She wrote to him and the *Daily Express* in early 1975 to complain that 'the new so-called "independent" Commission Against Corruption was not independent', noting that no charges could be laid without the permission of the Attorney General's Office. Elliott's claim regarding malpractices in the Legal Department was forwarded to the Secretary of State by Johnson. Johnson supported Elliott's campaign by making use of newspapers. For example, he was interviewed several times on Independent Television and London Broadcasting in February 1975. After the police unrest in 1977, Elliott wrote an open letter to the Hong Kong government and British MPs to urge the formation of a Royal Commission.[126]

Throughout the period Elliott, supported by her network of personal contacts in Hong Kong and London, argued that the current practices and amnesty 'posed a threat to law and public order'.[127] By the end of the 1970s, the campaign had however lost its earlier intensity. According to a MOOD report in 1977, there was 'little support' for Elliott's accusation that the state was an 'inhumane, oppressive administration' despite the existence of 'a certain degree of suspicion and distrust'.[128] By 1978, Elliott's view was 'represented in the press as very much a minority view'.[129] This suggests the ICAC had altered public perceptions: people believed that corruption was being controlled.

Government responses

The ICAC

As Yep has rightly argued, the creation of ICAC was a cumulative process which could date back to the 1960s.[130] In 1960, the Governor, Robert Brown Black, had accepted the recommendation that an expert should be appointed to review the organisation and operation of the Branch. Initially, the Committee suggested the appointment of 'a highly qualified expert on anti-corruption procedures from Scotland Yard' to take on the task.[131] The British government was uninterested:

> We have been considering this enquiry in consultation with the Home Office, and I am afraid that the result is not very encouraging ... No police force in the United Kingdom, even including the Metropolitan Police, has specially trained officers for this sort of anti-corruption work.[132]

The idea was dropped. Instead, a Special Working Party to review the Branch's organisation and operation was set up in 1961.

In 1962, locals started advocating the separation of the Anti-Corruption Branch from the police force:

> There was a strong feeling among those who were heard by the Working Party on Public Cooperation that the Anti-Corruption Branch should not be a part of the police force. It was stated that the public are reluctant to complain to the police of whom they are afraid of and there was danger in using police staff in the branch because they can put the techniques and knowledge which they acquire to bad use when, as frequently happens, they are posted to other branches of the force.[133]

The Secretary of Chinese Affairs agreed that 'on principle', there should be a separation. Nonetheless, 'in view of administrative difficulties', it was agreed that the Branch should remain with the police force. It was also believed that an institutional separation would be 'tantamount to implying that the police is not capable of becoming faithful'.[134] Besides, the Advisory Committee was aware of the danger that 'civilians permanently employed in such work would themselves become corrupted'. However, it 'reluctantly' argued that the Branch 'must continue to be staffed by serving members of the police force and must remain under the authority of the Commissioner of Police'.[135] In April 1962, to increase the efficiency of the Branch, two additional Senior Inspectors, two more Inspectors and five other Corporals were appointed.

The call for an independent organisation to investigate police corruption persisted throughout the 1960s. In 1969, the news that corruption and protection rackets existed in the mini-bus business attracted attention. Town Talk recorded that there was 'widespread support for the idea that corruption allegations should be investigated by an organisation separate from the police and for tougher legislation'.[136] The amendment of the Prevention of Bribery Bill dominated the public discourse in 1970: most people believed that 'the Anti-Corruption Branch should not locate in the police but independent or semi-independent'.[137] However, social discontent only escalated after activists and the press exploited the Godber incident in 1973.

The Godber case 'revived the demand for the Anti-Corruption Branch to be taken away from the police force and made an independent body'.[138] Through the CDOs, Town Talk, MOOD and the Chinese Press Review, the colonial administration monitored the view of the public. The event, according to the Governor, was 'a subject of raucous criticisms of both [the] informed and uninformed'.[139] The British government did not only face pressure from Hong Kong residents, but also those of its own country. Student movements and the campaigning of *China Mail* and MPs in the House of Commons in 1973 put pressure on the British government to intervene. British newspapers started reporting news about corruption in Hong Kong. *The Times*, for example, argued that unless Hong Kong's corruption problem could be eliminated, Britain's reputation would suffer.[140] The *Sunday Times* argued that corrupt Hong Kong police should be blamed for their failure to stop the flow of drugs.[141] *The Guardian* closely reported any development of cases of corruption and activists' speeches.[142] It even interviewed a former policemen in Hong Kong, who revealed 'how pervasive police corruption is and the compromises which even an honest policeman is forced to accept in order to survive'.[143]

Due to the extensive coverage of corruption in the press in both Hong Kong and Britain after the escape of Godber, in mid-1973 a large number of petitions started by individuals in Britain were received by the British government. For example, a group of 'complainants' petitioned the Minister of Foreign and Commonwealth Affairs and asked the state to start a 'direct immediate investigation into serious malpractices' in Hong Kong to avoid 'funny incidents' like 'Watergate'.[144] Robert Moore, a lecturer at the University of Aberdeen, even argued that refusal of the amendment of the Fugitive Offenders Act to extradite Godber was racist.[145] These petitions concerned the British government, creating opportunities to discuss the necessity of creating an independent Anti-Corruption Branch.

Shifting public attitudes in Hong Kong and Britain played an important role in the formation of the new ICAC. The Governor's decision to set up an inquiry to review the legislative and administrative measures for the prevention of corruption and investigate the escape of Godber was influenced by the changing public sentiment:

> But the man's escape has caused great disquiet. So far as I have been able to establish the facts surrounding his escape, while these highlight various legal problems, they indicate that there were considerable difficulties that inhibited the police from doing anything effective to prevent his departure. However, as you can imagine, this is hard for the public and press to accept, if stated by police or the government ... I have therefore, with the agreement of the Executive Council, set up an enquiry under the Commission of Enquiry Ordinance to report on the facts.[146]

On 13 June 1973, a one-man Commission of Inquiry was set up, led by Justice Alastair Blair-Kerr. As David Ford, the Director of GIS, suggested, the appointment of Blair-Kerr to be the Commissioner was 'a conscious decision' to 'bring the whole problem out into the open' in response to rising public discontent.[147] Due to the lack of public confidence in the police force, Blair-Kerr, a senior puisne judge, instead of a police officer, was appointed to be the investigator. To show that the colonial administration respected public opinion, it was announced in July 1973 that public views were invited. This move was welcomed by the general public.[148] The two Blair-Kerr reports would then be published in the public domain 'as soon as possible' due to 'considerable public interest'.[149] The Foreign and Commonwealth Office also agreed that increased administrative transparency in this inquiry would 'allay public suspicion that senior officials [had] helped Godber to leave the country'.[150] A press release was subsequently issued, announcing the acceptance of the report's recommendations to 'reassure the public about the vigour and sincerity of police action on corruption'.[151]

In terms of institutional changes, the British government was clearly aware of the 'good deal of pressure building for an UK appointed enquiry' in the colony. M. J. Macoun, the Overseas Police Adviser, supported the initial appointment of an external Commission of Inquiry to investigate corruption within the police force. He believed such an enquiry would be 'more desirable and effective' and could indicate the British government's determination 'to accept its responsibility as the administrating authority'.[152] Nevertheless, officials noted the potential public responses predicted by Town Talk: the setting up of an external inquiry would be 'a major blow to Hong Kong's amour propre'. It could also be seen as the British government's lack of confidence in the colonial government's ability to settle its own affairs. MacLehose was 'totally opposed to an outside enquiry'.[153] The idea was dropped in August 1973.[154]

On the other hand, the Foreign Secretary Alec Douglas-Home had made it clear he was 'inclined to the former course [separation]' as 'it would command greater public confidence'.[155] The detachment of the Branch from the police force 'would have sufficient immediate cosmetic effect to hold opinion in Hong Kong and also the House of Commons'.[156] Taking public opinion into account, MacLehose endorsed an independent branch:

> Clearly the public would have more confidence in a unit that was entirely independent, and separation from any department of the government, including the police. We have therefore decided, on the advice of the Executive Council to set up a separate Anti-Corruption Commission under a civilian Commissioner.[157]

The ICAC was designed to be a 'civilian organisation' containing few police elements and giving preference to local candidates rather than expatriates.[158] The revised language policy had allowed more Hong Kong Chinese who did not read English to work as civil servants. The private correspondence between high-ranked officials reveals that shifting public opinion played an important role in leading to the independence of the Anti-Corruption Branch.

Driven by shifting public sentiment, the ICAC was formed in February 1974, and consisted of three departments: the Corruption Prevention Department, the Operations Department and the Community Relations Department. It was headed by Jack Cater. John Prendergast, the former Director of the Special Branch, became the Director of Operations. To close the previous operational loopholes, the Commissioner possessed increased power. He was only responsible to the Governor and was empowered to appoint and terminate any officers without assigning reasons. He could also investigate suspected offences under the Prevention of Bribery Ordinance and examine practices in any government departments and public bodies. Most importantly, a number of new advisory bodies were set up within the ICAC in response to public opinion, in which members of the public were represented. For example, the Advisory Council on Corruption was set up to make recommendations to the ICAC on corruption matters. A Citizen Advisory Committee on Community Relations was also formed, representing the community, and was responsible for advising on the work of the Community Relations Department.[159]

Despite the implementation of numerous anti-corruption reforms since 1960, the Anti-Corruption Branch was not separated from the police force until 1974. Previous attempts made by different Governors to press for institutional reform were unsuccessful. Reform coincided with the agitation of social movements on this issue. These movements exploited the Godber incident. Public opinion was mobilised in the colony, and this must have put pressure on the Governor to renegotiate with the British government for an independent Commission. In England, questions were raised by anti-corruption activists in parliamentary discussions. Corruption in Hong Kong was widely covered in various newspapers, making it much more difficult for the British government to avoid instituting reforms. Archival evidence demonstrates that the colonial administration had been monitoring shifting public opinion closely through various covert mechanisms, which was then fed back into the policymaking process. Changing political culture eased institutional reform, the establishment of the ICAC in 1974.

Public reception to the ICAC's formation

Reform was welcomed. Town Talk stated that the 'government's decision to separate anti-corruption work from the police and the appointment of Mr. Jack Cater' had 'won almost universal approval'.[160] According to the Chinese Press Review, among the editorials which had commented on the second report of the Blair-Kerr Commission of Inquiry, 'most of them were satisfied with it as a whole' and 'showed faith in the new Commissioner and leader Mr. J. Cater'.[161] However, there were also negative responses. For instance, Elliott argued that the Commission only 'arrested a lot of small fry' and 'has made virtually no in road into the syndicates which control corruption'.[162]

Besides, the ICAC's unique power led to growing concern over potential power abuses. *Star* was worried that the new institution might become a 'second police force'. The new 'powerful armoury [of] legal weapons for "Cater raiders"' was 'almost unprecedented in Hong Kong's legal history'.[163] The Reform Club expressed similar concerns over the possibility that the Commission would turn into a 'secret police'.[164] *SCMP* urged the colonial administration to 'control the revolution': 'it is essential that the government remains vigilant and keeps more than a fatherly eye on this rapidly growing youngster, the ICAC Revolutions, even quiet ones, can get out of hand.'[165]

When the Arms and Ammunition Order passed in 1975 permitting ICAC officers to carry weapons in the course of duty, the public became extremely concerned about the 'excessive' power that the Commission possessed. Many deemed the legislation 'unnecessary' and failed to understand the decision. The fact that ICAC was not a military organisation and administrative staff received no special training irritated the public.[166] The speech made by Hilton Cheong-leen, a Legislative Councillor, in 1976, captured the public's fear: 'I would at the same time seek to remind the Commissioner that continuous vigilance and caution is at all times necessary to ensure that the powers given under the amended bill will not be abused.' Lo Tak-shing, another Legislative Councillor, regarded the new legislative reforms as 'quite exceptional and unprecedented'.[167] Contemporaries referred to the Commission as 'another Frankenstein'.[168] In response to criticism in the public domain, the administration set up an ICAC Complaints Committee in December 1977 to monitor and review the handling of complaints, identify any faults in its procedures and make recommendations to the Governor regarding its practice when necessary.[169]

The extradition of Godber

It was widely believed that Godber was able to escape because he was a British subject, protected by other senior officials in the colonial and British governments. According to Town Talk, 'many people urged that Godber be brought back for a fair trial' and 'did not understand why this could not be done'.[170] People felt that the colonial state 'should settle the Godber case expeditiously' to 'prevent trouble and disorder arising from increased resentment from all walks of life'.[171] To restore public confidence, MacLehose negotiated with London to return Godber for trial. However, the Fugitive Offenders Act enacted in 1967 created obstacles to the extradition as it outlined that return was only possible when the offence concerned constituted an offence to the law in both countries under the double criminality rule. Godber's failure to explain his 4.3 million HKD wealth was not a crime in British law. He could not be returned. Aware of popular sentiment on this issue, MacLehose repeatedly pressed for the amendment of the Fugitive Offenders Acts to return Godber:

> We consider it essential that the Fugitive Offenders Act be amended to allow for the extradition to Hong Kong of any person charged in Hong Kong with an offence carrying a maximum twelve months' imprisonment or more ... If the Fugitive Offenders Act is amended, it is highly desirable that the Amendment is made retrospective as to catch Godber. The public in Hong Kong will be deeply disappointed by an amendment which does not do so.[172]

In October 1973, aware of the escalating public discontent, MacLehose reiterated to the Foreign and Commonwealth Office that 'a decision that the law could not be amended to catch Godber would be received with disappointment and anger here'.[173] Andrew Stuart from the Hong Kong and Indian Ocean Department agreed: 'it is not a question of changing the law to catch one man, but of the case of Mr. Godber illuminating an illogicality in the law which might now be changed on general grounds.'[174] This was a legislative loophole. The British government had the ultimate control over the legislation of its dependent territories. MPs, such as Johnson, supported the amendment of the Act. Nevertheless, the Attorney General was 'most reluctant to consider an amendment'. He expressed strong opposition as he believed changing the law just to deal with a single case 'tended to produce "bad law"'.[175] Besides, if the ultimate goal was to extradite Godber, it would be necessary to change the law retrospectively. Godber would certainly 'get the wind' of the legislative proposal and attempt to leave the country.[176] The Home Office concluded it was 'not at the present convinced that it would be desirable or politically easy' to withdraw the double criminality rule.[177]

Shifting public opinion did not lead to changes in the Fugitive Offenders Act. Although the British government was trying to work with the colonial government to return Godber, abandoning centuries of common law tradition and core values of Anglo jurisprudence – the presumption of innocence and the right of the individual not to incriminate oneself – was considered problematic. In November 1973, the Home Office ruled that the amendment of the Act would only 'lay the government open to criticism' and it 'did not consider that a strong enough case had been presented by the Foreign and Commonwealth Office'.[178] The Chief Whip argued that the introduction of such retrospective changes would attract 'considerable opposition in the House of Commons'.[179] In early October 1973, Royle decided to drop the idea of amending the Fugitive Offenders Act. This suggests that public opinion could not pressurise the British government to implement legislative changes, especially when the Crown's reputation would be compromised and the change was applied to more than one single territory.

In 1974, Godber was only returned to Hong Kong because Ernest Hunt, another corrupt police superintendent, provided evidence of Godber's corruption as a witness.[180] The news of Godber's arrest in Britain came as 'a happy surprise to many people'.[181] According to MOOD, the Godber affair played an important role in restoring public confidence in the colonial state as 'the unrelenting efforts' of the Commission had 'left people in no doubt' to realise that 'the government means business'. It impressed those who formerly speculated the creation of the ICAC was 'window dressing' or 'pouring old wine into new bottles'.[182]

Political culture

The setting up of the ICAC had a huge impact on Hong Kong's political culture. With the introduction of new anti-corruption measures, increased education and the influence of the mass media, public engagement in politics increased. After the formation of the Commission, people were less reluctant to report corruption. Their fear of officialdom was greatly reduced. This changing political attitude formed a strong contrast with the conservative political culture in the early 1970s. Before the ICAC was set up, the public in general was either reluctant to engage in social movements or unwilling to disclose their identities when they were involved. Such reservation in politics could be observed when people reported cases of corruption and shared their views in newspapers anonymously. Campaigns, such as the *China Mail* one, emphasised that when dialling their hotlines, people were not obliged to give their names.[183] The speech made by the HKFS revealed a similar fear of officialdom: 'members of the public will be more than willing to talk about grievances providing government has shown its sincerity to guarantee the villains will be properly handled'.[184] As the previous chapter indicated, many believed that 'tackling the evils and inequalities' was 'rocking the boat'.[185]

State records reveal this political conservatism prevailed when people handled the issue of corruption. For example, in June 1973, it was noted that the response to Blair-Kerr's appeal for information from the public 'has been comparatively poor'. Blair-Kerr therefore had to reiterate that 'the appeal was still open' through the mass media. To minimise public anxiety, he repeatedly stressed that witnesses and people who offered evidence could be heard 'in chambers with complete confidentially'.[186] Prior to the formation of the ICAC, the only politically active group seemed to be the young generation, mainly the students. In the anti-corruption movement, the young workers in the working class, however, had become increasingly active, as an article in *CU Student* suggested:

> The anti-corruption campaign has demonstrated a good phenomenon, which is the unity between students and workers. The youth organisations that initiated this movement were not only student parties but also included many groups consisted of young workers. These young workers that were enthusiastic about social problems showed good leadership and positive social consciousness in the movement.[187]

The political culture shifted gradually after the formation of the ICAC. According to MOOD, with new anti-corruption measures being imposed, many people felt that the government was 'prepared to take a fair and honest attitude about its own failings and shortcomings' and was 'not afraid of washing dirty linen in public'.[188] It was noted that these moves 'have gradually built up public confidence in the government's open minded attitude and sincere interest in public reactions'.[189] The public was now 'in no doubt' that the colonial state was 'fully determined to suppress corruption'.[190] Compared to the 1950s, the public was now 'much more prone to take issue with the government over what they consider unjust official action'.[191] Due to the state's efforts in publicising and explaining its policies through the mass media and extended personal contact by the CDOs, people were more inclined to believe that 'public criticism and the pressure of public opinion can produce results' and the colonial administration had become increasingly 'sensitive and responsive'.[192] This phenomenon was particularly obvious among the 'young intelligentsia'.[193]

The number of complaints reflected increased popular involvement in eradicating corruption post-ICAC formation. Between 15 February and 31 December 1974, the ICAC received 3,189 complaints.[194] And during the twelve months before June 1975, over 7,000 reports were made with 3,408 concerned with corruption.[195] By June 1975, the ICAC received ten complaints per day on average.[196] However, it is important to note that most of these complaints remained anonymous, and the public 'maintained a rather sceptical attitude' towards the Commission.[197] Of the 3,189 complaints taken in the first ten months, only 1,063 reports contained adequate information to become actual cases on which full investigations were launched. The relatively low prosecution rate could be attributed to 'the reluctance or refusal of witnesses to provide the necessary evidence to substantiate complaints of corruption'. According to Prendergast, some of the anonymous reports had provided sufficient information about corruption. Yet, it was impossible to return to the complainants for further details, and hence investigations could not be launched.[198] Table 3.1 reveals that almost half of the complaints received by the Commission in the first fifteen months were made anonymously. To some extent, the high percentage of anonymous complaints shows people's persistent fear towards officialdom and their lack of confidence in the ICAC.

Middle-aged and elderly groups in particular showed 'fatalism inherited from traditional attitudes formed by experience under successive Chinese governments'. They rarely sought to question 'the wrongs of officialdom, or to contest its actions'.[199] The perception that politics was dangerous could be found in a number of Cantonese proverbs, such as 'officials have two mouths' (a traditional saying which means that authorities could always find excuse to justify their decisions), 'the poor should never attempt to fight the wealthy, or the wealthy to fight the officialdom' and 'the governor of a prefecture can commit arson with impurity, but the people are not even allowed to light their lamps'.[200] It was also commonly thought that despite public consultation, the colonial administration would 'in the end

Table 3.1 Complaints made to the ICAC

	June 1975	May 1975	Feb 1974–May 1975
Anonymous	187	192	3,148
Non-anonymous	81	83	1,553

HKRS 70-6-340-3, *ICAC Bulletin*, 2 June 1975.

take a decision rejecting some of the suggestions or recommendations from there'.[201] A small number of people even viewed the ICAC with 'resentment and fear' due to its image as 'an all-powerful Gestapo'.[202] As the rate of anonymous reports remained high and there were concerns that 'malicious' complaints would be made if complainants did not have to disclose their identities, the Commission was forced to announce in January 1976 that no action would be taken in relation to anonymous reports unless some form of corroboration was available.[203]

Mass media played an important role in the increase of political awareness and popular involvement in reporting corruption. According to professional market research findings, by 1976, over 90 per cent of the households in Hong Kong owned or had access to television sets.[204] Many high-income and middle-income families even owned more than one set. The convenient hire-purchase terms also enabled low-income families to rent second-hand and cheap TV sets.[205] The diffusion of television technology allowed people of different social classes to have the access to both state and non-state-funded TV programmes, which played an important role in the shift of general political culture. MOOD stated that 'the interest and attention of television views on public affairs programmes appeared to have [been] enhanced'.[206] To educate the public about corruption and encourage them to identify themselves while reporting cases, the ICAC produced a television drama named 'Quiet Revolution' in mid-1976. All three television companies in Hong Kong, despite differences in approach and style, produced programmes aiming at increasing 'exposure of social injustice' and 'airing public grievances and criticism of unsatisfactory social system, government policies or service'.[207] Commercial Television, for instance, produced a five-minute critical commentary named 'Sound Off' on current affairs, which was broadcast on weekday evenings. The show criticised 'the establishment' through 'ruthless exposure of misdeeds, maladministration or inhumanity of government', including cases of corruption. It also acted as the spokesman of 'the oppressed and inarticulate victims suffering in silence'.[208] Selected victims were interviewed. 'Sound Off' had 'a respectably high view rating' and had many grassroots viewers who were informed and encouraged to participate in the political public discourse. Rediffusion Television also produced a weekly thirty-minute current affairs programme named 'Life in Hong Kong', exploring different social problems including corruption, which 'obviously attracted a certain amount of attention'.[209] 'Focus' produced by Television Broadcast Limited claimed to 'give moral and public pressure support' for the 'down-trodden underdog' who were poor, oppressed or victimised. Although the credibility of the reports in these shows was questionable, they successfully raised awareness of social injustice and political misdeeds. MOOD reported that criticised topics often

Table 3.2 Percentage of identifiable complaints made to the ICAC

Year	Percentage
1974	35
1975	39
1976	47
First half of 1977	51

HKRS 70-8-2168, 'Summary of ICAC Annual Report', 2 August 1976, p. 3.

received extensive publicity and 'tended to become common subjects of dinner table or tea house conversations'.[210]

Influenced by the mass media and the changing reporting policy, the public was now more willing to identify themselves while reporting cases of corruption. Popular political attitudes shifted gradually:

> Members of the public are increasingly coming to the Commission's local offices not only to report corruption but also to seek advice, to give information about non-corruption criminal offences and even to lodge general complaints about rudeness, inefficiency or maladministration, as if with an all-purpose 'ombudsman'.[211]

In the first six months of 1977, 901 identifiable corruption complaints were received in total.[212] By mid-1977, it was estimated the percentage of identifiable complaints and people who reported corruption in person had increased (see Tables 3.2 and 3.3). Twenty per cent of the corruption complaints were made in person, compared to 6 per cent in 1975 and 18 per cent in 1976.[213] However, the average reporting rate of five to six cases per day was still lower than the average figure of ten reports per case in 1974. As MOOD has suggested, by 1977, many at the grassroots level remained silent and were 'not aware of the services available' due to 'simple ignorance, shyness or reluctance to approach government'.[214]

Although the percentage of non-anonymous reports had increased, the total and average monthly number of reports the ICAC received had both

Table 3.3 Percentage of corruption reports made in person

Year	Percentage
1975	6
1976	18
1977	20

HKRS 70-8-2168, 'Summary of ICAC Annual Report', 2 August 1976, p. 3.

Table 3.4 Number of reports received by the ICAC

Reports received	January–June 1976	January–June 1977	January–June 1978
For ICAC consideration	1367	901	575
(percentage of total)	(38.5)	(29.8)	(21.9)
(monthly average)	227.8	150.2	95.8
Referred to government/ departments/public bodies/ others (percentage of total)	2185 (61.5)	2125 (70.2)	2054 (78.1)
(monthly average)	364	354	312.3

FCO 40/1023, 'Comparative Statistics for the First Six Months of the Years: 1976, 1977, 1978', p. 1.

dropped. It decreased significantly, especially after 1977 (see Tables 3.4 and 3.5). This could be related to the partial amnesty granted to the police force in late 1977. Before 1974, the Commissioner of Police, Charles Sutcliffe, publicly asserted that he got the impression that the force was often being targeted by the press and people would 'not be satisfied until there is a scandal'.[215] After the ICAC was formed, the unease within the police force grew. Some police launched a campaign against ICAC officers in late May 1974. They complained about the 'harassing' and 'wild

Table 3.5 Modes of reports for ICAC consideration

Reports received	January–June 1976	January–June 1977	January–June 1978
Anonymous (percentage of total)	723 (52.9)	459 (50.9)	227 (48.2)
Non-anonymous (percentage of total)	644 (47.1)	442 (49.1)	298 (51.8)
In person	247	159	139
By telephone	179	144	85
By letter	94	55	15
Referred by government departments	124	104	59

FCO 40/1023, 'Comparative Statistics for the First Six Months of the Years: 1976, 1977, 1978', p. 1.

accusations' they had to face.²¹⁶ The Colonial Secretary, Denys Roberts, initially ruled out the possibility of granting a general amnesty in regard to corruption offences committed before the formation of ICAC: 'It would be totally wrong, and indeed a dereliction from the duty imposed by the law on the Commissioner, for the Commission to refuse to investigate past corruption where this emerged.'²¹⁷ However, tensions escalated in January 1977. A number of 'incidents of confrontations' emerged between the Commission's officials and police officers on duty in the street.²¹⁸ By October, Brian Slevin recognised 'the strain that these (ICAC) investigations have placed not only on individuals but throughout the force'.²¹⁹ With the police riot, an amnesty was granted on 5 November 1977.²²⁰ As a result, eighty-three investigations had to be dropped.²²¹ The amnesty was regarded by the public as a severe blow to the morale and efficiency of the ICAC, mainly due to the impression that the Commission became less active. As MacLehose had pointed out, 'since the "partial amnesty" on 5 November last year, the question in many minds has been whether things would slip back into the bad old ways'.²²²

Throughout the 1960s and 1970s, the most common way for ordinary people to address their grievances about corruption was not through reporting to the Anti-Corruption Bureau directly but through petitions. This was mainly due to a lack of trust in the Anti-Corruption Branch. Letters of complaint received by anti-corruption activists were mostly either anonymous or full names were not given. People did not want to reveal their names because they did not want to get themselves 'involved into troubles' and believed that in doing so, the 'authority might take revenge'.²²³ For example, a person who called himself 'a supporter of good law and order' wrote to Elliott in 1968. Elliott believed that such a practice 'indicates he fears victimisation'.²²⁴ It was also a prevalent practice for people to write to the press anonymously, raising concerns about corruption.²²⁵ This practice effectively protected the identities of the victims and raised concern about the issue in the public domain. Believing grievances would not be addressed by the colonial authorities, many wrote to politicians and royalty in the United Kingdom directly, both anonymously and non-anonymously.²²⁶ Although these cases were not neglected by the British authorities, they were often sent back to Hong Kong for investigation.

This petitioning culture did not cease after the formation of the ICAC. An anonymous person, for example, sent a petition to James Callaghan, the Foreign Secretary, complaining that 'the majority (95 per cent) of the British officers are crooks', and demanded the resignation of the chief Commissioner of Police and the dismissal of the remaining corrupt police officers.²²⁷ Numerous similar petitions continued to be received by the Foreign and Commonwealth Office after the mid-1970s.²²⁸ The petitioning culture remained in the late 1970s.[229] Elliott continued to receive a high number of petitions and anonymous letters complaining about corruption.[230] To some extent, this indicates the persistence of political conservatism and the lack of confidence in the ICAC.

The HAD conducted a MOOD opinion poll in 1980, assessing public impressions on the Commission six years after its establishment. The Commission itself was well known by the public: 'All respondents knew of the existence of the ICAC and its general aims.'[231] The ICAC hotline 266366 was in particular commonly known by the community.[232] The institutional change restored people's confidence in the colonial regime and was considered 'generally successful', except in the private sector.[233] Most respondents appreciated the extensiveness and effectiveness of the Commission's publicity and believed that it would handle all the complaints 'promptly and thoroughly'.[234] They felt that it 'has done a good job in building up a respectable community image' and 'successful efforts had been made towards [the] long term aim of inculcating, among the general public, a healthy attitude towards corruption'.[235] The report indicated a gradual change in the general political culture as it stated that there was 'a readiness' of the public to report corruption, with many young people being enthusiastic about joining the ICAC.[236] These comments and changes show increased political engagement and reduced fear of politics.

Nonetheless, MOOD also revealed the persistence of political conservatism:

> There was still a certain social stigma which discouraged direct involvement with or working in the ICAC. Less-educated housewives, for example, had said they would not like their children to work in the Commission. Some young people were also hesitant partly because they believed that their friends might keep them at arms' length or at least with some suspicion.[237]

It was indicated that work still had to be done to 'correct' the attitude of members of the grassroots level towards corruption.[238] Most importantly, despite the expression of 'readiness', 'the majority of the respondents did not have any direct contact with the Commission and its staff'.[239] This could be explained by the fact that the public, except for the students, who learned about the structure and duties of the ICAC through their Economic and Public Affairs syllabus, generally had superficial and 'sketchy' knowledge about the Commission and how it investigated corruption.[240] The fear of officialdom was not eliminated completely, which could be observed when respondents from various social groups still held the notion that ICAC officials would abuse suspects by arresting them in the early mornings or late evenings and have 'long hours of interrogation in very cold-air conditioned rooms'.[241]

Conclusion

Long before 1974, activists had called for either the separation of the Anti-Corruption Branch from the police force or the appointment of a Royal Commission of Inquiry. These demands were initially ignored by the British government. The creation of the ICAC was only made possible in 1973, when the press, student organisations and activists exploited the escape of Peter Godber from Hong Kong to Britain and mobilised public opinion. *China Mail*'s campaign to set up a hotline and conduct a survey successfully drew the attention of its young intellectual readers in Hong Kong. It also captured the attention of other newspapers and MPs, leading to further protest orchestrated by James Johnson and former civil servants in London. Signature campaigns and demonstrations initiated by student organisations led by the HKFS also received positive responses from the young generation, although some adult members of the society continued to criticise their political activism, denouncing it as a threat to political and social stability. Campaigners, notably Elliott, Johnson and Ellis, worked closely with each other and made good use of their connections with politicians and the mass media to pursue their cause.

These activists sought democratic reforms and social justice. To pressurise the colonial government to introduce new anti-corruption measures, they made good use of the press, publicising stories of corruption in the colonial bureaucracy. They presented the movement as endorsed by the majority of Hong Kong and noted that inaction risked social unrest. Anti-corruption dominated the public discourse. The extensive coverage in newspapers and on television in both Hong Kong and Britain led to increased petitions being sent to authorities in London. However, except the students, none of these activists organised demonstrations and adopted tactics of direct confrontation. The middle-aged and elderly groups within the middle and upper classes remained politically conservative.

Although the formation of ICAC and strengthening of anti-corruption legislation undoubtedly were outcomes of accumulated efforts made by successive Governors and activists since the 1960s, archival records suggest that the emergence of anti-corruption campaigns and the shift in public opinion after the escape of Godber were inseparable. Through covert opinion polling exercises and public consultations, the colonial government was able to monitor the situation closely, capture the society's prevailing mood and introduce changes accordingly. The appointment of Blair-Kerr, the separation of the Branch from the police force, the civilian composition of the Commission and the creation of the ICAC Complaints Committee were all direct responses to popular demands. These swift responses seem to indicate increased channels of political participation and some degree of 'decolonisation' in the bureaucratic mentality despite the absence of democratic reforms in Hong Kong. Nonetheless, local public sentiment did not always influence policymaking, especially when the metropole and other dependent territories were affected. Despite public discontent over the escape of Godber, the Home Office refused to amend the Fugitive Offenders Act to extradite the corrupt police officer as it was problematic to risk compromising British core legal values just to solve a specific political problem in Hong Kong. In this circumstance, the degree of 'public political participation' in policy formulation was limited.

The ICAC restored public confidence in the colonial state. With increased political transparency, education, state propaganda and the influence of the mass media, the political culture shifted. People were more eager to engage in politics and express their grievances. There were increased reports of crimes and corruption. However, this positive mood was shattered in 1977 by a partial amnesty granted to the police force. The fact that many people continued to petition either activists or the London authorities, instead of reporting to the Commission, indicates that the Commission had not fully gained the trust of the Chinese population. By 1980, although the Commission's success was widely acknowledged, many people, in particular the grassroots level and the less educated class, were still reluctant to contact and work in the ICAC, revealing the persistence of political conservatism among these groups in colonial Hong Kong.

Notes

1 Yep, *Silent Revolution*, pp. 7–8.
2 Yep, 'The Crusade against Corruption', p. 198.
3 Goodstadt, *Uneasy Partner*, p. 156; Carroll, *A Concise History*, p. 175.
4 Tsang, *A Modern History*, p. 276.
5 Hampton, 'British Legal Culture', p. 239.
6 Ibid., p. 224; Hampton, *Hong Kong*, pp. 145–59.
7 Hampton, 'British Legal Culture', p. 224.
8 Yep, 'The Crusade against Corruption', pp. 197–221.
9 Lam, *Understanding the Political Culture*, pp. 156–63.
10 Ibid., pp. 161–2.
11 Ibid., p. 163.
12 Hampton, 'British Legal Culture', p. 238.
13 Yep, 'The Crusade against Corruption', p. 205.
14 However, unlike conventional beliefs, these corrupt inspectors were mainly expatriates, notably Portuguese and Eurasians. See HKRS 163-1-2838, 'Corruption in Preventive Service: Commerce & Industry Department', H. W. E. Heath to Colonial Secretary, 27 July 1962, pp. 2–4.

15 Ibid., pp. 3–4.
16 Ibid., p. 19.
17 Yep, *Silent Revolution*, p. 197.
18 HKRS 70-6-339-1, 'Corruption in the Government', Chinese Press Review, no. 218, 8–14 March 1973.
19 MSS.13 7-6, Elsie Elliott to MacLehose, 29 March 1972.
20 HKRS 286-1-8, 'Prevention of Bribery Bill', Town Talk, 31 July 1969, p. 1.
21 Ibid.
22 HKRS 286-1-9, 'Prevention of Bribery Bill', Town Talk, 5 November 1970, p. 1.
23 HKRS 70-6-339-1, 'Is Corruption a Way of Life?', *HKS*, 8 February 1973.
24 HKRS 70-6-339-1, 'What You Think about Corruption', *China Mail*, 26 March 1973.
25 HKRS 70-6-339-1, Rodney Tasker, 'Ostriches Ignore Corruption', *China Mail*, 13 November 1973.
26 'Corruption in the Government', Chinese Press Review, no. 218, 8–14 March 1973.
27 HKRS 70-6-340-2, GIS, 'Extract from the Debate on the Address of the House of Commons on Wednesday, 31 October 1973', 8 November 1973, p. 4.
28 HKRS 70-6-339-1, '議員及市民多認為反貪污部門獨立 工作效率提高', *Sing Tao Man Pao* (*STMP* hereafter), 14 July 1973; 'Public Wants Separate Anti-Corruption Office', *HKS*, 30 July 1973.
29 HKRS 70-6-339-1, 'Corruption: Beware of Falling Overboard', *SCMP*, 12 October 1973.
30 HKRS 70-6-339-1, '應擴大反貪污權力', *Kung Sheung Evening News* (*KSEN* hereafter), 12 October 1973.
31 HKRS 70-7-76-2, 'Mail Memo', *China Mail*, 30 August 1972.
32 Among the readers, 32,000 were students, 16,000 were professionals and 11,000 were clerks. See ibid.
33 'What You Think about Corruption'.
34 'Richer Get Richer, Poor Get Poorer'.
35 HKRS 415-2-1, 'PC Asked Seller for Laisee', *China Mail*, 9 February 1970.
36 'What You Think about Corruption'.
37 Ibid.
38 'Richer Get Richer, Poor Get Poorer'.
39 HKRS 70-6-339-1, 'Corruption: You Don't Trust Police', *China Mail*, 12 March 1973.
40 HKRS 70-6-339-1, 'Graft Prove: Keep It Up', *China Mail*, 20 March 1973.
41 Ibid.
42 HKRS 70-6-339-1, 'China Mail Opinion: Make It Independent', *China Mail*, 6 June 1973.
43 HKRS 70-6-339-1, '香港人辦香港事', *TTYP*, 25 September 1973.
44 HKRS 70-6-339-1, 'Hong Kong Must Act on Its Own Over Graft', *HKS*, 24 September 1973.
45 HKRS 70-6-339-1, 'Question in Parliament: Hong Kong Corruption, MP Seeks Probe', *China Mail*, 23 March 1973.

46 Ibid.
47 HKRS 70-6-339-1, 'MP Alleges Hong Kong Police Graft', *The Guardian*, 28 March 1973.
48 HKRS 70-6-339-1, 'MPs to Prove Corruption', *China Mail*, 11 April 1973.
49 HKRS 70-6-339-1, 'A Letter to the Governor', *China Mail*, 20 September 1973.
50 Ibid.
51 HKRS 70-6-344-1, 'Corruption Hotline a Dead End', *China Mail*, 19 March 1974.
52 HKRS 70-6-344-1, 'Opinion: An Ugly Ultimatum', *China Mail*, 31 May 1974; 'Opinion: The Only Answer to Blackmail', *China Mail*, 6 June 1974.
53 The paper had been 'losing money for some time' despite 'changes of format and editorial staff' in 1973. See FCO 40/549, 'Closure of the China Mail', D. L. S. Coombe to K. Chesterman, 23 August 1974.
54 'Corruption in the Government', Chinese Press Review, no. 218, 8–14 March 1973.
55 HKRS 286-1-11, 'Corruption and Anti-Corruption', Town Talk, 19 July 1973, p. 2.
56 'Public Wants Separate Anti-Corruption Office'.
57 'The Anti-Graft Bill', *CU Student*, 2:8, 15 November 1970.
58 Ibid.
59 Hong Kong Federation of Students, 香港學生運動回顧 (Hong Kong, 1983), p. 78.
60 反貪污運動特刊: 中大學生會聲明 (*CU Student: Anti-Corruption Campaign Special Edition*), 25 October 1973.
61 '香港政府不敢正視葛柏事件', *CU Student*, 5:4, 15 April 1973.
62 香港學生運動回顧, p. 74.
63 Ibid., p. 76.
64 HKRS 70-6-339-1, 'Civic Association Calls for Independent Anti-Corruption Branch', *SCMP*, 20 July 1973.
65 FCO 40/453, Fung Tze Cheong, Acting President of the Hong Kong Federation of Student to Edward Heath, 17 August 1973.
66 The 70's Biweekly Group was known for its connections with left-wing bodies in Britain. See Lam, *Understanding the Political Culture*, p. 159.
67 FCO 40/453, 'Godber Case', Hugh Norman-Walker to FCO, 24 August 1973.
68 FCO 40/453, M. J. Macoun to Andrew Stuart, 23 August 1973.
69 Lam, *Understanding the Political Culture*, p. 159.
70 HKRS 70-6-339-1, 'Students to Form Anti-Graft Force', *SCMP*, 30 October 1973.
71 Ibid.
72 HKRS 286-1-11, 'Continuing Interest on Corruption', Town Talk, 16 August 1973, p. 1.
73 HKRS 413-1-6, 'Town Talk for the Week 29.8.73- 4.9.73', Town Talk, 4 September 1973, p. 1.
74 'Continuing Interest on Corruption', p. 1.
75 HKRS 413-1-5, 'Town Talk for the Week Ending 20.8.73', Town Talk, 23 August 1973, p. 1.

76 HKRS 413-1-6, 'Town Talk for the Week 8.8.71- 14.8.73', Town Talk, 16 August 1973, p. 1.
77 HKRS 413-1-7, 'Town Talk for the Week 14.8.73 to 20.8.73', Town Talk, 23 August 1973, p. 2.
78 FCO 40/453, 'Godber Case', Hugh Norman-Walker to FCO, 24 August 1973.
79 Ibid.
80 FCO 40/453, 'Godber Case', Hugh Norman-Walker to FCO, 28 August 1973.
81 HKRS 286-1-11, 'Anti-Corruption Rally', Town Talk, 6 September 1973, p. 1.
82 HKRS 286-1-11, 'Government's Determination to Fight Corruption Welcomed', Town Talk, 20 September 1973, p. 1.
83 'Anti-Corruption Rally', p. 1.
84 HKRS 286-1-11, 'Corruption Issues Kept Alive by Rally Summonses', Town Talk, 13 September 1973, p. 1.
85 'Town Talk for the Week 29.8.73–4.9.73', p. 1.
86 'Anti-Corruption Rally', p. 1.
87 Ibid.
88 HKRS 286-1-11, 'Anti-Godber Rally', Town Talk, 30 August 1973, p. 1.
89 HKRS 394-26-12, '1975 in Retrospect: Part II', MOOD, 8 January 1976, p. 2.
90 HKRS 413-1-4, 'Town Talk for the Week Ending 18.8.73', Town Talk, 20 September 1973, p. 1.
91 HKRS 70-6-339-1, 'Colony to Have Hive of Corruption Watchdogs', *The Guardian*, 11 October 1973.
92 FCO 40/544, A. C. Stuart to Mr. Rushford, 21 January 1974.
93 For example, Elliott admitted that she had been trying to get *China Mail* to investigate the case of a forged cheque, in which a woman was blackmailed by a policeman, Lau Hong Leung and a triad member. See MSS. 13 6-12, Elsie Elliott to Speary, 9 March 1973.
94 FCO 40/120, Nigel Fisher to Malcolm Shepherd, 22 April 1968.
95 MSS.13 7-6, Elsie Elliott to MacLehose, 10 March 1972.
96 FCO 40/451, Elsie Elliott to Anthony Royle, 24 June 1973.
97 FCO 40/1022, Elsie Elliott, 'Open Letter to the Hong Kong Government and Interested British MPs', 1978.
98 FCO 40/544, Elsie Elliott to Mr Stewart, 7 January 1974.
99 MSS.13 6-11, 'A Resident' to Elsie Elliott, 6 November 1971.
100 MSS.13 6-11, Elsie Elliott to Charles Sutcliffe, 31 March 1972.
101 FCO 40/120, 'A Supporter of Good Law and Order' to Elsie Elliott, 28 June 1968, enclosed in letter to Nigel Fisher, 5 July 1968.
102 MSS.13 6-12, Elsie Elliott to James Johnson, 17 April 1974.
103 HKRS 70-6-340-2, Extract from 'The Debate on the Address in the House of Commons on Wednesday, 31 October 1973', 8 November 1973, p. 4.
104 FCO 40/453, 'Call on Mr Amery by Mr James Johnson, MP, 3.00 pm', 9 August 1973, p. 2.
105 FCO 40/451, Parliamentary Question, Written Answer, 28 March 1973, pp. 339–40, extract from 'Debate on the Address in the House of Commons on Wednesday, 31 October 1973'.

106 Ibid.
107 FCO 40/453, R. B. Crowson to M. R. Guest, 8 August 1973.
108 For example, 'As I See with Elsie Elliott', *Star*, 28 January 1974 and Elsie Elliott, 'I Want the Whole System Cracked', *Star*, 28 August 1974.
109 HKRS 70-6-344-1, 'What the Star Thinks: A Step in the Right Direction', *Star*, 25 February 1974.
110 HKRS 70-6-339-1, 'Colony to Hive Off Corruption Watchdog', *The Guardian*, 11 October 1973.
111 HKRS 70-6-339-1, 'Anti-Elsie Plot Afoot, Says Former Policeman', *HKS*, 27 November 1973.
112 FCO 40/451, 'Corruption in Hong Kong, B.C.C.', Alan Ellis to Anthony Royle, *China Mail*, 1 April 1973; HKRS 70-6-339-1, 'MP Alleges Hong Kong Police Graft', *The Guardian*, 28 March 1973.
113 'Corruption in Hong Kong, B.C.C.', Ellis to Royle, p. 2.
114 FCO 40/453, Alan Ellis to A. C. Stuart, 20 August 1973.
115 FCO 40/451, 'Mr Alan Ellis', R. B. Crowson to M. J. Macoun, 5 April 1973.
116 FCO 40/451, 'Mr Alan Ellis – Ex-Probationary Inspector of Police, Hong Kong', M. J. Macoun to R. B. Crowson, 9 April 1973.
117 FCO 40/453, R. B. Crowson to M. R. Guest, 8 August 1973.
118 FCO 40/457, Alan Ellis to Anthony Royle, 7 December 1973.
119 HKRS 70-6-339-1, 'What the People of Hong Kong Have to Say', *China Mail*, 12 October 1973.
120 'What the People of Hong Kong Have to Say'.
121 HKRS 286-1-11, 'Blair-Kerr Report', Town Talk, 18 October 1973, p. 1.
122 HKRS 70-6-344-1, 'Worth Every Dollar Spent', *SCMP*, February 1975.
123 HKRS 70-6-339-2, 'Elsie's No.1 Aim: Beat Corruption! Move for Independent Probe Gains Support', *Star*, 24 January 1975.
124 HKRS 376-8-23, 'Hong Kong Reformer Critical of Anti-Corruption Efforts', *SCMP*, 30 December 1976.
125 HKRS 70-6-344-1, Elsie Elliott, 'Poor Who Have to Prove Their Innocence', *SCMP*, 27 August 1975.
126 FCO 40/1022, Elsie Elliott, Open Letter to the Hong Kong Government and Interested British MPs, 1978.
127 Ibid.
128 HKRS 925-1-1, 'An Assessment of the Government's Current Image and a Study of Community Aspirations', 9 February 1977, p. 1.
129 FCO 40/1023, MacLehose to FCO, 8 April 1978.
130 Yep, 'The Crusade against Corruption', p. 198.
131 HKRS 163-1-2505, 'Adviser for the Anti-Corruption Branch', Robert Brown Black to Secretary of State, 19 October 1960.
132 HKRS 163-1-2505, W. I. J. Wallace to Robert Brown Black, 20 December 1960.
133 HKRS 163-1-2505, 'Chapter VI: The Anti-Corruption Branch', enclosed in 'Sixth Report of the Advisory Committee on Corruption', A. P. Richardson to H. W. E. Heath, 18 January 1962, p. 23.
134 HKRS 163-1-2505, 'Anti-Corruption', P. M. M. Sedgwick to A. P. Richardson, 7 February 1962.

135 'Chapter VI: The Anti-Corruption Branch', p. 23.
136 HKRS 286-1-8, 'Corruption', Town Talk, 30 January 1969, p. 1.
137 HKRS 286-1-9, 'Prevention of Bribery Bill', Town Talk, 5 November 1970, p. 1.
138 HKRS 286-1-11, 'The Godber Case Grabs Headlines', Town Talk, 21 June 1973, p. 1.
139 FCO 40/451, 'Escape of Chief Superintendent Godber', MacLehose to FCO, 13 June 1973.
140 The Report of *The Times* on 23 September 1973 was translated to Chinese in '星期日泰晤士報撰文　抨擊香港貪污問題　呼籲來一次大肅清', *Express*, 24 September 1973.
141 FCO 40/453, 'Drugs, Brothels, Bribery and a British Colony's Police Force', *The Sunday Times*, 30 July 1973.
142 HKRS 70-6-339-1, 'MP Alleges Hong Kong Police Graft', *The Guardian*, 28 March 1973; 'Colony to Hive Off Corruption Watchdogs', *The Guardian*, 11 October 1973; FCO 40/457, 'Britain Cannot Send Back Hong Kong Policeman', *The Guardian*, 24 November 1973.
143 HKRS 70-6-339-1, 'Putting the Squeeze on Curry and Water', *The Guardian*, 12 October 1973.
144 FCO 40/451, 'Complainants' to Minister of FCO, 24 June 1973.
145 FCO 40/457, Robert Moore to editor of *The Guardian*, 24 November 1973.
146 FCO 40/451, 'Escape of Chief Superintendent Godber', MacLehose to FCO, 13 June 1973.
147 HKRS 70-6-340-2, 'The Not So Quiet Revolution', D. Ford's Speech to Rotary Club, 12 March 1975, p. 3.
148 HKRS 286-1-1, 'Corruption and Anti-Corruption', Town Talk, 19 July 1973, p. 2.
149 FCO 40/453, 'Second Blair-Kerr Report on Corruption', MacLehose to FCO, 27 September 1973.
150 FCO 40/452, 'Report on Godber Case', Douglas-Home to MacLehose, 13 July 1973.
151 FCO 40/452, 'Parliamentary Question on the Godber Case', MacLehose to FCO, 19 July 1973.
152 FCO 40/453, 'Alleged Corruption in Hong Kong Police', M. J. Macoun to R. B. Crowson, 8 August 1973, p. 1.
153 FCO 40/453, 'Mr Royle's Talk with Sir Murray MacLehose', M. R. J Guest to R. B. Crowson, 19 August 1973.
154 FCO 40/453, R. B. Crowson to M. R. Guest, 9 August 1973, p. 2.
155 FCO 40/453, MacLehose to John Prendergast, 9 August 1973.
156 FCO 40/455, 'Parliamentary Question', MacLehose to FCO, 15 October 1973.
157 Ibid.
158 FCO 40/558, 'Staffing of the ICAC', J. Cater to A. C. Stuart, 26 February 1974, p. 1.
159 FCO 40/558, GIS, 'New Council to Set Up to Advise on Ways to Fight Graft: Public Widely Represented on New Committees', 30 January 1974.
160 HKRS 286-1-11, 'Decisions on Anti-Corruption Applauded', Town Talk, 25 October 1973, p. 1.

161 HKRS 70-6-339-1, 'Second Report of the Blair-Kerr Commission of Inquiry', Chinese Press Review, 11–17 October 1973; HKRS 70-6-344-1, 'Independent Commission Against Corruption Bill 1974', Chinese Press Review, 13–20 February 1974, p. 1.
162 HKRS 376-8-23, 'Hong Kong Reformer Critical of Anti-Corruption Efforts', *The Times*, 30 December 1976.
163 HKRS 70-6-344-1, 'Cater's Raiders Get More Teeth: Second Police Force', *Star*, 16 March 1974.
164 HKRS 70-6-344-1, 'Reform Club Warns of ICAC as Secret Police', *HKS*, 27 October 1975.
165 HKRS 70-6-339-2, 'Controlling the Revolution', *SCMP*, 15 May 1975.
166 HKRS 70-6-344-1, '廉署調查員應否配槍?', *STMP*, 22 March 1975; '廉政人員武裝化', *HKT*, 24 March 1975.
167 HKRS 70-8-2168, Draft speech by Lo Tak-shing, Legislative Council, Independent Commission Against Corruption (Amendment) Bill and the Prevention of Bribery (Amendment) Bill, 10 March 1976.
168 HKRS 70-8-2173, Extract from an interview between Jack Cater, Brian Tisdall, Robert Ho and Michael Harrison, 'Corruption: The Crunch Years' (RTHK Production), 3 June 1976.
169 FCO 40/1022, 'Independent Commission Against Corruption Complaints Committee', R. G. B. Bridge to heads of departments, 20 December 1977.
170 'The Godber Case Grabs Headline', Town Talk, p. 1.
171 HKRS 286-1-11, 'Corruption Issues Kept Alive by Rally Summonses', Town Talk, 13 September 1973, p. 1.
172 FCO 40/453, 'Second Blair-Kerr Report on Corruption', MacLehose to FCO, 27 September 1973.
173 FCO 40/455, 'Blair-Kerr Report', MacLehose to FCO, 15 October 1973.
174 FCO 40/453, A. C. Stuart to E. Youde, 27 September 1973.
175 FCO 40/453, M. R. J. Guest to A. C. Stuart, 3 October 1973.
176 Ibid.
177 FCO 40/457, F. Graham-Harrison to Duncan Watson, 25 November 1973.
178 FCO 40/457, 'Note of a Meeting Held at the Home Office on 27 November 1973 to Discuss the Implications of the Double Criminality Rule in the Fugitive Offenders Act 1957, in Relation to Offences Committed in Hong Kong', pp. 2 and 4.
179 Ibid.
180 Ibid.
181 HKRS 286-1-12, 'The Return of Godber', Town Talk, 2 May 1974, p. 1.
182 HKRS 925-1-1, 'Changes in Public Attitude towards the Hong Kong Government', MOOD, 18 September 1975, p. 3.
183 HKRS 70-6-339-1, 'Fight Graft: Dial the Mail's Hot-line', *China Mail*, 7 March 1973.
184 HKRS 70-6-339-1, 'Now Students Support Anti-Graft Campaign', *China Mail*, 14 July 1973.
185 HKRS 70-6-339-1, 'What the Star Thinks: Rocking the Hong Kong Boat', *Star*, 2 August 1973.

186 HKRS 70-6-339-3, D. A. Richardson to Director of GIS, 12 July 1973.
187 '社論:反貪污運動的展望', *CU Student*, 5:8, 15 December 1973.
188 'Changes in Public Attitude towards the Hong Kong Government', p. 3.
189 Ibid., p. 2.
190 HKRS 394-26-12, '1975 in Retrospect, Part I', MOOD, 31 December 1975, p. 4.
191 'Changes in Public Attitude towards the Hong Kong Government', p. 2.
192 Ibid.
193 Ibid.
194 HKRS 70-6-340-2, Summary of *First ICAC Annual Report: A Year of Development and Consolidation*, 11 May 1975, p. 1.
195 HKRS 70-6-340-2, Answer given by David Ennals, Minister of State Foreign and Commonwealth Affairs to question asked by Victor Goodhew, MP in Written Answer in House of Commons, 6 August 1975.
196 HKRS 70-6-340-3, *ICAC Bulletin*, 3 June 1975.
197 HKRS 70-8-2168, 'The Social Impact of ICAC', speech made by L. K. Ding at the meeting of Kowloon North Lion's Club, 15 March 1977.
198 Summary of *First ICAC Annual Report*, pp. 1–2.
199 'Changes in Public Attitude towards the Hong Kong Government', p. 5.
200 Ibid.
201 Ibid.
202 '1975 in Retrospect, Part 1', p. 4.
203 HKRS 70-8-2168, GIS, 'Attention News Editors', 27 January 1976.
204 HKRS 925-1-1, 'The Impact of Television: Pt II: Entertainment Programmes', MOOD, 17 June 1976, p. 1.
205 Ibid.
206 HKRS 925-1-1, 'The Impact of Television Pt I – Public Affairs Programmes by Commercial Stations', MOOD, 9 June 1976, p. 1.
207 'The Impact of Television Pt I', p. 1.
208 Ibid, p. 2.
209 Ibid, pp. 3–4.
210 Ibid., p. 1.
211 HKRS 70-8-2168, 'Summary of ICAC Annual Report', 10 August 1976, p. 6.
212 HKRS 70-8-2168, GIS, 'Attention News Editors', 23 July 1977.
213 HKRS 70-8-2168, 'Summary of ICAC Annual Report', 2 August 1976, p. 3.
214 'An Assessment of the Government's Current Image and a Study of Community Aspirations', p. 5.
215 HKRS 70-6-339-1, 'You Are Preening Me from Getting Recruits: Police Chief Slams Press on Graft Stories', *HKS*, 24 March 1973.
216 HKRS 70-6-344-1, 'ICAC under Attack from Our Police', *HKS*, 31 May 1974.
217 HKRS 70-6-344-1, 'Full Amnesty for Graft Ruled Out', *SCMP*, 4 April 1975.
218 HKRS 908-1-43, 'Relations with ICAC', by C. L. Scobell, 18 January 1977.
219 HKRS 908-1-43, 'Investigation of Allegations of Corruption', by R. T. M. Henry, 27 October 1977.
220 The formation of the ICAC created anxiety among the police force. Many police complained that the investigation procedures were unfair. On 27 October

1977, a mass meeting was held, attended by 3,000 police officers. A petition was also signed by 11,000 of the 17,400 members of the force. A mutiny soon took place, with the police demanding an amnesty. The ICAC, however, continued to investigate cases. In September, 228 police officers were arrested. In November, tensions escalated and the atmosphere became increasingly militant. To bring the situation under control, a partial amnesty was granted on 5 November, making 1 January 1977 the 'cut-off date': investigations on corrupt crimes before this date were dropped and the police involved would not be prosecuted. See Yep, 'The Crusade against Corruption', pp. 212–13.
221 FCO 40/1022, 'ICAC and Amnesty', C. R. Staff to Quantrill, Thompson and Stewart, 9 January 1978.
222 FCO 40/1023, 'The ICAC', MacLehose to FCO, 6 October 1978.
223 'A Resident' to Elsie Elliott, 6 November 1971; MSS.13 6-11, Leung P.S. to Elsie Elliott, 18 September 1973.
224 FCO 40/120, Elsie Elliott to Nigel Fisher, 5 July 1968.
225 FCO 40/451, 'Retired Potato Hawker' petitioned editors of various newspapers, 16 June 1972.
226 FCO 40/451, Lee Yuk Tai to Edward Heath, 16 June 1973.
227 FCO 40/644, 'Corruption at All Levels in Hong Kong', anonymous letter to James Callaghan, 18 January 1975.
228 FCO 40/647, Pun Ting Chau to MacLehose, 20 September 1975; 'An Open Appeal for Justice', Pun Ting Chau to R. Goronwy Roberts, 25 September 1975; Same letter was sent to A. C. Stuart, C. V. Peterson, D. K. Timms, P. J. E. Male and D. Ennals.
229 FCO 40/828, 'An Illegal Judgement Without Trial', F. M. Tung to Elizabeth II, 29 July 1977; Cheung Chok-kap to FCO, 7 October 1977.
230 MSS. 13 7-3, 'Conspiracy for Justice' to Elsie Elliott, 30 June 1977.
231 HKRS 471-3-2, 'Public Impressions of the Independent Commission Against Corruption', MOOD, 4 March 1980, p. 1.
232 Ibid., p. 3.
233 Ibid., p. 5.
234 Ibid., p. 2.
235 Ibid., pp. 3–4.
236 Ibid., p. 5.
237 Ibid.
238 Ibid., p. 4.
239 Ibid., p. 2.
240 Ibid., p. 3.
241 Ibid.

4

The campaign against telephone rate increases

By the mid-1970s, the CDO Scheme and its covert mechanism had provided the colonial government with increased organisational capacity to monitor shifting popular sentiment and political activism. They also widened the channels of political participation. The colonial administration seemed to be more responsive to public opinion and facing up to its shortcomings. The formalisation of Chinese as the official language lowered state–society communication barriers. The Chinese population's stake in colonial administration was enhanced with the revised language requirements in appointments of civil servants. The setting up of the ICAC and the extradition of Godber restored public confidence in a reformist government. Distrust and resentment of officialdom was falling, in particular among the educated young generation. As a result, the general political culture in Hong Kong was shifting gradually. Despite persistent political conservatism in certain classes and age groups, people in general expected the government to be more effective and were willing to report corrupt practices. Intolerance towards 'corruption' is explored in this case study, a campaign against telephone rate increases in 1975.

In 1973, the Hong Kong Telephone Company reported a profit of $70 million, but it gained approval from the Advisory Committee on Telephone Services to increase the rental rate in early 1974. In August 1974, in response to cash shortages, the company was planning to apply for a further rental increase. It was, however, widely suspected that its business practices were corrupt. The anti-corruption campaign had focused on bureaucratic corruption. The campaign on telephone charges had a different target and was the largest-scale movement of consumer activism in Hong Kong in the 1970s.

Despite its scale and significance, the campaign has not been studied extensively. Reliant on published materials, Lam Wai-man's work provided an account of how different organisations, such as the Hong Kong Christian Industrial Committee, kaifong associations and chambers of commerce, collaborated and formed coalitions to protest against rate increases. Nonetheless, she did not examine the strategies and rhetoric employed by these activists and assess their effectiveness using robust methods. How the campaign was perceived by different social classes and age groups also has not been analysed.[1] This chapter uses both archival records and published sources to investigate how the colonial administration monitored, perceived and reacted to the campaign. It also highlights the shifting popular sentiment of different social classes and age groups towards the event, and how district organisations and political coalitions protested.

Increased press coverage and shifting public sentiment

The Hong Kong Telephone Company was a public utility company, granted a fifty-year monopoly in 1925. In 1951, the task of supervising the company was delegated to the Postmaster-General. Its dividends and levels of return were not subject to legal control, but when proposing a rental rate increase, it had to seek approval from the Legislative Council.[2] The company's performance was often poor. Customers had to wait for a long period of time before getting their telephone lines installed. To improve its quality of services and prevent further mismanagement, an advisory body, the Advisory Committee on Telephone Services, was set up in 1964.

In August 1973, the company requested an increase in the telephone rate, the first time in ten years. The increase came into effect in January 1974, raising the existing rentals for business lines by 17 per cent and residential lines by 19 per cent, respectively. As a result, the telephone rates for business lines rose from $350 to $410 per annum. For residential lines, the rentals increased from $235 to $280 per annum.[3] According to Town Talk, reactions to the increase were 'mixed'. Some housewives argued that the increase was 'too great'. Many white-collar workers, such as office executives in Central District and businessmen in Sham Shui Po and Mong Kok, however, did not mind the increase given that the company promised to improve its services. The general public mostly believed that rising telephone charges were 'inevitable' due to the increased cost of living.[4] The increase in early 1974 was therefore not opposed.

According to the report by the Advisory Committee on Telephone Services in 1972, Hong Kong Telephone Company's expansion plans were 'too conservative'. They only followed 'proven demand rather than assessing demand and meeting it as it arises'. By the end of 1972, the total waiting list had reached 38,271, compared with 31,177 in 1971.[5] Unless it altered its existing policy, the number of people waiting for telephone lines would not fall, an indicator that its performance had not improved. Table 4.1 reveals the disparity between demand and supply of telephone lines. Although the installation rate increased from 72.58 per cent in 1972 to 92.32 per cent in

Table 4.1 Applications received and lines installed by the Hong Kong Telephone Company

Year	Application received	Lines installed	Installations as percentage of applications
1972	163,537	118,708	72.58
1973	168,775	140,063	82.99
1974	125,068	113,890	91.06
1975	115,236	107,536	93.32
Total	572,616	480,197	83.86

HKRS 276-7-197, Telephone Service Statistics, November 1976.

1975, the company still failed to meet the demand. The *Star* recorded the public dissatisfaction about the company's service: 'Our phones are cheap ... Nonetheless, the waiting list is a barometer of the basic conflict of interest – and it is going up.'[6] To improve its service, the company invested in new technologies and planned an expansion programme. In May 1974, the existing microwave system was extended from Hong Kong to Kwai Chung and Yuen Long to Kwai Chung after the introduction of pulse-code modulation.[7] This microwave system improved transmission performance and also provided increased capacity for telephone channels. It also ensured that each telephone call was secret and no overhearing would occur between phone calls.

In August 1974, to finance its capital expansion programme, the Hong Kong Telephone Company sought approval from the Legislative Council for a 60 per cent increase in telephone charges. The company argued that compared to many other countries, Hong Kong's telephone rates remained low. While Hong Kong residential and business subscribers were paying $280 and $410 per annum, the charges were approximately $434 and $829 in Malaysia and $489 and $734 in Singapore. The difference in rentals was even greater in European countries. For instance, the rates were about $651 and $1,026 in Belgium and $810 and $1,140 in France.[8] The Telephone Company therefore believed that the proposed increase was justified. Nonetheless, these figures ignored differences in international costs of living and did not deflate rates by the prevailing income levels.

The capital expansion programme unfortunately coincided with an economic downturn. The growth rate of annual Gross Domestic Product fell from 14 per cent in 1973 to about 2.5 per cent in 1974 and 1975. The index of real daily wages for industrial workers also dropped from 159 in 1973 to 141 in 1974 and 137 in 1975. Unemployment rose.[9] Lam argued that 'the government kept the public in the dark' about the situation until mid-January 1975, and that triggered 'territory-wide outrage'.[10] As early as August 1974, however, there were rumours about the price changes. According to Town Talk, the proposed increase was 'vociferously opposed in all the districts'. For example, residents in Wan Chai and Yau Mai Tei condemned the increase as 'unreasonable', especially as the company had netted a $70 million profit in the previous year.[11] People also complained about the poor service. There were requests for interventions by the Consumer Council, which was set up in 1974 to enhance consumer welfare.[12] According to Y. K. Kan, the Chairman of the Consumer Council, the Council received 'a large number of complaints' about the proposed increase in telephone charges even though the Council had already issued a public statement suggesting that it would not look into the matter.[13]

In September 1974, reactions to the proposed increased remained 'strong and unfavourable'.[14] The Director of the Hong Kong Christian Industrial Committee, Raymond Fung, indicated to the press that his organisation, which consisted of fifty-two groups, including kaifongs, churches and students, would take 'drastic measures' to prevent the telephone rates from being raised.[15] Business groups also petitioned the colonial government. The New Territories General Chamber of Commerce, for example, wrote to the Secretary for the New Territories to express grievances over the rate increases. The group believed that the increase would cause 'an ill effect' on the economy and argued that a public utility company should not be 'earning excessive profit'.[16] The Sha Tin Chamber of Commerce also complained to the DO, arguing that an increase in telephone rate would 'accelerate inflation' and 'add [to] the difficulties of the public'.[17] Heung Yee Kuk expressed similar concerns.[18] In December 1974, the Universal Consumers Association publicly condemned the company's move to seek rental increases, and announced that it would make an 'all-out effort' to protest against the increase.[19] By late 1974, the proposed increase had received considerable attention from a range of different groups and organisations.

The proposed increase in telephone rates was widely reported and criticised by newspapers. *SCMP* for instance argued that the increase was 'an extremely irresponsible move', which 'completely ignored the current economic difficulties of the colony and the sentiment'.[20] During the week from 17 to 22 December, six newspapers showed 'strong objection' to the rumoured fee increase.[21] News coverage increased and the topic was covered in seventeen editorials in the last week of December, with most criticising the proposal.[22] The communist-leaning *Hong Kong Commercial Daily* argued that it was 'unreasonable' for the Telephone Company to seek another rate increase given its charges had been raised the previous year. It also believed that such an increase would lead to 'chain reactions' during the economic recession.²³ *Fai Po* asserted that the increase was 'most unfair' given the $70 million profit made by the Telephone Company in 1974.²⁴ *WKYP* suggested that that the Telephone Company should be nationalised to stop it from profiteering.²⁵

The adverse newspaper comments shaped public opinion and increased tensions between the company and its customers. According to Town Talk, there were 'mounting tensions' over the proposed telephone charge increases in early January 1975: 'CDOs received strong protests from every sector of the population.'²⁶ The main problem was the company's rate revision in early 1974. Another increase in such a short period of time seemed unjustifiable. From the public's perspective, the company was making profits, $70 million in 1973. The public did not realise the company had committed to buying cables and other equipment for expansion, which amounted to millions of dollars. It was difficult for people to understand why this increase was necessary. The argument was one of public versus private interest: during a time of inflation and rising unemployment, as a public utility company, the interest of the whole community should be placed above profiteering. Many suspected that the poor financial situation was the result of mismanagement and corruption. Town Talk also revealed that there was an 'unanimous view' that capital for expansion should be raised from shareholders instead of consumers.²⁷ The absence of an effective regulatory system to monitor the operation of the Hong Kong Telephone Company led the colonial government to become a target. Middle-aged kaifong and community leaders started pressing for a government statement on the proposed increase.²⁸ Some even radically suggested that the Telephone Company should be nationalised.²⁹

The widespread public reaction was due to the rate of take up of telephones. Table 4.2 reveals the increase in the number of direct lines from 1967 to 1975. The number of direct lines nearly tripled in less than ten

Table 4.2 Telephone take-up rate in Hong Kong (direct lines)

Year	1967	1968	1969	1970	1971	1972	1973	1974	1975
Lines/100	7.24	8.67	10.08	11.46	13.91	15.88	17.70	18.48	19.11
Station/100	9.13	10.74	12.44	14.14	17.02	19.38	21.65	22.75	23.60
Population, million	3.9	4	4	4.2	4	4.1	4.2	4.3	4.4

HKRS 276-7-407, 'Hong Kong Telephone Co. Ltd: Statistical Review', attached in 'Statistical Review', I. Cowley to General Manager, Assistant G. M. Administration, Mr. Gaut, Chief Account, Manager of the Engineering Branch, Manager, Operations, heads of divisions and heads of departments, 25 February 1976.

years, from 7.2 per 100 population in 1967 to 19.1 in 1975.[30] In other words, about a quarter of the population had everyday access to telephones. Those without lines used the telephones of their friends and families. By December 1974, there were 803,144 working lines in Hong Kong in total.[31]

Tensions escalated after F. L. Walker, the general manager of the Telephone Company, announced that the company had applied for a 70 per cent increase in telephone rate on 10 January 1975.[32] This led to extensive media coverage. In the second week of January, twenty newspaper editorials opposed the increase.[33] *Sing Tao Yat Pao* (*STYP*) and *KSDN* both described the proposed rate of increase as 'shocking'.[34] *STYP and Nam Wah Man Po* even cited the Star Ferry riots to warn the colonial government of the potential 'vicious chain reaction' which may be caused by the increase.[35] *WKYP, Oriental Daily* and *Hong Kong Commercial Daily* insisted that no increase should be allowed by the government.[36] Leftist newspapers expressed similar disapproval at the proposed rise of charge. *Wen Wei Po* suggested that as a public utility company which had close connection with people's livelihoods, such a frequent increase in rate was unacceptable.[37] *Ta Kung Pao* argued that it was 'too much' for the company to ask for a 70 per cent increase given its profit and the recent charge revision.[38]

Influenced by press opposition, the government and the public were further 'polarised'.[39] According to A. F. Neoh, the CDC of Kowloon, the public was 'resentful' that the Telephone Company had applied for a high percentage increase during a time when living standards were not rising.[40] Public discontent soon escalated: 'Community pressure[s] are rapidly building. In the past two weeks, C.D.O. have been feeling tensions in almost all their dealing[s] with the public. At every point of contact, [the] government stand [was] accused.'[41] On Hong Kong Island, it was observed that a large number of local organisations had 'reacted rather strongly' to the proposed rate increase. Many considered the reasons for the increase 'unjustified' and 'unacceptable'.[42] The campaign was strengthening, against a backdrop of economic problems and stimulated by adverse newspaper coverage of the company's proposal.

In mid-January 1975, Town Talk reported that the issue 'continued to dominate public attention'.[43] 'Some quarters' felt that an increase of about 20 per cent was reasonable and believed that any higher increase would only create an impression that the government was 'favouring the Telephone Company regardless of public interest'.[44] Residents at the grass-roots level in public housing estates complained that a 70 per cent increase would increase the rental to a level that was higher than their housing rent.[45] Housewives and factory managers considered whether to cut telephone lines, a de facto boycott of services. Those who possessed more than one line, such as shop tenants and firm operators, expressed great anger, claiming that they would cut down the number of lines to the minimum if the increase was approved.[46]

In late January, clarifications were made by the company through the mass media: the increase was necessary to prevent its bankruptcy. The company launched a counter-publicity campaign to justify its price increases. It argued that, as it had ploughed most of its profits into the expansion programme, it needed additional revenue to cover costs. However, this argument was not widely accepted. People demanded the publication of financial statements.[47] Many residents in Kowloon and Hong Kong opposed the proposed increase, and backed a planned mass rally.[48] Yet, this was not the consensual position: some residents believed that an increase of up to 20 per cent was acceptable.[49]

Political culture

The protest against telephone rate increases took a variety of forms that reveals the shifting political culture of the time, and highlights how campaigners were motivated by instrumental reasoning and ideologies, which were often intertwined. As Town Talk has revealed, many believed the proposed increase was simply unjust: 'There was still a persistent belief that the Telephone Company was making an excessive profit and that the proposed increases were unjustified.'[50] Similar attitudes could be observed in the newspaper coverage. For example, a reader named C. H. Ho wrote to the *SCMP* arguing that the company, 'one of the monopolies which are making huge profits every year', had 'no reason to raise telephone charges twice within a very short time'.[51] The concept of fairness provoked many to participate in the campaign:

> Why must the consumer pay for mismanagement in a company? The deficit arising is due to poor management planning and having worked themselves into a hole, Mr Walker expects the consumer to bale the company out by paying higher charges ... The Telephone Company is passing the buck for their management mistakes to the consumer.[52]

Others were involved due to their dissatisfaction in the company's lack of administrative and financial transparency:

> Up till now, the public is kept in total darkness. We are not given any consistent explanation as to why the increase is needed. Mr Walker, by his action, or lack of it, obviously does not feel responsible for the public ... But the day when major decisions affecting the public can be made without reference to the people is crumbling, even in colonial Hong Kong.[53]

STYP similarly recorded that the public believed that examination of the increase in telephone rentals should be made public.[54] These comments found in Town Talk and newspapers reveal instrumental and ideological concerns.

Rather than participating in a rally, many people chose to write to newspaper editors to express their grievances, indicating political conservatism.[55] Nonetheless, there were also some who were concerned that this incident could escalate, especially after Walker reiterated that most local people would not be able to understand the Telephone Company's accounts even if they were publicised. The impact of the riots of 1966 and 1967 had left a strong impression on people, making them fearful of social unrest. As Town Talk pointed out:

> Quite a number of people were apprehensive over the possibility of a repeated circumstances and tensions which resulted in the Star Ferry riots several years ago. They felt that the telephone increase affected practically everyone in Hong Kong and any opposition was likely to be supported by the majority of the population.[56]

Tsz Wan Shan estate dwellers informed the CDO that 'they were afraid that disturbances might break out if the government was to take the Telephone Company's side and disregard public feeling'.[57]

These concerns were not completely illegitimate. Indeed, on the opposite side of the spectrum, there were radicals who adopted extreme measures and rhetoric. As Town Talk pointed out, in 'more vehement circles', there was an explicit threat to resort to violence against the colonial state, including the use of bombs if the government ignored public opposition to the rate rises.[58] Posters featuring inflammatory slogans, such as 'Hang P. C. Woo', were placed in prominent locations, such as Waterloo Road and Pui Ching Road in Kowloon. This was a threat to use violence against the Chairman of the Telephone Advisory Committee because the Committee declared the proposed increase reasonable and Woo asked residents who could not afford to pay the rental to share telephone lines.[59] Graffiti art also included the slogans 'Hang Haddon Cave' and 'Hang P. C. Woo'. These were highly visual displays of protest. Artists daubed their remarks in red characters in various places in Kowloon. Although the Kowloon CDC believed that these visual protests may have been the work of a 'lunatic fringe', he also acknowledged that these extreme forms of protest indicated 'deep' 'public resentment'.[60] Such form of protest is revealing, indicating that the political culture in Hong Kong was not monolithically conservative. Radical means to voice grievances were sought when people's economic interests and livelihoods were threatened.

At a district level, the situation was tense. Kaifong associations and MACs, which represented a large number of middle-aged and elderly groups, joined the collective lobbies.[61] For example, Wong Tai Sin kaifongs met in early January 1975 to work out strategies to exert pressure on the colonial government. Choi Hung MAC declared publicly that it was opposed to the proposed increase.[62] The Hong Kong and Kowloon Joint Kaifong Research Council also petitioned the Legislative Council, arguing that any increases in telephone rate would 'create a chain reaction and lead to disturbances similar to the one that followed the Star Ferry fare increase several years ago'.[63] Many kaifongs and community organisations in Mong Kok, Shum Shui Po, Kwun Tong and the Western District by contrast decided to wait for the government to announce its stance before taking any further actions.[64] By mid-January, many kaifong groups kept pressing the CDOs in their areas for an official stance on the matter as they felt that the government 'had remained doggedly silent'.[65] Some had already taken action in the form of signature campaigns, such as the Choi Hung MAC. These grassroots organisations also started to liaise with voluntary agencies such as Caritas and the Society for Community Organisation, which had become 'generally interested in the issue'.[66] According to the Kowloon CDC, there was a growing tendency for the MACs to 'confederate into united fronts' in opposition to the telephone rate increase.[67] It was predicted that the formation of a broad alliance would 'offer fertile ground for consolidation of power for the more opportunistic' and there was little the government could do to prevent it.[68] In late January, the Choi Hung MAC handed in a petition with 1,000 signatures to the Universal Consumers' Association. The Tai Hang Tung Society for Community Organisation also put up banners in the estate to protest against the proposed increase.[69] This demonstrated that middle-aged and elderly groups could also be mobilised when their interests were threatened.

Resettlement estates formed their own lobbies. The Lei Cheng Uk Resettlement Estate Commercial and Industrial General Association, for example, petitioned the UMELCO, noting that the proposed increase was 'unanimously opposed' by their association. It submitted information on public opinion in its district, which suggested that approval to the rise would only 'accelerate social unease and bring about undesirable chain reactions'.[70] The Hong Kong and Kowloon and New Territories Manufacturing and Commercial Association started a signature campaign in Tsz Wan Shan, although it was noted that it 'has not been very effective'.[71] Residents in Ngau Tau Kok also petitioned the UMELCO, urging the government to 'be sympathetic with the citizens' and respect public opinion: 'It is a proper procedure of the government not to make any decision blindly in the matter and the public opinions should not be disregarded. It should be realised that "a small defect will gradually spoil the whole".'[72]

The colonial administration was aware of the escalating social discontent. Officials predicted that 'it will not be long before the other less formalised but influenced groups' follow.[73] This was proven correct. In late January 1975, a resettlement estate shop owner's lobby escalated its action. The group represented twenty-three estates but the impetus for the action came from the Ngau Tau Kok and Jordan Valley Estates. They submitted a petition to the Colonial Secretariat, protesting against the telephone charge increase. Government officials believed that if the colonial administration failed to respond, these organisations would escalate their action.[74] In February, ten representatives were sent by the Tai Wo Hau Resettlement Estate to meet with Oswald Cheung and Harry Fung, unofficial members of the Legislative Council, to voice their opposition on behalf of 3,000 telephone subscribers in the area. They reiterated publicly that they were opposed to any kind of increase and would cut the telephone lines if necessary.[75] Social movements actively sought governmental intervention when people's interests were at stake.

On 6 February, the Legislative Council unanimously approved the Telephone (Amendment) Bill, which enabled the company to increase the telephone rental rate by 30 per cent. Public opinion, however, appeared to have been influenced by the negative comments made by the mass media.[76] Many housewives and residents started to criticise the increase. They believed that the capital for expansion programme should be paid by shareholders instead of consumers, and no decision should be made before the Commission of Inquiry finished its investigation.[77] However, in February, the campaign subsided, with 'a cooling down of public vehemence', a contrast to 'the emotional outbursts' that had followed the announcement of the proposed 70 per cent increase a month earlier. The following observation was recorded in Town Talk:

> In almost all the districts, the general feeling was that the increase was inevitable and although certain kaifong groups still pledged support to anti-increase campaigns, they added they were not keen about taking drastic action. Leaders in the anti-rent increase movement in group A and B housing estates said that they would rather save their energy for more effective action over proposed rent increases for shops in housing estates.[78]

To assess shifting popular sentiment, the HAD instructed the CDOs to conduct an opinion poll. The CDOs in Hong Kong interviewed 824 people to assess public reactions on the increase. Forty-six per cent believed the increase was acceptable and 19 per cent had no comments. Only 35 per cent thought the decision was unacceptable. This finding was impressionistic as there was no previous survey data to compare it with. Nonetheless, most CDOs believed that the survey suggested that 'the emotion of [the] general public has subsided to a large extent'.[79] As Legislative Councillor Oswald Cheung had suggested, 'even a clever housewife cannot cook a meal without rice'.[80] By this point, although some popular misconceptions about the financial situation of the company remained, the public had started understanding why the increase was necessary. According to Town Talk, 'the television programmes and government press features certainly succeeded to a certain extent in explaining the issue'.[81] The 'middle class segments', such as some building contractors and businessmen, even became sympathetic to the financial difficulties the Telephone Company was experiencing.[82] The appointment of the Commission of Inquiry also helped to ease tensions:

> It was noticed that all districts [,] following the appointment of the Commission of Inquiry, public vehemence on this issue had cooled down considerably and over the Chinese New Year, very few comments on the issues were heard, the public generally welcomed the choice of members of the Commission, especially Sir Alastair Blair-Kerr as the Chairman.[83]

The campaign soon lost its momentum and waned in late February 1975.

The proposed increase in the telephone rental rate attracted universal attention from Hong Kong Chinese of different social classes and age groups. Participants were motivated not only by instrumental concerns, but also ideologies such as justice and fairness. They also anticipated increased transparency in the company's administration. The reports of CDOs and Town Talk reveal a shifting political culture in Hong Kong among the middle-aged and elderly groups, as well as the grassroots groups. Unlike previous campaigns, the middle-aged and elderly groups, such as the kaifong leaders, were less reluctant to engage in the protest. They were not afraid to express their grievances when their interests were at stake. While some activists considered cutting their telephone lines to boycott the Telephone Company, others took the initiative to organise signature campaigns and petitions. People at the grassroots level, such as residents in resettlement estates, also engaged in consumer activism because their livelihoods were directly affected. Their rhetoric was radical, in extremist form inciting violence in the slogans. These were, however, outliers. The memories of the Star Ferry riots in 1966 were fresh. People were genuinely concerned that the campaign might cause colony-wide social unrest, which they opposed. Direct confrontations did not occur. The political culture was on the whole liberal, advocating change via established political channels of communication.

Political activism

To protest against the proposed increases in telephone rates, organisations collaborated informally and formed three coalitions. The primary lobby group was the Christian Industrial Committee, headed by Raymond Fung, which was considered by the colonial state to be 'by far the largest political lobby' and 'the most successful'.[84] Formed in 1966, with an interest in labour welfare policy and industrial safety, the Committee was influential, connecting more than 350 separate organisations, including kaifong associations, clansmen association and many voluntary agencies.[85] It was driven by instrumental concerns and employed moderate language to exert pressure on the colonial government, requesting explanations of rate increases. Believing the increase would have a drastic impact on people's livelihoods, it petitioned the UMELCO from September 1974. It argued that the proposed increase was 'detrimental to Hong Kong's worsening economic life, as a community and as families' and that the support of UMELCO and the Consumer Council was needed.[86] The Committee then requested a formal appointment with P. C. Woo, the Chairman of the Advisory Committee.[87] Under the chairmanship of L. K. Ding, an Urban Councillor, the organisation was in close contact with a number of kaifong federal bodies, which involved influential figures in both the Research Council and the Kaifong Advancement Association. To coerce the Telephone Company to withdraw its proposed increase, Ding publicly compared the campaign against the telephone rate increase to the 1966 riots:

> It's the timing; the proposal for an increase in rates has come at a time when people are troubled enough by unemployment and so on. We should try to avoid the rebellion of 1966 when we had a massive scale riot over a nickel increase. This time it's not a nickel but hundreds of dollars.[88]

The Committee deployed the example of the 1966 riots to put pressure on the Telephone Company and the colonial government. It was argued that disturbances would follow if public opinion was neglected and concessions were refused. There were also plans to rally for external support from Labour Parliamentarians in London.[89] Together with some influential figures in multi-storey building groups, such as Lee Wan Yuen, Wong Hoi, Wong Ping Ho and Wong Cham, the Committee used its influence to request an interview with the Secretary of Home Affairs in January 1975, which the press and kaifongs in most districts were aware of.[90] The Committee's success in mobilising a large number of organisations within a short period of time shows its organisational capacity, built on an expansive social network.

Another lobby group was the Universal Consumers' Association, an organisation headed by Edmund Chow, Urban Councillor, and William Shum, civic candidate who was running for the coming Urban Council election. The Association aimed to 'reveal profiteering in wholesale and retail outlets, to work against product inferiority, to censor over-exaggerated advertisement, to press for more sources of supply of consumer goods and to fight against price ragging by franchise or monopoly'.[91] Most of the executive members of the organisation were middle-class professionals, such as lawyers, accountants and architects. The Association was supported by more than forty supporting associations and district committees, ranging from kaifong associations to business corporates in different districts. Organisations included, for example, Civic Association Hung Hom District, Hong Kong and Kowloon Mutual Aid Association, Kwai Chung Kaifong Association, the Reform Club, the Incorporated Owners of Pak Lee building and Daily Growth Investment Company.[92] Since December 1974, the Association had expressed discontent over the proposed increase through the press to mobilise public opinion.[93] On 10 January 1975, Chow held a public meeting at the Hong Kong University Students Alumni Association in Edinburgh House, which was attended by many kaifong leaders. According to a report by the Central CDO, the meeting was 'jam-packed with people overflowing into the corridor'.[94] It was attended mainly by 'middle-aged' men of secondary school education. Most of them were 'quite established'.[95] The meeting agreed to petition the Telephone Company and start a signature campaign. Another meeting was to be scheduled if the petition letter and signature campaign failed to produce any effect. In the petition to the Telephone Company, the Association urged the company to publicise its accounts:

> Although you maintained that the financial situation of your company was something confidential between your company and the government, we feel that the consumers are entitled to know as they will be directly affected if your proposed increase is approved. If you believe that your application for increase is not profit motivated, would it be possible if you could forward to us for our perusal and discussion a copy of the relevant statement of account of your company in support of your application submitted to the Telephone Advisory Committee?[96]

The signature campaign subsequently started on 15 January, when 1,000 forms, each catering for ten persons, were issued to commercial organisations, industrial groups, schools and kaifong associations. The campaign was backed by the public; 643 out of the 1,000 forms were returned by 31 January. The forms carried 5,250 signatures, presenting forty-three organisations and seventy-five schools. 4,777 people, approximately 91 per cent of the signatories, expressed their objection to charge an increase of any degree.[97] Compared to the Christian Industrial Committee, the Universal Consumers' Association initially adopted a tougher attitude. It 'unanimously' refused to concede to 'even 1 per cent increase in rates'.[98] The CDC believed that the group, which was unsympathetic to the government, 'present[ed] a grave stumbling block for any peaceful negotiation'; it believed that if there were any riots, it was 'entirely the working of the government'.[99] However, by mid-January, its 'no concession' position had shifted. The organisation surveyed the public to assess their views on the percentage of rate increase. In the questionnaire, six answers (20 per cent, 30 per cent, 40 per cent, 50 per cent, 60 per cent and 70 per cent) were provided. No increase was not an option.[100] This indicates that the Association had softened its position. In early February, to put pressure on the government, the Association sent the poll result to the UMELCO. The active engagement of the ordinarily pro-status quo and politically indifferent middle class in the campaign through the Universal Consumers' Association suggests that this group could be mobilised against the colonial state when their interests were affected. However, the Universal Consumers' Association received less support when compared to the Christian Industrial Committee as it 'obviously bent on the issue' to pull in votes for the upcoming election.[101]

A third organisation, the well-established Reform Club, also joined the rate increase protest. Yeung Li Yin and two other Reform Club candidates started a signature campaign. Forms were sent out to banks on behalf of Yeung to appeal for support.[102] To campaign effectively and exert pressure on the colonial government, in February, the Reform Club set up an ad hoc sub-committee which consisted of members such as Yeung, Messrs Napoleon Ng, Poon Tai Leung and Sung Pui. The sub-committee carried out a public opinion survey on the proposed rise in telephone charges. It issued 30,000 poll forms and distributed them to the public. In the end, 21,940 of the respondents were against the increase, with only sixty-nine of them supporting the proposed revision.[103] The Club submitted the results to the UMELCO. Nonetheless, the Reform Club campaign received less publicity than those organised by the Christian Industrial Committee and the Universal Consumers' Association. It was only briefly mentioned in Yeung's speech at the inauguration ceremony of the executive committee on 17 January. According to Neoh, its signature campaign was 'rather ineffective', similarly because of its underlying political motive of appealing for public support in the forthcoming election.[104]

A few other civic bodies took an interest in the protest. In early January, the Chinese Manufacturers' Association, which was set up in 1934 representing its members in various sectors of industry and trade, sent a letter to the Colonial Secretary, Denys Roberts, and P. C. Woo, warning that any rise in telephone rentals may 'touch off social discontent and further inflation'.[105] It described the proposed increase as 'untimely in the light of the present economic situations' and argued that it was 'wrong' to make subscribers finance the company's expansion programme. It was also 'beyond understanding' that the company could not operate in spite of the rental increase in 1974 and the 'sizeable net profit' of $70 million.[106] In late January, after the government approved a 30 per cent increase in telephone rates, the Chinese Manufactures' Association formed a new federal pressure group with twenty-two other industrial, commercial and civic organisations, including the most influential trade association, the Hong Kong Chinese General Chamber of Commerce; the Kowloon Chamber of Commerce, the kaifong federal bodies and the Kowloon Multi-storey Buildings General Association also were associated with this pressure group. This led to a jointly issued press statement on 30 January to protest against the 'unwise' increase and to demand that the company's accounts be made public.[107]

By late January, the main lobbies had coalesced. Two distinct categories emerged. The three main groups were relatively liberal and tended to believe in solving the issue through the adoption of a 'collaborative strategy', such as meetings and petitions. Some student organisations, however, believed that the matter could only be settled by 'conflicts', such as demonstrations, sit-ins and other direct actions.[108] In mid-January, the CDC of Kowloon had already observed that the young leftists would take advantage of the telephone rate issue to discredit the colonial state: 'New Left and student groups are known to be actively planning protest action. The telephone charges issue is precisely an issue which the radical new left groups have been waiting for and there is no doubt that it will be exploited to the full.'[109] The Hong Kong Youth and Students Association, which was headed by Siu Kai-chung, probably lined up student radicals such as Daily Combat and 70's Bi-Weekly Groups and maintained a close connection with left-wing secondary schools, the editors of the student publication *Student Go* and community groups in Ngau Tau Kok Estate.[110] On 16 January, the Association sent a petition letter to the Governor, in which the student activists presented themselves as orderly citizens who usually sided with the colonial state but only expressed concerns because the increase was unjust:

> The Hong Kong administration has weathered crisis after crisis. On each occasion we were the first to voice our support of the government and advised heated and heady young people against anti-government demonstrations ... However, this time the Hong Kong Telephone Company is applying for a 70 per cent increase in charges less than a year since the last increase. The Hong Kong public is shocked. We are of [the] opinion that the grounds whereon the Telephone Company rests its application are inadequate. If the increase came through, other public utilities would follow suit, aggravating inflation and miserable economic situation.[111]

They then warned the government of the potential consequence of the rate increase: 'Civil disturbances, could do neither government nor governed any good'.[112] To avoid being viewed as 'trouble-makers', they claimed that their stance had always been 'to abstain from unhappy incidents'. They also informed the Governor that they had already contacted the police force and the HAD to ensure that their rally was held smoothly.[113]

Although the government announced that a 30 per cent instead of a 70 per cent increase had been approved on 22 January, the Hong Kong Youth and Students Association did not cease to protest. On 26 January, the Association held a mass rally in Kowloon Park. It started with 100 members of the Association marching from the main gate of the park to the allocated site. During the rally, students expressed their anti-colonial agenda. The Association's Chairman, Sui Kai-chung, accused the colonial government of being 'capitalists' and 'exploiting the common people'; he demanded the state to give the public a full explanation as to why a 30 per cent rate increase was allowed. In addition, the Association urged the government to abolish the Telephone Advisory Committee. Instead, these bodies should be replaced by elected members and members of the public. The rally was attended by 2,000 people, including Urban Councillors Denny Huang and Elsie Elliott. Civic leaders from the three other lobbies, for example, Edmund Chow and L. K. Ding from the Christian Industrial Committee, Raymond Fung and William Shum from the Universal Consumers' Association and Cecilia Yeung from the Reform Club, also participated in the rally.[114]

This episode led to a clash between councillors and the colonial government and thus had the potential to open up discussions about the relationship between Hong Kong representative organisations and the executives. Significantly, Elliott advocated unofficial Legislative Councillors to resign in protest if the colonial government insisted on authorising a 30 per cent increase in telephone charges.[115] However, according to the assessment carried out by A. K. Chui, the Director of Home Affairs, the reaction to the rally was 'very mild and helpfully indifferent'.[116] Town Talk also reported that public reactions to the rally appeared to 'lack enthusiasm'.[117] Some residents believed that the small number of student participants could be attributed to the fact that the rally was held during exam periods.[118] It could also be explained by the public's general political indifference and reluctance to directly confront the government. By late January, it was evident that the campaign had not been effective: 'Public emotion cooled down significantly.'[119] This disappointed the student activists. In particular, the 'extremist groups' were 'talking loosely about organising another rally because these critics were dissatisfied or disappointed with the lack of impact from the first one'.[120] Apart from the Youth and Students Association, the relatively 'moderate' HKFS also launched a signature campaign to protest against the increase of the telephone rate and profiteering of public utilities at Ferry Wharves and in San Po Kong in late January.[121] On 5 February, the HKFS organised a sit-in jointly with the Hong Kong University Students' Union and Hong Kong Federation of Catholic Students outside the Legislative Council chamber. The sit-in was a joint action between ultra-leftist and moderate student groups. About 150 people were assembled. The signature forms, which contained 60,000 signatures, were hung up. To express their discontent over the 30 per cent rate increase, students made bonfires out of the signature forms they collected.[122] Such symbolic behaviour did not receive support from the public.

On the whole, student bodies and organisations in the educational sector protested in a relatively moderate manner. The College Student Association of Hong Kong, for example, issued an open letter to the Chairman of the Consumer Council on 23 January, urging the government to reform the public utility sector: the monopoly of the Telephone Company should come to an end as 'the company's own claim of insufficient present services clearly indicates an acute "shortage of supply"'.[123] This was supported by some secondary schools and universities. On 29 January, for example, forty-two representatives from secondary schools and universities distributed pamphlets to the public at the Star Ferry concourse. They also submitted an open letter to the Administrative Secretary of the UMELCO, urging the councillors to give full consideration to the matter and inform the public regarding their stance.[124] The Hong Kong Teachers Association issued a public statement to demand the government to carry out a thorough investigation on the financial condition of the Telephone Company, inspecting whether there were any inappropriate corrupt practices.[125] These were moderate protests, in a liberal tradition, requesting improved information and state regulation.

The campaign against telephone rate increases demonstrates that associations of different backgrounds collaborated and formed coalitions. Despite the employment of different strategies, all activists and participants expected the colonial government to intervene and regulate the telephone rate. One can observe that the upper and middle classes flexibly adjusted their attitudes towards informal political activities when their interests were threatened. Although the campaign was very much led by middle and upper-class opinion leaders, residents at the grassroots level also demonstrated a capacity for political mobilisation. Rather than remaining 'politically quiescent', kaifongs at a district level and residents in resettlement estates formed groups and joined political lobbies. These groups often exerted pressure on the government through informal moderate measures, such as sending petitions and organising signature campaigns. Compared to other social classes and age groups, students and the young generation who were critics of the colonial government employed more radical strategies, such as organising demonstrations and sit-ins, to confront the colonial state directly. Although the political culture in Hong Kong was diverse, in events like this where public interests were vastly affected, groups with different political attitudes and orientations set up alliances and collaborated informally and formally in the pursuit of a common goal.

Government responses and public reception

Since the Telephone Company announced its application to increase the telephone rate, the colonial government had been monitoring shifting popular sentiment through Town Talk and situation reports compiled by CDOs. The Hong Kong CDC instructed the CDOs of Western District, Eastern District, Central District and Wan Chai on 6 January 1975 to 'pay special attention to how the public reacts to the proposed telephone rate increase' and plan strategies to ease tensions.[126] These covert public opinion assessments impacted the colonial state's ruling strategies as they were passed to the Colonial Secretariat to inform decision making.[127] The CDCs of both Hong Kong and Kowloon were asked to provide the Secretariat of Home Affairs with the latest report on public reactions, including the main points that had caused public outcry. The Hong Kong Special Branch was also required to put forward comments. These reports were discussed during the Governor's Committee meeting on 10 January.[128] There was considerable pressure on the administration to address the 'extremely emotive attitude of the public' and 'defuse the issue'. Utilising the intelligence collected, the government first decided to encourage public debate and then to depoliticise the issue by setting up a special commission or a sub-committee for the Telephone Advisory Committee to investigate the legal status of the company.[129]

In early January, the colonial government was 'under fire' as its passive stance had 'created the impression that it is prepared to side with the company' and disregard the interests of consumers.[130] In response, the Kowloon CDC recommended the state to take a public stand on the issue as soon as possible by announcing that a decision had not been made and that the interest of consumers would be considered in the decision-making process. They also suggested that a public statement should be made to clarify that the responsibility to explain the company's financial accounts lay on the company itself, rather than the government.[131] During their engagement with the public, CDOs were also instructed to take a similar line. Observations of CDOs indicated that the possibility of bankruptcy had little credibility in the public's eyes, especially after the company has declared a profit of $70 million in 1974. The fact that the company was a monopoly also led the public to expect the government to investigate all other possible ways to finance its capital expansion programme before approving the rate increase.[132]

The telephone rate increase continued to be given 'top priority' in the City District Offices in early 1975.[133] CDOs observed that suspicion that corruption existed in the company prevailed. The public believed that the financial difficulties of the company could be attributed to 'serious errors in forecasting the demand and the need of telephone service' as this Forecast

Section was not managed by professional expertise. Being poorly managed, the company invested a substantial amount of capital in purchasing equipment and cables.[134] In view of this situation, the CDOs pointed out that the government was caught up in a 'dilemma':

> If the government does not agree to the proposal of the Telephone Company, then it will result in mass unemployment for which the government will be held responsible. If the government agrees to the Telephone Company's proposal and gives the company entirely what it wants then there will be tremendous pressure from all sectors of society, and the consequences of which can be very frightening.[135]

To ease tensions and prevent the company from going into bankruptcy, they recommended the government to consider the company's proposal 'very carefully'. Their source also suggested that an increase between 25 per cent and 30 per cent may be set as 'a tolerable limit' for the year of 1975.[136] If the company could survive the financial difficulties that year, 'it would be much better to increase their rates next year'.[137]

These high-level deliberations were kept secret from the public, but action was urgently needed, as noted by lower-level bureaucrats. In the face of a community 'united against the telephone increases', the Kowloon CDC argued that 'too much delay would only enable attitudes to firm up and radicals to exploit the situation still further'.[138] He proposed two strategies. The first was to take a public stand on the issue as soon as possible. The government should state clearly that it would 'weigh the consumers' interest against the case of the company' and 'take all possible steps to listen to public opinions on the issue'.[139] The second was to ensure that the issue had a 'gestation' so that both the cases of the public and the company could be 'seen in a rational perspective'.[140] The CDOs believed that 'the best way of taking the heat off the situation' was to enlarge the Advisory Committee with members from civic organisations. They also recommended that the public should be invited to share their views on the issue with the Committees. Once these consultative processes had been conducted, they advised that the Committees' recommendations be 'published' and 'debated' in the Legislative Council.[141] This would have been a significant reform of policymaking.

The CDOs' recommendations were being taken into consideration by the colonial government. On 9 January 1975, the Secretariat of Home Affairs assured the CDOs that no decision would be made before the receipt of recommendations from the Advisory Committee on Telephone Services. The government planned to give 'a detailed explanation and justification to the public on the decision taken'. A press statement was also issued on the same day by Denis Bray's office, which would have 'calming effect on public feeling'.[142]

On 13 January, these reforms were discussed by the Governor, the Colonial Secretary, the Secretary of Home Affairs, the Director of GIS, the Director of the Special Branch and the political advisors at the Government House. A number of departments which had been keeping a close eye on the telephone rate issue were also invited to feed into decision making at this point. The Special Branch reported that the issue 'was not one for high-level consideration among local Communists', and the Kuomintang elements in the colony followed the 'policy of avoiding direct confrontation' although some participated in the protest individually.[143] Nonetheless, according to the report, 'the real threat' came from 'the neutral groups', notably the 'New Left', some Urban Councillors and shop tenants. And the shop tenants, who would be seriously affected by the rental increase, were 'potentially the most dangerous'. The issue had become an 'emotive' issue and thus the public reaction was 'potentially strong'.[144] Although the Universal Consumers' Association was not considered a legitimate threat, it had gained 'a good degree of public support' and was likely to become 'the focal point of the organised protest'.[145] As the government 'had so far not prepared itself for facing a public outcry', a remedy was required 'to prevent the situation from getting out of hand'.[146]

The outcome of these deliberations was government approval of an increase as high as the public could bear to ensure the continued operation of the Telephone Company. The government expressed its dissatisfaction with the company's financial situation and recognised that the approved increase may not be sufficient in the long run. It also announced the appointment of a Commission of Inquiry, which consisted of a judge, a public accountant, 'a member of the public' and a government official.[147] To follow up the issue, the Governor requested the department heads present to give any further thoughts on the matter 'urgently' and reach agreement over an action plan with the Colonial Secretary. The Secretary of Home Affairs and the Director of GIS were then instructed to draft plans of a publicity campaign to ease tensions.[148] The radical option of consulting fully with the public and then orchestrating a debate in the Legislative Council was not pursued, giving the colonial government leeway to implement changes that did not follow public opinion completely.

The HAD continued to monitor shifting public opinion on the issue after the meeting. On 17 January, the Secretary of Home Affairs reported to the Governor that 'people were very cross' as they disliked monopolies, the proposed percentage increase and the proximity of this application to the last round. There was 'potential for strong public reaction'.[149] Therefore, it was recommended that the government should 'cultivate the stabilising forces that exist' within the majority of the activists who were willing to engage in discussion. To reduce discontent, the colonial government had to be seen to

The campaign against telephone rate increases 145

take public opinion into consideration. The Kowloon CDO was instructed to encourage people in his district to share their views. Nonetheless, it was stressed that 'one cannot maintain credibility for too long' and the government was urged to take a public stand as soon as possible. A suggestion was made that full examinations should be carried out to reassure the political lobbies that their views would be considered and any decision in the change in telephone rate would be made public.[150]

In a final settlement, announced on 22 January, the government set up a Commission of Inquiry that would investigate the company's management structure, debts, liabilities, profitability and future plans. It was also announced that the government would only approve a 30 per cent increase in telephone rentals and waive the company's royalties for 1974 and 1975. In return for the government's help, the company was asked to issue no dividends to its shareholders and accept a government-appointed director to its board.[151] Some of the proposals made by the CDOs were adopted.

The settlement was criticised. People believed that 30 per cent was 'still too high' and 'unjustified'.[152] The setting up of the Commission of Inquiry did not win popular support. People viewed it as 'a plot to mollify public emotions' and did not understand the logic of setting up the Commission now that a rate had been agreed. A minority supported the formation of the Commission as 'a good move'.[153] There were few comments made regarding the appointment of a director to the company's board and the arrangement regarding dividends. The public simply did not see the benefits.[154] The public 'at large' was 'aggrieved'. According to the City District Office staff in Kowloon, 'much frustration abounded' and their respondents were 'mostly highly charged with emotions'.[155] The government's image suffered 'another new low' as the increase 'served another grave blow' to it. Public confidence in the colonial administration was 'weakened'.[156]

To accurately assess public reactions to the increase, a random survey was conducted by CDOs in Hong Kong on 23 January. 1,376 people were interviewed and 92 per cent disagreed with the 30 per cent increase. Among those who were against the increase, 23 per cent insisted that no increase at all should be made. 34 per cent believed that 5 to 10 per cent was appropriate, while 7 per cent thought an increase of 11 to 15 per cent was appropriate. And 12 per cent suggested that an increase of 16 to 20 per cent was acceptable. Only 2 per cent supported an increase of 21 to 25 per cent.[157] Newspapers were also 'hostile'.[158] *Fai Po*, for example, reported that 'reaction from the public is still strong' and pointed out that the increase was 'absolutely unreasonable'.[159] The headline of *HKT* described the 30 per cent increase as 'a move against public opinion'.[160] Both *STYP* and *KSDN* criticised the government for not taking into consideration the potential chain reactions the increase would bring.[161] *STYP* also argued that the increase should not be made before the Commission of Inquiry had completed its investigation.[162] In view of the negative comments made by the newspapers, the Governor instructed that 'more should be done to put down [the] government's package across the press and to impress upon editors the danger of giving too much weight to irresponsible criticism'.[163]

By the end of January, despite the unpopularity of the 30 per cent rate increase, the campaign lost momentum. According to the CDC of Hong Kong: 'there are indications that the storm is gradually settling for the time being in the sense that the degree of hostility is subsiding'.[164] It was believed that if the decision on the percentage increase could be postponed until the findings of the Commission of Inquiry were made available, the public would find it 'more palatable'.[165] Similar findings were reported in Town Talk. It was true that some were still concerned that the government was 'playing a game of numbers' and arrived at its decision 'by mere haggling'.[166] Nonetheless, there was on the whole 'a very grudging acceptance' in the Chinese communities.[167] Kaifong associations in Sham Shui Po, for example, indicated that they were less inclined to join any protest actions planned in the future.[168] By early February, the public had 'by large accepted without query that the Telephone Company is in a very difficult financial situation'.[169] They were now prepared to contribute to enable the continual operation of the company. They were also convinced that the government had 'tried its best in finding the fairest and cheapest way so that burden falls in the right places'.[170] The issue was now merely one of the 'challenges to our public relations efforts' rather than 'a serious threat to our social order', although people were still 'in an unhappy mood about these bad times' and public concerns that the issue may turn into civil disorder remained.[171] The Director of Home Affairs noted that most people were 'very much on the government's side'.[172] The government concluded that it must respond to dissent by improving the flow of information from itself to the people: it must try 'hardest to convince them that government is very much on their side as well', presenting data and facts that were of 'paramount importance'. Government decisions must be communicated, including a refusal to make the accounts of the company public.[173]

The dispute had not led to a reform of modes of political communication. Once tensions had eased, the Legislative Council approved unanimously a 30 per cent increase in the telephone rate. On 8 February, the composition of the Committee of Inquiry was announced. The Committee consisted of Alastair Blair-Kerr, Gordon MacWhinnie, the Chairman of the Hong Kong Society of Accountants, John Soong, the Chairman and Managing Director of Mobil Oil in Hong Kong, C. P. Hung, the President of the Chinese Manufacturers Association, L. K. Ding, the Chairman of the Christian Industrial Committee, the largest lobby in the campaign and Lydia Dunn, the Director of Swire and Maclaine.[174] The Committee was dominated by business and professional elites.

The colonial government closely monitored shifting public opinion through its surveillance instruments, notably Town Talk and a range of situation reports generated by departments. CDOs were particularly active, making daily observations based on contact with the 'man in the street'. The HAD, the Division of GIS and the Special Branch also monitored political activism and popular responses towards the issue constantly. Reports and recommendations were passed to the Governor and advisory committees. Even in the absence of a democratic system of government, public sentiment shaped the government responses. Only a 30 per cent increase was approved, which was needed to keep the company out of bankruptcy. Informal consultation with the public, publicity campaigns and the appointment of a Commission of Inquiry were devised to respond to and weaken the campaign. A reformist colonial administration was increasingly responsive to public opinion as it was being reshaped by subtle shifts in political culture. However, these social and political processes did not create the conditions for more profound institutional reform.

Conclusion

Compared to many other issues, such as the increase in public housing rents, the increase in telephone rate was regarded by the Governor as 'potentially explosive', as people of all social classes and age groups were affected.[175] And the proposed rate increase generated 'colony-wide protest'. At least ninety-three organisations of different sectors and backgrounds took part.[176] Individuals of different social classes, including kaifongs and residents at the grassroots level, community leaders, Urban Councillors, clansmen, businessmen, workers, teachers and students, were motivated by both instrumental and ideological concerns. Many boycotted the Telephone Company, the main mechanism of protest which put pressure on the colonial government to limit or scrap the rate increase. This reveals how the political culture was shifting, with civic organisations mobilising and actively lobbying the government. Even the upper and middle classes, who often disapproved of political activism, joined the campaign and used informal political activities to express their grievances. In this instance, their material interests were threatened.

Different methods were used to put pressure on the Telephone Company and the colonial government. Learning from previous campaigns, moderate informal political channels, such as sending petitions, organising signature campaigns and writing to newspaper editors, were predominantly used.

These forms of political communication were fundamentally liberal but underpinning this civil action was a collective memory of 'civil disturbance' of the 1960s. However, on the margins, radical groups and radicalised individuals organised rallies and sit-ins to confront the colonial state directly. There were different political cultures, with the young generation more radical in outlook and in practice. Nonetheless, these student activists were also aware that most Hong Kong Chinese were politically conservative and did not want institutional reforms. To appeal for public support, students presented themselves as orderly citizens who complied with laws during the rallies. Regardless of differences in the methods adopted, the anti-telephone rate increase campaign shows that the Hong Kong Chinese would not hesitate to voice their opposition and demand the colonial government to intervene and regulate whenever their material interests were threatened.

The colonial government monitored social attitudes during the protest movements. Shifting popular sentiment was observed by CDOs, using mechanisms such as situation reports and the covert Town Talk. Departments, such as City District Offices, the HAD, the Division of GIS and the Special Branch, were all involved, checking political activism and compiling special reports for the Governor and his Committee. This reveals that the government had the capacity to conduct surveillance. By collecting intelligence on popular attitudes, the colonial government improved its decision-making capacity and sought to demonstrate that it was responding rationally to the protest and public opinion, showing that the mentality of colonial bureaucrats was to some extent moving towards 'decolonisation'. Official responses of the CDOs were tailored to the public and the public was consulted to increase political participation and alleviate general grievances. A Commission of Inquiry was also set up. This weakened the campaign.

These social and political processes had a moderate effect: the increase was set at 30 per cent, lower than the 55 per cent that was advised by the Telephone Advisory Committee. This outcome was symbolically important: it showed that a reformist colonial administration was responsive to shifting public opinion, and thus had the potential to further encourage the development of civil society, newspapers and social movements mobilising on specific issues.

Notes

1 Lam tried to quantify the public reactions by examining the 'amount' of public responses the movement triggered: 'The campaign generated a wide range of actions: at least eighteen letters to the government, 26 press conferences, four surveys, ten public meetings and three closed-door meetings.' *Understanding the Political Culture*, p. 170.

2. Ibid., p. 109.
3. HKRS 618-1-567, 'HK Telephone to Seek Another Rise in Rental Charges', *SCMP*, 26 August 1974.
4. HKRS 286-1-12, 'Increase in Telephone Charges', Town Talk, 17 January 1974, p. 2.
5. HKRS 70-7-472-2, 'Report of Telephone Services Advisory Committee', Daily Information Bulletin, 13 June 1973.
6. HKRS 70-7-472-2, 'Cheap but Too Slow!', *Star*, 16 June 1973.
7. Outside Japan, the Hong Kong Telephone Company was the second company to use this system, which was considered to comprise the 'most up-to-date and advanced techniques presently available'. HKRS 276-8-351, 'Extension of Hong Kong Telephone Microwave Network', New Release, 15 May 1975, pp. 1–2.
8. HKRS 618-1-567, 'Inflation Puts Up Phone Rental Charges', *SCMP*, 25 September 1974.
9. Leung, 'Social Movement as Cognitive Praxis', p. 360.
10. Lam, *Understanding the Political Culture*, p. 164.
11. HKRS 286-1-12, 'Increase in Telephone Charges', Town Talk, 29 August 1974, p. 1.
12. Ibid.
13. HKRS 276-8-137, Y. K. Kan to Colonial Secretary, 16 September 1974.
14. HKRS 286-1-12, 'Telephone Charges', Town Talk, 19 September 1974, p. 2.
15. HKRS 618-1-567, 'All-out Bid to Block Higher Phone Rates', *HKS*, 13 September 1974.
16. HKRS 276-8-137, Tang Tung-kwong to Yu Sau-leung, October 1974.
17. HKRS 276-8-137, Lau Ping-wah to CDO (Sha Tin), 2 October 1974.
18. HKRS 276-8-137, Heung Yee Kuk to Secretary for the New Territories, 1 November 1974.
19. HKRS 618-1-567, 'Move to Increase Telephone Rates Lashed', *SCMP*, 21 December 1974.
20. HKRS 618-1-567, 'Telephone Rate Rise Unwise, Ill-timed', *SCMP*, 25 September 1974.
21. HKRS 618-1-567, 'Increase in Telephone Charges', Chinese Press Review, no. 310, 17–22 December 1974, p. 1.
22. HKRS 618-1-567, 'Increase in Telephone Charges', Chinese Press Review, no. 312, 30 December 1974–7 January 1975, p. 1.
23. Ibid., p. 3.
24. Ibid., p. 4.
25. Ibid., p. 6.
26. HKRS 286-1-14, 'Mounting Tensions Over Telephone Increase', Town Talk, 9 January 1975, p. 1.
27. Ibid.
28. Ibid.
29. Ibid., p. 2.
30. HKRS 70-7-472-2, 'Seventeenth Periodical Report for the Period from 1st Jan to 31st Dec 1974', Advisory Committee on Telephone Services, 28 July 1975, p. 7.

31 Ibid., Appendix E.
32 HKRS 276-8-351, 'Hong Kong Telephone Company's Application for Rental Increase Statement by F. L. Walker, General Manager', New Release, 10 January 1975.
33 HKRS 618-1-567, 'Telephone Company's Application for Charges Increase', Chinese Press Review, no. 313, 7–14 January 1975, p. 1.
34 Ibid., p. 3.
35 Ibid., p. 4.
36 Ibid.
37 Ibid., p. 3.
38 Ibid.
39 HKRS 394-27-11, 'Telephone Charges Increase', A. F. Neoh to Deputy Director of Home Affairs, 13 January 1975, p. 1.
40 Ibid.
41 HKRS 394-27-11, 'Telephone Charges Increase', A. K. Neoh to Deputy Director of Home Affairs, 8 January 1975, p. 1.
42 HKRS 394-27-11, 'Situation Report on Items of Special Current Interest', S. T. Tam to E. P. Ho, 9 January 1975, p. 1.
43 HKRS 286-1-14, 'Pressure for Government Line on Telephone Increases', Town Talk, 16 January 1975, p. 1.
44 Town Talk did not specify the location of these residential quarters. See ibid.
45 Ibid.
46 Ibid., pp. 1–2.
47 HKRS 286-1-14, 'Increase in Telephone Charges', Town Talk, 23 January 1975, p. 2.
48 Ibid.
49 Ibid., p. 3.
50 Ibid., p. 2.
51 HKRS 618-1-567, 'Boycott Campaign Proposed', *SCMP*, 9 September 1974.
52 HKRS 618-1-567, 'Subscriber' and 'The Consumer Should Not Be Penalised', *SCMP*, 29 January 1975.
53 HKRS 618-1-567, 'Public Has a Right to Know', *SCMP*, 14 January 1975.
54 HKRS 618-1-567, '電話加費應公開審查', *Sing Tao Yat Pao* (*STYP* hereafter), 3 January 1975.
55 'The Consumer Should Not Be Penalised'; HKRS 618-1-567, 'Why Raise Charges Before Inquiry', *SCMP*, 30 January 1975.
56 'Mounting Tensions Over Telephone Increase', p. 2.
57 'Increase in Telephone Charges', p. 2.
58 'Pressure for Government Line on Telephone Increase', p. 1.
59 HKRS 618-1-567, 'Hang P. C. Woo Posters Appeared in Kowloon', *Tin Wong Evening News*, 9 January 1975.
60 'Telephone Charges Increase', Neoh to Deputy Director of Home Affairs, 20 January 1975, p. 1.
61 'Telephone Charges Increase', Neoh to Deputy Director of Home Affairs, 8 January 1975, p. 3.
62 Ibid.

63 HKRS 618-1-566, Yan Chi Kit, Hong Kong and Kowloon Joint Kaifong Research Council to members of the Legislative Council, 11 January 1975.
64 'Mounting Tensions Over Telephone Increase', p. 1.
65 'Pressure for Government Line on Telephone Increases', p. 2.
66 'Telephone Charges Increase', Neoh to Deputy Director of Home Affairs, 13 January 1975, p. 3.
67 Ibid.
68 Ibid.
69 'Telephone Charges Increase', Neoh to Deputy Director of Home Affairs, 20 January 1975, p. 4.
70 HKRS 618-1-566, Lei Cheng Uk Resettlement Estate Commercial and Industrial General Association to UMELCO, 3 January 1975.
71 'Telephone Charges Increase', Neoh to Deputy Director of Home Affairs, 20 January 1975, p. 3.
72 HKRS 618-1-566, Residents of District 9, Fuk Tak Village, Ngau Tau Kok to UMELCO, 17 January 1975.
73 'Telephone Charges Increase', Neoh to Deputy Director of Home Affairs, 13 January 1975, p. 2.
74 'Telephone Charges Increase', Neoh to Deputy Director of Home Affairs, 20 January 1975, p. 3.
75 HKRS 618-1-567, 'LegCo Men to Get Phone Petition', *SCMP*, 3 February 1975.
76 HKRS 618-1-567, 'Shift in Public Reaction towards Telephone Increase', Town Talk, 6 February 1975, p. 1.
77 Ibid.
78 Ibid.
79 HKRS 394-27-11, 'Assessment of Public Reaction on the 30% Increase of Telephone Charges', S. T. Tam to Deputy Director of Home Affairs, 6 February 1975.
80 HKRS 618-1-567, 'A Decision We Must Accept', *SCMP*, 6 February 1975.
81 HKRS 286-1-14, 'Grudging Acceptance of Telephone Increase', Town Talk, 30 January 1975, p. 2.
82 'Shift in Public Reaction towards Telephone Increase', p. 1.
83 HKRS 286-1-14, 'Increase in Telephone Charges', Town Talk, 20 February 1975, p. 5.
84 'Telephone Charges Increase', Neoh to Deputy Director of Home Affairs, 8 January 1975, p. 2; 'Telephone Charges Increase', Neoh to Deputy Director of Home Affairs, 13 January 1975, p. 2.
85 HKRS 394-27-11, 'Telephone Charges Increase', Neoh to Deputy Director of Home Affairs, 20 January 1975, p. 3.
86 HKRS 618-1-566, L. K. Ding to UMELCO, 10 September 1974.
87 HKRS 276-8-137, Raymond Fung, Hong Kong Christian Industrial Committee to P. C. Woo, 25 September 1974.
88 HKRS 618-1-567, 'Appeal to Oppose Telephone Rate Rise', *HKS*, 19 September 1974.
89 HKRS 618-1-567, 'MP Aid to Fight Phone Increases Sought', *SCMP*, 31 December 1974.

90 'Telephone Charges Increase', Neoh to Deputy Director of Home Affairs, 8 January 1975, p. 2.
91 'Consumerism, Free Competition and Public Policy', *CU Student*, 3:1, 15 January 1975.
92 HKRS 618-1-566, 'Universal Consumers Association Supporting Association & District Committees', (date unspecified).
93 'Move to Increase Telephone Rates Lashed'.
94 'Telephone Charges Increase', Neoh to Deputy Director of Home Affairs, 13 January 1975, p. 2.
95 HKRS 394-27-11, 'A Report on the Meeting of the Universal Consumers' Association Held on 10 January at the HKU Alumni Association Premises', Angus Miu Wah-On to CDC (Hong Kong), 11 January 1975, p. 1.
96 HKRS 276-8-137, William Shum to Manager of the Hong Kong Telephone Company, 13 January 1975.
97 HKRS 618-1-566, William Shum to the UMLECO, 3 February 1975.
98 'A Report on the Meeting of the Universal Consumers' Association Held on 10 January at the HKU Alumni Association Premises', p. 3.
99 Ibid.
100 HKRS 394-27-11, 'Situation Report on Items of Special Current Interest: Proposed Increase in Telephone Charges', S. T. Tam to Director of Home Affairs, 16 January 1975, p. 1.
101 'Telephone Charges Increase', Neoh to Deputy Director of Home Affairs, 20 January 1975, p. 2.
102 Ibid., p. 3.
103 HKRS 618-1-566, Brook Bernacchi to P. W. Primrose, 3 February 1975.
104 'Telephone Charges Increase', Neoh to Deputy Director of Home Affairs, 20 January 1975, p. 3.
105 'Telephone Charges Increase', Neoh to Deputy Director of Home Affairs, 13 January 1975.
106 HKRS 618-1-567, 'CMA Opposes Telephone Fee Increase', *SCMP*, 9 January 1975.
107 HKRS 394-27-11, 'Telephone Charges Increases Recent Development: Report No.2 on Public Reaction', A. K. Chui to Financial Secretary, Secretary for Home Affairs, Secretary for Economic Services and Director of Special Branch, 3 February 1975, p. 1.
108 Ibid., p. 2.
109 'Telephone Charges Increase', Neoh to Deputy Director of Home Affairs, 13 January 1975, p. 3.
110 'Telephone Charges Increase', Neoh to Deputy Director of Home Affairs, 20 January 1975, p. 4.
111 HKRS 394-27-11, Hong Kong Youth and Student's Association to MacLehose, 16 January 1975, p. 1.
112 Ibid.
113 Ibid.
114 HKRS 618-1-567, 'Phone Rates Protest Rally Draws 2,000', *SCMP*, 27 January 1975.

115 HKRS 618-1-567, 'Elsie Says LegCo People Should All Resign as a Protest', *Star*, 27 January 1975.
116 'Telephone Charges Increases Recent Development: Report No.2 on Public Reaction', Chui to Financial Secretary, Secretary for Home Affairs, Secretary for Economic Services and Director of Special Branch, 3 February 1975, p. 1.
117 'Grudging Acceptance of Telephone Increase', p. 2.
118 Ibid.
119 'Telephone Charges Increases Recent Development: Report No.2 on Public Reaction', p. 1.
120 Ibid.
121 HKRS 618-1-567, 'Students to Hold Signature Campaign against the Increase of Telephone Rental', *Highnoon News*, 31 January 1975.
122 HKRS 394-27-11, 'A Situation Report on Students Sit-in Outside Main Entrance of Colonial Secretariat on 5 February 1975 from 1:45 pm to 4:05 pm', Angus Miu Wah-on to CDC (Hong Kong), 6 February 1975.
123 HKRS 276-8-137, Open letter from Ho Chun Yan, the President of the College Student Association of Hong Kong to Consumer Council, 23 January 1975.
124 HKRS 618-1-567, 'Student to Submit Open Letter to UMELCO Councillors against the Increase of Telephone Rental', *STMP*, 29 January 1975.
125 HKRS 618-1-567, 'New Extracts of 3.2.75', 3 February 1975.
126 HKRS 394-27-11, 'Telephone Rate Increase', Peter Ng to CDOs (Western, Eastern, Central and Wan Chai), 6 January 1975.
127 Ibid.
128 HKRS 394-27-11, Extract of minutes from Directorate meeting, 7 January 1975.
129 HKRS 394-27-11, Extract of minutes from HAIG meeting, 6 January 1975.
130 'Telephone Charges Increase', Neoh to Deputy Director of Home Affairs, 8 January 1975, p. 1.
131 Ibid.
132 Ibid., p. 2.
133 'Telephone Charges Increase', Neoh to Deputy Director of Home Affairs, 8 January 1975, p. 3
134 HKRS 394-27-11, 'A Brief Report on the Latest Situation within the Telephone Company', p. 1.
135 Ibid.
136 Ibid.
137 Ibid.
138 'Telephone Charges Increase', Neoh to Deputy Director of Home Affairs, 13 January 1975, p.3.
139 Ibid.
140 Ibid., p. 4.
141 Ibid.
142 HKRS 276-8-137, 'Telephone Rate Increase', A. K. Chui to Secretary of Economic Services, 9 January 1975.
143 HKRS 394-27-11, 'Telephone Charges', record of a meeting held at Government House on Monday, 13 January 1975, p. 1.

144 Ibid.
145 Ibid.
146 Ibid.
147 Ibid., p. 2.
148 Ibid.
149 HKRS 276-8-137, Extract of minutes from Governor's Committee meeting, 17 January 1975, p. 2.
150 Ibid.
151 HKRS 618-1-567, 'Govt Orders Inquiry into Telephone Co', *SCMP*, 23 January 1975.
152 HKRS 394-27-11, 'Telephone Charges Increase', K. C. Lo to Deputy Director of Home Affairs, 23 January 1975, p. 1.
153 Ibid., p. 2.
154 Ibid.
155 Ibid., p. 3.
156 Ibid.
157 HKRS 394-27-11, 'Assessment of Public Opinion on the 30% Increase of Telephone Charges', enclosed in memo from S. T. Tam to Director of Home Affairs, 24 January 1975.
158 HKRS 276-8-137, 'Telephone Charges', extract of minutes from Governor's Committee, 24 January 1975.
159 HKRS 276-7-893, GIS, 'Announcement of Increase in Telephone Charges', 23 January 1975, p. 1.
160 Ibid.
161 Ibid.
162 HKRS 276-7-893, '電話費准加三成 滿城反對嘆聲', *STYP*, 24 January 1975.
163 'Telephone Charges', extract of minutes from Governor's Committee, 24 January 1975.
164 HKRS 394-27-11, 'Telephone Charge Increases', Peter Ng to Deputy of Director of Home Affairs, 30 January 1975, p. 1.
165 Ibid.
166 'Grudging Acceptance of Telephone Increase', p. 1.
167 Ibid.
168 Ibid.
169 'Telephone Charge Increase Recent Development: Report No.2 on Public Reaction', p. 3.
170 Ibid.
171 Ibid., p. 2.
172 Ibid.
173 Ibid.
174 HKRS 618-1-567, 'Blair-Kerr to Head Probe', *HKS*, 8 February 1975.
175 HKRS 394-27-11, Extract of minutes from Governor's Committee meeting, 17 January 1975.
176 Lam, *Understanding the Political Culture*, p. 167.

5

The campaign to reopen the Precious Blood Golden Jubilee Secondary School

The Precious Blood Golden Jubilee Secondary School dispute, which lasted from February 1977 to July 1978, was 'one of the most significant political acts' in the 1970s due to its scale and intensity.[1] After a decade of political turmoil in China, Hong Kong people increasingly identified themselves with the colony.[2] The legitimacy of the colonial state had also been enhanced by the implementation of reforms responding to popular demands, including legalising Chinese as the official language of Hong Kong and setting up the ICAC, as discussed in previous chapters. Nonetheless, the colonial government still faced challenges in the late 1970s. People engaged in informal and formal activities to press for political and social changes. With the establishment of the ICAC, the public began to believe that the colonial government was willing to face up to its shortcomings. The young generation became increasingly critical of the colonial administration. They were intolerant of any corruption. To express their grievances, they were willing to take direct action. The Precious Blood Golden Jubilee Secondary School dispute was the most commonly known example which involved student activism.

In early 1977, teachers found evidence of financial mismanagement at the Precious Blood Golden Jubilee Secondary School. The rumours of corruption, the warning letters issued by the Education Department, the new teaching contracts which prohibited teachers from engaging in political activities and the suspension of student extra-curricular activities led to a student campaign that captured the attention of the press and the public. Although the campaign presented a positive image of the school, the Education Department ordered its closure. This resulted in controversies and more political activism, which included sit-ins, signature campaigns, demonstrations and petitions. Young people were at the 'political centre' in this campaign and the 'society was divided' over the protest. For example, around 100 priests and sisters disapproved of the student activism and stated their support for the Education Department. Some newspapers also critiqued the campaign, arguing that students were being manipulated by radicalised teachers. As Lam Wai-man highlighted, the campaign raised concerns that radical political activism could undermine political stability.[3] This chapter reinvestigates this activism, exploring the impact of class and age.[4] In particular, it evaluates the organisational capacity and political culture of young people. It also uses policy files in Hong Kong and London to establish to what extent political activism influenced the colonial administration's ruling strategies.

Shifting sentiments of the teachers and students

The Precious Blood Golden Jubilee Secondary School was a Catholic government-aided college that opened in September 1973. In the 1970s, most schools in Hong Kong were academically oriented as success in examinations was the main way through which young people gained access to well-paid employment and, for a select elite, university education.[5] The colonial administration controlled the school curriculum to counter the spread of communist influence, with the study of contemporary China in the main not included. Political topics were confined to 'a description of the structure and functions of government departments'.[6] Contrary to most schools in Hong Kong, which placed an emphasis on examination performance and disciplines, the Precious Blood Golden Jubilee Secondary School experimented using a 'new' approach in education.[7] The school deemphasised examination results. Instead, it stressed the importance of 'discussions, dialogue, mutual assistance, respect' and adopted a 'questioning approach' in learning.[8] Students were exposed to matters of public affairs and debated social justice, and were trained to become responsible citizens. The school's innovative teaching style gained the approval of the School of Education at the Chinese University of Hong Kong, which selected the school for teaching observations for its students from 1973 to 1976.[9]

At the beginning of 1977, a number of teachers approached the principal, Sister Leung, about financial malpractices of the school and overcharging of student fees. These teachers suspected the school administration was corrupt. According to colonial records, Leung had recruited a number of teachers with 'Trotskyite views' and left the running of the school to one of them. She was also allegedly engaged in these fraudulent activities.[10] Teachers at the school reported Leung to the ICAC in February for financial mismanagement. Yet, no action was taken as the teachers refused to allow the ICAC to refer their allegations to the Education Department.[11] In spring 1977, a 'Trotskyite' teacher tried to blackmail Leung into letting his group take control of the school. Leung refused and resigned. The management committee was informed about her financial malpractice. The incident was then referred to the Education Department, which sent an audit team to inspect the school and reform its administration. The allegations of financial mismanagement coupled with reforms caused mass demonstrations and a two-day sit-in involving both teachers and pupils in June 1977.

This initial campaign led the Director of Education to send warning letters to the thirty-five teachers involved. Half of these teachers, led by Chan Chung Ling, demanded the withdrawal of these letters of complaint. With Sister Leung convicted in February 1978, they erroneously claimed that it was them who had revealed the school's financial mismanagement and hence were being victimised. Nonetheless, according to the Education Department, they had only reported these activities three days after the audit team was sent to the school and ten days after the school's management committee had informed the Director of Education regarding the possibility of financial mismanagement.[12] As a result, the warning letters were not withdrawn.

In September 1977, a new principal, Hilda Kwan, was appointed. Kwan took a firm stand. She dissolved the student union and suspended all activities. Many affected students were dissatisfied: 'Since the dissolution of the student union, the activities that were organised by it can no longer be held. And since some ordinary activities have been cancelled from the school calendar, such as Speech Day, Drama Day, we lack normal activities.'[13] Kwan also attempted to segregate the new students and teachers from the old ones by holding two assemblies daily: one for Form One students and one for students of Form Two and above.[14] The school however gave no public explanation of the financial mismanagement to the students. Students came to believe therefore that the school's administration was 'on the one hand, avoiding its responsibility; on the other hand, persecuting the teachers unreasonably'.[15] Discontent quickly increased. The school had poorly handled the allegations of institutional maladministration. A student tried to mobilise her peers and expressed her discontent over the school's unjust arrangement in *CU Student*:

> Just people! Don't fall! Or else the weak people walking in the dark will lose their only guiding light. Just people! Don't leave us! I am afraid I will lose my rationality because of this ... If you imprison the truth, [and] bury it under the ground, it will grow endlessly, and explosive power will accumulate. One day it will explode and override all obstacles.[16]

In April 1978, a new supervisor, Sister Lorraine Turcotte, sent out thirteen warning letters to the teachers involved. This new initiative, interpreted as an attempt to dismiss these teachers, escalated the protest. During the protest, four student representatives were suspended for two weeks and four others were warned for infringing the 'personal freedom' of the principal.

Students also alleged that they had been assaulted by non-academic staff, which led to increased discontent:

> On 1 May 1978, a morning with nice weather, students attended lessons like they did usually. The parents of three students were called one after another to see the principal. After that, their daughters were also being called to see the principal. They were being suspended for two weeks! Simply because they once represented the students to demand the school to investigate the school bag-searching incident; they were also engaged in actions 'seizing' the principal, vice-principal and other teachers, 'disrupting' the normal order ... We are angry, we hate that the school penalised its students unreasonably![17]

On 4 May, parents approached the Chairman of the Hong Kong Professional Teachers' Union, Szeto Wah, for assistance. Szeto attempted to contact the principal, the Education Department, the ICAC and the Catholic Board of Education to 'ease the situation'. This was to no avail. Szeto, nonetheless, received a reprimand from the Education Department for his involvement in the incident.[18] The chain of events was controversial as students believed they were being treated unfairly by a high-handed principal. Teachers were being viewed as victims in the disclosure of the school's fraudulent financial malpractice. The issuing of a reprimand, in particular, was contested as an infringement of union rights.

Political activism and increased press coverage

On 5 May, the Education Department issued a statement asserting that it had complete confidence in Kwan and sanctioned her to maintain discipline in the school. The government's endorsement led 440 students, eighteen teachers and twenty parents to march to Government House to petition the Governor. On 6 May, they marched to the Caritas centre next to the bishop's residence and requested to see the bishop. About twenty students camped outside his residence; several of them and their parents, and sixteen teachers, stayed outside the residence for two nights. About 300 students participated in the sit-in. They accused Kwan of being a fascist and the school of being corrupt.[19] They demanded the immediate resignation of Kwan, the resumption of classes of suspended students and the withdrawal of warning letters. They also requested the government to investigate the complaints from students that they had been assaulted and their school bags searched.[20] The sit-ins and demonstrations had made it impossible for any normal schoolwork to continue. As MacLehose noted, there was 'a danger of trouble escalating' and the organisation of the school might collapse under strain.

On 14 May, the Director of Education ordered the closure of the school.[21] It was announced that a new secondary school would be set up in September under the same principal and supervisor. New terms were included in the teachers' contracts. They were prohibited from engaging in political activities. Permission had to be obtained from the principal before anyone could put up posters and assemble. The use of school premises without permission was prohibited. The school management committee also reserved the right to dismiss any employees who failed to observe the new terms.[22] As a result, the sixteen teachers involved in the sit-ins were unable to extend their contracts. They complained to the Hong Kong Professional Teachers' Union. An ad hoc coalition was subsequently formed to engage in activism in support of the teachers: this included the All Hong Kong Committee to Strive to Reopen the Precious Blood Golden Jubilee Secondary School, which consisted of a range of representative social groups, including students organisations, educational bodies, religious groups and labour organisations.[23]

The incident was widely reported in newspapers. According to 'Opinions' in the Chinese Press Review, public opinion was divided on the government handling of the issue: 'at least eight papers came out in support of the Education Department's decision, but an equal number of papers disagreed with or had reservations about the move'.[24] *WKYP*, for instance, described the government decision as 'wise'.[25] Both *STYP* and *HKT* endorsed the government's measures, which they believed would 'win public support'.[26] *The HKDN* argued that the school's closure was the only way of 'ending the trouble quickly'.[27] Other newspapers were critical. *TTYP* captured the discontent of some parties involved: 'Students feel aggrieved. Teachers say it is revenge. And parents demand explanation.'[28] It condemned the decision made by the Education Department as 'undemocratic', 'bureaucratic', 'abrupt' and 'high-handed'. Closing the school was also deemed a typical example of 'colonialism'.[29] The leftist press, *Wen Wei Po* and *Ta Kung Pao*, also condemned the decision to close the school. *Wen Wai Po* argued that the state's move would only aggravate the situation and *Ta Kung Pao* believed that students' and parents' interests should be given 'the greatest weight'.[30] Community leader L. K. Ding accused the colonial government of showing 'the ugly aspects of colonialism'.[31]

In response to the school's closure, the Chairman of the Hong Kong Professional Teachers' Union, Szeto Wah, petitioned the Governor on 16 May. He justified the reopening of the school by arguing that the closure was not in the public interest: 'And the whole of Hong Kong was startled. The consequence that this decision may lead to will make people worry more.'[32] He requested the formation of a special committee, consisting of John Wu, the Roman Catholic bishop, Peter Cheung, the Vice Chairman of Diocesan Justice and Peace Commission, Father Thomas Kwan and Father John Tong, to carry out an 'in-depth fact-finding survey' to settle the affair fully.[33] Decisions regarding the alteration of the name and sponsoring organisation of the school, the retention of the principal and renewal of contracts with the teachers could not be made before the committee had finished its investigations.[34] The representatives of teachers, students and parents also petitioned Colvyn Haye, the Acting Director of Education. They claimed that the Education Department had only listened to the school authorities' 'one-sided report' before issuing the statement, which was evidence of 'prejudice and rashness'. The closure neglected 'the suggestion made by the public'. They protested that the 'high-handed policy' was against the wishes of parents, students and teachers, and demanded the reopening of the school.[35] To enlist public support, Szeto made use of the press and warned the public of the implications of the arbitrary incident. The rhetoric of 'law and order' was invoked: 'Closing the school is a rude move and is worrisome; if the policy is to continue the community will be [in] a state of disorder.'[36]

The campaign captured the public's attention. Newspaper coverage of the dispute expanded. According to 'Opinions', the incident 'continued to be a major talking point in the Chinese press and attracted no fewer than ten editorials'.[37] Although some newspapers were sympathetic, most reports disapproved of the campaign, an indication of political conservatism. *HKDN*, for example, felt that the 'major error' was the boycott of classes initiated by teachers and students.[38] *STYP* said that the campaign had developed into a social issue, which would 'adversely affect social stability': 'Anyone concerned with the security of Hong Kong is worried about the situation because Hong Kong is in a delicate position and any small trouble will bring undesirable effects.'[39]

One of the reasons behind this negative publicity was a perceived association with the leftists. In May 1977, a pro-Taiwan newspaper, *Wan Ren Jih Pao*, implied that it was the left-wing teachers who had blackmailed the principal.[40] By 1978, many newspapers suggested that the teachers were politically motivated. Some teachers were believed to have Trotskyite backgrounds. For example, Wai Wing-kwong, one of the teachers involved, was the President of Grantham College of Education Student Union from 1972 to 1973, when the Union was controlled by the pro-Chinese Communist fraction.[41] *SCMP* also speculated that the campaign was backed by leftist organisations, including the Marxists Revolutionary League, the Progressive Students and the October Review.[42] The potential connection between the campaign and leftists was also highlighted by a range of mainstream Chinese-language newspapers. *STYP* suggested that 'the issue is soon to blow up into a social campaign which smacks of a "mass struggle"'. The choice of the term 'mass struggle' associated the movement with the leftists, as this was a concept referring to Maoist strategies of political mobilisation.[43] *KSEN* condemned the 'group of subversive elements' as having 'ulterior motives' and 'waiting for the opportunities to disturb our social order to achieve their own ends'.⁴⁴ Some newspapers even compared the campaign with the 1967 leftist riots directly. *Oriental Daily* reported that a home-made bomb was found in the street:

> Looking back at 1967 when uncountable genuine and fake 'home-made bombs' were found, the consequence were casualties, disturbances of people's daily life and an economic recession ... The use of 'home-made bombs' is not the right way to solve the problem. It will only result in loss of lives or the problem of one school becoming the problem of the society as a whole.⁴⁵

The Express made similar connections, arguing that there were 'bad elements' 'exploiting innocent children', just like what happened in the 1967 riots.⁴⁶ This coverage linking the dispute with leftist activism deterred people from supporting the campaign, a conservative legacy of 1967.

The public's fear of disorder and political conservatism was also reflected in Sister Lorraine's public announcements. Her rhetoric revealed the society's emphasis on discipline and order:

> Discipline is the foundation of homes, schools and institutions which constitute civilised societies. If we sacrifice [it], we lose everything. There are ways and ways of complaining about alleged injustices. Sit-ins, marches, intimidation and abuse are not the right ways. The methods adopted by some teachers have disrupted one unhappy school, but the firm action of the authorities in closing the school rather than tolerate continued demonstrations of contempt for law, order and discipline there, must be supported by all right-thinking people.⁴⁷

She appealed for public support by suggesting that the Education Department's decision was right. Her speech reveals that 'radical' political activism was not mainstream.

How did newspaper coverage influence public opinion? According to MacLehose, 'there has not been much public sympathy for the sixteen teachers' and it appeared that most criticism against the school's closure derived from sympathy for the pupils whose education has been 'disrupted'.⁴⁸ This view was particularly common among the middle-aged and elderly groups, who showed 'strong misgiving and distrust towards the government in China' and remained 'the stronghold of anti-communist sentiments and convictions'.⁴⁹ Even the petition letter drafted by the Hong Kong Professional Teachers' Union acknowledged that 'the public at large and most sections of the press in Hong Kong' viewed the incident with 'indifference' and as an 'insult'.⁵⁰ The Hong Kong Subsidised Secondary Schools Council, for example, supported the closure of the school and argued that the Education Department had 'acted responsibly'. The Council believed that the campaign initiated by teachers and students had 'badly disrupted' the school's functioning and therefore the school should not remain open.⁵¹

The Hong Kong Council of the Church of Christ in China also issued a press release and endorsed the closure. It described the government's decision as a 'prompt action' which was 'justifiable' and disapproved of activism by students. It also appealed to the public to consider 'discipline as a prerequisite' for the operation of any schools in Hong Kong.[52]

Nonetheless, the campaign successfully solicited substantial support from some post-secondary students. About 370 post-secondary students, who were either Catholics or former pupils of Catholic schools, signed an open letter, demanding Bishop Wu to request the Education Department to reopen the school. These students intended to expand the publicity of the campaign by sending a petition to Pope Paul VI.[53] The Leimukshui Caritas Centre also handed in a petition to the bishop, urging him to consider the matter seriously. The petition was signed by more than 100 of its young members.[54] To press for the reopening of the school, Golden Jubilee pupils, wearing red arm bands inscribed with the slogan 'Return the Golden Jubilee to Us', gathered at the cathedral on the same day. The pupils were soon joined by more than 100 parents and 200 post-secondary students. They then issued a joint statement, revealing that they had formed an action committee to campaign for the reopening of the school. The statement claimed that they would continue having marathon sit-ins (two teachers at a time) and soliciting support from other organisations.[55] Some post-secondary students from the Chinese University of Hong Kong, the Hong Kong University and the Hong Kong Polytechnic University showed support for the movement by offering free tutorials to the affected students. About 200 of them volunteered to act as tutors. The HKFS was involved in coordinating the tutorials. The 400 students from the Golden Jubilee School were divided into nineteen groups, each led by a group of post-secondary students who had just finished their final exams. The tutorials started on 23 May 1978.[56]

In addition, the campaign was endorsed by staff in higher education. On 23 May, 205 staff and teachers from the University of Hong Kong issued a signed statement, expressing opposition to the Education Department's decision.[57] A joint statement urging the Education Department to investigate the matter before any interventions was signed by twenty-seven people.[58] A group of staff from the Chinese University of Hong Kong made use of newspapers to air their grievances. They claimed that they were 'astounded' by the Education Department's decision, which demonstrated that 'the true democracy is still beyond the reach of the people in Hong Kong'.[59] By suspending the operation of the school, they argued that the colonial administration had disregarded the feelings and grievances of the students, teachers and parents.[60] Apart from lecturers, twenty-four priests in Hong Kong issued a statement to express their 'deepest regrets'. They publicly endorsed the petition made by Szeto Wah and disapproved of the decision made by the Education Department, describing it as 'a judgement without trial for the sixteen teachers'. They also argued such 'injustice' should not be accepted by the Catholic Church.[61] In July, the campaign reached its climax. Thirty students from the Polytechnic and Baptist College escalated their action by starting a hunger strike outside the Bishop's Office, protesting against the school's closure.[62] The action was condemned by some newspapers. *KSEN*, for instance, argued that the hunger strikes 'make one feel that they have gone from reasoning to exerting pressure through threats'.[63] On 9 July, a demonstration was held, attended by 4,000 people. Four days later, a signature campaign was organised. 30,000 signatures were soon collected, indicating that the scale of the movement was considerable.[64]

Understanding their 'weak bargaining position' and possessing limited resources for mass mobilisation, as Lui and Chiu pointed out, activists often rallied the support of a third party to exert pressure on the colonial government.[65] The Golden Jubilee dispute was no exception. To press for the reopening of the school, activists attempted to obtain support in Britain. A pressure group, the Education Action Group, first petitioned MP Janet Fookes, informing her of the 'very shocking and unreasonable event' and persuading her to intervene in this 'arbitrary' and 'gross injustice'. They portrayed the closure of the school as a 'high-handed authoritarian attitude and action' which was widely condemned by community leaders, groups and organisations.[66] This petition led Fookes to write to David Owen, the Foreign Secretary, on 3 June 1978. On behalf of the students, parents and teachers, the Hong Kong Professional Teachers' Union also petitioned Gorowny Roberts, the Minister of State for Foreign Affairs, and a number of MPs, including Frank Hooley and Tony Benn, pressing for the reopening of the school. To enlist support, the organisation similarly claimed that the action taken by the Education Department was 'high handed, groundless and unjust', especially given that the sit-ins were 'peaceful'.[67] Although sit-ins and hunger strikes initiated by the students and teachers were not endorsed by the public, the rhetoric the Professional Teachers' Union employed strategically portrayed the school's closure as against the public interest:

> The high-handed measure of the Education Department has shocked the citizens of Hong Kong and the reluctance of the government to listen to the public opinions has prompted parents, teachers and students to decide to make representation to the members of Parliament in England despite the heavy expenses.[68]

In June, Wai wing-kwong and Fan May-yung, two of the teachers involved in the incident, visited London for two weeks to air their grievances to MPs.

The campaign attracted the attention of British MPs, in particular the Labour MP, Robert Perry, who asked eight questions regarding the Golden

Jubilee incident during parliamentary discussion on 28 June 1978. In the meeting of the Labour Party International Executive Committee, Joan Lestor also raised the subject of the Golden Jubilee dispute.[69] After some discussions, the Committee agreed to express concern and asked the Secretary of State for the provision of facts. They pressed David Owen for the publication of all the details of financial irregularities. They also wanted to ensure that no teachers were victimised.[70] On 20 July, the two teachers met with a group of Labour MPs, including Parry, James Johnson, James Lamond, Martin Flannery and Dennis Canavan. The activists seemed to have captured the sympathy of these MPs, who 'were mostly impressed with them and thought they had been treated shabbily'.[71] The campaign also received support from the Catholic Institute for International Relations, which believed that the incident was 'a blatant injustice'.[72] This foreign support put further pressure on the colonial government to respond to the campaign.

Apart from students and teachers of the school, a number of educational and religious organisations participated in the campaign, and they employed a wide range of strategies: organising demonstrations, sit-ins and signature campaigns, sending petitions and issuing public joint statements. To justify their demands, activists often presented the action taken by the colonial administration as unjust and against the public will. The rhetoric of 'law and order' was repeatedly invoked by activists who emphasised the potential negative consequences the arbitrary closure would have on the society's order. To exert pressure on the colonial state effectively, activists also solicited support from Labour MPs in London. The campaign, which captured the attention of people in the educational sector, shows the increasingly sophisticated organisational and networking skills of the young activists. Nonetheless, the campaign still met with opposition. Many newspapers disapproved of the student activism and compared the campaign with the 1967 riots, hinting that the activists were associated with violent leftists.

Government responses

Having been monitoring the situation closely, the colonial government assessed the potential public responses before making the decision to close the school:

> We expect the closure order to lead to some further demonstrations and a considerable amount of publicity in the press. The Professional Teachers' Union may complain that the sixteen are being unfairly treated. Some other schools may join in. But we doubt if support for the sixteen will be widespread, both because exams are now on and because their cause in itself will not be seen by many as worthy to support.[73]

To avoid similar events from reoccurring, the Executive Council advised the appointment of a Committee of Inquiry. Dr. Rayson Huang, the Vice Chancellor of the University of Hong Kong, a Legislative Councillor and a member of the Board of Education, became the Chairman.

After the school's closure, the colonial administration continued to monitor shifting public opinion through the CDOs and MOOD. The Foreign and Commonwealth Office used MOOD to assess responses to the campaign in Hong Kong. Most importantly, the content found in the telegram sent by MacLehose to the Foreign and Commonwealth Office on 31 May 1978 resembled closely the MOOD report published a week previously. On 24 May, MOOD described the mixed opinions found in society:

> Overall public reaction was still very mixed, different people taking different sides according to their own education background, convictions and basic attitudes. The government's publicity efforts to redress the balance during the next few days were successful to some extent in enabling the public to see the situation in better perspective ... Unfortunately, this message came rather late and the more critical sectors of the public were inclined to be incredulous ... There was still not much support for the sixteen teachers. Only radical students, free thinkers and critics of the government sympathised with them. However, there was much more sympathy towards the displaced students whose schooling had been thus disrupted ... Secondary and post-secondary students, were inclined to criticise the closure of the school as suppressive and draconian action.[74]

Similar records were found in the Governor's telegram:

> Vocal opinion is split fairly down the middle between those supporting and those opposing the government's action. Much of the criticism is directed at the closure itself and appears to have derived from sympathy for the pupils whose education has been disrupted ... There has not been much public sympathy for the sixteen teachers who claimed to have been victimised for revealing financial mismanagement of the school ... Nevertheless, the revelation of this earlier complaint has understandably caused confusion and some damage to the Education Department and government's credibility. Some people have clearly found it difficult to believe the true situation.[75]

The assessment by MOOD revealed that the secondary and post-secondary students were 'particularly sensitive and resentful to any government measure which appeared to them to be high-handed or dictatorial'.[76] In encountering the tutorial classes organised by radical post-secondary students, a non-interventionist approach was deliberately taken by the Education Department as it was believed that 'to do so [intervene] would have brought post-secondary students directly into the arena'.[77] It instead offered to place Golden Jubilee students in other schools.

The major intervention involved setting up a Committee of Inquiry. This was created to ensure that 'decisions would be taken on an intelligent understanding of community aspirations and sensitivities' and to respond to the call for 'more opportunities for public consultation'.[78] A 'public invitation' was issued to invite citizens to share their views on the incident.[79] Goronwy Roberts was aware of the public confusion regarding the incident, as revealed in MOOD. To reduce 'prevailing tension and distrust', he recommended the Director of Education to 'make public his findings of the financial mismanagement' of the school and make clarifications regarding the school's closure and its change of sponsorship.[80] The report of the Inquiry was soon published on 14 July. Public opinion influenced how the government responded to the incident, indicating changes in bureaucratic mentality and ruling strategies.

According to MOOD, the incident posed a debate about 'whether Hong Kong's education system aimed to produce such radical thinking graduates as teachers'.[81] There were worries that conflicts and danger would emerge if 'radical graduates like the Chan group were to be employed by institutions whose management and leadership belong to a conservative school'.[82] These concerns were central to investigations. On 5 October 1978, it was announced in the Executive Council that 'proposals to strengthen the Education Department will be put forward shortly'.[83] There would be 'extensive consultation'.[84] In the final report issued, the Committee of Inquiry urged the Education Department to 'examine whether it has sufficient capabilities in responding to grievances'. As the aided schools were not directly responsible for the colonial government, the Education Department was the statutory authority in charge of the operation of the sector. It was therefore crucial for the department to 'handle grievances at all levels' appropriately so that officials could understand 'the grassroots level, attitudes and feelings of the community they serve[d]'. By reviewing the department's capabilities, it could 'maintain the credibility of the government and the community's confidence in it'.[85] This strongly suggests that the government's perceptions of public opinion fed into the policymaking process; the channels of political participation were widened covertly in a state-controlled manner.

The colonial administration did not only monitor changing popular sentiment in Hong Kong, but also in Britain. The Hong Kong and General Department closely observed the situation in the United Kingdom and ruled that 'there has been no Parliamentary, press or public interest in the disturbances'.[86] Despite the lack of interest in Britain, William Quantrill pointed out that the financial mismanagement and the fact that the school's administrators 'were trying to take a more enlightened and progressive approach to education' could 'attract attention here', and hence 'win them more sympathy than they probably deserved'. He therefore suggested to 'keep ourselves informed'.[87] The publicity of the campaign expanded to Britain in mid-1978 when the teachers petitioned the MPs and visited London. When the teachers, with the support of the Labour MPs, requested to meet with the Minister of State in London, the Hong Kong and General Department assessed potential public responses:

> A blunt refusal to receive the teachers at all would however appear discourteous, and might attract criticism from the MPs and trade unionists who have interested themselves in this case. I therefore recommend that the teachers should be offered a meeting with officials as an alternative to one with the Minister of State.[88]

In the end, Robin McLaren met with the two teachers.

Although it was observed that the situation was 'beginning to quieten down' and 'press coverage is getting less extensive' in late May 1978, the colonial government continued to monitor popular sentiment. With the support of the Labour MPs, the activists pressurised the colonial state to make concessions. In July, the Committee of Inquiry recommended establishing an additional new school, Ng Yuk School, alongside the St. Teresa Secondary School (formerly Golden Jubilee Secondary School) to 'accommodate those who do not accept the arrangements announced by the supervisor'.[89] Parents and students were at liberty to enrol at either institution. To ease discontent among the teachers, the Committee of Inquiry advised that invitations of teacher post applications should be sent to those who were not offered a contract extension at St. Teresa Secondary School.[90] Before the Committee of Inquiry published the final report, the Executive Council assessed the public's potential response: 'It is considered that the Final Report is likely to be acceptable to the public at large, who would see it as [a] satisfactory end to an issue which might have had more serious repercussions on the community had it not been handled judiciously and expeditiously.'[91] This indicates that public opinion was taken into consideration in the policymaking process. Foreseeing the unlikelihood of public disquiet, the final report was soon translated into Chinese on 4 September and published in the public domain on 31 October.

The publication of the Final Report 'was widely reported by all dailies'.[92] All Chinese newspapers, except *HKT*, mentioned the report. The report stated that the decision to close the school should not be made by the Education Department alone, but by the Governor-in-Council. The report was widely welcomed by the press. *Ming Pao*, for example, described the investigation as 'impartial' and 'unbiased' and praised the 'reasonable recommendations', which could set an example in dealing with other disputes in the future.[93] *STYP* believed that the recommendations could prevent similar events from occurring.[94] *KSEN* called the report 'a piece of marvellous work' and said 'the public was satisfied' with it.[95] Even Urban Councillor Elsie Elliott publicly asserted that the proposals in the report were good, given that they were implemented by the colonial administration.[96]

This section has revealed how public opinion had influenced the colonial government in handling the Golden Jubilee disputes. Ever since the emergence of the campaign, the state monitored shifting popular attitudes towards the incident. This 'public opinion', which was collected through the covert formal institution of MOOD and the supervision of mass media, was subsequently fed back to high-ranked civil servants, directly influencing the state's ruling strategies. This demonstrates that, on the one hand, the government possessed the organisational means to understand the changing sentiments of the Chinese communities, a manifestation of 'covert colonialism'; on the other hand, the Hong Kong Chinese, in particular the young generation, were able to influence decisions made by the government although they still could not participate in politics through democratic elections.

Political culture

As Lam has pointed out, 'as more actions took place, divisions in the society regarding the dispute became increasingly explicit'.[97] On the one hand, there was political activism initiated by the teachers and students, supported by the youth; on the other hand, 'the culture of depoliticisation' prevailed.[98] It remains unclear whether social class and age had an important effect on the dispute. This section investigates the social composition of the protest using newspapers and official opinion polls.

Initially, the public 'at large did not pay much attention to the dispute'.[99] It was when the sit-ins at Caritas took place that the public engaged with the incident. The public in general was 'confused and bewildered by conflicting reports, accusations and recriminations from both sides'.[100] Before the closure of the school, the demonstrations and sit-ins had already attracted 'widespread criticism', particularly from parents, headmasters, the middle class and community leaders; they described this political activism as 'an undesirable and dangerous method of airing grievances by junior students'.[101] The adult members of society were politically conservative and inclined to view the teachers as 'trouble-makers' and 'rabble-rousers', who exploited the teenage students.[102] MOOD suggested that there was 'not much support for the sixteen teachers', especially after the school's closure and the appointment of the Committee of Inquiry.[103] Only 'radical students', 'free thinkers' and 'critics of the government' were sympathetic to their cause.[104]

These negative reactions were found in both Chinese and English-language newspapers. *SCMP* repeatedly denounced student activism. It labelled the two-day sit-in as 'extreme' and described it as 'militarism'. It asserted that 'the last thing Hong Kong wants is a wave of student militancy over real or imagined grievances at schools'.[105] Both *KSDN* and *The HKT* similarly condemned the 'trouble-makers' who had 'stirred up the students'.[106] The *KSDN* claimed that the dissenting teachers were 'politically motivated', whose aim was to 'destroy the free society in Hong Kong'.[107] The *HKDN* argued that the demonstrations and sit-ins led by the teachers 'run counter to the education system and the basic principles which the community cherished'.[108] *STMP* also believed that teachers should not offer any encouragement to students to organise political activities.[109] Teachers' and students' reluctance to redress their grievances through formal channels 'failed to win public support' and showed their case 'in a bad light'.[110] These views were particularly prevalent among middle-aged and elderly householders, who mostly supported the decision made by the Education Department.[111]

Most people regardless of age were unwilling to take sides in the campaign as they were confused about the chronological development of the event. This was partly because the event was not fully covered by media: 'the further friction and confrontation in the school that afternoon was not clearly reported and consequently not known by public'.[112] Most importantly, the communities in general 'were anxious to avoid "rocking the boat"'.[113] Most people disapproved of any action that might create political or social tensions: 'Harmony and stability of society were considered to be of paramount importance.'[114] Direct confrontations, such as sit-ins and hunger strikes, were considered 'radical actions' which 'could never get the support from the mass'.[115] Political conservatism continued to prevail among many in the colony, especially when the event did not directly affect people's lives.

Besides, the campaign itself failed to enlist public sympathy, probably because the propagation of causes such as 'injustice', 'democracy' and 'anticolonialism' was not particularly appealing to the general public. As MOOD has pointed out earlier, lower-income groups, especially blue-collar workers, were only concerned with their 'workaday livelihood' and 'problems affecting their family'.[116] They rarely worried or cared about other issues.[117] These grassroots groups remained 'largely indifferent' to how Hong Kong was governed provided that they were not affected.[118] In 1975, MOOD also had found that there was 'no general public aspiration or pressure for constitutional reform': 'Majority attitudes indicate a lack of enthusiasm about elections.'[119] The middle class either was 'indifferent' or advocated 'caution'.[120] Many doubted if a limited representative government would 'really make much difference'.[121] Rhetoric such as 'democracy' and 'anticolonialism' therefore did not generate substantial support from the local people, who might consider the closure of the school irrelevant to their daily livelihood.

By the late 1970s, the political culture of the young generation and social elites was, however, changing. As MOOD pointed out, attitudes towards the event 'varied considerably according to age and education background'.[122] During the early period, the teachers successfully lobbied support from some post-secondary students. A state opinion poll earlier in 1975 had suggested that students and youth tended to hold significantly different and unfavourable views of the colonial government than their elders.[123] Their 'idealistic outlook on life' led many of them to be 'intolerant of a paternalistic type of government', 'distrustful of compromise' and 'impatient in their wait for an egalitarian government'.[124] In 1975, it was predicted by MOOD that their pursuit of social and political participation would only continue to rise.[125] Despite the merits of the colonial administration's consultation policy, the young generation still became 'more aggressive and presumptuous'.[126] In the Golden Jubilee dispute, these post-secondary student leaders suspected Kwan of being 'reactionary and disciplinarian, and deliberately vindictive and suppressive against the Chan group'.[127] They urged the Education Department to carry out a detailed investigation before declaring its support for the new principal. Apart from secondary students, MOOD also reported that post-secondary students and the younger generation tended to criticise the closure of the school as 'suppressive'.[128] They were 'sensitive' and 'resentful' towards any state responses which appeared to them as 'high-handed' and 'dictatorial'.[129] Despite their disapproval of political activism, the established middle-aged bourgeoisie also did not support the government's measure. They believed that such 'strong line' policy would only threaten social order.[130] The Committee of Inquiry's Final Report attributed this political activism to increased education: 'In a progressing community like Hong Kong, with [a] steadily rising level of education, there is inevitably [a] trend of rising expectations and increasing social awareness.'[131] This was particularly true as the schooling in Hong Kong was moving towards the direction of 'mass access' in the 1970s. Universal primary education was achieved in 1971, followed by the implementation of three-year compulsory government-funded education in secondary schools in 1978.[132] The emergence of parents who were part of an educated 'large middle class' in the 1970s also made it increasingly difficult for schools to meet their high expectations.[133] As the incident has revealed, the political culture in Hong Kong was far from monolithic. Different attitudes were held by people in different social classes and age groups.

Conclusion

The Golden Jubilee incident was 'an eye-opener' for the public, in particular those with a conservative mindset.[134] In order to obtain attention from senior civil servants, the teachers and students exposed an example of 'corruption' to the public through the organisation of sit-ins and hunger strikes, and by attracting media coverage. During the campaign, the activists displayed a remarkable capacity for organisation. The networking capacity of activists gave them an effective way of communicating with post-secondary students, educational and religious organisations, and even MPs in London. They were able therefore to organise large-scale sit-ins and pressurise the colonial government to set up a Committee of Inquiry to monitor public opinion closely.

As for the colonial government, since the beginning of the campaign, state monitoring of public opinion – through systematic analysis of newspapers and using MOOD – informed how it managed the incident. This shows that the bureaucratic mentality was changing and the channels of political participation had been widened despite the extent to which it was still largely controlled by the state.

Lastly, the campaign shows how the political culture of the educated young generation and social elites, who were at the 'political centre', was changing. Motivated by ideological concerns, such as social justice, democracy and anti-colonialism, they engaged in different forms of political acts and gained support from their peers and the politicians. Despite considerable support from the post-secondary students and educational sector, the campaign failed to enlist support from the general public. Political conservatism was prevalent but attitudes differed from group to group. Most middle-aged and elderly people were conservative, worried about political stability. Some grassroots groups considered the campaign irrelevant to their lives. Middle-aged and elderly householders accused dissenting teachers and students of being troublemakers. In this case, however, conservatism arose from a perception reinforced by the press that the campaign was linked to leftist activism. Moreover, concepts such as 'injustice', 'democracy' and 'anti-colonialism' propagated by the activists were probably unappealing to many people concerned primarily with their livelihood, who lacked enthusiasm to engage in debates about how the state was governing a colonial society.

Notes

1 Lam, *Understanding the Political Culture*, p. 172.
2 Loh, *Underground Front*, p. 99.
3 Lam, *Understanding the Political Culture*, pp. 177–8.
4 Ibid., p. 180.
5 Morris and Sweeting, 'Education and Politics', p. 258.
6 Ibid.
7 FCO 40/1002, 'Summary of Event', Education Acting Group, 1978, p. 1.
8 Ibid.; The academic and apolitical orientation was strong in the education system in Hong Kong up until the early 1980s, see Morris and Sweeting, 'Education and Politics'.

9 'Summary of Event', p. 1.
10 FCO 40/1002, 'Precious Blood Secondary School', MacLehose to FCO, 12 May 1978.
11 FCO 40/1002, 'Precious Blood Secondary School', MacLehose to FCO, 31 May 1978.
12 'Precious Blood Secondary School', MacLehose to FCO, 12 May 1978.
13 '金禧學生週記一束', 金禧事件發展特刊 (*CU Student: Golden Jubilee Incident Special Edition*), 4 November 1977.
14 'Summary of Event', p. 2.
15 '金禧事件交代', 金禧事件發展特刊 (*CU Student: Golden Jubilee Incident Special Edition*), 4 November 1977.
16 '與金禧同學的一席話', 金禧事件發展特刊 (*CU Student: Golden Jubilee Incident Special Edition*).
17 Higher-form students' school bags were searched by non-academic staff without previous warnings and legitimate reasons. Many considered this a violation of privacy. See '校方剝奪了我們的權益有幾多?我數之不盡!', *CU Student*, 10:2, 14 June 1978.
18 FCO 40/1002, 'Union Chief Gets Reprimand', *SCMP*, 16 May 1978.
19 'Precious Blood Secondary School', MacLehose to FCO, 12 May 1978.
20 FCO 40/1002, 'Call for Principal to Resign', *SCMP*, 10 May 1978.
21 'Precious Blood Secondary School', MacLehose to FCO, 12 May 1978.
22 FCO 40/1002, 'Precious Blood Secondary School Dispute', MacLehose to FCO, 28 June 1978.
23 Lam, *Understanding the Political Culture*, pp. 176 and 178.
24 HKRS 70-8-1207, 'Opinions', Chinese Press Review, no. 69, 10–16 May 1978, p. 1.
25 Ibid.
26 Ibid.
27 Ibid.
28 HKRS 70-8-1207, '學生表示沉痛 教師指為報復 家長要求解釋', *TTYP*, 15 May 1978.
29 HKRS 70-8-1207, '蓋棺論功過 教署是罪人', *TTYP*, 16 May 1978.
30 'Opinions', Chinese Press Review, no. 69, 10–16 May 1978, p. 2.
31 FCO 40/1002, 'Government Picks Up Tempo', *HKS*, 16 May 1978.
32 FCO 40/1002, Szeto Wah to MacLehose, 16 May 1978, p. 1.
33 Ibid., p. 2.
34 Ibid.
35 FCO 40/1003, Letter from 'Representative of Teachers, Parents and Students' to Colvyn Haye, 19 May 1978.
36 HKRS 70-8-1207, '教協會長司徒華心所謂危談金禧 封校粗暴令人心憂 此風一長天下大亂', *STYP*, 15 May 1978.
37 HKRS 70-8-1207, 'Opinions', Chinese Press Review, no. 72, 31 May–6 June 1978, p. 1.
38 Ibid.
39 Ibid., p. 2.

40 Lam, *Understanding the Political Culture*, p. 172.
41 Back in 1972, Wai was convicted of unlawful assembly. See FCO 40/1002, 'Precious Blood Secondary School', MacLehose to FCO, 26 June 1978.
42 FCO 40/1002, 'HKU Chief to Lead Inquiry', *SCMP*, 17 May 1978.
43 'Opinions', *Chinese Press Review*, no. 72, 31 May–6 June 1978, p. 1. Maoism adhered to a 'mass-line' agenda, in which populism was emphasised. It was believed that the masses, including the rural peasants, embodied 'great social activism'. Revolutions could only be successful if the peasant mass were mobilised. See Meisner, *Mao's China and After*, pp. 41–5.
44 HKRS 70-8-1208, '陰謀者悄悄等候機會', *KSEN*, 29 May 1978.
45 HKRS 70-8-1208, '請收起土製菠蘿', *Oriental Daily*, 17 May 1978.
46 HKRS 70-8-1208, '當心,不要做別人的犧牲品!', *Express*, 19 May 1978.
47 FCO 40/1002, Extract from GIS, 21 May 1978.
48 'Precious Blood Secondary School', MacLehose to FCO, 31 May 1978.
49 HKRS 471-3-1, 'Current Attitudes of the Hong Kong Public towards China', MOOD, 23 October 1978, p. 3.
50 FCO 40/1002, 'The Parent-Teacher-Pupil Committee for the Reopening of the Precious Blood Golden Jubilee School', the Hong Kong Professional Teachers' Union to Gorowny Roberts, 30 June 1978.
51 HKRS 70-8-1204, 'Press Release on the Closure of the Precious Blood Golden Jubilee School', by Hong Kong Subsidised Secondary Schools Council, 22 May 1978.
52 HKRS 70-8-1204, 'The C.C.C. Express Concern', by Peter Wong, General Secretary of the Hong Kong Council of the Church of Christ in China, 22 May 1978.
53 'HKU Chief to Lead Inquiry'.
54 FCO 40/1002, 'School Girls "Enter" College', *SCMP*, 23 May 1978.
55 Ibid.
56 FCO 40/1002, 'Temporary Tutors Offer Help to Students', *HKS*, 23 May 1978.
57 Ibid.
58 Ibid.
59 FCO 40/1002, 'Government Must Review Decision on School', by 'Staff Members of the Chinese University of Hong Kong', *SCMP*, 20 May 1978.
60 Ibid.
61 'HKU Chief to Lead Inquiry'.
62 HKRS 457-3-140, 'School Sympathisers Begin Hunger Strike', *HKS*, 8 July 1978.
63 'Opinions', Chinese Press Review, 5–11 July 1978.
64 Lam, *Understanding the Political Culture*, pp. 177–8.
65 Lui and Chiu, *The Dynamics of Social Movements*, p. 8.
66 FCO 40/1002, Anthony Ha, Education Action Group to Janet Fookes, 24 May 1978, pp. 1–2.
67 'The Parent-Teacher-Pupil Committee for the Reopening of the Precious Blood Golden Jubilee School', p. 1.
68 Ibid., pp. 3–4.

69 FCO 40/1002, 'Labour Party NEC International Committee: The Golden Jubilee School, Hong Kong', David Stephan to Robin McLaren, 11 July 1978.
70 FCO 40/1002, Jenny Little to David Owen, 18 July 1978.
71 FCO 40/1002, 'Precious Blood School-Meeting with MPs', FCO to MacLehose, 20 July 1978.
72 FCO 40/1002, Eileen Sudworth, the Catholic Institute for International Relations to FCO, 14 July 1978.
73 Ibid.
74 FCO 40/1002, 'The Golden Jubilee Controversy', MOOD, 24 May 1978, p. 5.
75 'Precious Blood Secondary School', MacLehose to FCO, 31 May 1978.
76 'The Golden Jubilee Controversy', p. 5.
77 'Precious Blood Secondary School', MacLehose to FCO, 31 May 1978.
78 'The Golden Jubilee Controversy', p. 5.
79 'Precious Blood Secondary School', MacLehose to FCO, 31 May 1978.
80 FCO 40/1002, 'M.I.P.T', G. Roberts to FCO, 7 July 1978.
81 'The Golden Jubilee Controversy', p. 6.
82 Ibid.
83 FCO 40/1002, 'Final Report of the Committee of Enquiry of the Precious Blood Golden Jubilee Secondary School', Memorandum for Executive Council, 5 October 1978, p. 7.
84 Ibid.
85 FCO 40/1003, Rayson Huang and Maisie Wong, 'Precious Blood Golden Jubilee Secondary School: Final Report', Committee of Inquiry, 31 October 1978, p. 33.
86 FCO 40/1002, 'Trouble at the Precious Blood Secondary School', M. J. Upton to Q. Quantrill and R. McLaren, 2 June 1978.
87 FCO 40/1002, Note by W. Quantrill, 2 June 1978.
88 FCO 40/1002, 'Hong Kong: Precious Blood Golden Jubilee Secondary School', R. J. T McLaren to MacLehose, 3 July 1978.
89 'M.I.P.T'.
90 Ibid.
91 'Final Report of the Committee of Enquiry of the Precious Blood Golden Jubilee Secondary School'.
92 HKRS 457-3-141, Chinese Press Summary, 1 November 1978.
93 HKRS 457-3-141, Extract from Chinese Press Review, 2 November 1978, p. 1.
94 Ibid, p. 2.
95 HKRS 70-8-1206, 'Final Report on the Golden Jubilee Affairs', Chinese Press Review, 1–7 November 1978.
96 HKRS 457-3-141, Extract from Chinese Press Summary, 2 November 1978, p. 1.
97 Lam, *Understanding the Political Culture*, p. 176.
98 Ibid.
99 'The Golden Jubilee Controversy', p. 1.
100 Ibid.
101 Ibid.

102 Ibid., p. 2.
103 Ibid., p. 4.
104 Ibid.
105 HKRS 70-8-1208, 'A Firm "No" to School Militants', *SCMP*, 11 May 1978; FCO 40/1002, 'Discouraging School Sit-ins', *SCMP*, 19 June 1978.
106 HKRS 70-8-1207, 'Opinions', Chinese Press Review, no. 69, 10–16 May 1978, p. 1.
107 HKRS 70-8-1207, '學生及家長同感焦慮 就心未來學業問題 指擾事者應負全責', *Kung Sheung Daily News* (*KSDN* hereafter), 15 May 1978; 'Opinions', Chinese Press Review, no. 22, 15–21 June 1978, p. 2.
108 'Opinions', Chinese Press Review, no. 69, 10–16 May 1978, p. 1.
109 HKRS 70-8-1208, '保持良好學風', *STMP*, 20 June 1977.
110 'The Golden Jubilee Controversy', p. 1.
111 Ibid., p. 5.
112 Ibid.
113 Ibid.
114 Ibid.
115 FCO 40/1003, D. C. Bray to P. Leung, 24 July 1978.
116 HKRS 925-1-1, 'Public Attitude towards Living in Hong Kong', MOOD, 25 September 1975, p. 5.
117 Ibid.
118 HKRS 925-1-1, '1975 in Retrospect: Part II', MOOD, 8 January 1976, p. 4.
119 HK9S 925-1-1, 'Dr. L. K. Ding's Proposals for Constitutional Reform: Reaction Unenthusiastic', MOOD, 20 March 1975.
120 Ibid.
121 Ibid.
122 'The Golden Jubilee Controversy', p. 5.
123 HKRS 925-1-1, 'Changes in Public Attitude towards the Hong Kong Government', MOOD, 18 September 1975.
124 Ibid.
125 Ibid.
126 Ibid.
127 'The Golden Jubilee Controversy', p. 2.
128 Ibid., p. 5.
129 Ibid.
130 Ibid.
131 'Precious Blood Golden Jubilee Secondary School: Final Report', p. 33.
132 Sweeting, *Education in Hong Kong*, p. 237.
133 Morris, *Hong Kong School Curriculum*, p. 148.
134 'The Golden Jubilee Controversy', p. 6.

6

The changing immigration discourse and policy

> A small integrated community with resources appropriate to its size surely has a right to protection against an inundation of strangers. This is an internationally accepted principle, and Hong Kong's own pre-war and more recent history has shown that it can and must be applied when the situation becomes threatening – or when the government wakes up to its responsibilities to its established citizens. Why was the situation ever allowed to develop into the vast problem that now faces the government? Was it assumed that up to one million immigrants could be assimilated to an acceptable degree and in reasonable time?[1]

The piece was written in 1956 by Chief Secretary, Claude Burgess and was re-quoted by Secretary for Information, David Ford in a speech, 'The Price of Freedom' in June 1979. By then, the statement possessed a new meaning. To justify the new immigration policy, Ford employed Burgess's statement but deliberately omitted the answer provided by Burgess to these questions he raised in 1956:

> The answer to these questions may fall oddly on modern ears. The immigrants were admitted on humanitarian grounds alone and the problems to which they would give rise if they did not return or emigrate elsewhere were deliberately accepted. The first influx fled from the shattered economy and threat of famine which followed the Pacific War. The people who followed in the second influx voted with their feet against the new regime which was established when the Nationalists withdrew to Formosa. In either case the immigrants sought in Hong Kong something sufficiently important to themselves to necessitate the abandonment of their homes, the severance of family ties and the renunciation of traditional allegiances. No one will ever know what it cost them to abandon the land on which their ancestors had made their living. They were not denied what they sought, and Hong Kong accepted the burden which they brought with them in the name of humanity rather than because it had any special standing in the matter other than the accident of contiguity.[2]

Ford argued that Burgess's statement was 'as relevant today as it was 23 years ago'. The situation was different, however, in the 1970s because illegal immigration was 'unacceptably high' and the present rate of immigration would yield at least one and a half million people in three years. The central problem for Ford was that the increase would hinder the government's Ten-Year Housing Programme planned in 1972. Ford noted that this plan was 'ambitious': it aimed to rehouse 1.8 million people.[3] Ford's statement highlighted that immigration from China was a major problem for the colonial government and one that affected its relationship with Hong Kong people. This chapter examines the relationship between the changing public discourse on immigration and the colonial state's immigration policy. Illegal immigration became a serious issue in Hong Kong from the late 1960s because it strained the colony's under-developed housing stock and welfare and education systems.

Agnes Ku has argued that the colonial government's shift from 'a policy of tolerant acceptance' to exclusionary immigration practices – such as the introduction of 'Hong Kong belonger' as an immigration category, the deprivation of illegal immigrants' rights to apply for identity cards and the ending of the 'Touch Base' policy had 'unintentionally' invoked 'a set of inclusionary and exclusionary mechanisms', which transformed the refugee mentality of Hong Kong Chinese and gave rise to a new political culture in the 1970s.[4] This aligns with the consensus that Hong Kong's political, cultural and economic separation from mainland China gave rise to the Hong Kong identity in the 1970s.[5]

The public's attitude towards migrants had shifted since the 1940s and 1950s, the first wave of post-war migration. Nonetheless, historical work that focuses specifically on the 1970s is limited.[6] Hong Kong's political culture was changing during the 1970s, as previous chapters have demonstrated, but how did a reformist polity set a new policy towards immigration from China, and how did this relate to shifting public opinion? The chapter explores these dynamic effects by reconstructing unofficial discourse regarding immigration and linking this cultural analysis with policy changes. It argues that the relationship between popular discourse and policy was dynamic in the sense that new policy measures affected popular attitudes in the early 1970s and the relationship changed after the mid-1970s. These shifting relationships were further complicated by the changing state of international relations: new Hong Kong immigration policies were controversial in Taiwan and the PRC. They were used by the Nationalists to undermine communist China, which argued that the colonial government's repatriation policy was aiding the 'tyranny of enslavement and oppression'.[7]

Managing 'the problem of people'

In the early 1950s, as Chi-kwan Mark has pointed out, a 'lenient approach' was adopted by the colonial government in handling immigrants. From May 1950, there was a quota system which restricted the number of people entering from China to be equal to that of those leaving Hong Kong, but this policy was 'not strictly enforced'.[8] The colonial administration had limited internal funds for resettlement programmes, and piecemeal funding from the Nationalists, the US and the UN was insufficient for a comprehensive set of measures to support refugees. Seeking more financial support from Taiwan and the US also risked entangling Hong Kong in Cold War politics.[9]

Colonial policy changed from 1956. Earlier in 1951, the UN Convention Relating to the Status of Refugees defined 'refugees' as people who were unable or unwilling to return to their country of nationality due to a 'well-founded fear of persecution', which could be caused by various reasons such as 'political opinion, race, religion, nationality or membership of a particular social group'.[10] As Jordanna Bailkin argued, in the Cold War context, the term 'refugees' was a 'product of oppressive totalitarian regimes that preyed on their own citizenship'.[11] Employing it in Hong Kong therefore could lead to political controversies, in particular raising questions about the PRC's sovereign rights over these Chinese nationals and providing opportunities for the Nationalists to exploit this issue. The increase in Chinese immigrants also imposed strains on the colony's housing, welfare and education systems.

Understanding the implications of the term 'refugees' and realising the 'permanent nature' of inward immigration, the colonial government started labelling mainland immigrants as 'illegal immigrants' instead of 'refugees' and identified their influx as a 'problem of people' with serious economic, social and political implications.[12] The colonial government believed the ultimate solution to 'the problem of people' was to turn 'potential troublemakers into responsible residents' through 'local integration', which could also restore people's confidence after the 1956 riots.[13] Rapid industrialisation, which relied on low-cost labour, provided abundant job opportunities for immigrants. It also generated higher revenues for the government and allowed it to expand social services in line with population growth.

In 1962, Hong Kong experienced another influx of Chinese immigrants due to the Great Leap Forward, which caused famine across China. In response to the 'exodus', the Hong Kong government applied a 'turning back doctrine': illegal immigrants were to be returned once they crossed the border.[14] From 1962 to 1967, the government allowed, under a quota system, fifty legal immigrants to enter Hong Kong per day. It repatriated the rest. This policy was abandoned in 1967 'as a consequence of the trouble caused by the Cultural Revolution', when clashes and violence broke out repeatedly on the border.[15]

By the 1970s, the 'local integration' policy became impracticable due to the scale of immigration from China. The number of illegal immigrants increased at an unprecedented rate. The annual figure of illegal immigrants increased from less than 8,000 during the period from 1968 to 1970 to 18,000 in 1973. These figures did not include illegal immigrants that had successfully reached the urban area. It was estimated that 'for every one caught, two entered undetected' and 'the actual number of illegal immigrants from China might be anything from two times to three times the number detected by the police'.[16] The number of legal immigrants also increased from under 2,000 to nearly 74,000 in the same period.[17] It was estimated that about 56,000, 75 per cent of the total, would 'settle permanently' in the colony.[18] In 1974, the population density in some parts of Kowloon was 'ten times that of Tokyo'. The welfare system and housing were both under extreme pressure.[19]

Job opportunities and the relatively high level of economic development seemed to be the primary pull factors for migrants. As James Callaghan, the Secretary of State for Foreign Affairs, pointed out, 'in many cases the motive has been as much one of economic self-interest as a well-founded fear of political persecution'.[20] Many came to what they perceived as a 'paradise', 'with the hope of enjoying better living'.[21] The chaotic political situation in China during the Cultural Revolution also served as push factors, pushing people to escape to Hong Kong. The relative low quality of life, such as 'the day-to-day life of the commune', which was 'physically demanding and materially unrewarding', continued to motivate many to move to Hong Kong illegally.[22]

As Ford acknowledged, the scale of new immigration created a real problem for the colonial government, at a time when it was trying to increase per capita spending on social infrastructure, on housing in particular. It was estimated that an additional $300 million would have to be spent on housing, medical facilities and education due to the influx of population from China.[23] It was difficult for the colonial government to house all these migrants under the existing housing programmes.[24]

The 'Touch Base' policy reduced the number of illegal immigrants from 7,105 in 1974 to only 583 in the first half of 1975.[25] In the long run, however, it failed to stop the influx of immigrants from China. The number of both legal and illegal immigrants continued to rise. The daily average figure of legal immigration remained high. As Table 6.1 shows, in 1978, the average number of legal immigrants entering Hong Kong from China per day increased from ninety-two in January to 149 in April. The number of illegal immigrants was also showing a sharp increase, as shown in Table 6.2 which sets out statistics for the first quarter of 1978. The number of illegal immigrants arrested in April 1978 was the 'highest arrest figure since repatriation commenced on 30 November 1974'.[26]

Table 6.1 Legal immigration from China to Hong Kong in 1978

Month/1978	Average per day
January	92
February	97
March	114
April	149

FCO 40/1005, 'Entrants from China and Macao', by A. J. Carter, 3 February and 8 April 1978.

Throughout the late 1970s, additional measures were introduced to cope with the high level of immigration from China, such as the setting up of a Ship Searching Unit, the amendment of legislation to grant police the authority to arrest illegal immigrants who had stayed in Hong Kong for two years, the implementation of a new immigration bill to prosecute people aiding illegals and increased fines and imprisonment. Nevertheless, the number of illegal immigrants did not drop. During the 'peak time' in June 1979, the figure reached an average of 625 a day.[27] Up until October 1979, 57,000 illegal immigrants were arrested.[28] Press coverage on immigration increased and popular sentiment shifted, which forced Hong Kong to negotiate with China, ending the 'Touch Base' policy in October 1980.

Negotiating the 'Touch Base' policy

With the end of the economic embargo imposed by the US and the admission into the UN in 1971, China's relation with the West improved, providing an opportunity for the British and colonial governments to negotiate with the PRC over the issue of immigration. A number of factors, however,

Table 6.2 Number of illegal immigrants arrested in 1978

Month/1978	Number of illegal immigrants arrested
January	197
February	199
March	165
April	308

FCO 40/1005, 'Entrants from China and Macao', by A. J. Carter, 4 March and May 1978.

created obstacles to reaching a mutual agreement on Hong Kong's immigration control. First, immigration from China to Hong Kong had always been loosely regulated due to the tradition of free movement of people. To effectively reduce immigration, it was essential for China to agree to reduce the number of legal permits issued and receive illegal immigrants that were sent back by Hong Kong. Second, the differences in two legislative and judiciary systems constituted a problem. The colonial government had to develop a standard measure of repatriation that complied with colonial laws. Third, immigration policies enacted and implemented by Hong Kong had to have the backing of the British government, which might prioritise improved Sino-British relations over Hong Kong's interests. Fourth, to reduce the risk of international criticism, Britain had to adopt a consistent liberal humanitarian policy on immigrants. The complexities made swift resolution unfeasible. These factors hindered the repatriation process.

Before the early 1970s, there were no formal modalities on how illegal immigrants from China should be returned. There was neither agreement nor coordination between China and Hong Kong. The Guangdong Authorities often requested the return of particular groups of illegal immigrants after they had been living in Hong Kong for a long period of time. It was extremely difficult to arrest them when many of them had already gained residence and settled in the colony.[29] Also, Guangdong only pursued cases that were related to groups of criminals who had violated Chinese laws, often without a formal request from the Ministry of Foreign Affairs. Uncertainty regarding legal process further complicated the returning of illegal immigrants to China.[30] Given these complexities, the colonial administration needed to lay down modalities of returns before appropriate measures could be taken.

The increase in the scale of immigration combined with critical press coverage of the issue drove the colonial government to consider tightening immigration controls. The normalisation of Sino-British relations allowed negotiations with China to take place in November 1973. On 27 November, it was agreed that legal immigrants should be kept to seventy-five a day. Nevertheless, the daily flow of immigrants seemed to have exceeded this level.[31] In February 1974, regular meetings between Hong Kong's Political Advisers and New China News Agency's (NCNA) representatives were set up. The strategy was simple: first to reach an agreement with China on legal immigration before any discussions of illegal immigration. The aim was to keep the number of legal immigrants down to about fifty a day.[32] In a telegram to the Foreign and Commonwealth Office, the British Foreign Secretary Alec Douglas-Home stated that he would be 'grateful' if Political Advisers 'would confine yourself [themselves] to probing the latest Chinese position on legal immigration' and 'would not volunteer anything about illegal immigration'.³³ Given the legal complexity involved in returning illegal immigrants, MacLehose also preferred 'not to mention' this matter 'until Hong Kong introduced a control on legal immigration'.³⁴ By making arbitrary decisions regarding illegal immigration, the Governor was concerned that it 'would expose ourselves [the colonial government] to charges of corruption'.³⁵

For China, tightening control on illegal emigration was desirable. This was because illegal immigrants were 'very seldom refugees' but mostly 'young people from town who dislike[d] having been sent to work on farms or others who prefer[ed] the comparative ease of Hong Kong'.³⁶ Therefore, the absence of effective controls over illegal emigration would reduce the size of the labour workforce and subsequently the country's productivity. Through taking control over illegal emigration, China could also discourage Hong Kong's representations.

From the viewpoint of the colonial government, it was essential to 'separate the questions of immigration control and the extradition of wanted criminals'. Yet, the Chinese government often refused to comply with the requirements of the Extradition Ordinance and send witnesses to Hong Kong when requesting the return of some criminals back to China.³⁷ During a meeting in Shenzhen, NCNA representatives expressed that there were no difficulties for the Hong Kong authorities to return illegal immigrants caught at the frontier back in 1961 and 1962. The Political Advisor of Hong Kong therefore believed that what the Chinese government wanted was to 'return to the pre-67 situation' in which there was a quota of fifty legal immigrants a day and the colonial government returned all illegal immigrants detected at the borders.³⁸ However, since 1968, the regular control at the border had been lifted and the colonial government believed that illegal immigrants who had engaged in criminal activities should be viewed as a matter of extradition.³⁹ Despite the desire to return to the pre-67 situation, Chinese officials 'made [it] clear that they would object to the reinstitution of controls by Hong Kong on legal immigration on the pre-1967 pattern', as it would 'interfere with the "traditional rights of access of Chinese to Hong Kong"'.⁴⁰ Under this circumstance, how illegal immigrants were handled became the bargaining chip for Hong Kong in the negotiations. MacLehose believed that Hong Kong should strategically 'ignore [the matter of] illegals if the Chinese did not respond over legals'.⁴¹

On 3 May 1974, Goronwy Roberts granted approval to the Governor to start discussion with the NCNA over how illegal immigrants should be returned.⁴² Alan Donald, Hong Kong's Political Adviser, stressed the importance of establishing some general rules before taking action in individual cases.⁴³ On 27 August, the Political Adviser met the Director of Shenzhen Foreign Affairs Bureau to discuss the modalities. Donald questioned if China would receive all illegal immigrants sent by Hong Kong and emphasised the need for 'speed, smoothness and good judgement' in the method used.[44] During the meeting, the 'Chinese attitude was generally one of reasonableness'.[45] Representatives of the NCNA welcomed an effective approach of returning illegal immigrants. When it came to the discussions on returning criminals, there was 'however some disposition'.[46] In response, Donald had to stress that the British and Chinese legal systems were 'historically different'.[47]

During the negotiations, the colonial government had multiple alternative concerns. The Executive Council had given its approval to the idea of sending back illegal immigrants who were arrested before reaching the urban area based on the pre-1967 practice in November 1973. However, the Acting Governor wished to reconsult the Council in mid-1974 regarding the potential undesirable responses which may be created by revising the immigration policy.[48] There were also anxieties over possible international repercussions stirred up by international amnesty organisations. To avoid undesirable responses, MacLehose believed it was essential to distinguish Chinese immigrants from others from third world countries, particularly Vietnam.[49] Britain's political development was another 'complicating factor'.[50] If an agreement was not reached and implemented before a new British government was elected (a General Election was due in 1974), the revision of Hong Kong's immigration policy may have to be reviewed by the new government. If the negotiations were further postponed and changes were made by this new government, the colonial government may have faced 'accusations of bad faith' from the Chinese.[51] Since the subject was already an agenda in the Executive Council, the Governor found it difficult to further postpone the discussion.

The colonial government had assessed the potential public responses before the introduction of the 'Touch Base' policy. In the early 1970s, although the society was still sympathetic towards illegal immigrants, there were increased concerns over how population growth was straining social services. As MacLehose had pointed out, 'though people here would dislike a return to pre-67 practice, they are sufficiently disturbed by recent numbers [to] accept it'.[52] Lord Goronwy Roberts, the Parliamentary Under-Secretary for Foreign and Commonwealth Affairs, also believed that the majority of the public would acknowledge the need to relieve the pressure from housing and social services. It was predicted that only immediate relatives of immigrants would be 'more vocal'; the majority would be 'silent'.[53] The Executive Council also anticipated that people would understand the repatriation policy was necessary and accept it.[54] Nevertheless, as sympathetic attitudes still prevailed, it was expected that sometimes publicity given to a particular case would prevent the government from repatriating an illegal immigrant. The implementation of the 'Touch Base' policy would also be sharply criticised by Nationalist organisations, Christian groups and some expatriate newspapers in Hong Kong.[55]

On 22 October 1974, Gorowny Roberts agreed that a final agreement should be sought with the Chinese over the return of illegal immigrants on the basis of the meeting in Shenzhen on 27 August.[56] On 12 November, a final agreement was reached between Hong Kong and the NCNA: the colonial government 'in principle' would not allow illegal immigrants from China to either enter or stay in Hong Kong.[57] Hong Kong would start to return illegal immigrants from 30 November and the Guangdong provincial government would receive them according to the agreed procedures.[58] Under the 'Touch Base' policy, all illegal immigrants who were apprehended in the frontier area would be repatriated. However, to avoid public disturbance and unpleasant repercussions, those who had 'touched base' (reached the urban area) were allowed to stay. To minimise possible negative responses, officials were instructed to reiterate that the arrangements were a revival of pre-1967 policies, which were only put into practice because of the enormous increase in illegal arrivals. It was also emphasised that every single case was examined individually and people suffering from 'genuine hardship' were exempted from repatriation.[59]

Government officials played an important role in shaping the view that illegal Chinese immigrants were external threats to Hong Kong. The colonial administration continued the policy adopted since 1956, labelling them as 'illegal immigrants' instead of 'refugees'. In June 1974, Bill Collard, the Director of Immigration, publicly described Chinese immigrants as unwanted elements who strained Hong Kong's welfare system:

> We don't want and we don't need these people; they're no good to us and they can't go anywhere else because the country from which they originated many years ago simply don't want them back ... It's a very expensive business because all these people have to get accommodated and this means we've got to build more schools, hospitals and houses.[60]

After the implementation of the 'Touch Base' policy, police reports were issued regularly to further strengthen the negative image of Chinese immigrants. K. K. Pui, the Assistant Immigration Officer, for example, explicitly expressed in a speech to the Lion Club that many illegal immigrants were 'undesirables', 'swindlers, drug traffickers, racketeers, subversive elements and criminals': 'the illicit activities of these people constitute an immediate threat to law and order, and it is [of] critical importance they should be chased out of our city as soon as possible.'[61] The association between criminals and Chinese young illegal immigrants was still reinforced by officials in the 1980s. For example, in April 1981, the Deputy Director of Criminal

Investigation, Li Kwan-ha, stated that illegal immigrants were 'responsible for some 10 per cent of crime' and '35 to 45 per cent of major crimes such as bank robberies, goldsmith shop attacks and cases involving firearms' in Hong Kong.[62]

The capacity for Chinese immigrants to be identified as refugees in Hong Kong had been greatly reduced by the introduction of the 'Touch Base' policy and the associated rhetoric employed by the colonial state. Rather than being considered as 'refugees', Chinese immigrants fell into two categories: legal or illegal. The latter were now being portrayed as unruly criminals who bypassed legal procedures to enter Hong Kong and therefore should face repatriation. Along with shifting newspaper reporting, the public's perceptions of Chinese immigrants changed in the mid-1970s, paving the way for increased demands for a tighter immigration policy in the late 1970s.

Increased press coverage

In the early 1970s, newspapers were increasingly concerned about the 'exodus' from China. *SCMP* made the following observation and comment:

> A feeling of widespread concern verging on serious disquiet has been aroused by reports of the disturbingly large influx of people from the Chinese mainland ... There is no hope of many, if any, of them leaving. Hong Kong, in other words, is the end of the line ... Cooperation is needed by both sides in settling this, and it is to be hoped that this human flow is stopped as soon as possible.[63]

A similar sentiment was captured by the *Star*: 'the mystery surrounding the sudden upsurge in the number of immigrants from China deepened today'.[64] Ma Man-fei, the Secretary of the UN Association in Hong Kong, even accused China of treating Hong Kong as 'a litter bin': 'Hong Kong has always been a litter bin, right on China's doorstep. Anyone they don't want they just dump here.'[65]

The press typically portrayed the influx of Chinese illegal immigrants as a problem which had serious economic, social and cultural implications. *SCMP* held that Chinese illegal immigrants were 'illiterate, unskilled, unemployed, elderly or a combination of all four', who burdened Hong Kong's social welfare resources.[66] It also described these illegal immigrants as 'unassimilable and useless mouths' and stressed that they could hardly integrate due to cultural differences.[67] *STYP* similarly argued that immigrants from China were mainly people with a 'lack of labouring ability' and who were 'viewed by the Communist Party as unfit' and unable 'to make any contribution' to China.[68] Less frequently, newspapers implied that Chinese immigrants were criminals. For example, the *HKS* claimed that 'a number of well-planned holdups in recent years were carried out from China' and 'the problem of refugees-turned-bandits has already aroused the attention of the government'.[69]

The newspapers brought the ineffectiveness of state immigration control to the public's attention. For example, the *China Mail* labelled the current influx of Chinese immigrants as an 'immigration crisis' and denounced the colonial state for installing 'an effective wall of silence'.[70] When the 'Touch Base' policy was introduced in 1974, the subject was 'given prominence in most local papers'. According to a survey of local press, apart from the right-wing pro-Nationalist papers, 'all editorial comment has been understanding and favourable to the Hong Kong government's case'. A press report in early December 1974 suggested that newspapers had 'unanimously approved of the repatriation move'.[71] *WKYP* agreed that the repatriation policy was 'the only way to maintain the stability of the public of Hong Kong'.[72] *TTYP* expressed sympathy for the illegal immigrants but 'saw no point in objecting [to] the move'.[73] *Fai Po* also supported the 'new' policy: 'In face of the present economic recession, price inflation and rise of unemployment, we can no longer accept non-ceasing flow of illegal immigrants.'[74]

Nevertheless, the immigration discourse was not wholly anti-immigrant. From the early 1970s to the mid-1970s, some editorials and reports remained sympathetic towards illegal immigrants. For instance, *WKYP* regarded the move as 'inhumane'.[75] *KSDN* held that 'the refugees had provided considerable capital, technical skills and manpower for the industrial development of Hong Kong' and stressed that 'they would not have risked their lives to flee' if they 'had not been desperate'.[76] These opinions were not mainstream but reveal that some newspapers held a sympathetic stance towards illegal Chinese immigrants by the end of 1974.

As the scale of illegal immigration became public knowledge, the calls for a tighter immigration policy dominated the news discourse. The *Express* argued that only by strengthening the repatriation policy could Hong Kong's order be maintained.[77] In 1978, according to 'Opinions', most Chinese-language newspapers 'expressed concern over the problem of illegal immigration to Hong Kong'. For example, in November 1978, *TTYP* argued that, although 'Hong Kong should in principle not turn back those [who] seek political asylum here', it was 'common knowledge that Hong Kong is a small place and it would fall apart if it was forced to accept a large number of political refugees'. *KSEN* also pointed out that 'Hong Kong has already been placed in a difficult position by the influx of Vietnamese refugees from all directions' and therefore would 'not be able to cope with the situation'.[78] In 1979, there was increased criticism in both Chinese and English newspapers against the colonial government's lack of determination to put an end to the influx. According to *SCMP*, there was 'increasing dismay and growing concern' over the influx of people from both China and Vietnam, both 'legal' and 'illegal', and 'a growing sense of helplessness in official reactions as the daily figures mount'.[79] *Ming Pao*, during the week from 23 to 29 May 1979, devoted four editorials to the subject. It argued that the government's attitude was 'one of submission and resignation, lacking in both courage and determination'.[80] Similar views were expressed by the *Express*, which argued that Hong Kong could 'no longer afford to be soft-hearted' to these migrants.[81] The illegal immigrants were also considered burdens of the colony. *HKT* pointed out that the cost of repatriating illegal immigrants back to the mainland was high: 'the total sum of expenses reached $36,080.2' from January to April 1979. 'Generous taxpayers' ironically became 'hosts' of these illegal immigrants.[82] According to the *Star*, 'the call is growing for the government to change its policy on [the] illegal immigrant problem' as 'the current policy obviously is not working'.[83] In February 1980, the *SCMP* urged the colonial government to strengthen its immigration policy and stop issuing identity cards to illegal immigrants.[84] *The Sun* even called the influx 'an invasion' and said 'it must stop'.[85]

From the mid-1970s, newspapers started stereotyping Chinese illegal immigrants as criminals. This relationship between Chinese illegal immigrants and bad elements was established in *HKS* in 1976:

> Criminals responsible for many [of] Hong Kong's big payroll holdups and expertly planned robberies are believed to be illegal immigrants from mainland China. Police sources reported that the illegals have banded together in a loose association called the Big Circle. Detectives described the Big Circle members [as] having expertise, organisation and professionalism. They said that the illegal immigrants are tougher than ordinary street criminals ... Two of the Hong Kong's most wanted criminals who were involved in the $7.2 million Great Tunnel Robbery on 5 August last year are believed to be 'Dai Luk Chais [mainlanders]' or members of the Circle.[86]

In 1978, an editor of *KSDN* suggested that many young Chinese illegal immigrants 'still inherited the bad traditions of communism, which shaped their cruel personality'. He argued that many of these illegal immigrants 'would use measures, such as struggles, revenges and looting' to achieve their goals, especially those that were 'laid back' and 'do[did] not want to find a decent job'. These former Red Guards 'would be happy to see destruction of the social order, history, culture and ethnics under the name of "revolutions"'.[87] *KSEN* similarly pointed out that teenage illegal immigrants from China did not always have the ability to adapt and integrate into the society of Hong Kong. False expectation 'may stimulate them and provoke them to walk towards the "evil path"'. These 'black-market residents', the editor believed, were 'a major hidden trouble in Hong Kong'.[88] *STYP* and *HKS* also portrayed young Chinese illegal immigrants as criminals who 'wanted returns without efforts' and committed crimes with 'no remorse'.[89] Apart from the 'Big Circle Gang', other degradative discriminatory terms, such as 'Green Card Holders' and 'Ar Chan', were commonly inflicted by newspapers to describe Chinese illegal immigrants, differentiating them from the Hong Kong Chinese.[90]

While the society was gradually turning anti-immigrant, the pro-Taiwan press and rightists continued to portray illegal immigrants as victims and denounced the Chinese Communist regime:

> Under the tyranny of Mao's gang, people who risked their lives to come to Hong Kong have never stopped, the Mao's gang in particular again used 'investigating anti-revolutionaries' as an excuse to carry out a massacre on its people. People cannot tolerate it and therefore risk their lives to escape.[91]

Both *KSDN* and *HKT* repeatedly used the term 'compatriots' to label these Chinese illegal immigrants.[92] An editor, Yu Tin, advocated acceptance and tolerance in *HKT*. In one article, he denounced the repatriation policy as inhumane and argued that illegal immigrants ironically faced arbitrations that even animals would not need to face under the existing practice in the 'highly civilised' Hong Kong.[93] This propaganda, however only represented the opinion of a small minority, primarily Nationalist sympathisers. Since the 1970s, the increased press coverage triggered public discussion on the existing immigration policy. The negative image of Chinese illegal immigrants constructed by newspapers since the mid-1970s also influenced public sentiment towards Chinese immigrants, as discussed in the following section.

Shifting public sentiment and political culture

By the mid-1970s, many community leaders advocated a tighter immigration policy. The Chairman of Kowloon City Kaifong Association, Lui Fook-hong, for example, believed that 'both governments should be taking steps to stop them from coming in'. Chan Ling-fong, the Chairman of Kennedy Town Kaifong Association, also urged the colonial government to do 'something about this and give the situation top priority because it will upset our social plans'. As an Urban Councillor, Henry Hu believed the current policy should be revised: 'I would favour a move to stop these immigrants coming in, we cannot absorb many people in such a short time.'[94] In the mid-1970s, public attitudes shifted as a result of hostile comments made by public figures, the negative image of Chinese illegal immigrants constructed by the press and an increasingly crowded living environment. According to MOOD, during the 1950s, the general public in Hong Kong was sympathetic towards the Chinese immigrants and considered the immigration policy 'good' and 'humane'. Immigrants from China were often viewed as 'refugees seeking political asylum', whose attempt to move to Hong Kong would risk being 'harshly punished by the C.P.G'.[95]

The mid-1970s was a turning point when attitudes towards Chinese immigrants changed. Although the large-scale immigration from China had 'not aroused widespread of anxiety or strong feelings', there was increased hostility towards Chinese immigrants among people of different classes and age groups.[96] It was mainly due to the perception that the influx of mainland population to Hong Kong could be 'an impediment to the fulfilment of long-term social service projects'.[97] The perceived increasing difference between the locals and mainland Chinese in culture and experience further aggravated the anti-Chinese immigration problem. In the 1950s, locals believed that Chinese immigrants were able to adapt easily as they all had similar background and were brought up in China before the Chinese Communists seized power. Contrastingly, the young generation who grew up in China under the communist regime encountered enormous difficulties in adapting. Not only was 'their upbringing in present day China in many ways incompatible with the ways of life in Hong Kong', but many young Chinese immigrants' work ethic was considered questionable. According to MOOD, in 1975, many young Chinese immigrants were convinced that they could enjoy an easy life after they moved to Hong Kong. Many employers found these young immigrants 'unsatisfactory' and complained that they were 'lazy, unwilling to work too hard, difficult to manage or discipline, and quite ready to cause trouble'. Many Hong Kong Chinese held contemptuous attitudes towards Chinese immigrants and believed that growing up in an environment which had a different set of legal systems and hoping to seek instant benefit, they were 'prone to commit crime'.[98] The public's perceptions of Chinese illegal immigrants incorporated their negative characteristics found in official rhetoric and newspapers in the early and mid-1970s, demonstrating the influence of the latter on the former.

As the majority of the society expressed their hope to protect local interests, the 'Touch Base' policy had 'on the whole been tacitly accepted by the community'.[99] Although a number of posters appeared in Kowloon and Hong Kong Island on 1 December 1974, protesting against the introduction of the 'Touch Base' policy, they were 'the work of right-wing elements' and were soon 'removed by the police'.[100] According to the Governor's reassessment on 3 December, 'so far the public reaction has been calm' and people had accepted the revised immigration policy.[101] The 'new' immigration policy also received support from a number of community leaders and politicians, including Urban Councillors and representatives of kaifong associations. For example, Denny Huang endorsed the 'Touch Base' policy: 'We must face the fact that we are experiencing a population explosion. If the influx of refugees from China was allowed to continue, local residents would suffer, particularly in housing and jobs.' Elsie Elliott agreed that it was a difficult decision which should be implemented: 'So many of our people are unemployed. We can't let the refugees accept jobs with less wages, leaving our own people unemployed.'[102] Another Urban Councillor, Peter C. K. Chan, also showed support for the new immigration policy: 'In view of the present economic situation, we have already reached saturation point as regards population and cannot accept the burdens of illegal immigrants from other countries.'[103] The President of the Hong Kong and Kowloon Joint Kaifong Research Council, Yan Chi Kit, also believed that 'the government had no other choice' as it had 'carried the burden long enough'.[104]

Press sentiment and comments made by officials and community leaders further influenced public opinion, which had been monitored by the colonial government closely through MOOD. A government report in 1979 revealed that the public was increasingly anti-immigrant when compared to 1975. In this period, the scale of immigration to Hong Kong grew as migration from China was coupled by the influx of Vietnamese refugees in 1975. According to MOOD, there was considerable anxiety:

> Respondents were spontaneous and frank. They were worried about the vast numbers arriving daily and the correspondingly few refugees/immigrants leaving for resettlement elsewhere. Everyone was concerned about the social and economic consequences; working class people in particular strongly held the view that Hong Kong people should come first and that government should ensure that 'outsiders', be they ethnic Chinese refugees from Vietnam or immigrants from China, did not disrupt their livelihood, and the housing, medical and educational programme.[105]

Despite their sympathy for immigrants and refugees who only fled to Hong Kong due to political persecution, most Hong Kong Chinese believed that 'Hong Kong had no responsibility, let alone the resources, to accommodate the refugees even [though] most of them were ethnic Chinese'.[106]

By 1980, the majority in Hong Kong believed that no identity cards should be issued to illegal immigrants and called for putting an end to the 'Touch Base' policy. The *Express* carried out a random poll interviewing 1,000 people. Eight out of ten 'felt that the government should deport illegal immigrants who had successfully made [it] into the urban areas'. When asked why they favoured an end to the 'Touch Base' policy, 67 per cent of respondents believed that 'the influx had strained social and transportation services', 31 per cent felt that the exodus from the mainland 'would cause greater overcrowding' and 30 per cent believed they had worsened the problem of employment.[107] In a poll conducted in an open forum on Victoria

Peak on 22 September 1980, 185 people supported a deportation policy. Only eight people opposed it.[108] This suggests a shifted attitude towards Chinese immigrants in the late 1970s, influenced by the press and official rhetoric. In October 1980, MacLehose reported that 'pressure from public opinion for the government to deal with the problem is growing'.[109]

Hong Kong residents, however, did not treat all immigrants indiscriminately. MOOD captured locals' different attitudes towards immigrants from China, Vietnam and Southeast Asia. They perceived illegal immigrants from Southeast Asia as 'resourceful people who were able to buy their way here'.[110] They were therefore unlikely to rely on Hong Kong's public social services. In contrast to their antagonism towards the Chinese immigrants, a proportion of Hong Kong Chinese welcomed these Southeast Asian immigrants to settle in Hong Kong, believing that they could invest in the colony and boost the local economy. Coming from 'free [non-communist] societies', many locals believed that compared to the mainland immigrants, the Southeast Asians 'should have few problems in adapting themselves to life in Hong Kong'.[111] In the MOOD exercise conducted in 1979, most respondents believed that the Chinese immigration 'had even more serious implications' than the influx of Vietnamese refugees as 'the [Chinese] immigrants were here to stay'.[112] There was a 'strong resentment' against mainland immigrants, especially 'the young men and women who supposedly came here for a more leisurely life or material gains'. Many mainland Chinese could enjoy overseas remittances from their relatives in Hong Kong since a more open market was developed in China in the early 1970s. Subsequently, many families in China had lost their incentive to work as wages were low.

The conventional view was that illegal Chinese immigrants were responsible for crimes, such as the Hang Seng Bank robbery.[113] This impression coincided with the negative image of Chinese illegal immigrants constructed by the press. As bitterness towards the Chinese immigrants intensified, there was increased criticism of the colonial government. Many condemned the government's inconsistent policies and expected a firmer stand to be taken. Stricter and harsher anti-immigration measures should be implemented. For instance, some MOOD respondents recommended that Chinese visitors who entered with travel documents should not be given an extension to stay and permanent resident statuses. There should also be more actions taken against immigrants who had arrived in Hong Kong illegally. Some even suggested that 'boats arriving in the future should be towed away'.[114]

Despite the tighter immigration control advocated by the general public, 'anti-immigrant' attitudes were constantly shifting. Under some special circumstances, people believed it was acceptable to grant illegal immigrants permission to stay. The mass media often played an important role in shaping this humanitarian sentiment. The case of Chan Kwan-fong in early 1977 was one of the exceptional cases that received publicity and triggered shifts in attitude. Chan's husband was a citizen of Hong Kong. They had been separated for years as Chan's two attempts to enter the colony both failed and she was subsequently repatriated to China. In March 1977, Chan tried to enter Hong Kong again but was apprehended for the third time. Being uncertain about what punishment Chan would face upon her return, her husband, Lee Man-hung, started a campaign to obtain public support for Chan's permanent stay in Hong Kong. Their story was widely reported. In the end, Chan was allowed to stay. 'Opinions' captured the shifted public sentiment: 'The general consensus was that while there was a need to stop illegal immigrants from entering Hong Kong, humanitarian grounds must be given due consideration in individual cases.'[115]

For example, an editorial in *Oriental Daily* believed that 'the government should refuse illegal immigrants permission to stay here' in order 'to prevent a population explosion' but it 'should examine every case very carefully and make an appropriate decision based on its merits'.[116] The *Express* also praised the colonial government for dealing with Chan's case 'sensibly and reasonably'.[117] The editor of *HKDN* similarly claimed that 'the government has made a correct decision in allowing Chan Kwan-fong to stay here'.[118] The case of Chan Kwan-fong demonstrated that the anti-immigrant attitudes of Hong Kong Chinese were not static. In special contexts, humanitarian grounds were invoked and Hong Kong Chinese could be mobilised, supporting Chinese illegal immigrants to stay.

This period witnessed a shift of attitude towards mainland Chinese immigrants. A call for a tighter immigration policy emerged in the mid-1970s. Despite the absence of direct confrontation, such as demonstrations and sit-ins, there was a new critical discourse about immigrants and this intensified the pressure for policy changes. Since the mid-1970s, Chinese immigrants were being increasingly considered by the public to be inferior, not only when compared to local Hong Kong Chinese, but also compared to newcomers from Southeast Asia, primarily due to their perceived lack of language proficiency and economic skills, cultural differences and their association with illicit activities. Nevertheless, the flexible nature of attitudes towards immigrants should be acknowledged. As Chan's case has shown, Hong Kong Chinese were able to adjust their positions on the immigration issue flexibly, in response to the context. The escalating anti-immigrant sentiment should be attributed not only to the increasingly overcrowded living environment and strained social services, but also to the construction of negative images of mainland Chinese immigrants by the press and government officials. The prejudicial rhetoric adopted by the newspapers and bureaucrats in the early 1970s influenced the perception of Chinese illegal immigrants among Hong Kong Chinese. Holding a negative view towards illegal immigration, Hong Kong Chinese of different social classes and age groups increasingly engaged in a critical immigration discourse after the mid-1970s. Even the working class, which often distanced themselves from the political discourse, expressed their discontent towards the colonial state's immigration policy. This changing public opinion influenced policy changes, ending the 'Touch Base' policy in 1980.

Government responses

Initially, the 'Touch Base' policy reduced the number of illegal immigrants.[119] There were increased warnings against illegal emigration in China. According to intelligence sources, in mid-December 1974, 'leading cadres of all production teams in Pao-an County received via production brigades a commune directive that in all mass meetings, regardless of the main topic, verbal warnings against attempting to escape to Hong Kong should be issued'.[120] People were warned that the Hong Kong government had sought an agreement with China for the immediate repatriation of all illegal immigrants and they would all be returned. Nonetheless, in the long run, this Chinese policy failed to address illegal immigration.

Due to the increased anti-immigrant sentiment, more measures were introduced to detect illegal arrivals both in China and Hong Kong in 1976. For example, a Ship Searching Unit was set up within the Immigration Department in early 1976 to inspect vessels entering Hong Kong.[121] On the Chinese side, smugglers were given life sentences by the Chinese authorities.[122] In June 1976, a new legislative amendment was proposed to allow the police to prosecute illegal immigrants who had stayed in Hong Kong for two years. Most newspapers supported the change. *SCMP*, for example, described the bill as 'designed to plug a loophole in the Immigration Ordinance'.[123] In July 1976, the bill became law. It empowered the Immigration Department to arrest and remove illegal immigrants within a period of three years from the time they have overstayed in or entered Hong Kong. In June 1977, another new immigration bill was introduced to prosecute people aiding illegal immigrants. Before 1977, to fine and imprison aiders, evidence had to be provided in court to demonstrate that the person they assisted was of illegal status, which hindered the process. The new act solved this problem by allowing certificates issued by the Director of Immigration to be used as evidence in court proceedings.[124]

Yet, these new measures failed to put a halt to the influx. In May 1978, MacLehose was aware of the public's increasingly hostile attitudes towards Chinese illegal immigrants. He expressed to London that the colonial administration was 'becoming increasingly concerned' about the number of immigrants arriving from China. The Governor instructed Political Advisers to raise concerns to the Director of the NCNA. MacLehose, however, believed that the Chinese could only help in solving part of the problem by issuing exit permits to legal immigrants who had valid documentation for onward travel. MacLehose's main concern was with the 'overall numbers', which should be brought down to fifty a day at the maximum. Therefore, he proposed to the Foreign and Commonwealth Office the re-imposition of unilateral immigration controls at the border. However, that was only regarded as the 'ultimate weapon' which should be used if China refused to act on the immigration problem.[125] The Far Eastern Department and the Hong Kong and General Department both believed that 'the possibility of controls should not be mentioned' at this stage. Given 'the present state of our relations with the Chinese over Hong Kong', it was unnecessary to 'resort to threats of counter-measures in order to induce them to be cooperative'.[126] In the meeting between the Political Adviser and the NCNA in May 1978, Chui Yi, the Deputy Director of the NCNA, agreed to report the views expressed by D. C. Wilson to relevant departments in China.[127]

By the end of 1978, the 'problem of people' had escalated. The cumulative figure of legal arrivals from 1 January 1978 to 12 December 1978 totalled 64,770. What worsened the situation from the perspective of those who perceived higher immigration as a 'problem' was that among these legal immigrants, 61,916 did not have onwards visas, which meant that the majority of them were unable to travel further and would therefore stay in Hong Kong permanently.[128] The imposition of unilateral border controls on the Hong Kong side was once again brought to the agenda. However, D. T. Owen, the Director of Immigration, pointed out that imposing border controls on the Hong Kong side 'would present major political difficulties and could only be considered a last resort'. He believed that it should be made clear that Hong Kong would prefer China to control the flow, and stated that the colonial government would be forced to introduce unilateral control if the number did not reduce to an acceptable level.[129] China's opposition to the re-imposition of border controls was principled: Hong Kong was 'a Chinese territory temporarily under British administration', and not a 'British territory'. Any quota system and border controls, therefore, was viewed as a violation of a 'traditional right for Chinese nationals to enter Hong Kong'. And China, of course, had 'never officially recognised the legality of any systems of quota for entry of Chinese nationals into "Chinese territory"'.[130]

On 15 December 1978, Percy Cradock, the British Ambassador to China, met the Chinese Vice Foreign Minister, Zhang Wenjin, in Beijing. Cradock expressed concerns and hoped that the Chinese government would not issue any exit permits before valid visas for onward travel were acquired. Chang recognised immigration as 'an important and serious matter' and agreed that 'something would have to be done to solve the immediate problem'.[131] The Ambassador also suggested that Hong Kong should return people who had stayed longer than the period stated in their Chinese short-term exit or re-entry documents. This approach, however, was 'not practical', according to MacLehose:

> If we attempted to return the thousands who overstay, they would simply destroy their Chinese travel documents and either go underground or claim to be treated as illegal immigrants who had 'reached base'. We would then face the same dilemma as in dealing with illegal immigrants who 'reached based' in the urban areas, i.e. arresting them from the midst of their relatives and in crowded areas is virtually impossible; and the alternative of denying them legal documents to stay is equally unpalatable since it would create a substratum of people outside the law who would be vulnerable to all sort of pressure.[132]

The NCNA agreed. Alternative measures had to be sought. In January 1979, three changes were proposed and approved in the Executive Council: the distinction between immigrants from Guangdong and elsewhere in China should be abolished; the initial stay of all legal arrivals from China should be limited to twelve months; the initial stay of all illegal immigrants should be restricted to three months.[133] It was expected that these new practices would be 'welcomed by the public', especially by those who considered the previous colonial immigration policy illogical.[134] Although these changes would not completely solve the 'problem of people', they would at least cause those who stayed 'some inconvenience and expenses'.[135]

While being received positively by the general public in Hong Kong, the new policy attracted criticism from China. *Wen Wei Po* denounced the Immigration Department for changing its policy two times within three months and argued that the new measures 'resulted in the disappointment or anxiety of so many people'.[136] *Ta Kung Pao* argued that 'compatriots in China and people of Hong Kong are related in flesh and blood'. The new policy 'would naturally bring about problems and difficulties to [the] people concerned'.[137] These 'unpopular' measures, however, did not put an end to the immigration problem.

From the viewpoint of the Governor, the situation was extremely alarming: 'We cannot allow this situation to continue. The present rate would be the equivalent of over 100,000 a year for legal immigrants alone. With illegal immigration also running at a high level we could face a yearly total of 140-150,000.'[138] This rapid increase in illegal immigrants entering Hong Kong from China could be attributed to the relaxation in internal Chinese security: people were now able to move more freely than previously inside the country. In addition, the collapse of the back-to-the-countryside movement also led hundreds of thousands of exiled young people to return to cities where unemployment was running as high as 50 per cent. Natural disasters, such as floods in Huizhou, also played an important role in the rise of illegal immigrants in 1979. MacLehose pressed the British government for policy changes, arguing it was 'inevitable' to impose unilateral control.[139] Cradock agreed that a warning should be given to China.[140] In March 1979, the situation became so serious that MacLehose requested naval reinforcement.[141] The Political Advisor then met the representatives of NCNA to follow up the discussions. As expected, the NCNA suggested that 'the Chinese government would find it very difficult to accept an imposed quota in view of the traditional free movement between China and Hong Kong'. The meeting ended in a 'friendly' atmosphere but 'the NCNA gave no signs of a favourable response to the various ideas put to them'.[142]

Public opinion in Hong Kong shaped negotiations between MacLehose and the Foreign Office in London. In May 1979, as public discontent escalated, the Governor wrote to the Foreign and Commonwealth Office, proposing to inform the Chinese that a unilateral quota system would be re-imposed on legal immigrants:

> We are now facing a potentially explosive mixture of immigration problems which I think requires early actions ... and NCNA say the numbers will continue to drop. But they are still more than treble our target of 1,550 a month. NCNA persistently defer the discussions we have asked for because they have not yet authority for 'concrete measures' ... The public are becoming profoundly disturbed by these mounting Chinese and Vietnamese figures. They feel that they are being shot with both barrels ... There is therefore strong demand that the Hong Kong government should act in some way, and this demand will grow fast.[143]

However, the proposition put forward by MacLehose was opposed by both Cradock and Carrington, who believed that emphasis should be placed on the illegal problem instead as 'unilateral measures by Hong Kong to stem the legal flow would increase rather decrease pressure of illegals'.[144] In response to Hong Kong's request to lower the number of illegal immigrants, Shenzhen started an anti-illegal emigration campaign in June 1979. Banners were put up and new policies against illegal immigration were also broadcasted by radio in Guangzhou.[145]

Yet, the number of illegal immigrants increased again in the second half of 1979. Numerous potential emigrants 'were waiting for the dust [new anti-illegal emigration campaign] to settle before making an attempt to get away'.[146] The lack of coordination of the anti-illegal emigration campaign, which was first initiated by China in October 1977, also contributed to the increased number. For example, Zhongshan and Panyu Counties installed 'stringent anti-escape measures'. The militia in Zhongshan in particular, was 'exercising a high level of vigilance' and had set up a number of sentry posts.[147] However, in some areas, border controls were loosely regulated. An illegal immigrant from Shekou Commune suggested that the militia near Shekou was 'not active in arresting escapees but merely patrol[ling] the roads'.[148] The People's Liberation Army soldiers also patrolled counties in different ways. Some were patrolling with dogs, but some, such as soldiers in Shatou and Baishizhou were without dogs, which made it easier for people to elude the soldiers.[149] Severe weather conditions also hindered border checks. An illegal immigrant from Longgang Commune pointed out that 'many Commune members succeeded in reaching Hong Kong whenever storm condition prevailed'.[150] Gathering intelligence from both successful and unsuccessful escapees, illegal emigrants would avoid routes that were heavily patrolled. Fines and punishments also varied in different counties. For example, the Sai Heung Commune had taken no special anti-escape measures. Before July 1980, illegal emigrants who were arrested would face detention for fifteen days in the Reception Station. Even after July, they were only asked to pay a fine of RMB ¥35 and surrender a rice coupon. Penalties were not strictly enforced in a busy farming period when communes needed more manpower.[151] However, in Chashan Commune, escapees had to face both detention and fines. Their heads would also be shaved and they had to labour without pay for fifteen to twenty days.[152] Due to the lack of universal measures and the absence of close supervision of the implementation of anti-emigration measures, the problem of illegal immigration from China to Hong Kong persisted.

In September 1979, the lack of effectiveness of China's measures drove MacLehose to press London to reconsider the re-imposition of unilateral controls on legal immigration. He also proposed to separate immigrants without onward travel documents from other travellers at the border.[153] The plan, however, was put on hold because of the visit of Hua Guofeng to London in October 1979. The Foreign Office wanted to see 'what Hua and his party say in London' before taking any further steps.[154]

Alongside negotiations with China, a series of legislative amendments were passed in 1979 in the hope of solving 'the problem of people'. For example, fines and penalties against smugglers were increased in both the Merchant Shipping (Amendment) Ordinance and the Shipping and Port Control Ordinance, which were passed in January 1979.[155] The Immigration Ordinance was amended in May 1979, removing restrictions on both the detention period of illegal immigrants and the size of vessels in offences, empowering the Royal Hong Kong Regiment and the Royal Hong Kong Auxiliary Air Force in arresting illegal immigrants and altering the definitions of 'Immigration Assistant' to include other newly created ranks in the Immigration Department'.[156]

Despite these new measures, the spread of rumours encouraged emigration to Hong Kong illegally, leading to fluctuations in the influx rate in the late 1970s and early 1980s. The rumour that the People's Liberation Army would replace the local police force after Shenzhen became a Special Economic Zone led numerous people to attempt to enter Hong Kong in late 1980.[157] Throughout the early 1980s, the rumours of amnesty stemmed from the Royal Wedding in 1981 and the agreement of the Sino-British Joint Declaration in 1984 motivated many to attempt escaping.[158] Rumours of the spread of natural disasters also occasionally led to the influx of illegal immigrants from a few particular counties. Believing there would be an earthquake, a large number of people from Haifeng and Lufeng fled to Hong Kong by vessels to seek shelter in March 1981.[159] The influx of illegal immigrants could also be attributed to the increased number of smugglers who sought profit by offering boats to assist escapees.

In response to the rising public pressure, on 16 April 1980, Lewis Davies, the Secretary for Security, announced that the repatriation policy was 'under review'. In June, the representatives of the NCNA expressed their 'concern about this problem' and accepted that 'in Hong Kong the concern was even greater'.[160] In July, the public sentiment further escalated, forcing MacLehose to contact the Hong Kong and General Department again to press for policy changes. The number of illegal immigrants had been rising since early 1980. The total number of illegal immigrants being returned reached 31,380 during the period from 1 January to late June. The daily average number of illegal immigrants repatriated also increased from 248 in mid-June to 282 in late June (see Table 6.3). The Foreign and Commonwealth Office believed that time should be given for representations to take effect in Beijing on this 'delicate political issue'.[161] Nonetheless, in July, driven by increased public criticism and public expenditure, MacLehose continued to press for London's approval in revising Hong Kong's immigration policies:

> There are a number of factors which led me to modify this view ... (4) This means we could face a population increase this year from immigration alone, of at least 125,000 (excluding Vietnamese). This is on top of an increase of

Table 6.3 Statistics of illegal immigrants repatriated in 1980

	17–23 June	10–16 June	Cumulative total since 1 January 1980
Illegal immigrants repatriated	1,977	1,739	31,360
Daily average	282	248	187

FCO 40/1202, 'Immigration from China', MacLehose to FCO, 24 June 1980.

at least 180,000 last year. We cannot go absorbing population at this rate without very serious consequences for our wages, social services, and, ultimately, political stability. A new factor is that this is now realised by the public, because the steady accumulation of numbers has passed the point at which immigrants can be invisibly absorbed. Squatter areas are growing. The illegal immigrants are a noticeable and unruly element, and fellow feeling for them has evaporated. (5) The certainty of international recession, which inevitably will hit Hong Kong is also a major new factor which worsens this prospect. Because of (4) and (5) above, public opinion has noticeably happened [for] months, and there is increasing criticism in and outside the media of government's failure to act to change the 'reached base' policy. This criticism will grow as recession abroad affects the working population here.[162]

The Foreign and Commonwealth Office recognised 'the increased pressures over the last two months' but proposed that the policy should not be implemented before the Secretary of State visited Beijing in early October 1980.[163] To persuade the British government to accept the proposal as soon as possible, MacLehose stressed that 'opinion in Hong Kong was strongly in favour of the measures' in July.[164]

In September 1980, a new policy was set that an identity card must be carried when travelling to the New Territories. However, the calls for ending the 'Touch Base' policy were not muted by the introduction of the new law. In late September, MacLehose put pressure on the Foreign and Commonwealth Office again, arguing that the immigration issue 'cannot wait'.[165] On 1 October 1980, a meeting was held between Peter Carrington, the Secretary of State of the Foreign and Commonwealth Office, and the Chinese Foreign Minister. Carrington pointed out to Huang Hua that 'the situation was so serious that Hong Kong was planning to send back to China those who were successful in reaching the urban areas and had previously [been] allowed to stay' and China's cooperation would be needed.[166] When MacLehose met Huang two days later, he explained to him that changes in border controls were necessary. To deal with illegal immigration effectively, Hong Kong would soon declare that it was illegal for illegal immigrants to take up jobs and they would send back all illegal immigrants even they 'reached base'.[167] The Chinese side was in general cooperative. As Guo Jie, the Deputy Director of the Western European Department, had pointed out, the Chinese authorities had attempted to but could not solve the illegal immigration problem. Therefore, they 'appreciated the efforts on the British side and all necessary measures would have Chinese support'. To avoid another wave of influx of illegal immigrants, the new measure was deliberately kept secret.[168] On 8 October, the Hong Kong and General Department and Far Eastern Department both agreed that London should authorise MacLehose to enact new laws to end the 'Touch Base' policy.

MacLehose also should be 'given discretion to implement the scheme without further reference to Ministers'.[169] Two days later, the Governor visited Guangdong. It was finally announced on 21 October that the 'Touch Base' policy would end on 27 October after a three-day grace period was given to illegal immigrants to register. Identity cards were no longer given to immigrants, causing them to be unable to seek employment and public welfare. During the grace period, 6,952 people came forward for registration. And 4,068, which was about 59 per cent of them, were allowed to remain in Hong Kong.[170]

This section demonstrates that shifting sentiments towards Chinese illegal immigrants since the mid-1970s played an important role in ending the 'Touch Base' policy in October 1980. Through the CDO Scheme and MOOD, the colonial state was able to observe how popular discourses about immigrants were changing, and this information informed the revision of immigration policy, as the Governor put pressure on the British government to tighten controls. Although the character of colonialism in Hong Kong was changing, Britain prioritised relationships with China, which led to difficult and delayed negotiations that shaped changes to Hong Kong's immigration policy.

Conclusion

Throughout the 1970s and early 1980s, the influx of immigrants from China resulted in public discussions regarding the colonial government's immigration policy. Hong Kong Chinese of all social classes and age groups were engaged in an issue that directly and indirectly affected their daily lives. The mid-1970s was a turning point when attitudes towards mainland Chinese immigrants shifted. Mainland Chinese immigrants were stereotyped as 'inferior' due to the perceived cultural differences, lack of language proficiency and skills, and absence of work ethics. Nevertheless, public attitudes varied, with some invoking humanitarian concerns to pressurise the colonial government to grant residence to a particular group of illegal immigrants.

Shifting public opinion encouraged the colonial administration to change its immigration policy. The colonial government departed from 'local integration', the approach adopted in the 1950s when immigration was controlled at the border. The 'Touch Base' policy was introduced. Public attitudes influenced how MacLehose negotiated with the British government but the Foreign Office prioritised its relationship with China, which led to delayed revision in immigration policies.

The policy changes had long-term effects. The end of the 'Touch Base' policy and new immigration measures strengthened the boundary between

Hong Kong Chinese and mainland Chinese and reinforced the emerging 'Hong Kong political identity', influencing the colony's political culture in the 1980s. The new policy separated Hong Kong Chinese from mainland immigrants politically and highlighted cultural differences. It, arguably, laid the foundation for the emergence of a political definition of 'Hong Kong permanent resident' in the Sino-British Joint Declaration in 1984 and the Basic Law in 1990.

Notes

1. Hong Kong Government Printer, 'Chapter 1: Review – A Problem of People', in *Hong Kong Annual Report, 1956*.
2. Ibid.
3. HKRS 70-8-2093, D. Ford, 'Talk by Secretary for Information to the Y's Men's Club: The Price of Freedom', 7 June 1979, pp. 1–4.
4. Ku, 'Immigration Policies', p. 327.
5. Sinn, *Culture and Society*; Tsang, *Government and Politics*, pp. 246–8; Carroll, *A Concise History*, pp. 170–3; Ma and Fung, 'Negotiating Local and National Identifications', p. 173; Lui and Chiu, 'Social Movements', p. 110.
6. For historical work on Hong Kong's immigration policy in the 1970s, see Mok, 'Chinese Illicit Immigration'.
7. FCO 21/1274, Ho Ying-chin, President of the UN Association of the Republic of China to J. Selwyn and B. Lloyd, 6 December 1974.
8. Mark, 'The "Problem of People"', p. 1148.
9. Ibid., pp. 1151, 1153–8.
10. The UN High Commissioner for Refugees, 1951 Convention Relating to the Status of Refugees, also quoted in Bailkin, *Unsettled*, p. 2.
11. Ibid.
12. Mark, 'The "Problem of People", pp. 1148–51.
13. Ibid., pp. 1164–5.
14. Ibid., p. 1174.
15. FCO 21/1273, 'Immigration into Hong Kong', R. M. Evans to Youde, 30 April 1974.
16. FCO 21/1273, 'Illegal Immigration from China', A. E. Donald to W. G. Ehrman, 14 August 1974.
17. FCO 21/1273, 'Immigration from China into Hong Kong', by the Far Eastern Department, 30 April 1974, pp. 1–2.
18. Ibid., p. 3.
19. FCO 21/1417, P. J. E. Male to Terence Garvey, 7 January 1975.
20. FCO 21/1417, M. Ennals, Secretary General of Amnesty International to J. Callaghan, 8 January 1975.
21. FCO 21/1274, *Hong Kong Press Report*, 4–11 December 1974, p. 4.
22. HKRS 70-6-856-1, 'No High Jinks Behind the Hay-ricks: Peter Steward Talks to a China Refugee', *HKS*, 1 July 1973.

23 HKRS 70-6-856-1, 'Refugee on a Big Strain on Our Resources', *SCMP*, 19 November 1974.
24 Between 1970 and 1974, 367,000 people were being housed by the colonial government in public housing. For more details and figures, see Mok, 'Chinese Illicit Immigration', p. 347.
25 FCO 21/1420, 'Illegal Immigrants from China and Macao – July 1975', D. C. Readman to Secretary for Security, 13 August 1975, p. 2.
26 FCO 40/1005, 'Entrants from China and Macao', by A. J. Carter, 4 March and 4 May 1978.
27 FCO 40/1116, 'The Threat to Hong Kong', MacLehose to FCO, 9 October 1979.
28 HKRS 70-8-2093, Reply by the Secretary for Security to a question by the Hon. R. H. Lobo in the Legislative Council, 17 October 1979.
29 FCO 21/1273, MacLehose to FCO, 15 February 1974.
30 There were three categories of illegal immigrants which the colonial government had to handle differently. The first was refugees who were alleged to have committed crimes within China, which should be repatriated under the Chinese Extradition Ordinance. The second category was refugees that were alleged to have committed crimes in the act of escaping. For this category, if the escapes were justified, the means of escape would also be justifiable. The last category was refugees who had committed no crimes but had entered Hong Kong. See Mok, 'Chinese Illicit Immigration', pp. 348–9; FCO 21/1273, 'Immigrants from China to Hong Kong', A. C. Stuart to P. M. Kelly, 4 March 1974.
31 HKRS 70-6-856-1, 'Compromise on China Immigrants: London Agreeable to 75 Migrants a Day', *HKS*, 27 November 1973; 'Refugees Hit by Ransom Racket', *HKS*, 3 December 1973; 'Immigrant Flow from China up Again', *HKS*, 26 January 1974; 'China's Legal Immigrant Influx Doubled', *HKS*, 27 January 1974; 'China Intake Remains 100', *China Mail*, 1 April 1974.
32 FCO 21/1273, Youde to R. M. Evans, 21 February 1974; 'Immigration into Hong Kong', R. M. Evans to Youde, 30 April 1974.
33 FCO 21/1273, Alec Douglas-Home to FCO, 1 March 1974.
34 'Immigrants from China to Hong Kong', Stuart to Kelly, p. 1.
35 FCO 21/1273, 'Immigration into Hong Kong', MacLehose to FCO, 1 April 1974.
36 Ibid.
37 'Immigration into Hong Kong', Evans to Youde, 30 April 1974.
38 'Immigration from China', MacLehose to FCO, 8 March 1974.
39 'Immigrants from China to Hong Kong', Stuart to Kelly.
40 'Immigration into Hong Kong', Evans to Youde, 30 April 1974.
41 'Immigration into Hong Kong', MacLehose to FCO, 1 April 1974.
42 FCO 21/1273, 'The Return of Illegal Immigrants to China', by the Far Eastern Department, 14 June 1974, p. 1.
43 FCO 21/1273, 'Illegal Immigration from China', MacLehose to FCO, 27 June 1974.
44 FCO 21/1273, Roberts to FCO, 28 August 1974.

45 Ibid.
46 Ibid.
47 Ibid.
48 FCO 21/1273, 'Illegal Immigrants to Hong Kong from China', A. C. Stuart to Male, 30 August 1974.
49 Ibid.
50 Ibid.
51 Ibid.
52 'Immigration from China', MacLehose to FCO, 8 March 1974.
53 FCO 21/1273, 'Illegal Immigrants to Hong Kong from China', A. C. Stuart to Goronwy Roberts, 30 August 1974.
54 FCO 21/1273, 'Immigration from China', memorandum for the Executive Council, 10 September 1974, p. 6.
55 Ibid., pp. 5–6.
56 FCO 21/1273, 'Chinese Immigrants', James Callaghan to MacLehose, 22 October 1974.
57 The word 'in principle' was added to allow more flexibility for the colonial government, especially over cases of genuine hardship. See 'Illegal Immigrants from China', MacLehose to FCO, 14 November 1974.
58 FCO 21/1273, 'Illegal Immigration from China', MacLehose to FCO, 19 November 1974.
59 FCO 21/1273, 'Return of Illegal Immigrants to China', A. C. Glasworthy to D. March, 28 November 1974.
60 HKRS 70-6-856-1, 'Refugees: A "Crisis Level" Warning', *HKS*, 1 June 1974.
61 HKRS 70-8-2097, 'Immigration Fight to Keep Hong Kong Clean', *SCMP*, 9 September 1976.
62 HKRS 70-8-2094, 'Police Report No. 4', Police Public Relations Wing, Daily Information Bulletin, 30 April 1981.
63 HKRS 70-6-856-1, 'The Influx from China', *SCMP*, 7 November 1973.
64 HKRS 70-6-856-1, 'Refugee Mystery Deepens', *Star*, 9 November 1973.
65 HKRS 70-6-856-1, 'Peking is Using Hong Kong as a Litter Bin, Says Ma', *HKS*, 11 November 1973.
66 HKRS 70-6-856-1, 'China Exodus a Burden on Hong Kong Resources', *SCMP*, 7 November 1973.
67 HKRS 70-6-856-1, 'Useless Mouths', *SCMP*, 11 November 1973.
68 HKRS 70-6-856-1, '香港的大陸難民與移民', *STYP*, 8 November 1973.
69 HKRS 70-6-856-1, 'China Refugees Turn to Planned Robberies', *HKS*, 2 July 1973.
70 HKRS 70-6-856-1, 'The Wall of Silence', *China Mail*, 9 November 1973.
71 *Hong Kong Press Report*, 4–11 December 1974, p. 1.
72 Ibid., p. 3.
73 Ibid.
74 Ibid.
75 Ibid.
76 Ibid., p. 4.

77 HKRS 70-8-2097, '加強執行遞解條例 確保本港社會治安', *Express*, 9 September 1976.
78 In 1975, the US forces withdrew from Vietnam and Saigon was sized by the communist regime. Hong Kong therefore became a haven for Vietnamese refugees in the Cold War. See Wong, ' "Bat Lau Dung Laai", p. 280. HKRS 70-8-2097, Extracts of the articles of *TTYP*, 15 November 1978 and *KSEN*, 16 November 1978 were recorded in 'Opinions: A Weekly Summary of Chinese Editorials', Chinese Press Review, 15–21 November 1978.
79 HKRS 70-8-2103, 'Time to Turn the Tide of People', *SCMP*, 23 February 1979.
80 HKRS 70-8-2103, Extract from *Ming Pao*, 23 May 1979. It was recorded in 'Opinions: A Weekly Summary of Chinese Editorials', Chinese Press Review, 23–29 May 1979, p. 1.
81 Extract from *Express*, 25 May 1979, ibid., p. 2.
82 HKRS 70-8-2103, '港納稅人慷慨天天請客 難胞逃港被捕遣回 每人日耗港幣廿元 今年四個月伙食廿三萬六千元', *HKT*, 10 May 1979.
83 HKRS 70-8-2104, 'No Haven for Illegals', *Star*, 28 March 1980.
84 HKRS 70-8-2104, 'Time to Review Policy in Illegal Immigration', *SCMP*, 11 February 1980.
85 HKRS 70-8-2104, 'The Invasion Must Stop', *The Sun*, 2 October 1980.
86 HKRS 70-8-2097, A. Roddick, 'Chinese Militia-trained Robbers Band Together in a Big Circle', *HKS*, 17 December 1976.
87 HKRS 70-8-2097, '逃海外紅衛兵多成問題青年', *KSDN*, 4 May 1978.
88 HKRS 70-8-2103, '偷渡客成香港心腹大患', *KSEN*, 18 June 1979.
89 HKRS 70-8-2106, 'Jail for II Who Had No Remorse', *HKS*, 8 July 1981; '偷渡來港後竟不甘揮窮 大陸青年械劫傷人 兩罪判入獄五年半', *STYP*, 8 July 1981.
90 HKRS 70-8-2105, '綠印者衣錦還鄉 引起警方密切注視 疑屬專門打劫金舖大圈仔份子', *Express*, 18 January 1981; HKRS 70-8-2106, '阿燦劫金行五十萬 四人入獄九至十年', *Hong Kong Commercial Daily*, 28 October 1981; '三綠印客被控藏槍意圖行劫', *KSDN*, 4 November 1981.
91 HKRS 70-8-2097, '毛幫又屠殺香港魚民', *HKT*, 4 June 1976.
92 HKRS 70-8-2097, '但願人權尚在人間! 冒死逃港卅餘難胞 全被捕獲面臨厄運', *KSDN*, 29 December 1977; '七名男女難胞 昨晚摸黑逃港 不幸被白宮圴警崗發覺 山腳截獲等待遣解厄運', *HKT*, 26 April 1978; HKRS 70-8-2103, '難胞胞逃港創新紀錄 較前年增加四倍半', *HKT*, 8 January 1979.
93 HKRS 70-8-2097, 于田, '今恩足以及禽獸...', *HKT*, 23 September 1977.
94 HKRS 70-6-856-1, 'Stop the Refugees – Community Leaders', *China Mail*, 9 November 1973.
95 HKRS 925-1-1, 'Public Attitude Gradually Turning Anti-immigrant', MOOD, 9 October 1975, p. 1.
96 Ibid., p. 5.
97 Ibid., p. 1.
98 Ibid., p. 2.
99 Ibid.
100 FCO 21/1273, 'Illegal Immigrants: Local Press Reaction', MacLehose to FCO, 2 December 1974.

101 FCO 21/1273, MacLehose to FCO, 3 December 1974.
102 FCO 21/1417, 'China Refugees will be Sent Back', *SCMP*, 30 November 1974.
103 Ibid.
104 Ibid.
105 HKRS 925-1-1, 'Public Reactions towards Vietnamese Refugees and Chinese Immigrants', MOOD, 28 June 1979, p. 1.
106 Ibid., p. 2.
107 The result of the poll survey was quoted in HKRS 70-8-2104, M. Lee, 'Fed Up with Poor Relations: There is Increasing Pressure for an End to the Touch Base Rule for Illegal Chinese Immigrants', *Far Eastern Economic Review*, 21 March 1980, p. 22.
108 HKRS 70-8-2104, 'Majority Supports Deportation Policy', *SCMP*, 22 September 1980.
109 FCO 40/1203, 'Immigration', MacLehose to FCO, 7 October 1980.
110 'Public Reactions towards Vietnamese Refugees and Chinese Immigrants', p. 3.
111 Ibid., p. 4.
112 Ibid., p. 5.
113 Ibid, pp. 4 and 6.
114 Ibid., p. 2.
115 HKRS 70-8-2097, 'Opinions: Chinese Press Summaries', Chinese Press Review, 9–15 March 1977.
116 Extract of *Oriental Daily*, 13 March 1977 in 'Opinions: Chinese Press Summaries', Chinese Press Review, 9–15 March 1977.
117 Extract from '合情合理的決定:談港府處理陳桂芳事', *Express*, 13 March 1977 in 'Opinions: Chinese Press Summaries', Chinese Press Review, 9–15 March 1977
118 Ibid.
119 FCO 21/1420, 'Illegal Immigrants from China and Macao – July 1975', D. C. Readman to Secretary for Security, 13 August 1975, p. 2.
120 FCO 21/1417, Extract from the Hong Kong Police Special Branch Report, K. M. Draycott to B. H. Dinwiddy, 28 January 1975.
121 HKRS 70-8-2097, 'Daily Search for Illegal immigrants', *SCMP*, 5 January 1976; '三月來不斷檢查抵埗貨輪 港府展開特別行動 嚴厲搜捕台偷渡客', *STYP*, 19 January 1976.
122 HKRS 70-8-2097, 'Top Fishing Industry Man Gets "Life" in China', *Star*, 6 April 1976.
123 HKRS 70-8-2097, 'Bill Plugs Immigration Loophole', *SCMP*, 2 June 1976.
124 FCO 40/811, 'Memorandum for Executive Council: Immigration (Amendment) Bill 1977', 30 May 1977.
125 FCO 40/1005, 'Legal Immigration from China', MacLehose to FCO, 4 May 1978. A quota system of 'four-ins, five outs' was first introduced by the colonial government at the border in 1950 due to the influx of immigrants after the establishment of the PRC. China was not consulted. The system lapsed in 1952 due to the Chinese imposition of a system of entry and exit permits for Guangdong Province. However, due to increased immigration, the quota system

was reintroduced in 1955. It was changed to 'one-in, one-out'. The system operated until 1967 when the Cultural Revolution broke out. It ceased mainly because of the fear that officers may be abducted at the border. See FCO 40/1005, 'The "Quota" and Legal Immigration from China', by Security Branch, Government Secretariat, 18 May 1978, pp. 2–4, attached in 'Legal Immigration from China to Hong Kong', I. C. Or to J. Thompson, 31 May 1978.
126 FCO 40/1005, 'Legal Immigration from China', W. E. Quantrill to MacLehose, 5 May 1978.
127 FCO 40/1005, 'Record of Meeting in the Political Adviser's Office on May 1978', 9 May 1978, p. 2.
128 FCO 40/1007, 'Immigration from China', MacLehose to FCO, 13 December 1978.
129 FCO 40/1007, 'Immigration from China', D. T. Owen to Hong Kong, 11 December 1978.
130 'The "Quota" and Legal Immigration from China', p. 6.
131 FCO 40/1007, 'Immigration from China', P. Cradock to FCO, 16 December 1978.
132 FCO 40/1007, 'Immigration into Hong Kong', MacLehose to FCO, 29 December 1978.
133 Before 1979, Guangdong province residents were allowed to stay in Hong Kong 'unconditionally', 'regardless of the purpose or purposed length of stay' while immigrants from other parts of China would be given twelve months. Illegal immigrants who had registered for an identity card would also be given a stay of twelve months. FCO 40/1007, 'Memorandum for Executive Council: Immigration from China', 2 January 1979, p. 1.
134 Ibid.
135 'Immigration into Hong Kong', MacLehose to FCO, 29 December 1978.
136 FCO 40/1114, 'Immigration Policies Should be Humane and Reasonable', *Wen Wei Po*, 19 March 1979.
137 FCO 40/1114, 'Restrictions Unreasonable', *Ta Kung Pao*, 21 March 1979.
138 'Immigration into Hong Kong', MacLehose to FCO, 29 December 1978.
139 FCO 40/1114, 'Immigration from China', MacLehose to FCO, 16 February 1979.
140 FCO 40/1114, 'Immigration from China', P. Cradock to FCO, 17 February 1979.
141 FCO 40/1114, 'Naval Reinforcement', MacLeose to FCO, 10 March 1979.
142 FCO 40/1114, 'Immigration from China', MacLehose to FCO, 9 March 1979.
143 FCO 40/1115, 'Immigration', MacLehose to FCO, 25 May 1979.
144 FCO 40/1115, 'Immigration from China', Cradock to FCO, 28 May 1979; 'Immigration', Carrington to MacLehose, 28 May 1979.
145 FCO 40/1115, 'Illegal Immigration from China', MacLehose to FCO, 11 July 1979.
146 FCO 40/1116, 'The Threat to Hong Kong', MacLehose to FCO, 9 October 1979.
147 HKRS 908-1-82 'Implementation of Illegal Emigration Controls in China', J. M. Shannon to Secretary for Security, 24 October 1980, p. 5.
148 Ibid., p. 2.

149 Ibid.
150 Ibid., p. 4.
151 Ibid., pp. 5–6.
152 Ibid., p. 6.
153 FCO 40/1116, 'Immigration from China', MacLehose to FCO, 4 September 1979.
154 FCO 40/1116, 'Immigration from China', MacLehose to FCO, 18 October 1979.
155 Hong Kong Government Printer, *Legal Supplement No.1 to the Hong Kong Government Gazette Extraordinary*.
156 FCO 40/1118, 'Memorandum for Executive Council, Immigration (Amendment) (No. 2) Bill 1979', 31 May 1979, p. 1.
157 'Implementation of Illegal Emigration Controls in China', Shannon to Secretary for Security, 21 November 1980, p. 1.
158 HKRS 70-8-2106, 'II Amnesty Rumours Denied', in 'Opinions', Chinese Press Review, 22–28 July 1981; HKRS 70-9-588, 'Illegals Keep Pouring In', *SCMP*, 28 March 1984; 'More Illegals Floating in on Amnesty Rumours', *SCMP*, 20 September 1984.
159 HKRS 70-8-2094 'Attention NWS Editors: Tuesday 31 March 1981', Daily Information Bulletin, 31 March 1981.
160 FCO 40/1202, 'Illegal Immigration from China', extract from the record of meeting with NCNA, 10 June 1980.
161 FCO 40/1202, 'Governor of Hong Kong: Illegal Immigration from China', Youde to R. D. Clift, 4 July 1980.
162 FCO 40/1202, 'Illegal Immigration', MacLehose to FCO, 8 July 1980.
163 FCO 40/1202, 'Illegal Immigration', Carrington to Hong Kong, 16 July 1980.
164 FCO 40/1202, 'Illegal Immigration from China to Hong Kong', discussion between Mr Blaker and MacLehose, 14 July 1980.
165 FCO 40/1202, 'Cancellation of Secretary of State's Visit to China', MacLehose to FCO, 29 September 1980.
166 FCO 40/1203, 'Record of a Conversation between the Secretary of State and the Chinese Foreign Minister at 1 Carlton Gardens on Tuesday 1 October 1980 at 2.30 pm', by the Far Eastern Department, 6 October 1980, p. 1.
167 FCO 40/1203, 'Immigration', MacLehose to FCO, 3 October 1980.
168 FCO 40/1203, 'Immigration', P. Cradock to FCO, 16 October 1980.
169 FCO 40/1203, 'Hong Kong: Illegal Immigration from China', R. D. Clift to Mr Donald, 8 October 1980.
170 HKRS 70-8-2094, 'Reply by Secretary for Security to a Question by Dr. Rayson Huang in Legislative Council', Daily Information Bulletin, 13 May 1981.

7

The British Nationality Act controversy

The British Nationality Act, which passed in October 1981 and came into force in January 1983, was controversial in Hong Kong at a time when the colony's future status was being resolved via Sino-British negotiations. In March 1979, MacLehose raised the question of the New Territories lease with Deng Xiaoping when he visited China for the first time. Deng stated that Hong Kong was 'part of China' despite his agreement of 'respect[ing]' its 'special status'.[1] MacLehose delivered Deng's messages to the public in Hong Kong selectively. Rather than mentioning that Hong Kong must return to China by 1997, he stated that China would ultimately resolve the Hong Kong issue and informed investors that they could 'set their hearts at ease'.[2] Although MacLehose's visit to Beijing 'created a temporary sense of relief in Hong Kong', the British Nationality Act which affected 2.6 million Hong Kong people unsettled certain sections of the society, particularly the business elites, the industrial sector, the civil servants and the UMELCO.[3] For most Hong Kong Chinese, the right of abode was a delicate issue: it did not only deprive them of their current nationality, but also worried many who were convinced of the unsuitability of the PRC government. The older generation, who migrated from China to Hong Kong due to political turmoil, and the post-war baby boomers, who had adopted a capitalist lifestyle, were in particular fearful of the consequences of communist rule over Hong Kong.[4] Even for non-Chinese Hong Kong residents, this Act was considered problematic as their lack of Chinese nationality inherently meant that they were not eligible for a travel document if Britain did not provide one.

The most detailed study of Hong Kong's relations with the British Nationality Bill was conducted by Chi-kwan Mark. Mark examined the Act's origins and deliberation, Hong Kong's representation and local legislative changes after the agreement of the Sino-British Joint Declaration. According to Mark, the question of 1997 caused widespread fear among the UMELCO, who played a crucial role in lobbying the Conservative government to protect the status and rights of British subjects in Hong Kong.

The passage of the Act and the legislative changes which followed signified Britain's attempt to start decolonising Hong Kong in the early 1980s.[5] Mark Hampton has also discussed the Nationality Bill when examining the question of 'Chinese Britishness'.[6] He noted that most people accepted that it was 'unreasonable' to expect Britain to grant the right of abode to millions of Hong Kong Chinese, but felt that Britain was trying to distance itself from the responsibilities for Hong Kong citizens.[7]

This chapter focuses on how different sectors of Chinese society exerted pressure on the colonial government and lobbied the British government. Unlike previous case studies, the British Nationality Bill did not only affect Hong Kong but many other former British dependencies. The British government therefore prioritised domestic interests, that is, to control immigration, reduce pressure on its strained housing and social services and construct a 'racialised' sense of nationality, over the concerns of British subjects in Hong Kong. The sentiments of the people of Hong Kong were not decisive.

The Green Paper and the White Paper

In April 1977, the Labour government in Britain published a Green Paper titled 'British Nationality Law – Discussion of Possible Changes', which proposed that British citizenship should be limited to those that had close links with the United Kingdom and could be expected to identify themselves with the British society. It proposed the single classification of 'Citizens of the United Kingdom and Colonies' (CUKC) to be abandoned and replaced by two categories: 'British Citizens' (BC), who had automatic rights of access and abode in the United Kingdom, and 'British Overseas Citizens' (BOC), who had no automatic rights of access or abode in the United Kingdom, instead having these rights in their own territories of residence. The latter category consisted of British subjects in Asia and Africa and residents of dependent territories, including 2.5 million British passport holders in Hong Kong.[8]

The CUKC was created under the British Nationality Act passed in 1948. The Act did not only give citizenship to British subjects who had ties with the United Kingdom, but also to British subjects who did not, for any reason, acquire citizenship of another Commonwealth country.[9] As most of the Commonwealth countries became independent but had not passed their citizenship laws in the late 1940s, this Act provided that British subjects who had ties with Britain should be regarded as potential British citizens. In other words, if they failed to obtain citizenship in their countries of residence, they would become CUKC.[10] CUKC could acquire British citizenship easily by showing that they had ordinarily resided in the United Kingdom for twelve months. Since the Act only dealt with nationality and citizenship, few restrictions were imposed on the movement of CUKC – they were entitled to enter and leave the United Kingdom freely before the introduction of the Commonwealth Immigrants Act in 1962.[11]

However, a lot of problems emerged after the Act was introduced in 1948. One issue was that the status of British subjects without citizenship, which was supposed to be 'transitional', had persisted due to developments in independent territories. For example, the citizenship laws enacted by India and Pakistan in 1950 and 1951 withheld citizenship from many who were considered potential British citizens or British subjects. Kenya also did not grant citizenship to CUKC who were born in pre-independent Kenya by default unless at least one parent was born there. As a result, a 'significant number of people' remained CUKC even if they had few or no connections with the United Kingdom.[12] This also led to an influx of immigrants from the New Commonwealth to Britain in the 1950s and early 1960s, in particular from the West Indies, India and Pakistan, straining the housing and social welfare services and creating social and racial tensions.[13] Britain's transition from a diehard imperialist power to a power that attempted to increasingly distance itself from imperial legacies in the post-war period, together with increased race riots such as the Notting Hill riots of 1958, further facilitated the emergence of anti-immigrant sentiment at home.[14] To control immigration into the United Kingdom, the Commonwealth Immigrants Act, which stopped granting non-White people from the colonies and Commonwealth free access to Britain using a voucher system, was passed in 1962.[15] In 1971, the Immigration Act was introduced to allow only 'patrials', that is, people who were born in Britain or with at least one parent or grandparent born in Britain and who had resided in Britain before 1 January 1973, to have the right to settle in the country. Other 'non-patrials' were considered 'aliens' and needed to apply for permits to enter the United Kingdom.[16] However, by 1980, there were still approximately 950 million people across the globe that were considered 'British subjects' in law. Of these, 57 million were CUKC that were exempt from immigration controls. Due to the scale of the problem, the British government believed that it was necessary to control immigration from the Commonwealth and distinguish between CUKC, who had close ties with the United Kingdom and should be admitted to the country freely, and others, avoiding 'considerable uncertainty and misunderstanding, both at home and overseas, about the United Kingdom's obligations to its citizens'.[17] Margaret Thatcher wanted to reconstruct national identity creating a sense of 'Britishness' based on 'racial superiority'.[18] In the 1979 election, Thatcher and the Conservatives agreed to tighten immigration controls if they were elected.[19]

The British Nationality Act controversy 211

As Mark has argued, when the bill was discussed in Britain, it was unlikely that 'the future of Hong Kong after 1997' and 'the prospects of an influx of Hong Kong "refugees"' was 'uppermost' in British minds.[20] Yet, when the Green Paper was first published, the colonial government in Hong Kong reacted strongly as it believed that combining residents of the dependent territories and other British subjects into one single category was 'wrong in principle and totally unacceptable for Hong Kong' and argued that Hong Kong's British subjects should be able to retain the title of CUKC.[21] In October 1980, the Hong Kong government made strong representations on four aspects of the White Paper. First, 'British Dependency Citizen' could be an alternative and the future Hong Kong passport could continue to retain the wording 'British passport'. Second, a request was put forward to waive the requirement of entry certificates or visas for Hong Kong residents and other countries, particularly residents from the European Economic Community. Third, it was submitted that British citizens employed by the colonial government should retain the right to transfer their citizenship to children born in Hong Kong. Lastly, hopes were expressed for the British government to acknowledge the special position of expatriate businessmen when drafting the bill.[22]

Due to representations made by the colonial government and other remaining dependencies, the Conservative government proposed a third citizenship category named 'Citizens of the British Dependent Territories' (CBDT) for people that had a close connection with a British dependent territory.[23] In addition, it modified the position in the Green Paper; exemption was given to children born to parents with a close connection with the United Kingdom and who had spent a large proportion of their career abroad serving British interests. More importantly, the White Paper stated that the creation of this separate citizenship would 'in no way alter the relationship between those territories and the United Kingdom, nor the British government's obligations and commitments to the dependent territories and to their citizens'. The constitutional position of Hong Kong and the rules governing the entry of Hong Kong residents to Britain and other countries therefore should remain unchanged.[24]

Increased press coverage and political culture

The White Paper was 'accorded wide coverage in both Chinese and English press'.[25] Many editorials expressed anxieties over the proposed changes. For example, the *SCMP* suggested that the new proposed legislation was 'a gradual process of devaluation' of the status of passport holders of Hong Kong.[26] The *Express* argued that the new changes were 'discriminative' and would reduce Hong Kong people to 'second class citizens'. Given that Hong Kong residents were 'still closely connected with the United Kingdom', this series of amendments were 'unjust'.[27] *Ming Pao* pointed out that the proposed changes 'suit the needs of Britain rather than aiming at Hong Kong or other dependent territories' and urged the colonial government to 'make a careful study of the situation'.[28] Some of these editorials believed that the bill might adversely affect Sino-British negotiations. For example, *Ming Pao* argued that the new category 'CBDT' 'sounds offensive to China as well as to Hong Kong residents of British nationality' and would 'not to be of any help to arriving at a satisfactory settlement on the post-1997 issue':

> China being a big country, the absence of a suitable arrangement giving due regard to China's dignity and national feelings constitutes pressures on China to take back Hong Kong and Macao ... Britain and Hong Kong should cast their sight farther by refraining from doing or by trying to remove anything that may disturb Beijing.[29]

The increased press coverage captured the public's attention yet did not result in an uproar. According to the Secretary for Information, the White Paper received 'a cool reception in Hong Kong'.[30] At a grassroots level, views were 'muted'.[31] The Executive Council's memorandum made a similar observation: 'Public reaction to the Green and White Papers on British Nationality has initially been muted, probably mainly because leaders in the community did not wish to express publicly their concern and disquiet about the proposals.'[32] This could be attributed to the fact that many considered the bill to be a remote issue and were not interested in migrating to the United Kingdom. Compared to practical issues, such as 'bus fare increases and income tax allowance' which affected their everyday lives, the public was 'far less enthusiastic about the nationality law'.[33] This reflected the fact that the working class were driven by instrumental concerns.

Another factor that contributed to such public attitudes was that the purposes of Green Papers and White Papers were not well understood by the public: 'the majority of respondents did not know what a Green Paper was and could not tell the difference between a Green Paper and a White Paper.'[34] The terms 'Green Papers' and 'White Papers' were 'alien' ones.[35] Even 'interested observers', including those 'with a good educational background', misunderstood these British conventions of consultation. For example, many thought that proposals published in the Green Papers were 'firm government policies announced prior to implementation'.[36] The jargon was too 'difficult' for the public to understand unless 'they happened to have a good knowledge or background of subject through profession'.[37] The public was not familiar with the process of policy formulation and hence 'at large remained somewhat passive and indifferent'.[38]

However, certain social groups expressed concerns over the bill. For example, the business community was worried about the bill's implications; how it would affect investors' confidence and increase the difficulties of travelling abroad.[39] In addition, the young generation questioned how opportunities for admission into the United Kingdom and other countries for further education would be affected and were distressed about the bill's potential impacts on 'the future of Hong Kong generally'.[40] Members of the Heung Yee Kuk also showed concerns due to the substantial number of New Territories people residing in Britain.[41] The concerns commonly shared by these groups were largely practical: they were worried that the proposed change might represent 'an indefinable and distinct shift in the United Kingdom's attitude towards Hong Kong, with implications of relinquishing sovereign responsibilities in the future'. The new category of citizenship was perceived to have a 'discriminatory effect', turning Hong Kong people into 'second class citizens' and producing 'unfair and unnecessary' difficulties when they travelled.[42] Furthermore, civil servants were 'deeply distressed' and petitioned the Governor to express their 'grave concern', and their desire for 'anything but favourable treatment if Hong Kong were revert[ed] to China'; they noted that:

> China is a one-party communist state, its four modernisations notwithstanding. The recent trial of the Gang of Four has, if anything, re-emphasised that the communist justice bears no resemblance to the Queen's justice under which we were nurtured.[43]

Although people's major concerns were mostly about practical matters, the vague concept of 'Britishness' was invoked in petition letters and there was a general view that the new citizenship category should be changed. For example, in an anonymous petition, the proposed move was denounced as confusing and 'a kind of discrimination' against Hong Kong British subjects. The petitioner questioned the definition of 'close connection' and argued that there 'should not be different citizenships', especially because Hong Kong was part of the British Commonwealth.[44] At the end of the letter, to request the retention of the existing citizenship category, political allegiance to the Queen was shown by the petitioner:

> During the past 25 years, under the administration of Her Majesty's Government, Hong Kong has become more and more prosperous and stable. I strongly believe that the majority of Hong Kong residents wish Her Majesty Queen Elizabeth II to govern Hong Kong forever.[45]

Another petitioner similarly stressed the disappointment but noted that he/she 'will always give allegiance to Her Majesty Queen Elizabeth II in [the] future as in the past and present'.[46] However, according to MOOD in 1977, the majority of Hong Kong Chinese did not 'consciously think of themselves as British subjects or CUKCs' unless they sought to travel using a British passport.[47] When speaking of the Queen, many also called her 'Ying Lui Wong' (The Queen of England) rather than 'the Queen', suggesting that she was 'still to them very much an alien queen'.[48] A MOOD survey conducted in 1976 after the Queen's birthday also suggested that many 'ordinary households' considered the celebrations to be 'routine' and 'did not care a great deal about them'.[49] Even guests invited to attend the celebrations were 'largely indifferent'.[50] Many even said they 'would not be interested to come if invited to the same programme next year'.[51] MOOD also observed that there was 'no significant element of genuine historical sentiments, national pride or loyalty ties in the jovial spirit of community celebrations' during the Silver Jubilee of Elizabeth II.[52] Similar sentiments were displayed towards other royal figures. For example, when Prince Charles visited Hong Kong in March 1979, people were not overly 'enthusiastic or excited', although his visit was received positively.[53] Such 'favourable reaction', however, 'stemmed primarily from their good impression of the Prince who was described as charming, friendly and approachable' – not from some abstract sense of loyalty to the monarchy.[54] For Hong Kong Chinese, their 'allegiance' to Britain was based on instrumentalism.

Urban Councillors also argued that the three-tier citizenship scheme was discriminating against Hong Kong British subjects. For example, Denny Huang described the new bill as 'unreasonable and irresponsible'. Augustine Chung denounced the new nationality proposal for turning local Hong Kong people into 'second class citizens'. Edmund Chow claimed that under the new scheme, only British citizens could go to Britain without a visa. Ambrose Choi called for the repeal of this 'unfair law'. Wong Ming-kuen urged the British government to look after the interests of Hong Kong people rather than 'causing them inconvenience'.[55] However, the most vigorous opposition came from the UMELCO, led by Sze-yuen Chung and Oswald Cheung. Chung was an engineer who had been a senior unofficial member of the Executive Council since April 1980.[56] Cheung, a barrister by profession, joined the Executive Council in April 1980. These Unofficials, who were highly educated and had strong connections with Britain, believed that any changes should cause 'no erosion of any of the existing rights enjoyed by Hong Kong based on CUKCs'. They demanded the British government to ensure that the category CBDT would not result in third countries discriminating against Hong Kong people by imposing new restrictions on their travels. Most importantly, they argued that the bill should not create any impression of 'a weakening of constitutional relationship between Hong Kong and the United Kingdom'. The British nationality of Hong Kong people should also remain intact.[57]

With local press coverage and UMELCO campaigning, Hong Kong's opposition attracted considerable attention in Britain. For example, in its publication, the Hong Kong Research Project,[58] a London-based radical East Asian studies group founded by Walter Easey, a former Hong Kong police officer, called the new nationality proposal 'alarming' and urged for further amendments:

> The right to an internationally-recognised nationality is held to be one of the most important human rights anyone can possess. Rights to freedom, happiness and the rest are meaningless if no government will take responsibility whose only choices are between the refugee camp and the detention centre of immigration authorities all around the world ... the forthcoming attempt to downgrade your citizenship and nationality rights by a distant, cowardly and racist government is a disgrace.[59]

In January 1981, Paul Bryan, Chairman of the All-Party Anglo-Hong Kong Parliamentary Group, presented 'a long list of grievances, fears and details caused of concern'.[60] Bryan pointed out that people in Hong Kong, in particular young people, were 'deeply interested in the bill' because 'any alternation in citizenship means a great deal to people in practical terms'.[61] In particular, he argued that people would be placed into 'separate and lengthy immigration queues'.[62] The new bill was also presented as 'evidence' of the 'weakening' 'links between Britain and Hong Kong'.[63] The proposed change which required Hong Kong citizens to apply for naturalisation to become a British citizen was considered problematic: 'It would be wrong if aliens were in the position of finding it easier to become naturalised than Hong Kong citizens.'[64]

These debates led to amendments. First, a new clause allowed the CBDT to register as a British citizen after five years of residence in the United Kingdom. Under the original bill, CBDT would have had to apply for naturalisation, which was discretionary and needed language and other requirements to be met. Second, the Secretary of State gained the discretion to register a CBDT, who had not met the residence requirement, as a British citizen in special circumstances if he/she had been in paid or unpaid Crown service under the government of a dependent territory; the original White Paper only accepted Crown service under the British government. Third, another new clause was added to enable a person born in Hong Kong, who had not acquired CBDT status at his/her birth, to be registered as CBDT after ten years of ordinary residence in Hong Kong, regardless of his/her parents' statuses; the original bill only granted CBDT status to people if either a parent was CBDT or 'settled' in Hong Kong. Lastly, the rules of transmitting British citizenship or CBDT status to children born abroad were relaxed.[65]

The first reading of the British Nationality Bill took place on 14 January 1981 and the second reading was passed after debates in the House of Commons on 28 and 29 January 1981. During the second reading, Timothy Raison, the Minister of State at the Home Office, provided assurances to British subjects in Hong Kong, pointing out that 'there was no hidden motives behind the bill' and that the proposals were 'in no way directed particularly at Hong Kong' or 'intended to weaken our links', to which the British government 'attach[ed] great importance'.[66] The views of local Hong Kong people had been taken into consideration.

Public reception and political activism

Newspapers appreciated how Bryan had represented the bill's revisions. The *SCMP* labelled Bryan a 'champion'.[67] His intervention was 'welcomed and appreciated by many from all walks of life'.[68] Anxiety still prevailed in Hong Kong. The new citizenship category still attracted criticism. The *SCMP* pointed out that Britain had 'a strong obligation to ensure a fair deal for those who lived their lives under the protection of [a] British flag', especially because Hong Kong could never become independent:

> Hong Kong is not and never can be a sovereign state and despite its growing economic clout it is difficult to believe there can ever be an effective Hong Kong passport ... It remains British and as long as this connection continues, it is to that country that Hong Kong must look as the ultimate guardian and custodian of its affairs.[69]

The *Post* then argued that 'any arrangement' that deprived people with links to the United Kingdom of this right to claim 'the full protection of the British government and ultimately resident status in Britain' would be 'strongly resented'.[70] Many also failed to understand why it was impossible to adhere to one citizenship category and argued that 'the assurance does not go far enough and leaves a great deal still to be desired':

> British nationality always has been an all-embracing concept, covering not just those who dwell in various parts of the United Kingdom but in territories for which Britain continues to be responsible.[71]

The *SCMP* argued that because the bill made 'a distinction between the passport of one British citizen and another', it offended a 'principle of unity', with countries given 'a superior and inferior status'.[72] It argued that it was extremely unfair that while any United Kingdom citizen could enter Hong Kong without any hinderance, there was no reciprocity for Hong Kong citizens.[73]

The Nationality Bill stimulated public debate within Hong Kong centred on 'the worries' of businessmen'.[74] In February 1981, the Federation of

Hong Kong Industries petitioned the Home Secretary, William Whitelaw, to 'reinforce the serious concern of businessmen over the British Nationality Bill and future of Hong Kong citizens'.[75] The Federation, established by statue in 1961, and with 1,500 members, argued that there had been a 'general erosion' of 'confidence in Hong Kong's economic future'. The bill would further cause a 'drain' of 'talents and investment'.[76] It urged the Home Office to make changes to the bill to ensure that the British–Hong Kong relationship would 'continue to be as close as it has been'.[77]

Heung Yee Kuk was concerned because many New Territories people had moved to Britain. In his open letter, the Kuk's Information Officer, Donald Yap, invoking the idea of 'Britishness', urged the colonial government to 'protect the interests of Hong Kong people in negotiations with the British government' over the proposed bill. When arguing that all passports issued to British subjects should be 'exactly the same, whether in form or in name', the Kuk implied that Hong Kong people were 'the Queen's subjects' and hence they should be treated by foreign countries 'without distinction'. It also pushed for the rights of British nationals living in Britain to acquire British citizenship and advocated that children born in the United Kingdom and abroad to British subjects should automatically acquire British citizenship. This letter was printed in newspapers.[78]

The UMELCO, who were convinced that the bill would turn them into 'second class citizens', protested for amendments. To these unofficials, the bill created 'a psychological' problem linked to the '1997' question.[79] After the second reading of the bill was passed, senior unofficial members, Szeyuen Chung and Oswald Cheung, who were already in London attending the debate, met with the Secretary of State Peter Carrington and Whitelaw on 2 and 7 February 1981, respectively. On 7 February, Chung and Cheung also held a press conference in London, drawing the public's attention to their cause. They stated that Hong Kong people were 'particularly worried' about the effects of a new category of citizenship and subsequently raised three main problems. First, Hong Kong was concerned over the change in its citizenship status in the bill and would have preferred the situation to remain unchanged. Second, if there was to be a change, Hong Kong people would only welcome the idea of a separate citizenship for the dependent territories provided that assurances were given by Britain and the change would not involve an erosion of their rights vis-à-vis British citizenship. Lastly, there were anxieties that travel restrictions were to be imposed on citizens of this proposed category, which would in particular affect the ability of businessmen to travel freely, one of Hong Kong's 'strengths' in external trade.[80] Among all of these requests, the unofficials were in particular 'adamant' about preserving the existing position whereby a CUKC could acquire the right of abode in the United Kingdom after five years of residence: 'They are prepared to accept a process of registration for this purpose provided it is an entitlement, but are totally opposed to naturalisation because of the constitutional and practical erosion it would represent.'[81] For the same reason, they also argued that unofficials and officials in the Crown service should be able to become British citizens through registration rather than naturalisation.[82] In terms of nomenclature, although they 'remained unconvinced' that British citizenship should be subdivided, they accepted that the retention of CUKC was no longer practical and proposed that Hong Kong CUKCs should be now given the title 'British (Hong Kong) Citizens'.[83] In addition, they wished to retain the existing entitlement Hong Kong CUKC women and men had to register as British citizens when married to British partner.[84] Their campaign generated 'great pressure' on the Governor.[85] They also subjected British MP Anthony Royle to a 'a terrific lecture' when he visited Hong Kong.[86]

Government responses and unofficials' reactions

In response to Hong Kong's representations, Whitelaw proposed two concessions. The first was to allow any child born in Britain who did not become a British citizen at birth to acquire citizenship after ten years' continuous residence, irrespective of his/her parents' statuses.[87] This would help children who found it difficult to produce evidence of their parents' statuses at the time of their birth. The second amendment enabled people who acquired British citizenship by naturalisation or registration to transmit their citizenship to their children, in the same way as people who were citizens by birth.[88]

On 9 February 1981, twenty-four MPs were nominated to serve a Standing Committee that was set up to consider the bill. Two of its members, Raymond Whitney and Edward Lyons, subsequently visited Hong Kong on 12 February to gather 'first hand' information and the 'feelings of Hong Kong on the bill'.[89] They issued a public statement expressing sympathy to Hong Kong's case but argued that the objective of the bill and 'its limited practical effects' had not been 'fully understood in Hong Kong'.[90] They assured the unofficials that the British–Hong Kong link 'should be firmly maintained' and they would ensure that Hong Kong's concerns were conveyed to ministers and members of the Standing Committee.[91] However, the Nationality and Treaty Department in Britain was reluctant to make further concessions. As Hong Kong had the highest number of people in Crown service in the remaining British dependent territories, approximately 145,808 civil servants, police and auxiliaries, granting concessions might have led to a sudden influx of people into Britain: 'it is not realistic to think that if such a provision existed it could be left dormant until a crisis situation developed.' The Department was convinced that unofficials 'want[ed] British citizenship now'.[92]

Such concessions were not the main concerns of the unofficials. According to MacLehose, who was by 1981 an experienced Governor, the unofficials' close analysis of the bill led them to believe that there were 'clear erosions of even their existing positions', making them 'more sensitive to the psychological and political shock of having their existing citizenship legislated away'.[93] MacLehose believed that there would be potential repercussions which affected Hong Kong's political stability if the unofficials' sentiments were not handled sensitively:

> The combination of practical position and psychological aspects has acted like a catalyst. Concern that something must be done to reassure those on whom the colony depends for administration and order is one aspect. But though at present reactions are confined to the small, influential and articulate minority, if their legitimate fears are not calmed by a substantial response by H.M.G. this concern could spill over and affect the confidence of a much wider section of the population. This could be serious.[94]

The colonial government was also aware of the bill's economic consequences, as the change of status from CUKC to CBDT was 'likely to accelerate the emigration of the young well-educated part of the population' – 'the managers and entrepreneurs of the future'.[95] With a potential 'reduction in the likelihood of CUKCs being able to settle in Britain', those who could afford to do so might also seek to 'establish an appropriate status in another country'.[96] In short, the changes in citizenship category would 'accelerate' emigration, affecting Hong Kong's workforce and productivity.[97]

Cradock, the British Ambassador to China, advised against any changes, arguing that creating a separate status for Hong Kong people would be perceived by China as 'a move towards autonomy or a challenge to Chinese aims on the territory'.[98] Facing pressure exerted by the UMELCO, MacLehose 'had no alternative but to come to London' to consult the Secretary of State and convey Hong Kong's view to the Home Secretary and Minister of State in March 1981.[99] The Governor believed that he needed to visit London to 'cool the situation'.[100] Before his departure, the Executive Council agreed that assurances should be given to the public, stressing that the British government would continue to uphold the 'constitutional relationship with Hong Kong' and that 'Hong Kong's view on the bill have been, and will continue to be, represented to the British government through various channels'.[101] When meeting with Raison on 11 March, MacLehose stressed that because of 'a crisis of confidence' in Hong Kong, amendments were 'essential'.[102] The Minister of State reminded the Governor that 'a major concession has already been made in response to Hong Kong's wishes', that is, adding an extra category of citizenship, CBDT. He also stressed that the ministers had to 'balance the difficulties of Hong Kong against the [British] government's own problems', including repercussions on other dependent territories.[103] Raison was reluctant to enable Crown service in a dependency to count as fulfilling the residence requirements for naturalisation as British citizen as it would 'surely have serious repercussions', constituting an impression that this was 'an escape route' to Britain 'in the event of a Chinese takeover'.[104] He also rejected the proposed title 'British (Hong Kong) Citizen' as that 'strikes at the root of the aims of the bill', which was to avoid giving the idea that CUKCs 'should simply become British citizens'.[105]

These exchanges were shaped by MacLehose's perceptions of what Hong Kong wanted with respect to revisions to the bill. In the meeting with Whitelaw, MacLehose stressed the 'strong emotion' raised in Hong Kong focusing on nomenclature:

> People in Hong Kong now saw the [British Nationality] Bill as a fundamental attack on the relationship with the United Kingdom. It was an unpleasant feeling to have one's citizenship legislated away. Strong resentment was at present restricted to about 5 or 10 per cent of the population but they were the most articulate and influential section, and at any time resentment could become general and have wider political implications.[106]

The Governor suggested that a failure to make changes would result in 'a strong public reaction', which was 'highly undesirable' and would affect the morale of civil servants.[107] Whitelaw agreed that CBDT should have the right to register as British citizens after five years of residence, but 'had much more difficulty' with the proposal for a discretionary provision allowing the Home Secretary to naturalise persons who had served the Crown in dependent territories in special circumstances.[108]

Editors of *Ming Pao* and the *SCMP* welcomed these 'concessions' which signalled that 'London does heed the colony's view and the sentiments of the people of Hong Kong'.[109] Among the unofficials, however, there was an 'underlying uneasiness'.[110] They wanted to retain the reference to British nationality in a separate citizenship, using the title 'British National: Hong Kong Citizen' or 'British National: Citizen of Hong Kong' or 'British National: CBDT (Hong Kong)'.[111] A 'strong pitch for a change in the nomenclature' was subsequently made by Chung to Carrington on 30 March 1981. Chung argued that he 'could not see why nomenclature' could not make the fact that CBDTs would remain British nationals 'explicit', especially given that the Nationality and Treaty Department also acknowledged in private correspondence that CBDTs would remain British nationals under international law.[112] Carrington explained that the Home Secretary would not adjust the nomenclature, because 'an umbrella title' covering all these various categories would have nullified 'a principal objective' of the bill: 'to use titles which avoid giving the impression that a person might have rights in the United Kingdom, particularly the right of abode'.[113] The Nationality and Treaty Department had pointed out that although the term had a 'specialised meaning in international law', domestic law 'excluded' these 'Nationals' from abiding in Britain.[114] Chung, however, continued to press for the case of using the title 'British Subject, CBDT (Hong Kong)' or 'British National (Hong Kong Citizen)'.[115] As unofficials were 'not prepared to accept that the word "national" cannot fit in to what is after all a "British Nationality Bill"', tensions with the Governor deepened.[116] A United Kingdom minister had opposed separate citizenship 'absolutely': but unofficials still pressed the case.[117] On 24 April, MacLehose noted:

> But in spite of the value of the amendments made (for which I am grateful) the feeling has grown here that the [British Nationality] Bill is yet another dirty trick played on Hong Kong. This is not related to a desire for asylum or a proposal to upset the provisions of the Commonwealth Immigration Act of 1962, but to a belief that the new nomenclature creates a new nationality of reduced status.[118]

With Hong Kong's anticipated return to China, the adjective 'British' was considered important as it implied to people their 'continuing British nationality'.[119] According to MacLehose, this symbolic 'general issue' was becoming 'coupled with other things', in particular the lease.[120] The *SCMP* expressed a similar view, noting that opinions of British nationals in dependencies were not being respected and that there should be a referendum to ascertain the views of 'the vast majority of Hong Kong's British subjects'.[121]

Understanding 'the importance of a name, particularly to Chinese' and being influenced by the 'stormy meeting' he had at the Executive Council, MacLehose requested that the Foreign and Commonwealth Office pressurise the Home Office to enable CBDT to carry the prefix 'British National' on Hong Kong passports.[122] The Nationality and Treaty Department refused the request, which they described as based on 'sentiment' not 'substance' and that 'merely served' elitist elements.[123] One of its officials declared that '*Civis Britannicus*' was 'dead'.[124] Despite the resistance of the Home Office, the Foreign and Commonwealth Office backed MacLehose and Hong Kong's proposal. Richard Luce, the Minister of State for Foreign Affairs, argued that it was a 'cosmetic' problem, that is, generating 'a false' impression of 'weakening' ties.[125] Carrington agreed and was 'convinced' that they must do what they could to meet UMELCO's request.[126] The Home Office ministers, however, were under the impression that the colonial government would not campaign for further changes after the new clauses on registration and

Crown Servants had been added.[127] The Governor recognised that 'no further amendments' to the bill were 'possible';[128] but the UMELCO continued to lobby the Secretary of State and MPs, expressing their 'growing concern' about 'the uncertainty' of the retention of British national status, which they considered to be 'a matter of paramount importance'.[129] However, Carrington explained to the unofficials that the Home Secretary simply 'found it impossible to accept' the proposed nomenclature.[130] Reassurance was, however, given to the unofficials that the absence of the term 'British Subject' or 'British National' on passports would 'not affect the right or commitment' of the British government to CBDTs: Britain would continue to 'afford consular protection and represent their interests internationally'.[131]

The Hong Kong government sought to manage the reactions of Hong Kong people. To this end, the GIS released a statement to newspapers, pointing out that some of Hong Kong's concerns had been taken into account and amendments had been made. The British government's commitment to Hong Kong remained unchanged and CBDTs were not 'second-class' citizens. Efforts would also be made to ensure that third countries were aware of the new category of citizenship and CBDTs could continue to travel on passports described as 'British passport Hong Kong' on the cover with the citizenship title 'CBDT' inside.[132] Bryan also stressed that the views of Hong Kong had shaped amendments, and consultation was not a mere 'public relations exercise'.[133]

At the end of the third reading, to assure Hong Kong, Raison reconfirmed that all CBDTs would remain United Kingdom nationals and Britain would offer them consular protection. The passport would include the word 'British' on the cover and the name 'Hong Kong', with 'Citizen of the British Dependent Territories–Hong Kong' likely to be in the citizenship column.[134] Accepting that further representations would be counterproductive, UMELCO declined to send a delegation to London.[135] The mood of the UMELCO was 'one of disenchantment and resigned acceptance'.[136] MacLehose reported that 'generally speaking' the bill 'was now fairly satisfactory to Hong Kong'.[137]

The Gibraltar amendment and public reception

In July 1981, the House of Lords announced the passage of a new clause which provided British subjects in Gibraltar the entitlement to register as British citizens.[138] This reignited debates in Hong Kong, leading to 'widespread concern and sharp reaction'.[139] Unofficial meetings became 'quite heated'.[140] Unofficials believed that 'in the light of the Gibraltar amendment', at least some 'specific administrative arrangement' could be done for Hong Kong to emphasise people's Britishness in the passport.[141] Differential treatment was perceived as unfair, with unofficial Legislative Councillor Yuet-keung Kan declaring that the Gibraltar amendment was 'wrong' and represented 'another nail in Hong Kong's coffin'.[142] Urban Councillor Hilton Cheong-leen petitioned Whitelaw on behalf of the Hong Kong Civil Association, urging the British government to recognise CBDTs, along with British citizens, as 'a common "British Nationality"'.[143] MacLehose was pragmatic enough to realise that the British government would not 'accept the extension of the same registration privilege to Hong Kong', and he believed that the colonial government's 'primary concern' should be to allow CBDTs to retain their British nationality.[144] Under the public and official pressure in Hong Kong, efforts were made by the Governor and the Secretary of State to convince the Home Office to alter the nomenclature. The Home Office, however, believed that 'premature concessions' should not be made due to a fear that this would 'jeopardise the chances of defeating the Gibraltar amendment'.[145] It therefore turned down Hong Kong's proposal on 13 October 1981.

As 'things have taken a most unhappy turn' in Hong Kong, in particular among the unofficials, MacLehose recommended the Home Office to accept a new amendment proposed by Lord Geddes, which was to provide for an alternative title of 'British Dependent Territories Citizens' (BDTC) and press for the case for the title 'British (Hong Kong) Citizen' to be used in passports. However, due to the firm stance held by the Home Office, there did 'not appear to be any possibility of providing for the description "British (Hong Kong) Citizen"' to be used in the passports.[146] Such a proposition was further rejected by the Clerk of the Parliament on the ground of 'its similarity with an earlier unsuccessful amendment' tabled by Lord Elwyn-Jones.[147] Lord Geddes subsequently tabled another amendment on 20 October, proposing to substitute the title of BDTC for CBDT.

As Chi-kwan Mark has argued, the unofficials were not worried about immigration rights but were more interested in preserving their present political position and maintaining confidence in Hong Kong's future.[148] Such requests therefore should not be interpreted as evidence of political allegiance to Britain. According to MacLehose, the UMELCO were 'principally concerned' whether the British government would accept its responsibilities for its dependent territories citizens when 'Hong Kong ceased to be British': they could become 'stateless' on leaving Hong Kong or would have to stay and 'become Chinese'.[149] Geddes' proposed amendment brought 'the word order of all three main categories of citizenship into line' and was supported by Whitelaw and passed in the House of Lords.[150] BDTCs were granted the rights of abode in Hong Kong and could transmit their statuses to the next generation.[151] The British Nationality Bill was enacted on 30 October 1981 and the British Nationality Act 1981 came into effect on 1 January 1983.

224   Covert colonialism

Public morale still had to be managed. On 11 November, therefore, Hong Kong's Commissioner in London, Jack Cater, stated that 'Hong Kong must accept the assurances given by [the] United Kingdom Minister' that the Act would 'in no way alter the United Kingdom government's relations with, and its commitment to, Hong Kong and its people'. Cater pointed out that he understood that 'while Hong Kong would have preferred no change at all' – and the change was an 'unpleasant and unwelcome shock' – the Act's effects on Hong Kong citizens' rights and interests would be 'neutral'. He also reminded the public that the Act was already 'a considerable improvement on the Bill as it was first presented in January', although the Act did not specify that Hong Kong people would remain British.[152]

Conclusion

The British Nationality Bill controversy demonstrates that the colonial government understood the importance of being responsive to public opinion, and consequently the Governor sought to persuade the Foreign and Commonwealth Office to put pressure on the Home Office to make amendments. This provides further evidence of a 'decolonisation' in the mentality of British bureaucrats representing Hong Kong people.

Heightened by the anticipated takeover of China in 1997, unofficials and business elites were concerned about the practical effects of the bill – for example, their ability to travel internationally: but the bill also had symbolic importance. A notion of 'Chinese Britishness', with an allegiance to the Queen and the British government, was invoked to demand that the new category of citizenship include the terms 'British National' and 'British (Hong Kong) Citizen'. The underlying motivation to take a stand related to the anticipated consequences of retrocession, implying that 'allegiance' to the British government was fluid. As in the 1970s, residents wrote to newspapers to express their concerns. Petitions were also issued. A degree of political conservatism persisted. Indifference was prevalent among the working class at the grassroots level.

Although the unofficials and Governor made strong representations to the British Parliament, they merely gained minor concessions. The British government prioritised its domestic interests over the concerns of British subjects in Hong Kong, and only made changes if they were confined to Hong Kong, did not compromise British interests and did not have repercussions for other British dependencies.

The nationality of BDTCs became a critical issue in Sino-British negotiations from 1982 to 1984 as under Chinese law, all Hong Kong Chinese residents were considered 'Chinese nationals' and the Chinese government did not recognise dual citizenship. The associated rights of BDTCs, such as British consular protection and the use of British passports, were not recognised.[153] The British and colonial governments accepted that BDTC in Hong Kong needed to be removed after 1997. Its existing rights could only be retained under a new category.[154] The Chinese and British in the end came to an agreement that BDTCs in Hong Kong could 'continue to hold British nationality after 1997 without the Chinese having formally to agree to this or to the concept of dual nationality'.[155] However, this did not end the controversy. The British Nationality Bill laid a foundation for further changes in Hong Kong British subjects' nationality in the 1990s and after 1997. Under the Hong Kong (British Nationality) Order of 1986, permanent residents of Hong Kong who were British Dependent Territories Citizens by 30 June 1997 could register for British National Overseas (BN(O)) citizenship.[156] Holders of BN(O) passports originally were not granted the right of abode in Britain. However, due to China's increased intervention in Hong Kong, a new immigration route to the United Kingdom was open to BN(O) status holders from 31 January 2021. This change, which the British government claimed to reflect 'the United Kingdom's historic and moral commitment to those people of Hong Kong who chose to retain their ties to the United Kingdom', provides a pathway for millions of BN(O) holders and their dependents to live, study and work in Britain and obtain citizenship after five years of residence.[157] The scheme, however, should also be interpreted as a policy to complement the new 'Global Britain' in the post-Brexit context and a means to continue attracting skilled labour.[158] It is also a result of the changing Sino-British diplomatic relations. Sino-British tensions are rising, as increased parliamentary calls for intervention in human rights abuses in Xinjiang and the decision to strip Huawei's involvement from Britain's 5G network have demonstrated.[159] This change in geopolitical dynamics also facilitated the emergence of the BN(O) visa route, which led to increased Sino-British hostility with Beijing stating that China would 'no longer recognise' the BN(O) passports for Hong Kong Chinese as travel and identity documents.[160] By August 2021, nearly 65,000 Hong Kongers had applied for this new BN(O) visa scheme.[161] The legacy of the British Nationality Act is still felt in today's Hong Kong.

Notes

1 Mark, 'To "Educate" Deng', p. 165.
2 Carroll, *A Concise History*, p. 177.
3 Ibid., p. 178.
4 Mark, 'To "Educate" Deng', p. 166.

5 Mark, 'Decolonising Britishness?', pp. 565–90.
6 Hampton, *Hong Kong*, Chapter 6.
7 Ibid., p. 169.
8 HKRS 565-9-5, 'Information Paper on the British Nationality Law', Paul F. Brown to heads of departments, branch secretaries, CDOs and DOs, 5 March 1981, p. 1.
9 HKRS 1443-1-10, 'Outline of Proposed Legislation: British Nationality Law', 1980, p. 1.
10 During the transitional period, they remained British subjects but were without citizenship. This status was supposed to be 'temporary' and 'non-transmissible'. See 'Information Paper on the British Nationality Law', p. 2.
11 Ibid.
12 'Outline of Proposed Legislation: British Nationality Law', p. 3.
13 Mark, 'Decolonising Britishness?', p. 566; also see Layton-Henry, *The Politics of Immigration*; Brown, *Global South Asians*.
14 Schofield, *Enoch Powell*, Introduction.
15 Mark, 'Decolonising Britishness?', p. 566.
16 Ibid.
17 'Outline of Proposed Legislation: British Nationality Law', pp. 4–5.
18 Mark, 'Decolonising Britishness?', pp. 566–9; Paul, *Whitewashing Britain*, pp. 183 and 189.
19 Mark, 'Decolonising Britishness?', p. 569.
20 Ibid.
21 'Information Paper on the British Nationality Law', p. 1.
22 Ibid., p. 3.
23 Ibid., p. 2.
24 Ibid.
25 HKRS 605-1-16, 'White Paper on British Nationality: A Summary of Public and Media Reaction', 31 July–September 1', September 1980, p. 1.
26 HKRS 605-1-16, 'Process of Devalued Citizenship', *SCMP*, 15 August 1980.
27 HKRS 605-1-16, '歧視香港人的國籍法', *Express*, 31 July 1980.
28 HKRS 605-1-16, '研究修改香港居民身份法例', *Ming Pao*, 1 August 1980.
29 HKRS 605-1-16, '中國的民族情緒與自尊', *Ming Pao*, 2 August 1980.
30 'Information Paper on the British Nationality Law', p. 2.
31 Ibid., p. 10.
32 FCO 53/693, 'Memorandum for Executive Council: British Nationality Bill 1981', Council Chamber, 28 February 1981, p. 10.
33 HKRS 1443-1-10, ' "英"國籍法與香港', *STYP*, 31 January 1981.
34 HKRS 163-13-68, 'Green Papers: Post-Mortem on an Interesting Consultation Exercise', MOOD, 3 May 1978, p. 1.
35 Ibid.
36 Ibid.
37 Ibid., pp. 2–3.
38 Ibid., p. 4.
39 'Information Paper on the British Nationality Law', p. 10.

40 Ibid.
41 Ibid.
42 Ibid., p. 2.
43 FCO 40/1330, E. P. Ho to MacLehose, in 'MIPT', MacLehose to FCO, 31 January 1981.
44 HKRS 605-1-16, Anonymous letter to Director of Immigration, 7 August 1980.
45 Ibid.
46 HKRS 605-1-16, Tong H. Y. Ko to Director of Immigration, 2 August 1980.
47 HKRS 471-3-1, 'Silver Jubilee Celebrations: A Day of Fun and Entertainment', MOOD, 11 May 1977, p. 1.
48 Ibid.
49 HKRS 925-1-1, 'Queen's Birthday Celebrations', MOOD, 28 April 1976, p. 1.
50 Ibid., p. 2.
51 Ibid.
52 'Silver Jubilee Celebrations', p. 1.
53 HKRS 471-3-1, 'Visit of Prince Charles', MOOD, 8 March 1979, p. 7.
54 Ibid.
55 'White Paper on British Nationality: A Summary of Public and Media Reaction', p. 1.
56 FCO 40/1330, 'New Nationality Legislation: Call on the Secretary of State by Hong Kong Unofficials 2 February 1981', R. D. Clift to Private Secretary, 30 January 1981.
57 HKRS 489-4-20, 'British Nationality Bill', L. M. Davies to branch secretaries, heads of departments, CDOs and DOs, 11 January 1981, p. 2.
58 HKRS 605-1-16, 'Immigration, Nationality and Hong Kong: New Proposals Downgrade Citizenship and Threaten Human Rights', by Walter Easey, Hong Kong Research Project, 11 June 1980, attached to 'UK Nationality Law: Article by Mr Walter Easey', I. C. Orr to Secretary for Security, 5 September 1980, p. 7. For information about the Project, see Hampton, *Hong Kong*, p. 48.
59 'Immigration, Nationality and Hong Kong', by Easey, pp. 9–10.
60 HKRS 489-4-20, 'Sir Paul Welcomes Whitehall Pledge', *SCMP*, 28 January 1981.
61 HKRS 489-4-20, Extracts from a Debate on the British Nationality Bill on January 28, in Written Answer in the House of Commons, 26 January 1981. Bryan's speech was also quoted in 'Sir Paul Welcomes Whitehall Pledge', *SCMP*, 28 January 1981.
62 Ibid.
63 Extracts from a debate on the British Nationality Bill on 28 January 1981.
64 Ibid.
65 Ibid.
66 HKRS 489-4-20, Information released to news editors by GIS on 30 January 1981.
67 HKRS 1443-1-10, 'Sir Paul to be Our Champion: Fight over Nationality Bill Looms', *SCMP*, 28 January 1981.
68 HKRS 489-4-20, 'Hopes and Fears in the Nationality Bill', *SCMP*, 29 January 1981.

69 Ibid.
70 Ibid.
71 HKRS 489-4-20, 'Why Not a Single British Passport?', *SCMP*, 2 February 1981.
72 Ibid.
73 Ibid.
74 FCO 53/692, H. C Tang, Chairman of the Federation of Hong Kong Industries to William Whitelaw, 20 February 1981.
75 Ibid.
76 Ibid.
77 Ibid.
78 HKRS 1443-1-10, 'Spell Out Effects of Nationality Bill: Kuk', *SCMP*, 23 April 1981.
79 FCO 53/692, 'Nationality Bill: Background to HK's Request (Annex A)', in 'Nationality Bill: Essential Facts', by Hong Kong and General Department, 6 March 1981, p. 2.
80 HKRS 1443-1-10, Information released to news editor by the GIS, 7 February 1981.
81 FCO 53/692, 'Nationality Bill', MacLehose to FCO, 3 March 1981.
82 Ibid.
83 Ibid.
84 Ibid.
85 Ibid.
86 HKRS 1443-1-10, Kelvin Sinclair, 'Whitelaw to Get HK View', *SCMP*, 16 February 1981; FCO 53/692, 'Hong Kong: New Nationality Legislation: Mr. Clift's Minute of 19 February Below', A. E. Donald to W. J. Adams, 19 February 1981.
87 'Information Paper on the British Nationality Law', p. 5.
88 Ibid.
89 Ibid., p. 6.
90 FCO 53/692, Statement by Mr. Edward Lyons Q.C., M.P. (Labour Bradford West) and Mr. Ray Whitney O.B.E., M.P. (Conservative, Wycombe) on Conclusion of Their Visit to Hong Kong February 12–16 1981, 16 February 1981, pp. 1–2.
91 Ibid.
92 FCO 53/692, 'Nationality Bill: Hong Kong', W. Jones to W. J. Adams, 23 February 1981; FCO 40/1333, Parliamentary Question for Written Answer (Question Asked by John Tilley), 1 April 1981.
93 FCO 53/692, 'Nationality Bill', MacLehose to FCO, 3 March 1981.
94 Ibid.
95 'Memorandum for Executive Council: British Nationality Bill 1981', p. 9.
96 Ibid.
97 Ibid.
98 FCO 53/693, 'Nationality Bill', P. Cradock to FCO, 18 March 1981.
99 FCO, 53/692, 'Hong Kong: Call on the Secretary of State by State by Sir Murray MacLehose', P. Morrice to A. Donald, E. Youde and Private Secretary, 2 March 1981.

100 Ibid.
101 FCO 53/693, 'Memorandum for Executive Council: British Nationality Bill 1981', 28 February 1981, p. 11.
102 FCO 53/692, 'Meeting on British Nationality Bill with Governor of Hong Kong', from D. H. J. Hilary to Boya Smith, 6 March 1981.
103 Ibid.
104 Ibid.
105 Ibid.
106 FCO 53/693, Meeting between the Home Secretary and MacLehose, 11 March 1981, p. 2.
107 Ibid.
108 FCO 53/692, 'Hong Kong: New Nationality Legislation', from R. D. Clift to Private Secretary, 11 March 1981.
109 HKRS 1443-1-10, Editorials in *Ming Pao* and *SCMP*, 1 April 1981.
110 FCO 53/693, 'New Nationality Law', MacLehose to FCO, 17 March 1981; 'Nationality Law', MacLehose to FCO, 17 March 1981.
111 Ibid.
112 FCO 53/694, 'Nationality Bill', MacLehose to FCO, 30 March 1981. According to the Nationality and Treaty Department, ' "Nationals" is an international law term which denoted the relationship between an individual and the state which claim[s] to represent his interests in the sphere of international relations'. See FCO 53/693, 'Nationality Bill', W. Jones to A. R. Rushford, 17 March 1981.
113 'Nationality Bill', MacLehose to FCO, 30 March 1981; FCO 53/694, 'Meeting with Sir S Y Chung', Peter Carrington to Hong Kong, 30 March 1981.
114 FCO 53/694, 'Comments on Hong Kong Telegram No. 443', W. Jones to W. J. Adams, 24 April 1981.
115 FCO 53/692, 'Nationality Bill', MacLehose to FCO, 31 March 1981.
116 FCO 53/694, 'Nationality Bill', MacLehose to FCO, 7 April 1981.
117 FCO 53/694, 'From Jones', P. Carrington to MacLehose, 9 April 1981.
118 FCO 53/694, 'Nationality Bill', MacLehose to Youde, 24 April 1981.
119 Ibid.
120 FCO 53/695, 'Nationality Bill', MacLehose to Youde, 29 April 1981.
121 HKRS 489-4-20, 'Of Invective and "Propaganda" ', *SCMP*, 19 April 1981.
122 'Nationality Bill', MacLehose to Youde, 29 April 1981; 'Nationality Bill', MacLehose to Youde, 24 April 1981
123 FCO 53/695, 'NTD Comments on Hong Kong's Proposals for a Collective Nationality Title "British (or UK) National" ', by W. Jones, 29 April 1981.
124 Ibid.
125 FCO 53/695, 'Hong Kong: Nationality Bill', Richard Luce to P. Carrington, 1 May 1981.
126 FCO 53/695, 'Nationality Bill', P. Carrington to W. Whitelaw, 4 May 1981.
127 FCO 53/695, 'Nationality Bill', P. Carrington to MacLehose, 9 May 1981.
128 FCO 53/695, 'Hong Kong Nationality Bill', P. A. R. Blaker to P. Carrington, 19 May 1981.

129 FCO 53/696, 'British Nationality Bill 1981', S. Y. Chung to P. Carrington, 22 May 1981; 'Nationality Bill, HK', M. J. M. Rickerd to Hong Kong and General Department, 29 May 1981.
130 FCO 53/696, 'Reply to Sir S Y Chung's Letter', P. Carrington to MacLehose, 8 June 1981.
131 Ibid.
132 HKRS 489-4-20, Information released by GIS to news editors, 5 June 1981.
133 HKRS 489-4-20, Full Text of a Speech by Sir Paul Bryan, MP (Conservative) in the House of Commons on 4 June 1981 during the Third Reading Debate on the British Nationality Bill 1981.
134 HKRS 565-9-5, Extract from a Speech by Mr. Timothy Raison, Minister of State, Home Office in the House of Commons on 4 June 1981 when Winding Up the Third Reading Debate on the British Nationality Bill (Annex D), attached to 'British Nationality Bill 1981', L. M. Davies to branch secretaries, heads of departments, CDOs and DOs, 11 June 1981.
135 FCO 53/696, 'Call by the Governor of Hong Kong on the Secretary of State', 23 June 1981.
136 FCO 53/696, 'British Nationality Bill 1981', S. Y. Chung to P. Carrington, 27 June 1981; 'British Nationality Bill', Jack Cater to FCO, 30 June 1981.
137 FCO 53/696, 'Governor's Press Confidence', Jack Cater to Beijing, 22 June 1981.
138 Under the new amendment (clause 10), CBDTs of Gibraltar, by virtue of their status as British nationals under the Treaty of Rome and membership in the European Community, would be entitled to be registered as British citizens on application without meeting any other requirements.
139 FCO 53/696, 'British Nationality Bill', J. Cater to FCO, 23 July 1981.
140 FCO 53/696, 'British Nationality Bill'. A. E. Donald to W. J. Adams, 24 July 1981.
141 FCO 53/696, 'British Nationality Bill', J. Cater to FCO, 21 July 1981.
142 HKRS 1443-1-10, 'Another Nail in Our Coffin', *HKS*, 24 July 1981.
143 FCO 53/697, Hilton Cheong-leen, Hong Kong Civil Association to William Whitelaw, 2 September 1981.
144 FCO 53/697, 'MIPT', MacLehose to FCO, 9 October 1981.
145 FCO 53/697, 'Nationality Bill', P. Carrington to MacLehose, 9 October 1981; 'British Nationality Bill: Citizens of the British Dependent Territories', C. J. Walters to Stephen Gomersall, 13 October 1981.
146 FCO 53/697, 'Nationality Bill', MacLehose to FCO, 15 October 1981; 'British Nationality Bill: Hong Kong', R. D. Clift to Lord Trefgarne, A. E. Donald, W. J. Adams, Howells and W. Jones, 16 October 1981.
147 FCO 53/697, 'MIPT', MacLehose to FCO, 16 October 1981.
148 Mark, 'Decolonising Britishness?', p. 578.
149 FCO 53/698, 'Nationality Bill', MacLehose to FCO, 26 October 1981.
150 Mark, 'Decolonising Britishness?', p. 578; FCO 40/1336, FCO to Hong Kong, 19 October 1981.
151 Mark, 'Decolonising Britishness?', pp. 578–9.

152 HKRS 489-4-20, GIS, 'Sir Jack Speaks on Nationality Act', 11 November 1981.
153 Mark, 'Decolonising Britishness?', p. 579.
154 Ibid., p. 580.
155 Ibid., pp. 581–2.
156 Ibid., p. 583.
157 'Guidance: Hong Kong British Nationals (Overseas) Welcome Programme – Information for Local Authorities', last updated on 29 July 2021, www.gov.uk/guidance/hong-kong-uk-welcome-programme-guidance-for-local-authorities.
158 Brexit means that the freedom of movement for citizens of the European Union members was repealed, followed by a points-based immigration system, which in effect 'liberalised' immigration in Britain into a 'level playing field for people from all over the world'. See Benson, 'Hong Kongers', p. 6. And according to the BN(O) survey conducted by the Home Office, many visa holders are professionals: 69 per cent of the visa holders hold bachelor or higher degrees, 39 per cent are in professional occupations, and 26 per cent are in associate professional occupations. See Home Office, 'Research and Analysis: Hong Kong BN(O) Survey Results', 31 January 2022, Tables 8 and 9.
159 Benson, 'Hong Kongers', p. 13.
160 'China Will "No Longer Recognise" UK-issued BNO Passports for Hong Kongers', *HKFP*, 29 January 2021.
161 'Nearly 65,000 Hong Kongese Have Applied for BN(O) Visa Scheme So Far Amid Exodus under National Security Law', *SCMP*, 26 August 2021.

8

Overt public opinion surveys and shifting popular attitudes towards proposed and implemented constitutional reforms

As Denis Bray, the Secretary for Home Affairs, observed in a 1982 speech, the Hong Kong government could not be 'changed by an election' – which was a 'norm' 'outside the western world' – but the territory provided 'a special set of civil liberties': it was, he argued, a polity like 'nowhere else'.[1] As previous chapters have explored, the colonial administration possessed 'a very extensive consultative machinery', including the Legislative and Executive Councils, the UMELCO office, the Urban Council, the Green Papers, ad hoc Commissions of Inquiry and channels to get in contact with traditional organisations and bodies, such as kaifong associations and MACs.[2] Covert polling mechanisms, which were becoming increasingly sophisticated, also widened channels of political participation. Archival records indicate that by the late 1970s, Town Talk and MOOD were no longer the only covert opinion monitoring mechanisms. During the 1970s, the colonial government introduced other similar covert exercises of different scales and with different areas of focus. For example, the Resettlement Department compiled Squatter Talks, which monitored the attitudes and opinions of inhabitants living on Crown land unlawfully towards various issues, ranging from views towards community facilities and traffic problems to crime and utility prices.[3] It also produced Estates Talk, which examined the 'gossip' of residents living in resettlement estates, sharing the reports with the HAD.[4] The CDOs collated Flash Points, a more 'spontaneous' version of MOOD with a smaller sampling size, which analysed 'public attitudes on day-to-day events or sensational district happenings and the sway or trends of public feelings' twice a week as soon as they emerged.[5] In addition, through the subject-oriented Stop Press, they reported and assessed incidents in particular districts.[6] The emergence of these exercises suggested that the surveillance system developed by the colonial government to monitor public opinion had been expanded considerably and had become increasingly sophisticated. However, how did these covert consultative forms of colonialism, which were an imperfect substitute for democratic elections, evolve as constitutional reforms were discussed in the last years of colonial rule?

The first section of this chapter investigates the introduction of the City and New Territories Administration and elections in District Boards in 1982. Although the reforms were not introduced with the goal of 'democratising Hong Kong', they widened the channels of political participation. The second section examines why scientifically organised public opinion surveys conducted by commercial firms and universities were commissioned by the colonial government. The third and fourth sections explore constitutional reforms at the level of the Executive and Legislative Councils and how they affected 'covert colonialism'. The last section reveals changing popular attitudes towards constitutional reforms and explores to what extent, as is to be expected, political cultures varied across society.

Democratisation at district level

In May 1982, Ng Chak-lam, the Principal Assistant Secretary for Hong Kong, claimed that government officials were now 'directly exposed to public opinion' and that there was 'no evidence that the government has failed to respond to it either out of ignorance or of interference by special interest groups'.[7] A system of consultative politics, however, had limitations, as argued by politicians-cum-activists. For example, in 1980, at the annual debate at the Urban Council, Elliott argued that 'while there was an intention on the government's part to find out the nature of that [communication] gap, there was no intention to bridge it'; the 'expensive public relations unit' was only set up to 'cover up the gap and paint beautiful pictures'.[8] A persistent critique of the government, the *SCMP*, argued that the CDO Scheme has not led policymakers to 'listen':

> For ten years, the CDOs have tried their best to do a job which, in the circumstances, is basically contradictory at worst and ill-defined at best. On the one hand they are supposed to be the 'eyes and ears' of the administration. They are also supposed to explain government policy to the governed. On the other hand, the people who seek the help and advice of the CDOs expect their complaints to be explained to the policymakers, in the hope that policies can be amended for their greater good.[9]

The report also mentioned Town Talk and MOOD. However, the paper seemed to hold a sceptical attitude towards the covert opinion polling exercises which the public vaguely understood:

Some years ago, CDOs were known to produce a weekly document called Town Talk, nowadays changed to the more reflective title of MOOD. It is said that this document is a compilation of what CDOs hear in the course of their work in their various localities. We have no information as to how this compilation is done but even a cursory onlooker of the vast organisation of the HAD will see that the 'public opinion' which is set in print each week for the consumption of the government must depend heavily on the width of the contacts of each officer in the department.[10]

As Suzanne Pepper has argued, the government merely made subtle adaptations in response 'to changing circumstances'.[11] In 1980, a Green Paper proposed District Boards, and in 1981, after issuing a White Paper, it announced that a 'more systematic form' of District Administration had been drawn up.[12] Due to the 'continuing shift and expansion' of the Hong Kong population, the task of administering Hong Kong had simply 'become increasingly complicated'.[13] In the face of the administrative challenge, a City and New Territories Administration was formed, and District Boards were subsequently created. In total, there were ten districts in the urban areas and eight in the New Territories, each served by one District Board and District Management Committee. All Boards and Committees were set up by March 1982.[14] These reforms were an 'acceleration' of 'regionalisation of government departments' and the 'delegation of greater authorities' to 'district representatives'.[15] Political participation in community affairs was also enabled through these reforms, with residents able to raise issues through their district representatives. In October 1982, the first District Board election was held.[16] Anyone aged twenty-one years old or older and who had lived in Hong Kong for at least seven years was eligible to vote in the election.[17] The District Boards advised the government on the wellbeing of district residents and workers, the provision and use of public services and facilities, the adequacy and priorities of government programmes and the use of public funds allocated to the district for community activities and work.[18] A 'Meet-the-Public' scheme also allowed the public to either ring up a District Board's Secretariat or go to a District Office in person to make an appointment with a District Board member.[19] District Board members therefore gained 'first-hand information of local problems as well as the needs of residents and their views on government policies and measures'.[20] In 1983, reforms were carried out in the Urban Council. The number of its total members increased from twenty-four in 1973 to thirty in 1983, and the number of its elected unofficials also rose from twelve in 1973 to fifteen in 1983.[21] Although both the District Boards and Urban Council were merely advisory bodies that did not possess executive power, the changes provided increased channels for the public to participate in district affairs and express their views to the policymakers, paving the way for further democratisation.

Scientifically organised public opinion surveys conducted by commercial firms and universities

Until late 1980, the HAD continued to use MOOD to assess public opinion but also sought to use 'untapped' sources to gain an enhanced understanding of public attitudes.[22] There were, however, significant perceived gaps in its knowledge, notably on the views of residents of the New Territories and on trade unionists.[23] Understanding the limitations of its existing mechanisms for gathering data, the HAD started enlisting professional expertise to solicit public opinion.[24] In October 1974, the department requested funds to commission commercial polling organisations;[25] and in 1977–8, a special budget for 'Public Opinion Surveys' was created, providing $400,000.[26] Even so, officials had reservations. One official noted that, of more than twenty market research specialist companies in the yellow pages in 1977, 'nearly all' had 'no experience' and their staff seemed to have had 'no scientific training', and just wanted a 'way to make easy money'.[27] According to the Director of GIS, of the three reliable firms – namely International Research Associates (IRA), Spectrum and Survey Research Hong Kong (SRH) – only the latter could undertake 'accurate' independent surveys; the IRA had 'a tendency to produce the results that they believed their clients require' and Spectrum had soon gone out of business.[28]

Moreover, although the methodologies used by these firms to collect and analyse data were 'scientific', they remained problematic. For example, although the SRH's technique claimed to capture a representative sample 'of all households in Hong Kong', officials questioned this claim, arguing that 'no attempt' had been made to quantify the magnitude of sampling error.[29] Details on the 'doubtful' sampling method were not available, and it was noted that lists of squatters were 'out of date' and that those paying rents in subdivided properties needed to be included.[30] The fact that a third of people did not respond to requests to be surveyed also 'biased' the results.[31] Furthermore, the colonial government was reluctant to grant private firms access to state records to improve sampling methods because this would constitute 'a degree of disturbance' to the government's operations and provide commercial organisations with access to information that could be used in subsequent commercial commissions.[32]

Despite these shortcomings, commercial fees were 'prohibitive' and so most surveys continued to be undertaken in-house.[33] The higher number of supervisors and enumerators required for these exercises posed logistical and staffing problems for the department.[34] Due to the limited capacity the HAD had to deal with increased requests for surveys from various departments, it was proposed that increased numbers of public opinion surveys should be conducted by post-secondary colleges and semi-governmental agencies, in preference to commercial consultancy firms.[35] The choice of university students, who had 'increasing social awareness' and engagement in 'a growing number of community projects', to serve as enumerators could also be attributed to the fact that they could 'harness their enthusiasm and energy', which might create a stabilising effect.[36] In 1977–8, three surveys, part of the government's Green Papers costing $278,154.62, were conducted by the University of Hong Kong with the HAD. In 1978–9, a public opinion survey on social facilities in Sau Mau Ping and Lam Tin was also carried out by the Hong Kong Polytechnic in collaboration with the department.[37] To ensure that findings were not subject to bias, before a consultant was engaged, his/her credentials and political allegiances were vetted.[38] It is important to note that despite the increased involvement of external organisations, the HAD continued supervising the surveys closely, such as designing the questionnaire, selecting the population coverage with the Census and Statistics Department and finalising the survey report, ensuring that it provided 'a sufficient injection of resources' to 'make the exercise a successful and meaningful one'.[39]

The 1980s saw the increased use of scientifically organised surveys by the HAD. For example, in January 1983, it started a series of bi-monthly telephone surveys to monitor public opinion on the government's overall performance, expected level of personal and household income and general impressions of the employment situation. In each survey, a random sample of 993 respondents aged fifteen to sixty-four was interviewed. The surveys had a small sampling error of merely 3 per cent and a confidence level of 95 per cent as 90 per cent of households in Hong Kong had telephones by that time.[40] Despite internal reservations, the HAD also relied on external companies and other government departments to conduct overt public opinion surveys. For example, in 1984, the IRA was responsible for undertaking a series of surveys with a sampling size of 2,000 interviewees from January to March to investigate 'public opinions and attitudes, thoughts and feelings, perceptions and depositions, sentiments and empathy' towards the 'government as a whole and various departments', and also their 'roles and/ or functions, services and provisions, efforts and performances, actions and programmes, projects and activities, policies and standards'.[41] To understand the shifting public opinion towards the Sino-British agreement, a Public Opinion Assessment Office was set up in 1984.[42] In 1991, the Hong Kong Public Opinion Research Institute was also set up under the University of Hong Kong's Faculty of Social Science.[43]

How did the expansion of polling affect the 'communication gap' between the government and Chinese society? According to the opinion poll conducted by the HAD in conjunction with the IRA in 1984, the public remained 'critical of' government communications with half of the respondents commenting that they were 'poor' and only 19 per cent believing that state–society communications were 'good' (this had fallen from 26 per cent in 1982), while 65 per cent felt that channels were 'inadequate'. Regarding the performance of the District Offices, only three in ten of the respondents agreed that DOs were doing 'a good job of collecting and reflecting public opinion to policymakers', as compared to 47 per cent in the 1982 survey.[44]

The HAD was consequently reorganised in April 1985. The Opinion Survey Unit (OSU) was transferred to the Administration Headquarters. The OSU belonged to the Community Information Unit and was headed by a Senior Statistician, assisted by a Senior Statistical Officer and a Statistical Officer. The OSU primarily carried out public opinion surveys of 'a territory-wide nature'. However, when the needs arose, it also conducted surveys on a district or regional basis. In addition, it supervised surveys commissioned to private research companies, and when opinion surveys were launched in the district, the unit offered help to individual District Boards. The Senior Statistician in particular would 'tender technical advice on the feasibility and methodology of the proposed surveys'. In cases when surveys were contracted out to a private firm, the past performance of the company was assessed.[45] In 1985–6 and 1986–7, a sum of $450,000 was provided for surveys.[46] The colonial state was still committed to bridging the communication gap between itself and Chinese society.

Constitutional reforms of the Executive and Legislative Councils

In 1984, the Sino-British Joint Declaration guaranteed that Hong Kong would become in 1997 a SAR of the PRC. Subsequently, increased constitutional reforms were introduced to fulfil the agreement of 'Hong Kong people ruling Hong Kong' and 'a high degree of autonomy'; electoral politics gradually replaced the paradigm of undemocratic consultative politics.[47] Consequently, in 1984, a Green Paper was issued to consult the public's views on the future development of representative government. The Paper suggested that a substantial number of unofficial members of the Legislative Council should be elected indirectly by an electoral college and using functional constituencies, with the number of appointed unofficial members reduced gradually. These proposed changes would be introduced in 1985 and 1988. After the 1988 election, a review should be carried out to decide what further development to be pursued. For the Executive Council, it was proposed that the majority of the appointed official members would be replaced progressively by unofficial members of the Legislative Council, retaining only a small number of appointed and ex-officio members. In due course, the Governor would be replaced as president of the Legislative Council by a presiding officer elected by unofficial Legislative Councillors. These arrangements would be implemented in 1988 and 1991.[48] In 1985, a White Paper was published, with the objective of establishing 'a future system of representative government in Hong Kong' which was 'rooted firmly in the community' and thereby 'more directly accountable to the people in Hong Kong'. It also provided for changes in the composition and methods of selecting members to the Legislative Council: to accomplish the aim of having 'a reasonable balance in the membership' between elected and appointed unofficial and official members. The changes would 'safeguard the essential features' of the 'present society' and 'ensure a smooth transition for Hong Kong' from a British colony to a SAR, granting Hong Kong a 'high degree of autonomy'.[49] According to the White Paper, elections of the Legislative Council would be held in September 1985 for twenty-four unofficial members who would hold office for three years. Twelve would be elected by the electoral college, which consisted of all members of the District Board, the Urban Council and the provisional Regional Council.[50] District Board members were grouped into ten geographical constituencies, which were also known as 'populist' constituencies, as each represented approximately 500,000 people. The members of the Urban Council and provisional Regional Council formed two special constituencies. Each of these constituencies returned one member to the Council. The other twelve Legislative Councillors would be elected by nine functional constituencies, which represented commercial, industrial, financial, labour and social services sectors of the community and the teaching, legal, medical and combined engineering, architecture, planning and surveying professions.[51] The number of the appointed members was scheduled to fall from thirty to twenty-two, and the number of official members from sixteen to ten.[52]

Using the device of Green and White Papers, the government consulted the public about electoral reforms but the White Paper stated that the representative political system should only be 'developed gradually and progressively' and should not put 'at risk those factors which have secured the social stability and economic prosperity of Hong Kong'.[53] Arguably the key risk factor was the attitude of the PRC, and in August 1985, Xu Jiatun, the Director of the Hong Kong branch of the NCNA, expressed that he was 'worried' that the colonial government 'was moving too far and too fast with the development of representative government'. He suggested that Hong Kong had long been governed under a system which 'provided freedom without democracy', implying that representative government was 'not needed to ensure continued freedom after 1997'.[54] In October of the same year, Zhou Nan, the Director of the NCNA, stated that the Sino-British Joint Declaration was 'based on the assumption that things in Hong Kong after 1997 would be "preserved as they are today except sovereignty"', and he identified elections as a 'big jolt' that required 'discussion and exploration'.[55] According to the colonial records, the Chinese concerns were twofold. First, the Chinese government did not want the British to announce decisions about major constitutional reforms before the promulgation of the Basic Law in 1990, due to a fear that it would give the impression that 'important provisions in the Basic Law had been imposed' on Hong Kong by 'pre-emptive actions' of the British.[56] Second, the Chinese government had 'long been highly suspicious about direct elections', even though they claimed that they were not opposed to them 'in principle'.[57]

During the meeting of the Joint Liaison Group in Beijing in late November 1985, Britain and China both 'agreed on the need to achieve convergence between any reforms to the structure of government in Hong Kong before 1997 and the structure of government of Hong Kong SAR after 1997', with discussions to be conducted 'without preconceived ideas'. However, it was also noted that the convergence must be subject to China's basic policies towards Hong Kong and that the British government was responsible for the administration of Hong Kong with the objective of 'maintaining and preserving its economic and social stability' during the transitional period.[58] In the face of China's opposition, reform elements were dropped in the Green Paper in 1987. For example, it stated that 'only very few [citizens] have suggested that there should be a rapid move towards having a substantial proportion of Legislative Council members directly elected'. Also, rather than aiming at developing a local government which was 'firmly rooted' in Hong Kong and 'accountable' to the locals, the 1987 Green Paper was only framed as a political review that encouraged the 'widest possible response'.[59] In the 1988 White Paper, it was proposed that direct elections should be introduced to the Legislative Council in 1991 rather than 1988.[60] In 1991, the Governor appointed eighteen official members and three ex-official members; eighteen members were elected by the geographical constituencies directly and twenty-one members were elected by the functional constituencies.[61]

After the Tiananmen incident of 1989, the British government sought to advance democratisation in Hong Kong, as electoral reforms were perceived as a way to safeguard Hong Kong's autonomy, to bolster confidence and stabilise the economy.[62] In 1992, Governor Chris Patten announced reform proposals: that the voting age should be reduced from twenty-one to eighteen; the number of directly elected seats in the Legislative Council should be increased from eighteen to twenty, a number which was specified in the Basic Law for Hong Kong's legislature in 1997; the multiple-seat geographical constituencies should be changed into single-seat ones; that all forms of 'corporate voting' should be replaced by 'individual voters' in the functional constituencies; that nine new functional constituencies should be added; that crossed membership of the Executive and Legislative Councils should end; that the Governor would give up the presidency of the Legislative Council; that power and financial resources should be delegated to the District Boards, whose members would be fully and directly elected; and that ten members of the 400-member selection committee specified under the Basic Law should be elected directly by elected members of the District Boards.[63]

For China, these proposals represented an 'open defiance of its stated policy'; it stated 'constantly and firmly' that the Governor should withdraw the package of reforms.[64] According to Douglas Hurd, the Foreign Secretary, this reaction was 'out of all proportion to the modest nature of these proposals'.[65] The colonial government also observed how China had started 'a campaign of intimidation and abuse' using the left-wing press, and by intimidating Legislative Councillors and directors of British and Hong Kong companies.[66] The left-wing media even noted that sending in the People's Liberation Army 'could not be ruled out'.[67] The NCNA questioned 'what price the economically motivated but politically apathetic Hong Kong people would like to pay for the Governor's constitutional proposals', implying that the locals 'would not wish to see a chaotic situation stirred up by the Governor and his supporters by pressing ahead with his proposals'.[68] According to Douglas Hurd, these statements were 'designed to talk down the Hong Kong stock market to unnerve investors'.[69] By February 1993, Patten believed that China had accepted that the Legislative Council, which it perceived as an advisory organ that did not represent public views in Hong Kong, would pass the reform package.[70] Under Patten's reforms, the Legislative Council was fully elected for the first time in 1995, but the Chinese government refused to endorse this elected Legislative Council and set up a 'provisional legislature', which began to function before 1997.[71] As Goodstadt noted, inevitably Sino-British relations deteriorated.[72]

Covert colonialism in the 1980s and 1990s

Archival records indicate that covert qualitative opinion polling exercises were still conducted by the colonial government throughout the 1980s and 1990s. DOs and the HAD needed to 'gauge people's perceptions and gut reactions about various issues'.[73] There was, for example, a series of papers titled 'Know the People' which began in mid-1983, providing government officials with 'a basis for assessing likely public reaction to important policies or measure[s]' and allowing them to review the 'popularity of existing services' and future demand new ones. A representative sample of people aged between fifteen and sixty-four, who accounted for 70 per cent of the population, were interviewed; half were Hong Kong born; 89 per cent were Chinese; slightly more than half of them had received secondary education; and 40 per cent lived in public housing. In addition, the HAD sought to capture the attitudes of different social groups in various districts by organising regular discussion groups. For example, in a survey in 1984, eight to ten professional and managerial workers aged between twenty-five and fifty in Central and Western Districts, eight to ten blue-collar clerical workers aged between twenty-five and fifty in Wong Tai Sin, and eight to ten students and housewives aged between eighteen and thirty-five in Sha Tin participated in the same discussion group to identify questions for a future survey.[74]

Into the late 1980s, the District Boards continued to carry out covert public opinion exercises to 'poll public views on controversial issues, find out public reaction to existing and proposed policies or actions' and 'detect changes in public attitudes towards long standing issues'. The opinion of the 'silent majority' was sought and the attitude of specific groups towards particular issues was investigated.[75] For example, in 1987, research was done by the District Administration to ascertain the needs and aspirations of the youth and examine the youth services and provision available in Hong Kong. People's views towards services for the elderly in ageing public housing estates were collected and fed into policymaking processes.[76]

There was also a general polling exercise named Talking Points, undertaken by the District Boards. Talking Points was 'a weekly record of issues of current interest collected from a small number of respondents in both urban and New Territories districts' by City and New Territories Administration liaison staff, issued every Friday. Similar to MOOD, it captured the shifting sentiments of the community which were relayed to high-ranked bureaucrats, including those working at the Foreign and Commonwealth Office in London. Using a small and unrepresentative sample, Talking Points did not claim to be 'totally authoritative'; but it was perceived as providing 'a valuable guide to what the public is [was] saying'.[77] Although it is unclear what year MOOD evolved into Talking Points, it is evident that Talking Points was compiled until at least November 1992.[78] The government obviously continued to monitor the mass media. The GIS's daily GIST reviewed news and views of interest to the government, taken from about twenty Chinese papers, radio and television.[79] Weekly and monthly summaries of magazine articles were also collated to provide a detailed account of press and magazine editorial comments which were of interest to the government.[80] Although these covert qualitative exercises survived in the 1980s and 1990s, they were less important because of the expansion of quantitative opinion polling and because electoral reforms were finally widening channels of political participation.

Shifting political culture: popular attitudes towards democratisation

The colonial government continued to monitor popular attitudes. What did these polling exercises reveal about the extent of grassroots support for democratic reforms? The analysis explores changes across distinct time periods.

1982–5

According to an opinion poll conducted by the HAD in 1982, a year when electoral reforms were introduced at the district level, the general public had little desire for major constitutional reforms, meaning that the government had 'no clear mandate for changes'.[81] This was confirmed by the 'Know the People' survey of 1983. Although the research revealed that the majority of the respondents, about 60 per cent, disagreed with the statement 'I never worry about tomorrow', suggesting that 'people like to hear future development plans and talk about them with a glint in the eye', many remained socially conservative.[82] Not only did the older people 'tend to stick to their old fashioned ways', many young people also admitted that 'they hold [held] conservative views and seem[ed] to attach as much to traditional values as the older generation'. Although it is unclear whether this social conservatism was extended to the political domain, the survey asserted that it would be 'presumptuous' to 'count on the support of the younger generation for introducing measures that challenge traditional values and perceptions'.[83] Such measures, by implication, would include constitutional reforms.

By 1984, opinions were 'obviously different'. Although those who wanted change was 'still less than half', appointing Legislative Councillors was 'no longer considered appropriate', and officials anticipated that 'public support for [constitutional] changes' would continue to 'increase'.[84] This shift in attitude was probably shaped by the Sino-British negotiations as there had been 'considerable dismay' in Hong Kong about the extent to which Hong Kong would be allowed autonomy after it was returned to China.[85] In 1985, public distrust towards China deepened. According to Governor Edward Youde, writing at the end of the year, there was 'a substantial increase in suspicion about Chinese intention post-1997', with concerns that China would 'intervene again before 1997 on important issues'.[86] There was, however, no consensus, with business elites opposed to direct elections, and 'a comparatively small but vocal group' of lawyers, pressure group activists and the English-language press in favour of creating a 'bulwark against excessive Chinese interference in Hong Kong affairs post-1997'.[87] Anxiety about Hong Kong's future was eased after the signing of the Sino-British Joint Declaration but there was also a sense that the government 'have [has] not gone far enough' to democratise Hong Kong.[88] The Green and White

Papers of 1984 and 1985 revealed that the public was 'generally in favour of' reforms.[89] There were also some 'renewed demands' for the introduction of direct elections to the Legislative Council; but most people agreed that it was 'essential' not to 'put at risk the harmony and stability of Hong Kong by introducing too many major constitutional reforms too rapidly'.[90] Hong Kong people supported moderate reforms but covert and overt polling revealed them to be conservative, prioritising social stability over rapid and radical democratisation.

The voter turnout rate in District Board elections might provide a better insight into attitudes towards reform. According to Youde, the 1985 District Board election yielded a 'very satisfactory result' and demonstrated 'support for the steps' the state was taking to 'develop progressively a more representative system of government'.[91] During the voter registration exercise in August and September 1984, the number of registered voters increased from 900,000 to over 1.4 million. In the election, a total of 476,530 people voted, which was equivalent to 37.5 per cent of the 1.27 million registered voters in the constituencies where the seats were contested. Although the percentage was not particularly high and was about the same as the percentage of registered voters in the 1982 election, there was an increase of almost 134,000.[92] The elected candidates also came from 'a wide variety of social backgrounds' and were 'significantly younger than those returned at previous elections', with 55 per cent aged between twenty-one and forty.[93] This shows that the young generation and many adults became less reluctant to participate in politics through formal political channels. For the Legislative Council election, the turnout was also 'very high': almost 100 per cent in the electoral college constituencies; among the functional constituencies, 97.2 per cent in the social services constituency and 86.4 per cent in the legal constituency. The lowest was the industrial constituency, which had a turnout rate of 45.2 per cent.[94] These statistics demonstrate that the willingness of the public, especially among the younger generation and adults, to engage in politics through formal political channels had increased, albeit marginally and selectively.

With the franchise being extended, new political parties and civil society groups ran for elections in the Legislative Council and District Boards.[95] 'Embryonic political parties' were formed by people of different social classes and occupations from 1983, such as the Meeting Point composed of intellectuals and former student activists, the Hong Kong Affairs Society formed by middle-class professionals, the Progressive Hong Kong Society established by pro-China conservative business and professional elites, and the Hong Kong Forum and the Association for Democracy for People's Livelihood which catered for grassroots interests and advocated for democracy.[96] The capacity of these political parties to mobilise support and run electoral campaigns remained limited. As Ma Ngok has pointed out, these groups 'from below' had 'very limited resources' and 'small membership'; they did not have elaborate political programmes and party organisation.[97] Youde even disputed whether 'the situation in Hong Kong' was yet 'ripe for political parties', noting that even the capitalist class was not able to 'form a coherent, disciplined and organised political party'.[98] During the District Boards election, he also noted that new political 'coalitions' had emerged but that they were far from 'combined political parties' and were usually 'individuals loosely banded together' to increase publicity and share electoral expenditures.[99] There had been, as Ma has argued, 'a movement of political participation from below', with candidates gaining improved campaigning skills, but there was no party political system of contrasting and coherent programmes.[100]

1986–8

In 1986, following 'the low point' of December 1985 when Xu Jiatun made remarks about the British 'deviation' from the Joint Declaration agreement, there was a 'gradual improvement in confidence in the future'.[101] The government reported that the media expected that both the British and Hong Kong governments would bring 'themselves in line with Chinese thinking'.[102] By 1987, the colonial government felt that there was a general understanding that democratisation 'cannot go further', as bound by the Basic Law.[103] Direct elections were perceived as 'a symbol of the Chinese government's willingness to allow the SAR a genuine measure of autonomy'.[104] Therefore, the issue of constitutional reforms had 'continued to attract the greatest public interest', with views divided, and, arguably, beginning to polarise:

> Those strongly in support of direct elections maintain they are the only way of ensuring the evolution of a genuinely representative government, capable of sustaining the 'high degree of autonomy' provided for in the Joint Declaration. Those against argue that the Hong Kong community is not ready for such a development, which could be destabilising. The debate is now focusing increasingly on the timing of the introduction of direct elections and the proportion of Legislative Council members to be selected by this method.[105]

At a grassroots level, people were 'more interested in getting on [with] their daily lives' and had 'little comment' on direct elections.[106] These people did 'not wish to see the 1987 review leading to dramatic changes' even if this meant, in the eyes of reformers, 'a perpetuation of undesirable colonial features in the present system of government'.[107] There was still 'a wide measure of [the] public' that supported the retention of 'a substantial appointed element' in the Legislative Council.[108] Business and professional groups remained 'conservative' in outlook on constitutional matters, with direct elections of up to 25 per cent of the Legislative Council 'tolerable', and they were becoming doubtful about 'the wisdom' of introducing direct elections in 1988.[109] High-ranked colonial bureaucrats, such as Executive Councillors Lydia Dynn, Chung Sze-yuen, Tse Chi-wai and Peter Wong Chak-cheung, were also politically conservative, endorsing the idea of constitutional reforms within the confines of the forthcoming Basic Law.[110] By contrast, intellectuals within the middle class, such as Martin Lee, Szeto Wah and Yeung Sum, supported direct elections to the Legislative Council by organising mass rallies, lobbying MPs in London and petitioning Prime Minister Margret Thatcher.[111]

In 1987, despite the untimely death of Youde, 'public confidence' that Hong Kong would remain prosperous and stable strengthened, with the Hang Seng Index reaching 'a record-high'.[112] There were, however, simmering concerns and there was an observed 'strong' tendency of some residents to consider emigration.[113] Attitudes towards reforms moreover remained divisive.[114] Business interests continued to oppose the rapid introduction of direct elections, as the middle-class intellectuals pressed for further democratisation. For example, in 1986, the Joint Committee for the Promotion of Democratic Government (JCPDG) led by Martin Lee and Szeto Wah was formed. The JCPDG, which consisted of ninety-five groups from various sectors and social backgrounds, was a cooperative platform for pro-democracy groups that sought to press for the introduction of direct elections in the Legislative Council in 1988 and 'a more democratic political formula' in the Basic Law.[115] The colonial government anticipated that, consequently, attitudes would 'polarise even further'.[116] However, the drafting of the Basic Law and constitutional debates did not capture the attention of members at the grassroots level, who were 'genuinely uninterested in the matter'.[117]

1989–97

The Tiananmen incident in 1989 changed Hong Kong's political culture, especially among the students and new generation, who became even more anti-establishment. These young actors tended to resort to 'less formal and more spontaneous modes of action' and distanced themselves from the 'electoral politician[s]'.[118] And for the conservatives and democrats, despite political differences, the incident encouraged them to 'strengthen the case for protection rooted in a strong locally based political authority with as many built-in legal and institutional safeguards as possible'.[119] Political parties were moreover expanding, and further stimulating public discourse. For example, within the pro-democracy camp, the Meeting Point, the Hong Kong Affairs Society and the Association for Democracy and People's

Livelihood united to support the democratic movement in Beijing; and these activists and politicians became members of the Alliance in Support of Patriotic Democratic Movements of China, and then, in April 1990, they formed the United Democrats of Hong Kong, which secured a 'landslide victory' in 1991, taking fourteen out of eighteen directly elected seats.[120]

The shape of the new electoral politics was complete when in 1994 the pro-Beijing Hong Kong Progressive Alliance was formed, merging with the Liberal Democratic Federation of Hong Kong in 1995. New political parties also emerged. For example, a group of Legislative Councillors and pro-democracy activists formed the Frontier in 1996 and Legislative Councillor Christian Loh formed the pro-democracy Citizen's Party in 1997. The pro-Beijing activists and unionists also formed the Democratic Alliance for the Betterment of Hong Kong, which later became the main rival of the democrats in Hong Kong's elections.[121] Political mobilisation extended to grassroots movements.[122] There was evidently increased political engagement. However, the level of political participation through formal political channels remained relatively low. For instance, in the 1991 Legislative Council election, only 1.86 million of the 3.7 million eligible voters registered, with a turnout rate of less than 40 per cent.[123]

During the Sino-British dispute over constitutional reforms in 1992, polling exercises provided insights into the pragmatism of Hong Kong people. Some respondents argued that the negotiation documents should be made 'more transparent to the public' and felt that both sides 'did not represent' the 'full interest of the Hong Kong people'; but many respondents preferred to 'see the prevailing freedoms and stability continue rather than democracy' and suggested the Legislative Council should focus on welfare services proposals rather than political reforms, indicating political conservatism.[124] Amid worsening Sino-British relations, people 'expressed a preference for the upholding of the stability and prosperity of the territory even it meant slowing down the pace of democratisation'.[125] Society was, however, split. The opinion polls conducted by the University of Hong Kong's Social Science Research Centre revealed Hong Kong's 'well-established community commitment to "democratisation"' and 'a high level' of commitment to 'the principles of constitutional reforms'.[126] For example, the poll undertaken on 23 and 24 September 1992 shows that 58 per cent of the respondents still wanted more directly elected Legislative Council seats even though that was not included in the 1992 constitutional reform proposal. In the survey done on 9 October 1992, 79 per cent of the respondents agreed that Hong Kong people 'needed to stand up for democracy', with 52 per cent saying they personally were willing to make such a stand.[127] The poll revealed 'solid support' for the 1992 constitutional package, including the proposals on functional constituencies, the

Election Committee and the 'through train'.[128] Moreover, according to M. J. J. Hanson, Hong Kong's Information Coordinator, this support for reform was 'not a short-run polling phenomenon' but 'has remained firm over the last eighteen months'; with 'a clear majority' refusing 'to abandon its principles', and creating a 'solid bedrock of support' for the 1992 constitutional package.[129] Furthermore, the colonial administration was aware that its support remained 'steady and solid', with the public retaining a 'capacity to reach its own assessment of Hong Kong's political needs even in the face of strident Peking propaganda'.[130] Despite different views towards the pace of democratisation, the changing political culture and increased political resilience in this period prepared the Chinese communities to become more actively involved in politics through both formal and informal political channels in post-handover Hong Kong.

Conclusion

This chapter has explored democratisation at district and central levels in Hong Kong in the last two decades of colonial rule. At the district level, with the formation of the City and New Territories Administration and introduction of elections to District Boards in 1982, the channels of political participation in community affairs had been widened. However, the reform did not represent an attempt of the colonial state to introduce democratisation at the district level or a response to popular demands for constitutional reforms. Instead, it was only launched to cope with administrative difficulties caused by the rising population in the increasingly urbanised New Territories. This reform paved the way for constitutional reforms in the mid-1980s. After the Sino-British Joint Declaration was agreed in 1984, reforms were proposed and introduced to the Legislative and Executive Councils, marking the beginning of an era of democratisation and the gradual decline of the paradigm of 'consultative politics'. Green and White Papers were used to consult with the public. Due to opposition from China and the prevalence of political conservatism in certain sections of the society, reforms were only introduced slowly, with direct elections delayed.

Generally, Hong Kong people favoured democratisation but business and industrial sectors largely opposed the introduction of direct elections to the Legislative Council, while middle-class intellectuals and the younger generation were dissatisfied with the pace and extent of reform. At the grassroots level, people remained indifferent or conservative, prioritising social stability over enhanced political rights. Although the Tiananmen incident in 1989 changed attitudes towards constitutional reforms, positioning on this issue became polarised.

Democratic reforms led to the emergence of political parties and civil society groups, and mobilisation, which deepened in the 1990s, was not confined to middle-class professionals, business elites and intellectuals, as there was also grassroots involvement. Even though the level of public engagement in elections remained low, demonstrated for example by the relatively low turnout rate in the Legislative Council election in 1991, political cultures were changing.

Lastly, covert forms of colonialism survived because of the government's hesitation at contracting out surveys to non-governmental bodies, which adopted unrepresentative sampling methods, charged expensive service fees and may have used government data for private purposes, and its concern that rapid democratisation would lead to administrative difficulties and political instability. Moreover, the HAD worked with external organisations to improve polling; persisted with in-house exercises, with the pioneering MOOD being transformed into the innovative Talking Points; and continued to monitor reports in the mass media. The importance of covert qualitative opinion polls, however, declined in the 1980s and 1990s. By then, the colonial government required more reliable and representative samples of public opinion. With Hong Kong's anticipated return to China and increased democratic electoral reforms being introduced, covert polling declined relative to other mechanisms used to gauge public attitudes.

Notes

1 HKRS 70-8-3698, 'Hong Kong: A Unique Society', Speech by the Hon. D. C. Bray at the Zonta Club of Hong Kong's November Luncheon on Wednesday, 24 November 1982, pp. 1–2.
2 Ibid., p. 2; HKRS 70-8-3698, 'A Matter of Opinion', Speech by Ng Chak-lam at the Luncheon Meeting of the Lions Club of Hong Kong Central on 7 May 1982, pp. 1–5.
3 HKRS 302-1-17, Resettlement Department, 'Squatter Talk', January and February 1971.
4 HKRS 302-1-17, Resettlement Department, 'Public Opinion in Estates', attached to 'Estates Talk', Billy C. L. Lam to Secretary for Home Affairs, 25 March 1971.
5 HKRS 163-13-68, HAD, 'Public Consultation Mechanism', for discussion at the meeting on 15th September 1978, 14 September 1978, p. 2. In fact, 90 per cent of the MOOD topics were based on public feedback picked up from Flash Points. See HKRS 455-4-2, 'Outline of Draft Proposals from the Wiggham Study', 1979.
6 HKRS 934-11-41, Community Relations Division, HAD, 'A Review of the Modus Operandi of H.A.D.'s Feedback Mechanism', 19 September 1978,

attached to memo from Alice Lai to CDCs, CDOs and Community Information Unit, 29 September 1978, p. 2.
7 'A Matter of Opinion', pp. 9–10.
8 HKRS 70-8-3698, Urban Council Annual Debate, 15 January 1980, p. 3.
9 HKRS 570-3-34, 'Gap That is Far from Bridged', *SCMP*, 5 November 1979.
10 Ibid.
11 Pepper, *Keeping Democracy at Bay*, p. 188; Lo, *The Politics of Democratisation*, p. 70. In fact, even by the 1990s, public opinion was not the primary factor that motivated changes at the district level. For example, the public was not always consulted regarding the composition of District Boards and the Municipal Councils. In 1990, it was noted by the Executive Council that 'the public should not be consulted' on the proposals of the composition of District Boards and Municipal Councils, 'just as they are not to be consulted over changes to the Legislative Council in 1991'. This was because carrying out consultation would merely 'give rise to presentational problems' and 'stimulate public debate about the lack of formal consultation about changes to the Legislative Council'. See FCO 40/2863, 'Memorandum Executive Council: Composition of the District Boards and the Municipal Councils in 1991', by Executive Council Chamber, 18 January 1990, p. 5.
12 HKRS 570-3-34, 'The Role of the HAD', speech by the Hon. G. Barnes to the Hong Kong Management Association, 11 May 1981, p. 4.
13 FCO 40/1797, 'MIPT: Joint Liaison Group: Developments in Representative Government', Geoffrey Howe to Hong Kong, 19 November 1985; HKRS 1536-1-3, *A Guide to District Administration*, 1982, p. 1.
14 Ibid.
15 'The Role of the HAD', p. 4.
16 Ibid., p. 5.
17 *A Guide to District Administration*, p. 3.
18 Ibid., pp. 1–2.
19 Miners also mentioned the 'Meet-the-People [Public]' sessions in *The Government and Politics*, p. 185.
20 HKRS 545-4-151, GIS, '"Meet-the-Public" Scheme an Effective Change', 13 July 1989.
21 Miners, *The Government and Politics*, pp. 167–8.
22 In the Wiggham Report, bureaucrats continued to discuss MOOD's limitations and suggested methodological changes to it. It is highly likely that the mechanism was still in use in the 1980s. HKRS 455-4-2, 'Wiggham Report on Community Information', Alice Lai to CDOs and CDCs, 14 February 1980, p. 1.
23 Ibid.
24 HKRS 934-11-41, Extract of Minutes from HAD Meeting, 15 March 1978, p. 1.
25 'Wiggham Report on Community Information', p. 8.
26 HKRS 163-13-68, HAD, 'A Review of the Modus Operandi for Public Opinion Surveys, Community Relations Division', 9 November 1978, p. 1.

27 HKRS 163-13-68, 'Survey Research Green Papers', Blundell to A. K. Chui, 15 October 1977.
28 Ibid.
29 HKRS 163-13-68, 'Comments on the Sampling Aspects of the Survey on the Public's Attitudes towards Elected Representation in Legislative Council', attached to 'Evaluation of the Reform Club Survey on Elected Members of LegCo', D. S. Whitelegge to A. K. Chui, 12 May 1978, p. 2.
30 Ibid.
31 Ibid.
32 HKRS 163-13-68, 'Evaluation of the Reform Club Survey on Elected Members of Legco', D. S. Whitelegge to A. K. Chui, 12 May 1978.
33 HAD, 'A Review of the Modus Operandi for Public Opinion Surveys, Community Relations Division', p. 4.
34 Ibid.
35 Ibid., p. 6.
36 Ibid., p. 5.
37 Ibid., p. 1.
38 Ibid., p. 5.
39 Ibid., p. 3.
40 HKRS 500-4-16, Home Affairs Branch, Government Secretariat, 'Summary of Results of an Opinion Poll in September 1983', September 1983, p. 1.
41 HKRS 1443-4-38, 'Home Affairs Branch HK Government Public Opinion Survey Report', by International Research Associates (HK) Ltd., 7 May 1984, pp. 1 and 4–5.
42 Lo, *The Politics of Democratisation*, p. 106.
43 The Institute, however, split from the university and became an independent body in 2019. See the website of Hong Kong Public Opinion Research Institute, www.pori.hk/about-us.html?lang=en.
44 'Home Affairs Branch HK Government Public Opinion Survey Report', p. 34.
45 HKRS 1443-4-38, 'Public Opinion Surveys', Allan Chow to DOs, 2 May 1985, pp. 1–2.
46 Ibid., p. 2; HKRS 1443-4-38, 'Public Opinion Surveys', K. K. Au to Dos, 7 April 1987.
47 Lam, "'Consultative Politics' Refined', p. 125.
48 FCO 40/1637/2, 'Green Paper on the Future Development of Representative Government in Hong Kong', D. C. Bray to FCO, 11 July 1984.
49 FCO 40/1792, 'MIPT: White Paper on the Future Development of Representative Government: Redraft of the Chief Secretary's Speech', Youde to FCO, 7 January 1985.
50 The provisional Regional Council was set up in 1985 by the colonial government to offer similar services offered by the Urban Council in Kowloon and Hong Kong Island to the New Territories.
51 'MIPT: White Paper on the Future Development of Representative Government: Redraft of the Chief Secretary's Speech'.
52 Ibid.

53 Ibid.
54 FCO 40/1796, 'Development of Representative Government: Comments by Mr Xu Jiatun', 2 August 1985.
55 FCO 40/1796, 'Hong Kong Agreement: Sir Peter Blaker's Meeting with Chinese Vice Foreign Minister', Youde to Beijing, 25 October 1985.
56 FCO 40/1927, Cabinet Defence and Overseas Policy Committee Sub-Committee on Hong Kong, 'Representation Government: Memorandum by the FCO', October 1986, p. 7.
57 Ibid., p. 8.
58 FCO 40/1923, 'MIPT: Representative Government, The Basic Law and the 1987 Review', Youde to FCO, 21 March 1986.
59 Hong Kong Government Printer, *Green Paper: The 1987 Review of Developments in Representative Government*, pp. 4 and 26-7; Lo, *The Politics of Democratisation*, p. 85.
60 Ibid.; Hong Kong Government Printer, *White Paper: The Development of Representative Government*, p. 4.
61 Tsang, *A Modern History*, p. 250.
62 Lo, *The Politics of Democratisation*, pp. 88, 109–11.
63 Pepper, *Keeping Democracy at Bay*, p. 243; Tsang, *A Modern History*, p. 256.
64 Ibid., p. 259; FCO 40/3627, 'Weekly Situation Report', C. Patten to FCO, 10 December 1992.
65 FCO 40/3627, 'Chinese Tactics: The Business Community', Douglas Hurd to Hong Kong, 11 December 1992.
66 FCO 40/3627, 'Hong Kong Future: Press Coverage: (9.12–15.12), Patten to FCO, 15 December 1992.
67 FCO 40/3625, 'Hong Kong: Latest Chinese Scare Tactics', P. F. Ricketts to Hum and Goodlad, 19 November 1992.
68 FCO 40/3627, 'Constitutional Development: Sino-British Negotiations: China News Agency Commentary', Patten to FCO, 14 December 1992.
69 'Chinese Tactics: The Business Community', Hurd to Hong Kong.
70 FCO 40/3932, 'Constitutional Development: Press Reports', Patten to FCO, 12 February 1993.
71 Goodstadt, 'China and the Selection', p. 732.
72 Ibid.
73 HKRS 1443-4-38, 'Community Information: Know the People Series: No. 1, Appendix X, Home Affairs Branch, Government Secretariat', attached to 'Know the People Series: No. 1', Sarah Wu to District Commissioner Tsuen Wan and DOs, 10 August 1983, p. 1.
74 HKRS 602-1-7, 'Discussion Groups for HAD', attached to 'Survey on Basic Attitude towards Political Concepts', Robin Ip to Diana Tang, 30 August 1984.
75 HKRS 1443-4-39, 'General Circular No. 4/88, Public Opinion', by P. K. Y. Tsao, 11 January 1988, p. 3.
76 HKRS 1443-4-39, 'Public Opinion Surveys', Dominic Cheung to DOs, 31 July 1987.
77 'General Circular No. 4/88, Public Opinion', p. 4.

78 Talking Points was first mentioned in archival records in the year of 1988. See ibid. For the latest issue of Talking Points which the author could find, see FCO 40/3575, 'Sino-British Dispute over Hong Kong's Constitutional Development', Talking Points, 6 November 1992.
79 It was recorded that GIST was first prepared by the Information Branch in the HAD in 1974. See 'Wiggham Report on Community Information', p. 4.
80 The Opinion report was compiled by the Public Relations Division as early as in 1974 as well. See ibid.; 'General Circular No. 4/88, Public Opinion', pp. 4–5.
81 HKRS 1443-4-38, Home Affairs Branch Government Secretariat, 'Report on a Poll on What People Think About the Government Generally (1984)', (Second Benchmark Survey on Public Attitudes), June 1984, p. 3.
82 'Community Information: Know the People Series: No. 1', p. 2.
83 Ibid., pp. 4–5.
84 Home Affairs Branch Government Secretariat, 'Report on a Poll on What People Think About the Government Generally (1984)', p. 3.
85 FCO 40/1798, 'Hong Kong: Representative Government', A. C. Galsworthy to D. C. Wilson, 19 December 1983.
86 FCO 40/1798, 'State Councellor Ji Pengfei's Visit', Youde to FCO, 16 December 1985.
87 Ibid.
88 FCO 40/1798, 'MIPT: Visit to Hong Kong by State Councilor Ji Pengfei', Youde to Beijing, 4 December 1985.
89 'MIPT: Joint Liaison Group: Developments in Representative Government', Howe to Hong Kong.
90 'MIPT: White Paper on the Future Development of Representative Government: Redraft of the Chief Secretary's Speech', Youde to FCO.
91 FCO 40/1794, 'Hong Kong District Board Elections', Youde to FCO, 8 March 1985.
92 Ibid.
93 FCO 40/1794, 'Hong Kong District Board Elections', Youde to FCO, 14 March 1985.
94 FCO 40/1796, 'Hong Kong Elections', Youde to FCO, 27 September 1985.
95 Lam, "'Consultative Politics" Refined', p. 125; Lo, *The Politics of Democratisation*, p. 20.
96 Ma, *Political Development*, p. 137.
97 Ibid., pp. 102 and 137.
98 FCO 40/1798, 'Hong Kong Agreement: Restricted: Basic Law', Youde to FCO, 11 December 1985.
99 'Hong Kong District Board Elections', Youde to FCO.
100 Ma, *Political Development*, p. 137.
101 HKRS 394-29-53, 'General Mood in Hong Kong: Report for the Governor', Carrie Yau to SDA DRSs, RSs and PASs, 12 August 1986.
102 HKRS 394-29-53, 'General Mood in Hong Kong', by Administrative Services and Information Branch, Government Secretariat, 1 September 1986, p. 6.
103 HKRS 394-29-53, 'Situation and Mood in Hong Kong', Hong Kong to Youde, 1 September 1986.

104 FCO 40/1923, 'Representative Gov, the Basic Law and the 1978 Review', Youde to FCO, 21 March 1986.
105 Cabinet Defence and Overseas Policy Committee Sub-Committee on Hong Kong, 'Representation Government: Memorandum by the FCO', pp. 4–5.
106 FCO 40/1928, Local Intelligence Committee, 'LIC Hong Kong Recent Developments of Intelligence/Security Interest', 28 October 1986, p. 5.
107 Cabinet Defence and Overseas Policy Committee Sub-Committee on Hong Kong, 'Representation Government: Memorandum by the FCO', p. 9.
108 Ibid., p. 5.
109 Ibid.
110 Lo, *The Politics of Democratisation*, p. 102.
111 Ibid., p. 104.
112 HKRS 394-29-53, City and New Territories Administration, 'Contribution to Security Branch's Report on Hong Kong Opinion and Mood', 12 January 1987, p. 1.
113 Ibid.
114 Ibid.
115 Ma, *Political Development*, p. 138; Sing, 'Economic Development', pp. 482–504.
116 City and New Territories Administration, 'Contribution to Security Branch's Report', p. 1.
117 Ibid.
118 Ma, *Political Development*, p. 205.
119 Pepper, *Keeping Democracy at Bay*, p. 216.
120 Ma, *Political Development*, p. 138.
121 Ibid., pp. 139–40.
122 Ibid., p. 203.
123 Pepper, *Keeping Democracy at Bay*, p. 231.
124 FCO 40/3575, 'Sino-British Dispute over Hong Kong's Constitutional Development', Talking Points, 6 November 1992, p. 1.
125 FCO 40/3578, 'Governor's Visit to Beijing', Talking Points, 30 October 1992, p. 2.
126 FCO 40/3932, 'Community Attitudes towards Constitutional Development: Recent Opinion Poll Trends', attached to 'Opinion Polls', M. J. J. Hanson to Peter Ricketts, 14 October 1993, p. 2.
127 Ibid., p. 3.
128 Ibid., p. 2.
129 Ibid., p. 4.
130 FCO 40/3932, 'The Mood of the Community', Hong Kong to FCO, 31 December 1993.

Conclusion

Using under-explored evidence derived from archives in Hong Kong and the United Kingdom, this book has uncovered changes to Hong Kong's state–society relations from 1966 to 1997, a time when other British colonies were undergoing or had completed decolonisation. It brought the hitherto disjointed research on 'state' and 'society' together by showing how the undemocratic colonial government in Hong Kong improved political communications with Chinese society and how political activism and shifting public opinion influenced the policymaking process. As revisionists have pointed out, colonial Hong Kong was far from a 'minimally-integrated social-political system'. After the Star Ferry riots in 1966 and the leftist-inspired riots in 1967, the colonial government sought to enhance its legitimacy to prevent further political turmoil. Political stability in the colony was crucial for future Sino-British negotiations, which would determine the destiny of Hong Kong. Democratic reforms became unfeasible as these jeopardised Sino-British relations. To instil a sense of belonging among the Hong Kong Chinese and enhance its legitimacy, the colonial government changed its ruling strategies and introduced 'covert colonialism' – a secret qualitative polling exercise that could be used as a substitute for representative democracy by providing state agencies with information about the prevailing attitudes of its residents. With this information, the colonial government had the potential to improve policymaking. First known as Town Talk, renamed as MOOD and then Talking Points, this mechanism increased the government's organisational capacity to conduct surveillance and monitor shifting opinions of Chinese society; it widened the channels of political participation for ordinary people by transferring public opinion into the policymaking process in a state-controlled manner without provoking China or further politicising the Chinese population. This technique provided a unique solution for a colonial state governing Hong Kong; it also increased and limited the ability of the public to influence the policymaking process. To enhance the diversity and representativeness of the data collected, the HAD and CDOs expanded their contact lists, invested in increased manpower and experimented with new methodologies adopted in the polling exercise. This highlights the colonial government's urge to develop a reliable and effective institutional mechanism to obtain better understandings of popular sentiment without introducing democratic electoral reforms.

The six case studies have shown how polling constructed 'public opinion' of different age groups, social classes and occupations, and how these constructions influenced administrative, legislative and institutional changes. Administrative agencies, such as the City District Offices and the Hong Kong Special Branch, were instructed to monitor shifting press sentiment, activists' activities and changing public opinion. The CDOs, in particular, attempted to capture attitudes of different social classes and age groups in their geographic areas; they also offered strategies and provided practical advice, helping to resolve social tensions. This intelligence circulated within the senior civil service among colonial bureaucrats and policymakers. Special Committees or Commissions of Inquiry also consulted the public, with their members carefully chosen and consisting of people of diverse backgrounds, included politicians, social elites, businessmen and community leaders. Based upon the situation reports from CDOs and the Special Branch, and using information uncovered by ad hoc bodies, the colonial administration adjusted policies, liaising with the British government. Institutionalised covert polling exercises and monitoring mechanisms affirm that the colonial government had the desire and organisational capacity to adjust policies as the sentiments of Chinese society shifted. The colonial government became increasingly responsive to public opinion.

These ruling strategies were the product of trans-colonial and transnational processes. The CDO Scheme introduced to Hong Kong in 1968 was an adaptation of the 'old tactic of imperial rule to new circumstances'.[1] A DO programme had long been used in rural Africa and Asia.[2] As archival evidence has shown, a similar institution had also been set up in Singapore prior to 1968, known as People's Association and Citizens' Consultative Committees. In addition, MOOD used Japan's Osaka Feedback Scheme and Monitor System for National Policy as blueprints. Hong Kong drew on lessons learned from overseas.

Public discourses have often depicted colonial Hong Kong as an unusual colonial regime that had a 'relatively enlightened' political system but nostalgia for the past and current political concerns should not be allowed to distort our understanding of British colonialism in Hong Kong. As this book has revealed, although the colonial government had become increasingly responsive to demands raised by Chinese society since the late 1960s, it did not always pay heed to public opinion. The case studies demonstrate the circumstances under which activists and Chinese society were more likely to succeed in exerting pressure on the colonial government. The following three conditions often enhanced the likelihood of the public to press for administrative, legislative and institutional changes successfully. First, if the movement involved people of different age groups and social classes, and was on a large scale, the colonial government would normally set up a Commission of Inquiry and respond to public opinion to avoid undesirable repercussions. Second, the colonial state was more likely to get permission from London to introduce changes if those changes were only confined to Hong Kong, instead of affecting other dependent territories. Third, interventions by British and colonial governments were shaped by perceptions of how the reputation of the British government internationally was being influenced by events and social processes in Hong Kong. In other words, if the requested changes had impacts beyond the colony, such as affecting legislation in other dependent territories, and if diplomatic relations between the British government and other countries might be adversely affected by the reform of colonial governance in Hong Kong, political activism did not necessarily lead to changes to colonial policy.

To reiterate, the wider interest of the British government and the state of Sino-British relations outweighed the importance of shifting popular sentiment in the policymaking process. With respect to the anti-corruption campaign, for instance, the Home Office was opposed to retrospective legislative changes and believed any precedent would affect other dependent territories. There was no attempt therefore to amend the Fugitive Offenders Act. The British government's concerns over Sino-British relations delayed immigration controls. Major concessions also could not be given in the enactment of the British Nationality Act as it was closely linked to the internal policies of Britain's Conservative Party and would have had an impact on remaining dependencies. When introducing democratic electoral reforms in Hong Kong after 1984, China's potential reactions evidently played a more important role in shaping the pace and form of constitutional changes than the changing public opinion. Similarly, if the situation involved practical issues which could not be solved by the colonial government, popular demands were not met. For example, in the case of the campaign against the telephone rate increases, the Legislative Council did not introduce a bill to cap rate increases; the colonial administration was concerned that the company would go bankrupt if rates did not increase. In short, safeguarding the colonial and British governments was a prerequisite for any changes that complied with public opinion. This was also precisely why the polling mechanisms remained covert before the democratisation of the 1980s.

Nevertheless, the colonial administration's new appreciation of the attitudes and needs of the Hong Kong people did reshape Hong Kong–London relations. Official perceptions of popular opinion influenced how the Governor engaged with the Foreign and Commonwealth Office regarding institutional changes. Hong Kong and London did not always agree. While the colonial administration paid close attention to the needs of the Chinese communities, the British government was concerned primarily with domestic interests and Sino-British relations; their interests rarely aligned. In such instances, the Governors used new evidence of political activism and changing public opinion to justify and press for reforms and, sometimes, the reversal of London's decisions. As Chapter 3 has shown, although the creation of an independent Anti-Corruption Branch separating from the police force was debated as early as in the 1960s, both the colonial and British governments did not endorse the notion of institutional change until a number of anti-corruption campaigns emerged and press coverage reporting corruption increased. When London was reluctant to introduce unilateral border controls, the colonial government drew on evidence regarding popular discourse of immigration. MacLehose repeatedly informed the Foreign and Commonwealth Office of the widespread public discontent over the existing immigration policy, which had failed to stop illegal Chinese immigrants from entering Hong Kong. In late 1980, he finally persuaded the British government to approve the new immigration legislation, ending the 'Touch Base' policy. Similarly, MacLehose used public confidence as a reason to press for Hong Kong's interests in the British Nationality Act. Together with the pressure from the Foreign and Commonwealth Office, the Home Office and Parliament had to revise certain clauses in the bill although further adjustment to the nomenclature could not be made. In these cases, the changing political culture altered policy.

This book has further debunked the myth of political apathy and stability in Hong Kong by offering detailed analysis of the political culture and activism of Chinese society in the late colonial era. The political culture in Hong Kong may seem conservative compared to other British colonies, such as Malaya and Kenya, where violent insurgencies of a larger scale that advocated overthrowing the colonial governments broke out. However, Hong Kong's society was not free from social conflicts and political instability. During the 1970s, the general political culture of Chinese society experienced changes. There was increased political activism. In the early 1970s, the general political culture in Hong Kong remained relatively conservative. Most people were reluctant to disclose their identities in discursive debates via newspapers and petitions. They avoided engaging in social movements. Nonetheless, by the mid-1970s, the political attitudes of many Hong Kong Chinese had changed. Reforms had gradually built up public confidence in the government. The formalisation of Chinese as the official language in 1974 improved political communications and enhanced the stake of Hong Kong Chinese in politics by introducing simultaneous interpretation in the Councils and amending the language requirement for working in the government. The setting up of the ICAC in 1974 showed that the public was determined to work with the colonial government in eliminating corruption. With increased political transparency, supported by colonial propaganda and mass education, hostility and apprehensiveness towards officialdom reduced. People were more willing to report crime and corruption, showing a rising readiness to raise their concerns and engage in public affairs. They increasingly stood up for their own rights and were willing to express their grievances publicly. Different social classes and age groups mobilised to participate in social movements and public discourse across a range of issues, and were especially active if their material wellbeing was perceived to be under threat as in the case of immigration, and actually under threat as with the case of telephone rate increases. The diversity of participants strongly suggests that a new form of political activism was pervasive. Although political activism advocated reforms within the existing political framework, it still had longer-term repercussions for colonial governance.

Due to the changing political culture, collaborative and overt strategies used in a range of social movements were gradually accepted as appropriate means to express grievances. Chapters 2 to 7 revealed common mass-mobilisation strategies. To pull resources together, activists set up ad hoc coalitions. Most groups did not confront the colonial state directly. Instead, they expressed their grievances through informal channels, using petitions, signature campaigns, open letters and surveys. Activists deployed rhetoric, such as 'people's livelihood', 'public interest', 'political stability' and 'law and order'; abstract ideas, such as democracy, nationalism, anti-colonialism and 'Britishness', were less appealing. Activists requested concessions and warned that administrative intransigence would cause political disturbance and lead to economic decline. There were extremists whose letters and posters included death threats. Nevertheless, they were on the margins of society, and had limited political impact. As collaborative strategies were considered rational and were widely endorsed by the public, their use was more likely to put pressure on the colonial government effectively. These experiences of collaboration and mass mobilisation in the 1970s proved to be important to many of these activists, who through which learned to pull their resources together, organise political coalitions and parties and run for indirect and direct elections in the 1980s and 1990s.

Nonetheless, political conservatism persisted. Sit-ins and demonstrations were still not widely endorsed by Chinese people, with such political activities limited to social elites, especially the younger generation in higher education. This may have been a legacy of the leftist riots of 1967. Many contemporaries considered direct confrontation radical and expressed their worries about 'rocking the boat' – about undermining the colony's political stability. Activists who confronted the colonial government were deemed as 'trouble-makers' and 'rabble-rousers'. The demonstrations of the anti-corruption campaign were poorly attended. The Precious Blood Golden Jubilee Secondary School dispute was another notable example where teachers and students lost the support of the public due to their 'radical' sit-ins and hunger strikes.

Attitudes towards constitutional reforms were also conservative, influenced by the China factor. Even when the colonial polity started opening up in the mid-1980s, which allowed the organisation of political parties and increased political participation in elections, many people remained cautious. Constitutional reforms were supported by Chinese society in principle but rapid democratisation was not. There was a persistent fear that China would intervene and take over Hong Kong early, and enhanced political rights could only be achieved at the expense of political stability and social harmony.

The political culture varied in accordance with class and age. In general, both the upper and middle classes opposed political activism and were staunch supporters of the status quo. The upper class considered participating in informal political activities as incompatible with their status, viewing this with disdain and concern. The middle class, who had by and large succeeded in going some way up the social ladder through hard work and persevering effort, also did not wish to lose that position and tended to be pro-establishment. They were politically informed but conservative. The grassroots level, despite possessing considerable capacity for political mobilisation, remained relatively politically indifferent on issues which they considered remote and as not directly affecting their livelihoods. The political culture also differed in accordance with age. While middle-aged and elderly members of the society were politically conservative, the young generation, particularly intellectuals and those in higher education, had a completely different political outlook. Direct confrontation, the more 'radical' approach, was only adopted by a younger generation seeking to exert pressure on the colonial government. Nevertheless, political attitudes and orientations cannot always be generalised neatly in accordance with people's social class and age group. One characteristic these groups shared in common was that their political attitudes and orientations were fluid and subject-oriented. Ideological concerns and instrumental reasoning did not only intersect but were sometimes inseparable. People could be mobilised and were willing to adjust their political stance when their interests were at direct stake. For example, as the Chinese as the official language movement showed, the young generation was divided; students in secondary schools sometimes were more reluctant to engage in political activism. Since the mid-1980s, the middle class was also evidently divided with the business and professional sectors opposing rapid democratisation and the intellectuals arguing that this was the only way to safeguard Hong Kong's autonomy.

The colonial government's changing attitudes towards constitutional reforms also redefined what 'pro-establishment' meant in Hong Kong in the 1980s and 1990s, with the business elites and conservative senior officials increasingly forging an alliance with the Chinese government and the pro-democracy intellectuals becoming the colonial government's ally in pushing democratic electoral reforms. This affirms the heterogeneity and fluidity of political culture in Hong Kong, rejecting the claim of 'political apathy' that prevailed in earlier sociological studies.

The importance attached to 'covert colonialism' gradually declined because the colonial government increasingly relied on scientifically organised overt opinion polls and the need to widen the channels of political participation through covert measures had been greatly reduced by the 1980s. It had been an indispensable part of Hong Kong's colonial statecraft and survived until 1997. Post-colonial Hong Kong remains far from being a democracy. Under the Sino-British Joint Declaration agreed in 1984, British sovereignty in Hong Kong ended in 1997. Hong Kong, however, was to retain a 'high degree of autonomy' under the principle of 'One Country, Two Systems' for fifty years. SAR retained legislative and judiciary independence, as well as freedom of speech and of assembly until 2047; but these rights have been eroded and state–society tensions have grown. Political activism became a new norm, and activists adopted radical strategies.[3] In response, the SAR government used repressive measures, including the enactment of the National Security Law in 2020. The society as a result became extremely polarised. And instead of responding to changing public opinion at a local level, candidates running for District Councillor elections were vetted; many were disqualified. For example, Joshua Wong was barred from running in the District Council election in 2019 because of his calls for 'self-determination'.[4] By early October 2021, a total of thirty-nine opposition District Councillors were ousted after the oath-taking ceremonies. Some were disqualified even before that.[5] While it is certain that covert strategies and techniques of 'co-option' used during the colonial era would no longer work in today's Hong Kong because of the radically different political culture and political system, these recent developments and the findings of this monograph have posed important questions which need to be further examined:

- How has the state surveillance system evolved in post-colonial Hong Kong?
- Did the 'covert exercises' adopted during the colonial era survive beyond 1997?
- When and why did the political culture start shifting drastically in post-colonial Hong Kong?

- What impacts do variations in social class, age, gender, educational level and geographical location have on a person's political attitude and orientation?
- Is the legacy of British rule still felt in Hong Kong?
- How should we position ourselves in history?

Examining how governance, surveillance and political culture shifted and transitioned from colonial to post-colonial Hong Kong not only enriches academic discourse in history and post-colonialism but also provides us with further insights into politics and tensions in today's Hong Kong.

Notes

1 Jones and Vagg, *Criminal Justice*, p. 412.
2 Ibid.
3 See for example, Lee and Sing (eds), *Take Back Our Future*; Lee et al., 'Hong Kong's Summer of Uprising', pp. 1–32; Dapiran, *City on Fire*; Mok, 'Hong Kong Protests: How Did We Get Here?', *The Diplomat*, 21 June 2019.
4 'Disqualifying Joshua Wong', *Wall Street Journal*, 31 October 2019.
5 '17 Opposition Hong Kong District Councilors Have Oaths of Allegiance Challenged; 20 More Disqualified', *SCMP*, 8 October 2021.

Select bibliography

Primary sources

Unpublished official documents

The National Archives, Kew, United Kingdom

Colonial Office

    CO 129/2

Foreign and Commonwealth Office

FCO 21/1273	FCO 40/1003
FCO 21/1274	FCO 40/1005
FCO 21/1417	FCO 40/1007
FCO 21/1418	FCO 40/1022
FCO 21/1420	FCO 40/1023
FCO 40/42	FCO 40/1114
FCO 40/113	FCO 40/1115
FCO 40/120	FCO 40/1116
FCO 40/292	FCO 40/1118
FCO 40/329	FCO 40/1202
FCO 40/341	FCO 40/1203
FCO 40/451	FCO 40/1330
FCO 40/452	FCO 40/1333
FCO 40/453	FCO 40/1336
FCO 40/455	FCO 40/1637/2
FCO 40/457	FCO 40/1792
FCO 40/536	FCO 40/1794
FCO 40/544	FCO 40/1796
FCO 40/549	FCO 40/1797
FCO 40/558	FCO 40/1798
FCO 40/644	FCO 40/1923
FCO 40/645	FCO 40/1927
FCO 40/647	FCO 40/1928
FCO 40/704	FCO 40/2863
FCO 40/811	FCO 40/3575
FCO 40/828	FCO 40/3578
FCO 40/1002	FCO 40/3625

Select bibliography 263

FCO 40/3627
FCO 40/3932
FCO 53/692
FCO 53/693
FCO 53/694

FCO 53/695
FCO 53/696
FCO 53/697
FCO 53/698

The Public Records Office, Hong Kong

HKRS 70-3-26-2
HKRS 70-3-26-3
HKRS 70-6-249-2
HKRS 70-6-339-1
HKRS 70-6-339-2
HKRS 70-6-339-3
HKRS 70-6-340-2
HKRS 70-6-340-3
HKRS 70-6-344-1
HKRS 70-6-856-1
HKRS 70-7-76-2
HKRS 70-7-472-2
HKRS 70-8-1204
HKRS 70-8-1206
HKRS 70-8-1207
HKRS 70-8-1208
HKRS 70-8-2093
HKRS 70-8-2094
HKRS 70-8-2097
HKRS 70-8-2103
HKRS 70-8-2104
HKRS 70-8-2105
HKRS 70-8-2106
HKRS 70-8-2168
HKRS 70-8-2173
HKRS 70-8-3698
HKRS 70-9-588
HKRS 160-1-23
HKRS 160-4-4
HKRS 163-1-2176
HKRS 163-1-2505
HKRS 163-1-2838
HKRS 163-13-68
HKRS 276-7-197
HKRS 276-7-407
HKRS 276-7-893
HKRS 276-8-137
HKRS 276-8-351
HKRS 285-1-1
HKRS 286-1-8
HKRS 286-1-9
HKRS 286-1-11
HKRS 286-1-12
HKRS 286-1-14

HKRS 302-1-17
HKRS 376-8-23
HKRS 394-26-12
HKRS 394-27-9
HKRS 394-27-11
HKRS 394-29-53
HKRS 413-1-2
HKRS 413-1-4
HKRS 413-1-5
HKRS 413-1-6
HKRS 413-1-7
HKRS 413-1-9
HKRS 415-2-1
HKRS 455-4-2
HKRS 455-4-4
HKRS 457-3-140
HKRS 457-3-141
HKRS 471-3-1
HKRS 471-3-2
HKRS 488-3-36
HKRS 489-4-20
HKRS 489-4-25
HKRS 500-4-16
HKRS 502-2-4
HKRS 545-4-151
HKRS 565-9-5
HKRS 570-3-34
HKRS 602-1-7
HKRS 605-1-16
HKRS 618-1-566
HKRS 618-1-567
HKRS 742-15-22
HKRS 908-1-43
HKRS 908-1-82
HKRS 925-1-1
HKRS 934-11-41
HKRS 934-17-34
HKRS 934-17-47
HKRS 1443-1-10
HKRS 1443-1-13
HKRS 1443-4-38
HKRS 1443-4-39
HKRS 1536-1-3

Private papers

Elsie Tu Papers, Hong Kong Baptist University Library

MSS.13 6-11
MSS.13 6-12
MSS.13 7-3
MSS.13 7-6

Published official documents

Hong Kong Census and Statistics Department, *Hong Kong Population and Housing Census: 1971 Main Report* (Hong Kong, 1972).

Hong Kong Census and Statistics Department, *Hong Kong 1981 Census Main Report: Analysis* (Hong Kong, 1982).

Hong Kong Government Printer, *Hong Kong Annual Report, 1956* (Hong Kong, February 1957).

Hong Kong Government Printer, *Hong Kong Urban Council, Official Record of Proceedings* (Hong Kong, October 1964).

Hong Kong Government Printer, *Report of the Working Party of Local Administration* (Hong Kong, November 1966).

Hong Kong Government Printer, *Official Report of Proceedings* (Hong Kong, February 1968).

Hong Kong Government Printer, *The Second Report of the Chinese Language Committee: Oral and Written Communication between Government and the Public* (Hong Kong, April 1971).

Hong Kong Government Printer, *The Third Report of the Chinese Committee: Court Proceedings and the Language of the Law* (Hong Kong, June 1971).

Hong Kong Government Printer, *The Fourth (and Final) Report of the Chinese Language Committee: General Translation and Interpretation Services, Hong Kong's Educational System, Chinese as an Official* Language (Hong Kong, July 1971).

Hong Kong Government Printer, *Legal Supplement No.3 to the Hong Kong Government Gazette* (Hong Kong, January 1974).

Hong Kong Government Printer, *Hong Kong Legislative Council, Official Report of Proceedings* (Hong Kong, February 1974).

Hong Kong Government Printer, *Legal Supplement No.1 to the Hong Kong Government Gazette Extraordinary* (Hong Kong, January 1979).

Hong Kong Government Printer, *Green Paper: The Further Development of Representative Government in Hong Kong* (Hong Kong, 1984).

Hong Kong Government Printer, *Green Paper: The 1987 Review of Developments in Representative Government* (Hong Kong, 1987).

Hong Kong Government Printer, *White Paper: The Development of Representative Government: The Way Forward* (Hong Kong, 1988).

Newspapers, magazines, media and student newsletters

Chinese newspapers

Express/Fai Po
Highnoon News
Hong Kong Commercial Daily
Hong Kong Daily News

Hong Kong Times
Kung Sheung Daily News
Kung Sheung Evening News
Ming Pao
Nam Wah Man Po
Oriental Daily
Sing Tao Man Pao
Sing Tao Yat Pao
Ta Kung Pao
Tin Tin Yat Po
Tin Wong Evening News
Truth Daily
Wah Kiu Man Po
Wah Kiu Yat Po
Wan Ren Jih Pao
Wen Wei Po

English newspapers and media

China Mail
Daily Express
Hong Kong Free Press
Hong Kong Standard
Hong Kong Times
Lausan
New York Times
South China Morning Post
Star
The Diplomat
The Guardian
The Sun
The Sunday Times
The Times
Tiger Standard
Wall Street Journal

Magazines and student newsletters

CU Student
Far Eastern Economic Review
Undergrad
University Bulletin

Secondary sources

Books and book chapters

Alanbrooke, Viscount, *Triumph in the West, 1943–46* (London, 1959).
Almond, Gabriel A. and Verba, Sidney, *The Civic Culture: Political Attitudes and Democracy in Five Nations* (Princeton, 1963).

Anderson, Benedict, *Imagined Communities: Reflections on the Origins and Spread of Nationalism* (London, 1983).
Bailkin, Jordanna, *Unsettled: Refugee Camps and the Making of Multicultural Britain* (Oxford, 2018).
Bickers, Robert and Yep, Ray (eds), *May Days in Hong Kong: Riot and Emergency in 1967* (Hong Kong, 2009).
Borstelmann, Thomas, *The 1970s: A New Global History from Civil Rights to Economic Inequality* (Princeton, 2012).
Breuilly, John, *Nationalism and the State* (Manchester, 1982).
Brown, Judith M., *Global South Asians: Introducing the Modern Diaspora* (Cambridge, 2006).
Cain, P. J. and Hopkins, A. G., *British Imperialism: 1688–2015* (Harlow, 2001).
Carroll, John, *A Concise History of Hong Kong* (Hong Kong, 2007).
Cheung, Gary Ka-wai, *Hong Kong's Watershed: The 1967 Riots* (Hong Kong, 2009).
Dapiran, Anthony, *City on Fire: The Fight for Hong Kong* (London, 2020).
Darwin, John, 'Hong Kong in British Decolonisation', in Brown, Judith M. and Foot, Rosemary (eds), *Hong Kong's Transitions, 1842–1997* (London, 1997), pp. 16–32.
Darwin, John, *The Empire Project: The Rise and Fall of the British World-System, 1830–1970* (New York, 2009).
Daunton, Martin, *Just Taxes: The Politics of Taxation in Britain, 1914–1979* (Cambridge, 2002).
Endacott, G., *A History of Hong Kong* (Hong Kong, 1964).
Endacott, G., *Government and People in Hong Kong, 1841–1962: A Constitutional History* (Hong Kong, 1964).
England, Joe, *Hong Kong: Britain's Responsibility* (London, 1976).
Grimal, Henri, *Decolonisation: The British, French, Dutch, and Belgian Empires, 1919–1963* (London, 1978).
Goodstadt, Leo F., *Uneasy Partners: The Conflict between Public Interest and Private Profit in Hong Kong* (Hong Kong, 2005).
Hampton, Mark, *Hong Kong and British Culture* (Manchester, 2015).
Hampton, Mark, 'The Uses of Monarchy in Late-colonial Hong Kong, 1967–97', in Aldrich, Robert and McCreery, Cindy (eds), *Monarchies and Decolonisation in Asia* (Manchester, 2020), pp. 225–42.
Hampton, Mark and Mok, Florence, 'Remembering British Rule: The Uses of Colonial Memory in Hong Kong Movements', in Roberts, Matthew (ed.), *Memory and Modern British Politics: Commemoration, Tradition and Legacy, 1789 to the Present* (Accepted, in press).
Harper, T. N., *The End of Empire and the Making of Malaya* (Cambridge, 1999).
Harrison, Henrietta, *China: Inventing the Nation* (London, 2001).
Ho, Pui-yin, *The Administrative History of the Hong Kong Government Agencies, 1841–2002* (Hong Kong, 2004).
Hodgkin, Thomas, *Nationalism in Colonial Africa* (London, 1956).
Hong Kong Federation of Students, 香港學生運動回顧 (Hong Kong, 1983).
Hopkins, A. G., 'Macmillan's Audit of Empire, 1957', in Clark, P. and Trebilcock, C. (eds), *Understanding Decline: Perceptions and Realities of British Economic Performance: Essays in Honour of Barry Supple* (Cambridge, 1997), pp. 234–60.
Jin, Yaoru, 香江五十年憶往 (*50 Years of Memories in Hong Kong*) (Hong Kong, 2005).

Jones, Carol and Vagg, Jon, *Criminal Justice in Hong Kong* (London and New York, 2007).
King, Ambrose Y. and Lee, Rance P. K. (eds), *Social Life and Development in Hong Kong* (Hong Kong, 1981).
Lam, Kay, '"Consultative Politics' Refined: The Precarious Development of Civic Engagement in Post-colonial Hong Kong", in Lui, Tai-lok, Chiu, Stephen and Yep, Ray (eds), *Routledge Handbook of Contemporary Hong Kong* (New York, 2019), pp. 123–38.
Lam, Wai-man, *Understanding the Political Culture of Hong Kong: The Paradox of Activism and Depoliticisation* (New York, 2004).
Lau, Siu-kai, *Society and Politics in Hong Kong* (Hong Kong, 1982).
Lau, Siu-kai and Kuan, Hsin-chi, *The Ethos of the Hong Kong Chinese* (Hong Kong, 1988).
Layton-Henry, Zig, *The Politics of Immigration: Immigration, 'Race' and 'Race' Relations in Post-War Britain* (Oxford, 1992).
Lee, Ching Kwan and Sing, Ming (eds), *Take Back Our Future: An Eventful Sociology of the Hong Kong Umbrella Revolution* (Ithaca, New York and London, 2019).
Leung, B. K. P., *Perspectives on Hong Kong Society* (Oxford and New York, 1996).
Leung, B. K. P., 'Social Movement as Cognitive Praxis: The Case of the Student Movement and Labour Movement in Hong Kong', in *East Asian Social Movements: Power, Protest and Change in a Dynamic Region* (New York, 2010), pp. 346–64.
Linstrum, Erik, *Ruling Minds: Psychology in the British Empire* (Cambridge, MA, 2016).
Lo, Shiu-hing, *The Politics of Democratisation in Hong Kong* (New York, 1997).
Loh, Christine, *Underground Front: The Chinese Communist Party in Hong Kong* (Hong Kong, 2010).
Louis, Wm. Roger, 'Public Enemy Number One: Britain and the United Nations in the Aftermath of Suez', in Lynn, Martin (ed.), *The British Empire in the 1950s: Retreat or Revival?* (Basingstoke, 2006), pp. 186–213.
Low, D. A., 'The Asian Mirror to Tropical Africa's Independence', in Gifford, Prosser and Louis, Wm. Roger (eds), *The Transfer of Power in Africa: Decolonisation, 1940–1960* (New Haven, 1982), pp. 1–29.
Lu, Xun, 'The American Cold War in Hong Kong, 1949–1960: Intelligence and Propaganda', in Roberts, Priscilla and Carroll, John M. (eds), *Hong Kong in the Cold War* (Hong Kong, 2016), pp. 117–40.
Lui, Tai-lok, 那似曾相識的七十年代 (*The Old-so-Familiar 1970s*) (Hong Kong, 2012).
Lui, Tai-lok and Chiu, Stephen W. K., 'Social Movements and Public Discourse on Politics', in Ngo, Tak-wing (ed.), *Hong Kong's History: State and Society under Colonial Rule* (London, 1999), pp. 101–18.
Lui, Tai-lok and Chiu, Stephen W. K., *The Dynamics of Social Movements in Hong Kong* (Hong Kong, 2010).
Ma, Eric Kit-wai Ma, *Culture, Politics and Television in Hong Kong* (London, 1999).
Ma, Ngok, *Political Development in Hong Kong: State, Political Society, and Civil Society* (Hong Kong, 2007).
Mark, Chi-kwan, 'Crisis or Opportunity? Britain, China, and the Decolonisation of Hong Kong in the Long 1970s', in Roberts, Priscilla and Westad, Odd Arne (eds), *China, Hong Kong, and the Long 1970s: Global Perspectives* (Basingstoke, 2017), pp. 257–77.

Mark, Chi-kwan, *The Everyday Cold War: Britain and China, 1950–1972* (London, 2017).
Meisner, Maurice, *Mao's China and After: A History of the People's Republic* (New York, 1977).
Miners, Norman, *The Government and Politics of Hong Kong* (Hong Kong, 1975).
Morris, Paul, *Hong Kong School Curriculum: Development, Issues and Policies* (Hong Kong, 1996).
Moser, Claus and Kalton, Graham, *Survey Methods in Social Investigation* (London, 1971).
Moss, Peter, *No Babylon: A Hong Kong Scrapbook* (Lincoln, 2006).
Ngo, Tak-wing, 'Colonialism in Hong Kong Revisited', in Ngo, Tak-wing (ed.), *Hong Kong's History: State and Society under Colonial Rule* (London, 1999), pp. 1–12.
Paul, Kathleen, *Whitewashing Britain: Race and Citizenship in the Postwar Era* (Ithaca, 1997).
Peden, G. C., *The Treasury and British Public Policy 1906–1959* (Oxford, 2000).
Pepper, Suzanne, *Keeping Democracy at Bay: Hong Kong and the Challenge of Chinese Political Reform* (Lanham, 2008).
Roberts, Priscilla, 'Introduction: China and the Long 1970s: The Great Transformation', in Roberts, Priscilla and Westad, Odd Arne (eds), *China, Hong Kong, and the Long 1970s: Global Perspectives* (Basingstoke, 2017), pp. 1–30.
Robinson, Ronald, 'Non-European Foundations of European Imperialism: Sketch for a Theory of Collaboration', in Owen, Roger and Sutcliffe, Bob (eds), *Studies in the Theory of Imperialism* (London, 1972), pp. 117–42.
Schofield, Camilla, *Enoch Powell and the Making of Postcolonial Britain* (Cambridge, 2013).
Scott, Ian, *Political Change and the Crisis of Legitimacy in Hong Kong* (Hong Kong, 1989).
Sinn, Elizabeth, *Power and Charity: The Early History of the Tung Wah Hospital, Hong Kong* (Hong Kong, 1989).
Sinn, Elizabeth, *Culture and Society in Hong Kong* (Hong Kong, 1995).
Sweeting, Anthony, *Education in Hong Kong, 1941 to 2001: Visions and Revisions* (Hong Kong, 2004).
Tsang, Steve, *Government and Politics: A Documentary History of Hong Kong* (Hong Kong, 1995).
Tsang, Steve, *Hong Kong: An Appointment with China* (London, 1997).
Tsang, Steve, 'Realignment of Power: The Politics of Transition and Reform in Hong Kong', in Li, Pang-kwong (ed.), *Political Order and Power Transition in Hong Kong* (Hong Kong, 1997), pp. 31–52.
Tsang, Steve, *A Modern History of Hong Kong* (London, 2004).
Wallerstein, Immanuel, *Africa: The Politics of Independence* (New York, 1961).
Wang, Gungwu, 'Hong Kong's Twentieth Century: The Global Setting', in Roberts, Priscilla and Carroll, John M. (eds), *Hong Kong in the Cold War* (Hong Kong, 2016), pp. 1–14.
Welch, Stephen, *The Political Culture Theory* (Oxford, 2013).
Wong, Aline K., *The Kaifong Associations and the Society of Hong Kong* (Taipei, 1972).
Wong, John D., '"Bat Lau Dung Laii": Shifting Hong Kong Perspectives Toward the Vietnamese Boatpeople', in Roberts, Priscilla and Westad, Odd Arne (eds), *China, Hong Kong, and the Long 1970s: Global Perspectives* (Cham, 2017), pp. 279–301.

Wong, Man Fong, 中國對香港恢復行使主權的決策歷程與執行 (*China Resumption of Sovereignty over Hong Kong*) (Hong Kong, 1997).
Yeo, Kim Wah, *Political Development in Singapore, 1945–1955* (Singapore, 1973).
Yep, Ray (ed.), *Negotiating Autonomy in Greater China: Hong Kong and Its Sovereignty Before and After 1997* (Copenhagen, 2013).
Yep, Ray, 靜默革命:香港廉政百年共業 (*Silent Revolution: 100 Years of Development of Hong Kong in Anti-corruption*) (Hong Kong, 2014).

Journal articles

Anderson, David M., 'British Abuse and Torture in Kenya's Counter-insurgency, 1952–1960', *Small Wars & Insurgencies*, 23:4–5 (2012), pp. 700–19.
Benson, Michaela, 'Hong Kongers and the Coloniality of British Citizenship from Decolonisation to "Global Britain"', *Current Sociology* (2021), pp. 1–19.
Clayton, David, 'From "Free" to "Fair" Trade: The Evolution of Labour Laws in Colonial Hong Kong', *Journal of Imperial and Commonwealth History*, 35:2 (2007), pp. 263–82.
Clayton, David, 'From Laissez-faire to "Positive Non-interventionism": The Colonial State in Hong Kong Studies', *Social Transformations in Chinese Societies*, 9:1 (2013), pp. 1–20.
Darwin, John, 'Empire and Ethnicity', *Nations and Nationalism*, 16:3 (2010), pp. 383–401.
Fung, Chi Keung Charles, 'Colonial Governance and State Incorporation of Chinese Language: The Case of the First Chinese Language Movement in Hong Kong', *Social Transformations in Chinese Societies* (2021), ahead of print.
Gallagher, John and Robinson, Ronald, 'The Imperialism of Free Trade', *The Economic History Review*, 6:1 (1953), pp. 1–15.
Goodstadt, Leo F., 'China and the Selection of Hong Kong's Post-Colonial Political Elite', *The China Quarterly*, 163 (2000), pp. 721–41.
Hampton, Mark, 'British Legal Culture and Colonial Governance: The Attack on Corruption in Hong Kong, 1968–1974', *Britain and the World*, 5:2 (2012), pp. 223–39.
Hoadley, J. S., 'Hong Kong is the Lifeboat: Notes on Political Culture and Socialisation', *Journal of Oriental Studies*, 8 (1970), pp. 206–18.
Hoadley, J. S., 'Political Participation of Hong Kong Chinese: Patterns and Trends', *Asian Survey*, 13:6 (1973), pp. 604–16.
Hyam, Ronald, 'The Primacy of Geopolitics: The Dynamics of British Imperial Policy, 1763–1963', *Journal of Imperial and Commonwealth History*, 27:2 (1999), pp. 27–52.
King, Ambrose Y., 'Administrative Absorption of Politics in Hong Kong: Emphasis on the Grass Roots Level', *Asian Survey*, 15:5 (1975), pp. 422–39.
Ku, Agnes S. M., 'Immigration Policies, Discourse, and the Politics of Local Belonging in Hong Kong (1950–1980)', *Modern China*, 30:3 (2004), pp. 326–60.
Lau, Siu-kai, 'Chinese Familism in an Urban-Industrial Setting: The Case of Hong Kong', *Journal of Marriage and Family*, 43:4 (1981), pp. 977–92.
Lee, Francis L. F., Yuen, Samson, Tang, Gary and Cheng, Edmund W., 'Hong Kong's Summer of Uprising: From Anti-Extradition to Anti-Authoritarian Protests', *China Review*, 19:4 (2019), pp. 1–32.
Lethbridge, H. J., 'Hong Kong Cadets, 1862–1941', *Journal of the Hong Kong Branch of the Royal Asiatic Society*, 10 (1970), pp. 36–56.

Louis, Wm. Roger and Robinson, Ronald, 'The Imperialism of Decolonisation', *The Journal of Imperial and Commonwealth History*, 22:3 (2008), pp. 462–511.

Low, Choo Chin, 'The Repatriation of the Chinese as a Counter-insurgency Policy during the Malayan Emergency', *Journal of Southeast Asian Studies*, 45:2 (2014), pp. 363–92.

Ma, Eric Kit-wai, 'Reinventing Hong Kong: Memory, Identity and Television', *International Journal of Cultural Studies*, 1:3 (1998), pp. 329–49.

Ma, Eric Kit-wai and Fung, A. Y. H., 'Negotiating Local and National Identifications: Hong Kong Identity Surveys 1996–2006', *Asian Journal of Communication*, 17:2 (2007), pp. 172–85.

Mark, Chi-kwan, 'Defence or Decolonisation? Britain, the United States, and the Hong Kong Question in 1957', *Journal of Imperial and Commonwealth History*, 33:1 (2005), pp. 51–72.

Mark, Chi-kwan, 'The "Problem of People": British Colonials, Cold War Powers, and the Chinese Refugees in Hong Kong, 1949–62', *Modern Asian Studies*, 41:6 (2007), pp. 1145–81.

Mark, Chi-kwan, 'Lack of Means or Loss of Will? The United Kingdom and the Decolonisation of Hong Kong, 1957–1967', *The International History Review*, 31:1 (2009), pp. 45–71.

Mark, Chi-kwan, 'To "Educate" Deng Xiaoping in Capitalism: Thatcher's Visit to China and the Future of Hong Kong in 1982', *Cold War History*, 17:2 (2017), pp. 161–80.

Mark, Chi-kwan, 'Decolonising Britishness? The 1981 British Nationality Act and the Identity Crisis of Hong Kong Elites', *Journal of Imperial and Commonwealth History*, 48:3 (2020), pp. 565–90.

Mok, Florence, 'Public Opinion Polls and Covert Colonialism in British Hong Kong', *China Information*, 33:1 (2019), pp. 66–87.

Mok, Florence, 'Chinese Illicit Immigration into Colonial Hong Kong, c. 1970–1980', *Journal of Imperial and Commonwealth History*, 49:2 (2021), pp. 339–67.

Mok, Florence, 'Disseminating and Containing Communist Propaganda to Overseas Chinese in Southeast Asia through Hong Kong, the Cold War Pivot, 1949–1960', *The Historical Journal* (2021), pp. 1–21.

Mok, Florence, 'Town Talk: Enhancing the "Eyes and Ears" of the Colonial State in British Hong Kong, 1950s–1975', *Historical Research* (2021), pp. 1–22.

Morris, Paul and Sweeting, Anthony, 'Education and Politics: The Case of Hong Kong from an Historical Perspective', *Oxford Review of Education*, 17:3 (1991), pp. 249–67.

Ng, Kenny K. K., 'Inhibition vs. Exhibition: Political Censorship of Chinese and Foreign Cinemas in Postwar Hong Kong', *Journal of Chinese Cinemas*, 2:1 (2008), pp. 23–35.

Ng, Michael, 'When Silence Speaks: Press Censorship and Rule of Law in British Hong Kong, 1850s–1940s', *Law & Literature*, 29:3 (2017), pp. 425–56.

Schenk, Catherine R., 'Decolonisation and European Economic Integration: The Free Trade Area Negotiations, 1956–58', *Journal of Imperial and Commonwealth History*, 24:3 (1996), pp. 444–63.

Scott, Ian, 'Bridging the Gap: Hong Kong Senior Civil Servants and the 1966 Riots', *The Journal of Imperial and Commonwealth History*, 45:1 (2016), pp. 131–48.

Sing, Ming, 'Economic Development, Civil Society and Democratisation in Hong Kong', *Journal of Contemporary Asia*, 26:4 (1996), pp. 482–504.

Turnbull, C. M., 'British Planning for Post-war Malaya', *Journal of Southeast Asian Studies*, 5:2 (1974), pp. 239–54.
Van Der Weyden, Martin B., 'Covert Colonialism', *The Medical Journal of Australia*, 189:4 (2008), p. 185.
Voinea, Camelia Florela and Neumann, Martin, 'Political Culture: A Theory in Search for Methodology. An Editorial', *Quality & Quantity*, 54 (2020), pp. 335–60.
Wong, Aline K., 'Chinese Community Leadership in a Colonial Setting: The Hong Kong Neighbourhood Associations', *Asian Survey*, 12:7 (1972), pp. 587–601.
Yep, Ray, 'The Crusade against Corruption in Hong Kong in the 1970s: Governor MacLehose as a Zealous Reformer or Reluctant Hero?', *China Information* 27:2 (2013), pp. 197–221.
Yep, Ray and Lui, Tai-lok, 'Revisiting the Golden Era of MacLehose and the Dynamics of Social Reforms', *China Information*, 24:3 (2010), pp. 249–72.

Index

5G networks 225

Advisory Committee on Telephone Services 125, 126, 143
Advisory Council on Corruption 104
Africa 2, 4, 17, 29, 46, 209, 255
All Hong Kong Committee to Strive to Reopen the Precious Blood Golden Jubilee Secondary School 159
All Hong Kong Working Party to Promote Chinese as Official Language (WPCOL) 57–9, 71, 75
All-Party Anglo-Hong Kong Parliamentary Group 215
Alliance in Support of Patriotic Democratic Movements of China 246
anti-China sentiment 1, 189
Anti-Corruption Branch 87–90, 92, 94, 101–2, 104, 113, 115, 257
Anti-Corruption Commission 98, 104
Anti-Corruption and Narcotics Branch 87
anti-Extradition Bill protests 1, 18
anti-imperialism 93
Arms and Ammunition Order (1975) 105
Association for Democracy and People's Livelihood 9
Attorney General (Hong Kong) 68, 100, 106

back-to-the-countryside movement (China) 195
Bailkin, Jordanna 178
Baishizhou 197
Baptist College 58
  Student Union 73, 163
Baptist University 86
Basic Law (1990) 9, 16, 201, 239–40, 244–5
Beijing 1, 7, 10, 18, 194, 198–9, 208, 225, 239, 246
Belgium 127
Benn, Tony 163
Bernacchi, Brook 55
Big Circle Gang 188
Bishop of Hong Kong 158, 159, 162
  Office of 163
Biweekly Group 94
Blair-Kerr, Alistair 103, 105, 108, 115, 135, 146
Blaker, D. J. R. 65
bombs 60, 132, 161
Bourdieu, Pierre 54
Bray, Denis 143, 232
Brexit 225, 231n.158
Britain
  Conservative government 208, 210–11
  Conservative Party 98, 256
  diplomatic relations with China 18, 225, 256
  'East of Suez' policy 7
  Labour government 3, 96, 209

Index 273

Labour Party 8, 68, 88, 91, 94, 97–8, 136, 163–4, 167
Parliament 68, 93, 136, 163, 223, 224, 257
'British Citizens' (BC) 209
British Commonwealth 3, 209–10, 213
'British Dependency Citizen' 211
'British Dependent Territories Citizens' (BDTC) 223, 224–5
British empire 2, 4–5
  development projects in 3
  earnings from 3
'British (Hong Kong) Citizens' 218, 220, 223, 224
'British National: Hong Kong Citizen' 220–1
British National Overseas (BN[O]) 225, 231n.158
British Nationality Act (1981) 10, 16, 48, 208–9, 223, 225, 256, 257
  Standing Committee 218
'British Overseas Citizens' (BOC) 209
Bryan, Paul 215–16, 222
Burgess, Claude 176–7

Cadet Selection Board 30
cadet system 7, 31
Callaghan, James 113, 179
Campaign for Chinese as an Official Language (CCOL) 57–9
  Federation for the Promotion of Chinese as an Official Language in Hong Kong 57
Canavan, Dennis 164
Cantonese 58, 65, 67, 69, 71, 76
Caritas 133, 158, 162, 168
Carrington, Peter 196, 199, 217, 220–2
Carroll, John 13, 24
Cater, Jack 91, 104–5, 224
Catholic Board of Education 158
Catholic Institute for International Relations 164
Cave, Haddon 132
Census and Statistics Department 43–6, 236

Commissioner 44
Central District 38, 76, 126, 137, 142, 241
Chan Chung Ling 157
Chan Ho-tin, Andy 1
Chan Kwan-fong 191–2
Chan Ling-fong 188
Chan, Peter C. K. 190
Chan Yat-sun 55
Charles, Prince 214
Chashan Commune 197
Cheong-Leen, Hilton 77, 105, 223
Cheung, Oswald 134–5, 214, 217
Cheung, Peter 159
Chief Justice (Hong Kong) 68, 90
Chief Whip 107
China
  admission to the UN 180
  Hong Kong policy 6, 193
  intervention in Hong Kong 1, 225, 242, 259
  US trade embargo 6, 87, 180
China Mail 14, 87, 88, 89–92, 94, 96–100, 102, 108, 115, 186
'Chinese Britishness' 209, 224
Chinese Civil Servants Association 57, 75
Chinese Communist Party 11, 60, 76, 185
Chinese Language Branch 69
Chinese Manufacturers' Association of Hong Kong 57, 79n.30, 138, 146
Chinese Press Review 27, 62, 102, 105, 159
Chinese University of Hong Kong 56–7, 64, 92, 162
  Chinese–English Dictionary project 56
  Chung Chi College 57, 58
  CU Student 70
  School of Education 156
Choi, Ambrose 214
Choi Hung 133
Chow, Edmund 99–100, 136–7, 140, 214
Chui, A. K. 140

Chui, James 60–1, 66
Chui Yi 194
Chung, Augustine 214
Chung, Sze-yuen 214, 217, 220–1, 245
Citizen Advisory Committee on Community Relations 104
'Citizens of British Dependent Territories' (CBDT) 211–12, 214–15, 219–23
Citizens' Consultative Committees (Singapore) 33, 255
Citizen's Party 246
'Citizens of the United Kingdom and Colonies' (CUKC) 209–11, 214, 217–20
City District Commissioners 33
City District Officers (CDO) 8, 11, 24–6, 32–9, 41–8, 53, 58, 63–5, 69, 72, 74–7, 88, 92, 102, 125, 129, 133–5, 142–8, 165, 200, 232–4, 254–5
  District Monthly Meetings 33
City and New Territories Administration 233–4, 241, 247
Civic Association Hung Hom District 137
Civis Britannicus 221
Clark, A. T. 63
Cold War 4–6, 12, 29, 178
Collard, Bill 184
College Student Association of Hong Kong 74, 141
colonial administration (Hong Kong) 5, 7, 9, 24–7, 30–2, 35, 49n.9, 55, 62, 69–72, 77, 88, 103, 105, 125, 134, 147, 156, 164, 168, 200, 232, 247, 255–7
  English-language requirement 8
  legitimacy of 8, 17, 86, 155, 254
  recruitment of elites 11
Colonial Office 27
  Information Department 27
  Press Division 27–8
Commerce and Industry Department 87

Commercial Television 110
Commissioner of Police 92, 99, 101, 112–13
  see also Sutcliffe, Charles
Committee of Inquiry 16, 146, 165–8, 170
Commonwealth Immigration Act (1962) 221
Confucianism 11, 82–3n.109
consular protection 222, 225
Consumer Council 128, 136, 141
corruption 8, 29, 39, 85, 87–93, 103, 107–9, 111, 113–15, 125, 129, 155, 182
  anti-corruption campaigns 14–15, 48, 85–90, 95–100, 115, 125, 256–9
  see also Anti-Corruption Branch; Independent Commission Against Corruption (ICAC)
counter-insurgency measures 4
Cradock, Percy 194–5, 219
Crown Service 215, 218–20
Cultural Revolution 7, 60, 178–9, 205–6n.125

Daily Combat 139
Daily Express 100
Daily Growth Investment Company 137
Darwin, John 4–5, 7
David, E. B. 29
Davies, Lewis 198
decolonisation 2–7, 14, 17, 26, 36, 48, 70, 254
Democratic Alliance for the Betterment of Hong Kong 246
Deng Xiaoping 10, 208
Development, Training and Research Division 69
devolution of power 6–7, 25, 26, 32, 37
Diaoyu Islands 68, 94
Ding, L. K. 136, 140, 146, 159
Diocesan Justice and Peace Commission 159

Director of Home Affairs 39–40, 69, 140, 146
  see also Chui, A. K.
Director of Immigration 184, 193, 194
District Boards 9, 234, 237–8, 240–1, 243–4, 249n.11
  elections 16, 233, 247
  Secretariat 234
District Management Committee 234
District Watch Force 31
Donald, Alan 182–3
Douglas-Home, Alec 103–4, 181–2
Dunn, Lydia 146–7

Easey, Walter 215
Eastern District 72, 142
Education Action Group 163
Education Department 32, 155–63, 165–7, 169–70
Egypt 3
Election Committee 240, 247
electoral reform 4–5, 8–9, 16, 17, 37, 46, 238–9, 241–2, 248, 255–6, 260
Elliott, Elsie 55, 65, 86–8, 96–100, 105, 113–15, 140, 168, 190, 233
Ellis, Alan 87, 98–100, 115
Elwyn-Jones, Lord 223
emigration
  from China 182, 193, 196–8
  from Hong Kong 10, 219, 245
Endacott, George 10
England 8, 76, 94, 104–5, 163
Estates Talk 232
Executive Council 6, 28, 58, 68, 103–4, 165–7, 183, 195, 212, 214, 219, 221, 232, 237, 247
Extradition Bill (2019) 1, 18
Extradition Ordinance 182, 202n.30
European Economic Community 211
European Free Trade Area 3

Fai Po 129, 145, 186
Fan May-yung 163
Far Eastern Department 194, 199

Far Eastern Economic Review 58
Ferry Wharves 140
films 12, 24
Fisher, Nigel 96
Flannery, Martin 164
Flash Points 232, 248n.5
Fookes, Janet 163
Ford, David 103, 176–7, 179
  'The Price of Freedom' 176
Foreign and Commonwealth Office 26, 48, 67, 69, 96, 98–9, 103, 106–7, 113, 165, 181, 194, 196, 198–9, 221, 224, 241, 256–7
foreign exchange 5
Foreign Secretary (UK) 91, 103, 113, 163, 181, 240
Four Modernisations 213
Fourth International 94
France 76, 127
Frankenstein 106
freedom of speech 93, 260
Frontier 246
Fugitive Offenders Act (UK) 85, 94, 102, 106–7, 116, 256
Fung, Charles 54
Fung, Harry 134
Fung, Raymond 128, 135, 140
Fung, Sir Kenneth Ping-fan 61

Gang of Four 213
Geddes, Lord 223
gender equality campaigns 13
Germany 3
Gestapo 110
Gibraltar amendment 222–3
'Global Britain' 225
Godber, Peter 86, 88–95, 97–8, 102–4, 106–7, 115–16, 125
Golden Jubilee incident (1978) *see* Precious Blood Golden Jubilee Secondary School
Goodstadt, Leo 7, 240
Goronwy Roberts, Lord 166, 183, 184
Government House 33, 144, 158

Government Information Service (GIS) 28, 32, 51n.91, 62, 64, 103, 144, 147–8, 222, 235
  GIST 241
  see also Colonial Office
Grantham College of Education Student Union 160
Great Leap Forward 60, 178
Great Tunnel Robbery 187
'Green Card Holders' 188
Green Papers 9, 44, 209–12, 232, 234, 236–7, 239
  'British Nationality Law–Discussion of Possible Changes' 209
Guangdong Province 181, 184, 195, 200, 205n.125, 206n.133
Guardian, The 91, 98, 99, 102
Guo Jie 199

Haifeng 198
Hampton, Mark 85–6, 98, 209
Hang Seng Bank robbery 191
Hang Seng Index 245
Hanson, M. J. J. 247
Haye, Colvyn 160
Heath, Edward 93
Heung Yee Kuk 54–5, 57, 128, 213, 217
Hilton Cheong-leen 77, 105, 233
Ho, C. H. 131
Ho, Stephen Y. S. 38
Hoadley, J. S. 11, 53
Home Affairs Department (HAD) 25, 35, 39–45, 47, 68, 134, 140, 148, 232, 234–7, 240–2, 248, 254
  Community Information Unit 42–3, 237
  Deputy Director 39, 42–3
Home Office (UK) 101, 107, 116, 216–17, 221–4, 231n.158, 256, 257
Home Secretary (UK) 217, 219–22
Hong Kong
  autonomy of 1, 9–10, 73, 219, 237–9, 242, 244, 259–60

  Director of Education 67, 157–60, 166
  economic development of 13, 53, 179
  Governor 1, 6, 26, 36, 41, 62, 66–8, 86, 90–1, 101–6, 139–40, 144–7, 158, 182–3, 194, 200, 213, 218–24, 238–40, 256–7
  Gross Domestic Product 9, 127
  handover 1, 2, 10, 16
  as 'laissez-faire' state 2, 10
  Political Advisers 181–2, 194
  Secretary for Information 176, 212
  treaties 5
  wages in 10, 127
Hong Kong Affairs Society 9, 243, 245
Hong Kong and General Department 166–7, 194, 198, 199
Hong Kong and Indian Ocean Department 99, 106
  Overseas Police Adviser 99, 103
Hong Kong and Kowloon and New Territories Manufacturing and Commercial Association 133
Hong Kong and Kowloon Joint Kaifong Association Research Council 54, 133, 190
Hong Kong and Kowloon Mutual Aid Association 137
'Hong Kong belonger' 177
Hong Kong (British Nationality) Order (1986) 225
Hong Kong Chinese General Chamber of Commerce 139
Hong Kong Christian Industrial Committee 125, 128
Hong Kong Civil Association 223
Hong Kong Commercial Daily 128, 130
Hong Kong Council of the Church of Christ in China 162
Hong Kong Daily News (HKDN) 66, 159, 160, 169, 192
Hong Kong Federation of Catholic Students 141
Hong Kong Federation of Students (HKFS) 57–61, 66–8, 70–3, 92–5, 108, 115, 141, 162

Chinese Language Study
  Committee 61
Language Action Committee 60
Hong Kong Forum 243
Hong Kong General Chamber of
  Commerce 64
Hong Kong Medical and Health
  Services 32
Hong Kong National Party 1
'Hong Kong permanent resident' 201
Hong Kong Police Force 32, 60, 87–92,
  96–7, 99, 101–5, 112, 115–16,
  140, 257
  amnesty granted to 112, 116
  Anti-Corruption Branch 87–90, 92,
    94, 101–2, 104, 113, 115, 257
  Inspectorate 87
Hong Kong Polytechnic University 162
Hong Kong Professional Teachers'
  Union 158–9, 161, 163
Hong Kong Progressive Alliance 246
Hong Kong Public Opinion Research
  Institute 236
Hong Kong Public Records Office 14
Hong Kong Research Project 215
Hong Kong Society of Accountants 146
Hong Kong Special Branch 104, 142,
  144, 147–8, 255
Hong Kong Standard (HKS) 62, 88, 97,
  185–6, 187–8
Hong Kong Subsidised Secondary
  Schools Council 161
Hong Kong Teachers Association 141
Hong Kong Telephone Company
  125–7, 129, 139
Hong Kong Times (HKT) 64, 88, 145,
  159, 167, 169, 187–8
Hong Kong University 160, 236, 246
  Faculty of Social Science 236
  Social Science Research
    Centre 246
Hong Kong University Students' Union
  60, 64, 140
  Alumni Association 137
  Current Affairs Committee 55
  Undergrad 56, 70, 72–3

Hong Kong Youth and Students
  Association 139–40
Hooley, Frank 163
House of Commons (UK) 68, 96, 102,
  104, 107, 216
House of Lords (UK) 97, 222, 223
housing 9, 16, 28, 39, 130, 134, 147,
  177–9, 183, 190, 209, 241
  see also Housing Authority; Ten-Year
    Housing Programme
Housing Authority 31
Hu, Henry Hung-lick 55, 66, 188
Hua Guofeng 197
Huang, Denny Mong-hwa 57–60,
  64–6, 70–1, 74, 76, 140,
  189–90, 214
Huang Hua 199
Huang, Rayson 165
Huawei 225
Huizhou 196
Hundred Flowers Movement 60
Hung, C. P. 146
Hung Hom Kaifong Association 100
hunger strikes 163, 169,
  171, 259
Hunt, Ernest 88, 107
Hurd, Douglas 240

immigration (to Hong Kong)
  176–81, 186, 189–95, 209–10,
  215, 256, 258
  illegal 9, 181–2, 186, 193, 196–9
  repatriation 177, 178, 181, 183–8,
    192, 193, 198, 202n.30
Immigration Act (UK) 210
Immigration Department 193,
  195, 197
  Ship Searching Unit 180, 193
Immigration Ordinance 193, 197
immigration policy 16, 48, 176–7,
  181, 183, 185, 187–93, 195, 198,
  200, 257
  'turning back doctrine' 178
  see also 'Touch Base' policy
Incorporated Owners of Pak Lee
  Building 137

Independent Commission Against
  Corruption (ICAC) 8, 15, 85–7, 91,
  95, 99–102, 104–16, 123–4n.220,
  125, 155, 156, 158, 258
  Community Relations
    Department 104
  Complaints Committee 106, 115
  Corruption Prevention
    Department 104
  Economic and Public Affairs
    syllabus 114
  Operations Department 104
Independent Television (ITV) 100
India 210
  independence (1947) 3
indirect rule 26
industrialists 10, 75
  relocation of industry to China 10
inflation 128–9, 138–9, 186
Inland Revenue Department 75
Inspector General of Colonial Police 98
International Marxist Group 94
International Research Associates
  (IRA) 235–6
International Socialists 94
investment 3, 10, 217

Japan 82n.109, 255
  occupation of Hong Kong 27
Japanese Monitor System for National
  Policy 44
Johnson, James 68, 87, 91, 98–100,
  106, 115, 164
Joint Committee for the Promotion
  of Democratic Government
  (JCPDG) 245
Joint Liaison Group 239
Jones, Daniel 91
Jordan Valley 134
Juvenile Courts 69

Kaifong Advancement Association 136
kaifong associations 28–32, 38, 42, 46,
  49n.19, 54, 57, 75, 95, 125, 128,
  132–7, 139, 141, 146–7, 189, 232
  membership of 30

Kan, Y. K. (Yuet-keung) 128, 223
Kennedy Town Kaifong Association 188
Kenya 210, 257
King, Ambrose 11, 48n.7
Korea 6
Korean War 6, 87
Kowloon 30, 33, 37, 44–5, 65, 71, 74,
  86, 130–3, 142–3, 145, 179, 189
Kowloon Chamber of Commerce 139
Kowloon City 75–6
  District Council 76–7
Kowloon City Kaifong Association 188
Kowloon Multi-storey Buildings
  General Association 139
Kowloon Park 140
'Know the People' 240, 242
Ku, Agnes 177
Kung Sheung 57
Kung Sheung Daily News (KSDN) 88,
  130, 145, 169, 186–8
Kung Sheung Evening News (KSEN)
  88, 160, 163, 167, 186–7
Kuomintang 11, 13, 144
Kwai Chung 45, 127
Kwai Chung Kaifong Association 137
Kwan, Father Thomas 159, 170
Kwan, Hilda 157–8
Kwun Tong 37, 95, 133

labour legislation 9
Labour Party (UK) 8, 68, 88, 91, 97,
  98, 136, 163–4, 167
  International Executive
    Committee 164
  Young Socialists 94
Labour Relations Bill 42
Lai, David 37, 65, 74
Lai, Helen 92
Lai, T. C. 64
Lam Hung-chow 59
Lam Tin 236
Lam Wai-man 13, 54, 86, 125, 148n.1,
  155, 168
Lamond, James 164
Lau Siu-kai 11
  'utilitarianist familism' 11

Lee Man-hung 192
Lee, Martin 245
Legislative Council 6, 9, 61–2, 65, 69, 77, 98–9, 126–7, 133–4, 140, 143–4, 146, 237–40, 246, 249n.11, 256
　elections 9, 16, 238, 240, 243–8
　Financial Committee 68
Lei Cheng Uk Resettlement Estate Commercial and Industrial General Association 133
Leimukshui Caritas Centre 162
Lestor, Joan 164
Leung, M. 72
Leung, Poon Tai 138
Li, F. K. 61, 64, 68, 77
Li Kwan-ha 185
Liberal Democratic Federation of Hong Kong 246
Lin Yutang 56
Lingnan College 58
Lion Club 184
literacy 4
Lo Tak-shing 105
Loh, Christian 246
London 2, 6, 26, 40, 68, 91, 96, 163, 167, 215, 217, 219, 245
　see also Britain
London Broadcasting 100
Longgang Commune 197
Lord Brockway 97
Lord Shepherd 97
Luce, Richard 221
Lufeng 198
Lui Fook-hong 188
Lyons, Edward 218

Ma Man-fei 185
Ma Ngok 12, 244
MacLehose, Murray 8, 10, 68, 86, 90, 96, 103–4, 106, 113, 158, 161, 165, 182–3, 191, 193–200, 208, 219–23, 257
Macoun, M. J. 103
MacWhinnie, Gordon 146
Magistrates' courts 69, 87

Malaya 4–5, 257
　deportation of Chinese from 4
Malayan Emergency (1948) 4
Malayan Spring 4
Malayan Union 4
Malaysia 127
Mao Zedong 5, 188
Mark, Chi-kwan 6–7, 178, 208–9, 211, 223
Marks, Kenneth 91
Marxists Revolutionary League 160
mass media 14, 27, 43, 94, 107–8, 110–11, 115–16, 131, 134, 168, 191, 241, 248
Mau Mau Uprisings 4
May Fourth movement 72–3, 82–3n.109
McDouall, J. C. 30
McLaren, Robin 167
'Meet-the-Public' scheme 234
Meeting Point 9, 243, 245
Merchant Shipping (Amendment) Ordinance 197
Migrated Archives (Hanslope) 15
Miners, Norman 11
Ming Pao 167, 187, 212, 220
Minister of Foreign and Commonwealth Affairs 102
Misdemeanours Punishment Ordinance (1898) 87
Mobil Oil 146
Mong Kok 37, 95, 126, 133
Moore, Robert 102
Morse Park 95
Movement of Opinion Direction (MOOD, 1975) 17, 25–6, 41–8, 100, 102, 107–8, 110–11, 114–15, 165–6, 168–71, 188–91, 200, 213–14, 232–5, 241, 248, 255
　Committee Organisers 43
Mutual Aid Committees (MACs) 42, 132–3, 232

Nam Wah Man Po 130
narcotics 28, 31, 98
National Archives 14

National Security Law (2020) 1, 18, 260
National Service Ordinance (Singapore) 4
National Union of Students (UK) 61, 68
nationalism 13, 46, 59, 71–3, 76–8, 258
  anti-colonial 4–5
  Malay 4
Nationalists 5, 176–8, 184, 186, 188
  see also Kuomintang
nationality 71, 178, 208–10, 212, 214–16, 220–5
Nationality and Treaty Department (UK) 218, 220–1, 229n.112
naturalisation 71, 215, 218, 220
Neoh, A. F. 130, 138
New Asia College 58
New China News Agency (NCNA) 181, 182–4, 194–6, 198, 238, 240
New Commonwealth 210
New Kowloon 45
New Territories 28, 44–5, 47, 49n.21, 54, 59, 199, 213, 217, 234–5, 241, 247
  lease 208
New Territories General Chamber of Commerce 128
Ng Chak-lam 76, 233
Ng, John 65
Ng, Napoleon 138
Ng Yuk School 167
Ngau Tau Kok 133–4, 139
Norman-Walker, Hugh 68, 95
Northcote Teachers Training College 58
nostalgia 1, 255
Notting Hill riots 210

October Review 160
Official Languages Bill (1974) 53, 69, 77–8
'One Country, Two Systems' 10, 260
Open Door Policy 10
Opinion Survey Unit (OSU) 237
Oriental Daily 160–1, 192
Osaka Feedback Scheme 44, 255

Owen, D. T. 194
Owen, David 163–4

Pakistan 210
pamphlets 14, 59–60, 68, 71, 94, 141
Panyu County 196
Pao-an County 193
passports 209, 211, 214, 216–17, 221–3, 225
  'British passport Hong Kong' 222
  'Citizen of the British Dependent Territories–Hong Kong' 222
Patten, Christopher 1, 9, 16, 239–40
Pendry, Tom 88
People's Association (Singapore) 33, 255
People's Liberation Army 197–8, 240
People's Republic of China (PRC)
  see China
Pepper, Suzanne 234
Perry, Robert 163
political parties 17, 243–4, 245–6, 248, 259
polling and surveys 17–18, 25, 40–1, 46, 48, 115, 138, 233, 235–6, 240–3, 246–8, 254–5
  methodologies 12, 25, 38–41, 44–5, 47, 235, 237, 255
  'Public Opinion Surveys' 235
Pope Paul VI 162
Postmaster-General 126
Powell, Enoch 99
Precious Blood Golden Jubilee Secondary School 155–6, 159, 167, 259
  Committee of Inquiry Final Report 166–7, 170
  St. Teresa Secondary School 167
Prendergast, John 104, 109
Prevention of Bribery Bill (1970) 86, 88, 102
Prevention of Bribery Ordinance (1968) 85, 87, 92, 104
Prevention of Corruption Ordinance (1948) 87
Progressive Hong Kong Society

Progressive Students 160
propaganda 4, 6–7, 27, 94, 116, 188, 247, 258
Public Opinion Assessment Office 236
Public Relations Office 24, 25–8, 31, 46
Pui Ching Road 132
Pui, K. K. 184

Qing dynasty 93
Quantrill, William 166
Queen Elizabeth II 6, 213–14, 217, 224
  Silver Jubilee 214
  'Ying Lui Wong' 214
'Quiet Revolution' (TV programme) 110

racketeering 88, 184
radio 39, 196, 241
Raimondi College 58
Raison, Timothy 216, 219–20, 222
Reception Stations 197
Red Guards 187
Rediffusion Television 110
  'Life in Hong Kong' 110
Reform Club 55, 105, 137–8, 140
'refugee mentality' 11, 177
refugees 29, 60, 178, 182–6, 189–90, 202n.30, 211, 215
  and asylum 189
  Vietnamese 187, 190–1
Regional Council 238, 250n.50
Rent Collectors 89
representative government 16, 169, 237–8, 244
Resettlement Department 23n.89, 32, 34, 232
responsible government 4
Rigby, Sir Ivo 90
Right of Abode 10, 16, 208–9, 217, 221, 223, 225
riots 4, 46, 96, 210
  in 1956 11, 23n.89, 178
  in 1967 7, 11, 17, 25, 28, 32, 53, 56–7, 60, 73, 85, 91, 132, 161, 164, 254, 258
  by police 113

Star Ferry 7, 11, 13, 25, 28, 32, 53, 85, 97, 130, 132, 135–7, 254
Roberts, Deny 113, 138
Royal Commission of Inquiry 96, 98, 100, 115
Royal Hong Kong Auxiliary Air Force 197
Royal Hong Kong Regiment 197
Royle, Anthony 60–1, 67–8, 99, 107, 218
rule of law 1, 99
  in Hong Kong 1

Sai Heung Commune 197
Salmon, G. M. B. 64
San Po Kong 140
Sau Mau Ping 236
Scotland Yard 89, 101
Scott, Ian 24, 53
Second World War 2, 6, 27
Secretariat for Chinese Affairs (SCA) 24–5, 27–8, 30–1, 46, 51n.65
  Assistant Secretary 29–30, 63
  Secretary 28–33
  Training Unit 32
Secretariat for Home Affairs 34, 37–9, 51n.65, 68, 82n.102
Secretary of State 100, 164, 179, 199, 215, 217, 219, 222–3
Senior Community Development Officers 31
Senkaku Islands
  see Diaoyu Islands
Sha Tin Chamber of Commerce 128
Sham Shui Po 63, 126, 146
Shatou 197
Shekou Commune 197
Shenzhen 10, 182, 184, 196, 198
  Foreign Affairs Bureau 183
Shipping and Port Control Ordinance 197
Shui, Dominic 72
Shum, William 136, 140
signature campaigns 13, 17, 59–60, 92, 94–5, 115, 133, 135, 137–8, 140–1, 147, 155, 163–4, 258

Sing Tao Man Pao (STMP) 66, 88, 169
Singapore 4, 5, 33, 127, 255
  Chinese language campaign 4
  communist infiltration of 4
Sino-British Joint Declaration (1984) 9, 10, 16, 198, 201, 208, 236–8, 242, 247, 260
Sino-British relations 7, 10, 181, 208, 225, 240, 246, 254, 256–7
  normalisation of 181
Sir Robert Black Teachers Training College 58
Sister Leung 156–7
sit-ins 139–41, 148, 155, 157–9, 161–4, 168–9, 171, 192, 258–9
Siu Kai-chung 139
Slevin, Brian 113
smuggling 98, 193, 197–8
Special Committees 18, 159, 255
So, C. P. 75
So, James 58, 72, 74, 76
Social Labour League 94
social security system 8
social welfare 9, 185, 210
Society for Community Organisation 133
Society to Promote Chinese Education 57
'sojourner mentality' 13, 53
Solidarity 94
Soong, John 146
'Sound Off' (TV programme) 110
South China Morning Post (SCMP) 76, 89, 96, 100, 105, 128, 131, 160, 168, 185–7, 193, 211, 216, 220–1, 233
Southeast Asia 6, 57, 191, 192
Soviet Union 3
Special Administrative Region (SAR) 1, 237–9, 244, 260
Special Economic Zones 10, 198
Special Working Party 101
Spectrum 235
Squatter Talks 232
squatting 4, 28, 39, 199, 235

Sterling Area 3, 6
Steveson, M. A. B. 64
Stewart, Andrew 99
Stop Press 232
Stuart, Andrew 106
Student Go 139
student newsletters 14, 53, 56, 70, 72
Suez Canal (crisis) 3, 7
Sun Yat-sen 93
Sunday Times, The 102
Sung Pui 138
surveillance 17, 23n.110, 25–6, 36, 43, 48, 147–8, 232, 254, 260–1
Survey Research Hong Kong (SRH) 235
Sutcliffe, Charles 92, 112
Sweetman, J. 61
Swire and Maclaine 147
Switzerland 98
Szeto Wah 158–60, 162, 245

Ta Kung Pao 130, 159, 195
Tai Hang Tung Society for Community Organisation 133
Tai Wo Hau Resettlement Estate 134
Taiwan 6, 13, 57, 83n.118, 160, 177–8, 188
  Formosa 176
Talking Points 25, 46, 241, 248, 252n.78, 254
Technical College 58
Teesdale, E. B. 31
Telephone Advisory Committee 132, 137, 140, 142, 148
Telephone (Amendment) Bill 134
telephone rates 15, 126–8, 135–7, 139, 143, 256
television 13, 39, 110, 115, 135, 241
  availability of 110
  public affairs programmes 110
Television Broadcast Limited (TVB) 110
  'Focus' 110
Ten-Year Housing Programme 9, 177
Tenancy Inquiry Bureaux 31, 34
tenancy tribunals 69
Thatcher, Margaret 10, 210, 245

Thirteen Anti-Corruption Group 94
Tiananmen Square 10, 16, 239, 245, 247
Tiger Standard 58
Tin Tin Yat Po (*TTYP*) 66, 159, 186
Todd, Ronald Ruskin 30
Tokyo 179
Tong, Father John 159
'Touch Base' policy 8, 16, 177, 179–80, 183–6, 189–90, 193, 199–200, 257
Town Talk (1968) 17, 25–6, 33–41, 43–8, 57, 64, 76–7, 88, 92, 94–6, 100, 102–3, 105–6, 126–7, 129–32, 134–5, 140, 142, 146–8, 232–4, 254
　Liaison Assistants 34
　Liaison Officers 31, 34
　quota sampling 37–8, 45–7
trade unionists 167, 235, 246
Trench, David 62–3, 86
triads 87–8, 119n.93
Trotskyism 156, 160
Truth Daily 66, 73
Tsang, Steve 24
Tse Chi-wai 245
Tsim Sha Tsui 75
Tsin Sai-nin 75, 100
Tsuen Wan 44, 45
Tsz Wan Shan 132, 133
Tu, Elsie *see* Elliott, Elsie
Tung Wah Hospital 28
Turcotte, Sister Lorraine 157

unemployment 39, 127, 129, 136, 143, 186, 196
United College 58
United Democrats of Hong Kong 246
United Nations (UN) 3, 60, 178, 180
　Association in Hong Kong 185
　Charter 3
　Convention Relating to the Status of Refugees 178
United States (US) 3, 5–7, 87, 178, 180
Universal Consumers Association 128, 133, 136–8, 140, 144

Unofficial Members of the Executive and Legislative Councils (UMELCO) 68, 133, 136, 138, 141, 208, 214–15, 217, 219, 221–3, 232
Urban Council 6, 7, 24, 31, 33, 55, 59–60, 65, 69, 74, 136, 232–4, 238
Urban Services Department 55

Victoria Park 95
Victoria Peak 190–1
Vietnam 183, 187, 190, 191
Vietnam War 7, 204n.78
　British support of 7
visas 194, 211, 214, 225, 231n.158

Wah Kiu 57
　Wah Kiu Man Po (*WKMP*) 64, 66
　Wah Kiu Yat Po (*WKYP*) 62, 66, 74, 129–30, 159, 186
Wai Wing-kwong 160, 163
Walker, F. L. 130–2
Wan Chai 64, 128, 142
Wan Ren Jih Pao 160
Wang Gungwu 5
Watergate 102
Waterloo Road 132
Watt, Nigel J. V. 32
Wen Wei Po 130, 159, 195
West Indies 210
Western District 95, 133, 142, 241
White Papers 16, 211–12, 215, 234, 238–9, 242–3, 247
Whitehall 91
Whitelaw, William 217–18, 220, 223
Whitney, Raymond 218
Wilson, D. C. 194
Wilson, Harold 93
Wong, C. K. K. 63
Wong, Joshua 260
Wong Ming-kuen 214
Wong, Peter Chak-cheung 245
Wong Tai Sin 58–9, 72, 74, 133, 241
Wong Tai Sin Kaifong Welfare Association 59

Woo, P. C. 61, 90, 132, 136, 138
Working Party on Public
    Cooperation 101
Wu, John 159
Wu Shing-sheun 100

Xinjiang 225
Xu Jiatun 9, 238, 244

Yan Chi Kit 190
Yang, T. L. 64
Yap, Donald 217
Yau Ma Tei 92, 128
Yau Wai-ching 1

Yep, Ray 85–6, 101
Yeung, Cecilia 140
Yeung Li Yin 138
Yeung Sum 245
Ying Wa College 74
Youde, Edward 242–5
Yu Tin 188
Yuen Long 127

Zhang Wenjin 194
Zhongshan County
    196–7
Zhou Enlai 5
Zhou Nan 238

EU authorised representative for GPSR:
Easy Access System Europe, Mustamäe tee 50,
10621 Tallinn, Estonia
gpsr.requests@easproject.com

www.ingramcontent.com/pod-product-compliance
Lightning Source LLC
Chambersburg PA
CBHW051603230426
43668CB00013B/1966